CRIMES
OF THE 20TH CENTURY

A CHRONOLOGY

CONTRIBUTING WRITERS:

BILL G. COX
BILL FRANCIS
WILLIAM J. HELMER
GARY C. KING
JULIE MALEAR
DAVID NEMEC
SAMUEL ROEN
BILLIE FRANCIS TAYLOR

Crescent Books

Louis Weber, C.E.O.
Publications International, Ltd.
7373 North Cicero Avenue
Lincolnwood, Illinois 60646

Permission is never granted for commercial purposes.

Printed and bound in USA.

8 7 6 5 4 3 2 1

ISBN 0-517-05246-6

Library of Congress Catalog Card Number 91-60667

This edition published by Crescent Books
Distributed by Outlet Book Company, Inc.
A Random House Company
225 Park Avenue South
New York, New York 10003

The descriptions of the crimes or persons contained in this book are strictly the opinion of the publisher and are based on news reports, court records, and other reference materials, and do not reflect the guilt or innocence of any individuals mentioned herein.

Photo Credits:

Atlanta Historical Society: p. 61. **AP/Wide World:** cover, pp. 11, 15, 64, 81, 85, 91-92, 98, 104, 108, 113, 117, 123, 147, 149-150, 155-156, 162, 164, 166-167, 170, 172, 174, 177, 179-180, 182, 184-186, 198, 200-202, 205, 208, 210-211, 213, 216-217, 220, 222, 224, 226, 228, 231-232, 235-236, 238-247, 251-252, 255, 257, 260, 262, 264-271, 273, 275, 279, 281-287, 289-298, 300, 303-316. **Buffalo Bill Historical Center:** p. 46. **Gene Daniels/Black Star:** cover, pp. 195, 230. **Denver Public Library/Western History Department:** p. 47. **Cleveland State University Library:** pp. 32-33. **Kansas State Historical Society:** p. 193. **LaPorte County Historical Society:** pp. 48-49. **Library of Congress:** pp. 19, 26-27, 38, 60, 100, 169, 203, 212, 225, 250. **National Archives:** pp. 119, 122, 124, 141, 148, 163. **National Baseball Library/Cooperstown:** pp. 70-72. **Omaha World-Herald:** p. 24. **Pinkerton's Inc:** pp. 21, 25, 44, 136. **Popperfoto:** pp. 96, 218-219, 249. **Rice University:** p. 22. **UPI/Bettmann Newsphotos:** cover, pp. 7, 9, 17, 36, 40, 50-53, 56, 58, 62, 66, 68, 75-77, 79, 83, 86-90, 93-94, 99-100, 103, 106, 109-110, 114-115, 118, 120-121, 125-127, 129-130, 134, 138, 143, 154, 157, 159-160, 165, 168, 171, 176, 178, 183, 188, 191-192, 214-215, 221, 223, 225, 227, 254, 258, 274, 277-278, 299, 301-302, 317. **Wyoming State Museum:** pp. 30-31.

CONTRIBUTING WRITERS:

BILL G. COX has been a newspaperman for 45 years, covering the police beat and the courts. Currently a general columnist, Mr. Cox has written about the true-crime field since 1958.

BILL FRANCIS has operated as an investigator in the law enforcement field for 19 years. He is also a free-lance writer who has written a number of nonfiction detective stories.

WILLIAM J. HELMER is a former senior editor for a major magazine and author of two books. He holds an M.A. in history and has written numerous articles concerning true-crime subjects.

GARY C. KING is a free-lance crime writer whose articles appear regularly in various true-crime publications. Having contributed to other true-crime books, Mr. King is now working on his own.

JULIE MALEAR has 20 years of experience in newspapers and magazines. Currently a free-lance writer and author, she concentrates on criminal subjects and hopes to have another book published soon.

DARRELL MOORE is a video producer whose work has covered the true-crime and political history fields. Mr. Moore is a also free-lance writer who has written books about the film industry.

DAVID NEMEC is a free-lance writer and the author of a number of crime and mystery novels. Mr. Nemec, who formerly worked as a parole officer, is also a baseball historian and novelist.

SAMUEL ROEN has written hundreds of published stories in the true-crime field, which has been his focus for several years. The author of several books, Mr. Roen is busy working on yet another.

BILLIE FRANCIS TAYLOR is a free-lance writer-editor and librarian with over 20 years of experience writing and editing true-crime stories. She also is a former high school and university teacher.

TABLE OF CONTENTS

INTRODUCTION

LAWBREAKING IS AS OLD AS THE LAW, PLAGUING MANKIND over the centuries. Today, crime seems to be increasing rapidly all over the world. Countless studies have examined the ways in which society responds to crime. It is not surprising that this foreboding increase in antisocial behavior has had a sharp impact on the attitudes of ordinary people, affecting the rich and poor alike.

Yet for all their fear of crime, people also find it alluring. Murder has always been a major theme in serious literature. And movies and television series celebrate the heroes of crime on both sides of the law. The smashing success of *The Godfather* movies and television series such as *America's Most Wanted* and *Unsolved Mysteries* are proof of crime's power to fascinate. Gory real-life crimes are equally savored, and clever ones are appreciated. The Great Train Robbery in 1963, possibly the world's most lucrative robbery, drew admiration in newspapers throughout the world.

Perhaps the most notable and touching crime of the century occurred on March 1, 1932, with the kidnapping of Charles Lindbergh, Jr., the 20-month-old son of the famed aviator. In this crime, the involvement of the general public probably exceeded anything known before. For more than four years, every development of the case was chronicled in minute detail by the press. Millions became armchair detectives, and thousands of spectators gathered daily at the Lindbergh home.

Many psychiatrists believe that, hidden in the psyche, all people have criminal impulses that are controlled so well that they themselves are not even aware of them. But news of a murder or other violent crime releases these repressed feelings, allowing people to experience crime on a vicarious basis, safely and legally.

Walter Bromberg of the University of the Pacific once wrote, "Society loves its crime but hates its criminals." To satisfy this love, *Crimes of the 20th Century* offers the reader a safe insight into the villains, victims, and crimes that have, unfortunately, helped shape the last 90 years or so.

20TH CENTURY CRIME AND THE FBI

At the turn of the century, the U.S. had thousands of law enforcement units operating at the federal, state, and local levels. (As many as 40,000 such units currently exist across the nation.) This diversity made nationwide law enforcement difficult; wanted criminals simply crossed state lines into different areas of police jurisdiction. To combat this, Congress established the Bureau of Investigation in 1908, providing the Department of Justice with a permanent crime investigation agency. The early years of the Bureau of Investigation were not particularly distinguished, owing to its restricted powers.

One of the first major changes in modern crime history was the ratification of the 18th Amendment in 1919. Better known as "Prohibition," it created criminals out of almost the entire U.S. population. Organized crime saw this as an extremely lucrative opportunity. Bootlegging became the largest U.S. industry, employing over 800,000 people. When these operations began, there were several small gangs. Eventually, the stronger ones merged, squelching smaller rivals. With this power, mobsters such as Al Capone began to earn a strange kind of respect, even from businessmen and politicians.

According to some accounts, Al Capone, right, and partner Johnny Torrio killed 500 people to control Chicago's bootlegging market.

In 1924, J. Edgar Hoover, the Bureau's new Director, quickly raised the FBI's standard of recruitment; all agents had to be either qualified lawyers or accountants. They were dubbed "G-men" or "government men." In 1924, the Bureau established an Identification Division with 800,000 fingerprints, which became the world's greatest fingerprint collection. Between the two world wars, Hoover's men excelled in dealing with Prohibition and gang warfare.

The 1930s saw the end of one phenomenon and the birth of another. The onset of the Great Depression in 1929 and the election of President Franklin Roosevelt eventually brought about a new consciousness concerning the nation's worsening situation. After the shocking Lindbergh case, kidnapping and other crimes became the province of the FBI in 1932. Then followed the repeal of Prohibition with the ratification of the 23rd Amendment in 1933. That caused the underworld to stumble, but it soon recovered, refocusing into other lucrative fields. At the same time, bands of hoodlums and thugs sprang from the Depression-ravaged rural Midwest and Southeast. Driven by poverty, hatred, and plain meanness, these bandits terrorized America. Names like John Dillinger, Ma Barker, Bonnie and Clyde, Pretty Boy Floyd, and Baby Face Nelson became well known for their vicious and mindless crimes.

In 1935, the Bureau was designated "the Federal Bureau of Investigation." By 1949, of 261 kidnapping cases dealt with by FBI agents, only two remained unsolved. In 1939, President Franklin Roosevelt made the FBI responsible for all internal security matters, including counterespionage and antisabotage measures.

Today, police jurisdiction at a national level in the U.S. is carried out entirely by the FBI. It provides central services for all identification, technical, forensic, and statistical requirements. The Bureau runs a central crime laboratory at its headquarters in Washington, D.C., making its highly sophisticated facilities available to even the smallest police force.

In 1967, the FBI set up the National Crime Information Center (NCIC) in Washington, D.C., which linked together law enforcement agencies at all levels nationwide. The NCIC's main computer can be accessed from computer terminals at police departments in any state. Within minutes, the fingerprints and photographic identity of a suspect can be checked. The computer stores complete information on wanted persons, including their Social Security and driver's license numbers.

As law enforcement has became more sophisticated, so have the criminals. Drug trafficking and use gained in popularity in the 1960s, and today, the drug war is one of the major issues facing society.

REAL CRIMES TURNED INTO BOOKS AND MOVIES

In the past, Hollywood glorified hardened criminals like John Dillinger, Al Capone, and Bonnie and Clyde. More recently, there have been books and movies about many contemporary crimes, including mothers who murder their own children (e.g., *Small Sacrifices*); husbands who kill their wives (*Blind Faith*); and young men who kill for power and money (*Billionaire Boys Club*).

The Manson family killings horrified the nation in 1969. The idea of cult members blindly following their leader through a ritualistic killing spree to the tune of "Helter

During a two-year crime spree, Clyde Barrow, right, and Bonnie Parker were responsible for a dozen deaths and countless robberies.

Skelter" seemed insane. This case was later made into a movie. The nation was at once terrified and mesmerized by the murders.

In February 1970, a similar cultlike killing took place when a family was brutally attacked and murdered, save Jeffrey MacDonald, the head of the household and the sole survivor. The public was shocked when MacDonald, the husband and father of the victims, was later charged with the murders. Found at the scene had been an *Esquire* magazine article detailing the Manson family murders. Jeffrey Mac-Donald apparently had studied it well. In 1983, Joe McGinniss wrote *Fatal Vision,* a book that detailed the Mac-Donald case and discussed the efforts apparently taken by MacDonald to mimic the cult killings. *Fatal Vision* was so popular that it was later made into a movie. That is one of the most widely known examples of real-life horror transformed into books and movies.

SCOTLAND YARD IN THE BEGINNING

In Great Britain in 1829, Sir Robert Peel introduced a bill in Parliament "for improving the police in and near the Metropolis." The bill became law and created England's first Parliament-mandated police force. A thousand uniformed men, nicknamed "Blue Devils" or "Bobbies," went on patrol in London's streets. The Metropolitan Police originally set up its headquarters in Westminster, occupying buildings entered through Great Scotland Yard. That center of police activity in London was soon called "Scotland Yard." The name remained even when the location of its headquarters was changed—it simply became New Scotland Yard. The Metropolitan force is the largest in England, with about a quarter of that country's total police manpower.

In addition to policing the greater London area, the Metropolitan force maintains criminal records including fingerprints for the whole country. It also runs the national bureau for Interpol (the International Criminal Police Organization), protects VIPs, and provides assistance when required by other police forces. The Criminal Investigation Division (CID), formed in 1878, has made Scotland Yard world famous. The CID runs specialized departments such as the Fingerprint and Photographic Branch, Criminal Record Office, Fraud Squad, Flying Squad, and Special Branch.

There is one factor that sets the British police apart from their counterparts around the world: They do not carry firearms. The recent growth of terrorism, however, has necessitated the carrying of guns by officers having special protection duties.

The Police National Computer in Hendon puts ordinary police officers throughout England in touch with a wealth of information in minutes. It was the speed of this information network and the judgment of the officers at the scene that lead to the 1981 capture of the Yorkshire Ripper, Peter Sutcliffe.

FORENSIC MEDICINE

Centuries ago, it was recognized that in order to properly investigate a crime, evidence must be collected. The objective was to solve the puzzle of what had happened and who was responsible. Eventually, forensic medicine was developed from the efforts put forth to meet this objective.

Captain Jeffrey MacDonald, second from the right, is escorted by an MP and two federal agents to the funeral for his wife and two daughters. Nobody knows whether they were killed by Capt. MacDonald or hippies.

Forensic medicine and forensic pathology are used to aid criminal investigations, in most cases, a suspicious death. Employing a victim's body to determine the circumstances surrounding a homicide used to be dependent on what a doctor could deduce from an autopsy. Those observations and the techniques developed from them are largely responsible for the development of specialized areas such as toxicology, hair and fiber analysis, and blood grouping.

In modern forensic medicine, after a crime has been discovered, the first step is the identification of a body (if there is one) and the connection of a person to the crime. Fingerprint analysis and blood grouping are employed regularly to meet those two objectives.

Next, in a homicide, the physician will try to determine the cause of death. If a weapon was used, the doctor will attempt to identify it. Perhaps an autopsy will allow the doctor to extract a bullet or two, which can then be linked to a murder weapon. A rope employed to hang a victim might be of an uncommon weave or fiber. Perhaps a weapon used to bludgeon a victim had left behind an impression of the weapon itself on the victim's body or clothes.

Once the cause of death has been determined, the responsibility for the death is explored. Was it suicide, murder, or accident? This can be difficult to determine. The presence of a suicide note does not preclude murder, just as multiple gunshot wounds do not rule out suicide.

New techniques and methods are being developed today in response to the different types of evidence encountered. The identification of a criminal might be accomplished by examining a bite mark left on a victim and matching it to the culprit, as was done in Ted Bundy's case.

The concepts behind many of today's analyses sprang from the imaginative mind of Sir Arthur Conan Doyle approximately one century ago. Modern techniques often appear to be as magical as Sherlock Holmes made them seem. However, science is at the core. It seems unbelievable that a man can be convicted of murder based on something as tiny as a dog hair, but that's what convicted Wayne Williams, the Atlanta Child Killer. That example is proof that no piece of evidence is too small or insignificant.

FINGERPRINTING

Centuries ago, fingerprints were used as signatures on Chinese and Egyptian pottery. This sparked the interest of several scientists and hobbyists throughout the years who began collecting fingerprints. Prints from relatives and identical twins were examined. Word spread that no two people have the same fingerprints. At the 1904 World's Fair, a Scotland Yard inspector lectured on the use of fingerprints for identification, and several people tried to implement it as a replacement for the existing method, which involved body measurements.

For identification purposes, fingerprints are generally taken in ink after an individual's arrest. They also are used to compare with any unintentional prints left by the criminal at the crime scene. The fingers and palms of the hand have raised and lowered areas arranged in specific patterns. When the raised areas make contact with a surface and the perspiration from the skin is transferred to the surface, a latent (hidden) print can result. These prints are normally invisible until developed by a professional. Originally, prints were developed by applying fingerprint powder with a brush. The powder was made mostly of lampblack (fine black soot) and was attracted to the moisture on the areas that the skin had touched. This worked well on most smooth surfaces, but on paper and similar items, the perspiration soaked into the absorbent fibers of the paper, inhibiting the development of the fingerprint.

In the mid-1950s, two Swedish scientists became interested in a chemical normally utilized to separate biological samples. They had heard complaints that this chemical inadvertently developed fingerprints on tests that were being run and interfered with their results. Those two scientists realized the chemical's potential for the intentional development of fingerprints by police officers. Today this chemical, ninhydrin, is utilized in the most productive technique for developing prints on paper items.

Twenty years later, another accident led to an important discovery. By using the fumes of the household adhesive known as "superglue" (cyanoacrylate ester), a white coating can be applied to a print, making the print visible and allowing it to be lifted from the same surface over and over again. Previously, a surface would have been dusted with powder, the print lifted with tape, and the tape placed on a paper to preserve the print. Without employing superglue fumes first, the print could be removed from the surface on the first lift. If it were processed with superglue fumes, the coating would keep the print from being removed by lifting or being accidentally wiped away.

Lasers also emit light that can make an invisible print visible. Also, prints can be treated with laser dyes to enhance the visibility of the print.

Dust prints, either fingerprints or shoe prints, are often left at the crime scene. Those prints have always been hard to preserve. Recently, electrostatic lifters have had good success. An electrostatic lifter uses a power supply to electrically charge a metallized lifting film called "mylar," attracting dust particles to it. That transfers the dust print to the mylar, where it can be transported or easily photographed. An electrostatic lifter has even been known to lift footprints off carpeting.

WIRETAPPING AND SURVEILLANCE

The American intelligence community began prior to World War II. Sosthenes Behn, a flamboyant wheeler-dealer, was the founder and chairman of the International Telephone and Telegraph Corporation (ITT). His title, "the Prince of Telephones," summed up both his power over world communications and the aristocratic methods with which he wielded it. Throughout World War II, ITT facilities communicated intelligence information to the Allies and the Axis, while Behn himself reported directly to the U.S. Secretary of War (and indirectly, it's suspected, to Nazi Hermann Göring).

Amazing as it sounds, current surveillance technology includes transmitters so small that they can fit on the back of a fly and miniature television cameras no more than three inches square. There are also photographic reconnaissance satellites and light-intensification lenses that enable pictures to be taken by starlight.

Surveillance has become a part of Western life, with watchful eyes in banks, supermarkets, department stores, and airports. In people's homes, telephones are "monitored" at the discretion of the Service Observation Bureau (SOB), a section of the Bell System with millions of wiretaps in operation. The SOB can also monitor selected customers' movements and speech through cable television with an optical wiretap that uses existing wiring. The PSE (Psychological

Stress Evaluator), originally developed for the CIA and Army, records stress and truthfulness remotely, without the subject's knowledge.

DNA TYPING

DNA, or deoxyribonucleic acid, is the genetic blueprint of life for most living organisms. It carries a code that determines the makeup of a human being, including such characteristics as eye and hair color. The DNA of no two individuals is alike, with the sole exception being identical twins. It is this almost universal difference in every person that is of benefit to forensic scientists.

In 1985, the scientific community was introduced to the concept of DNA fingerprinting. News of the DNA analysis spread like wildfire. In what has been a short period of time, U.S. forensic laboratories are now performing DNA analysis on criminal cases. Computer databases are also being established nationwide to store the coded DNA patterns of convicted sex offenders. Legislation has been passed or is in the works in many states that will require all convicted sex offenders to give a sample of their blood to the authorities so the felons' DNA patterns can be stored in a computerized database.

COMPUTERS IN LAW ENFORCEMENT

Computerization has greatly increased the speed at which information can be processed. This additional speed could save an officer's life. Computers are also becoming essential due to rising crime rates and cuts in funding law enforcement.

Perhaps one of the most familiar areas of advances in computerization is seen when an officer stops a vehicle.

Within a few minutes, the license plate number can be reported and a check made to determine the owner of the car. Most states have this capability. They can also access the NCIC (National Crime Information Center) to see if a vehicle has been reported stolen or if the owner of the car is wanted by the police. Recently, some cities have placed the computers inside the police vehicles, allowing the officers to access the records directly, without relying on a dispatcher. In addition, reports can be entered electronically from the crime scene.

An increasingly popular system automatically stores and retrieves photographs. It can also create an "electronic lineup" for witnesses. The video image of an arrested suspect could be entered along with data such as crime type, age, sex, race, and physical characteristics. That information would then be stored on a tamperproof optical disk. Later, it might be possible to capture live photos at remote sites and enter them into a central database.

Another valuable use for computers has been the collection of data concerning sex-motivated crimes. Thus, similarities between one sex crime and thousands of previous crimes can be examined. Data can also be combined to generate statistics on sex-crime trends.

Another useful computer advancement involves a device known as "live scan." It electronically records fingerprint ridge characteristics that would normally be recorded by placing a thin layer of printer's ink over the suspect's fingers and rolling them across a card. That older process transfers the inked ridged areas of the fingers onto the card for a permanent record. With live scan, the fingers are placed onto a piece of glass, where they are scanned by infrared or laser light. The scanned images are digitally recorded by a computer, and a special printer can produce a fingerprint card. This method is faster, cleaner, and requires little operator training. Live scan could also be very valuable when an alias is used or an unknown deceased body is found because it produces an immediate identification if that person's fingerprints are already in the system.

Probably the greatest incentive for funding centralized computer systems for storing fingerprint data came from the 1979 capture of the Hillside Strangler through the use of a new system in California. Originally, that equipment was called AIDS (Automated Identification System), but it was later changed for obvious reasons. The current name, AFIS (Automated Fingerprint Identification System), applies to three main systems, but their objectives are all to allow the speedy comparison of inked and crime scene fingerprints. The FBI is trying to bring together the almost 30 states that have AFIS equipment and the ones that will be obtaining it in the future, so they can interact with the FBI. In this way, the millions of fingerprint cards submitted to the FBI could be processed more effectively.

PSYCHOLOGICAL PROFILES OF CRIMINALS

The FBI has a new Behavioral Science Unit that employs psychological profiling to develop a "description" of the likely perpetrator. This can include age, sex, race, economic background, and educational level. Profiling proves most helpful in the more violent or bizarre cases.

In the past, most murder cases were committed by an acquaintance of the victim. During the last two decades, the percentage of crimes in which the killer knew the victim dropped steadily. It has always been difficult to link a crime to someone who has had no prior contact with the victim.

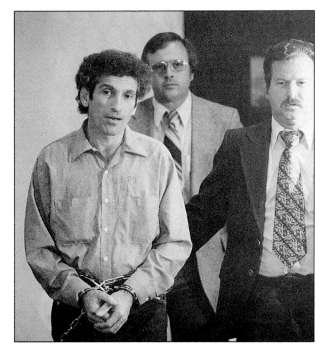

Angelo Buono, above, and his cousin Kenneth Bianchi, committed the Hillside Strangler murders. When shown irrefutable evidence, Bianchi confessed and, in order to strike a deal, implicated Buono.

In the 1950s, the New York City police enlisted the aid of psychologist James A. Brussel to identify "the Mad Bomber of New York." After examining notes written by the Bomber, Brussel described him in detail. Amazingly, George Metesky was captured shortly thereafter in Waterbury, Connecticut, fitting Brussel's profile almost perfectly, even down to the double-breasted suit.

A profile is a short, vivid biography that highlights those characteristics that would be most noticeable or unusual. This sketch tries to determine why the criminal is acting as he or she is, so future actions can be predicted. According to the FBI, the best profilers are investigators, not psychiatrists or psychologists, although a knowledge of psychology is helpful.

Officially, the FBI began profiling in 1978. To build up a base of information, the FBI interviewed serial murderers and rapists. In 1980, the FBI began training profilers for field work. During 1984, they achieved an accuracy rating of 75 to 80 percent. Profiling has been employed in cases involving the Boston Strangler, Charles Manson, Son of Sam, Richard Speck, and the Yorkshire Ripper.

THE ECONOMIC IMPACT OF CRIME

Everybody is a victim of crime. Even if you are not among the millions victimized directly each year, you pay for crime in the following ways:

- In the many billions of tax dollars expended on an out-dated system of criminal justice;
- In escalating insurance premiums;
- In inflated prices on goods and services, to compensate for shoplifting, employee dishonesty and theft, and executive embezzlement;
- In inflated prices for or rentals on residences, to compensate for construction employees stealing tools and materials, the faking of contractor payrolls, and the bribing of municipal employees;
- In poorer education for children resulting from the widespread vandalism of schools; and
- In the hundreds of millions of dollars spent by citizens for do-it-yourself security (e.g., locks, alarms, guns, and watchdogs).

White-collar criminals include the stock broker who uses inside information to reap a profit, the bank president who lends depositors' money to himself or herself, the defense manufacturer who overcharges the Pentagon for weapons, and the company that illegally dumps toxic waste. Recently, savings and loan scandals have cost U.S. consumers billions of dollars.

Although it is difficult to measure the direct costs of corporate crimes, they appear to dwarf those costs associated with the more highly publicized street crimes. In addition, approximately 28,000 deaths and 130,000 serious injuries are caused annually by dangerous products, many of which are manufactured by unscrupulous, penny-pinching companies that want to make a profit at any cost.

Everyone probably knows people who cheat on their income taxes by understating their income. If everybody reported all their income, the U.S. Gross National Product (GNP) could increase by one trillion dollars. Other sources of underground income include drug profits, bribery, prostitution, fraud, pornography, and stolen goods.

To assess the economic impact of blue-collar crime, a variety of available information sources, such as police agencies, insurance companies, trade associations, books, newspapers, and scholarly journals, can be used. The economic impact of blue-collar crime in both the public and private sectors is estimated to be over $40 billion annually.

AGE AS IT RELATES TO CRIMINALS

Statistics show that young people have a higher crime rate (i.e., they commit more crimes) than older persons. Age appears to have an important effect, directly or indirectly, on the frequency and type of crime committed.

Charles Manson arrives in court with a clean-shaven face, a short haircut, and a swastika carved in his forehead.

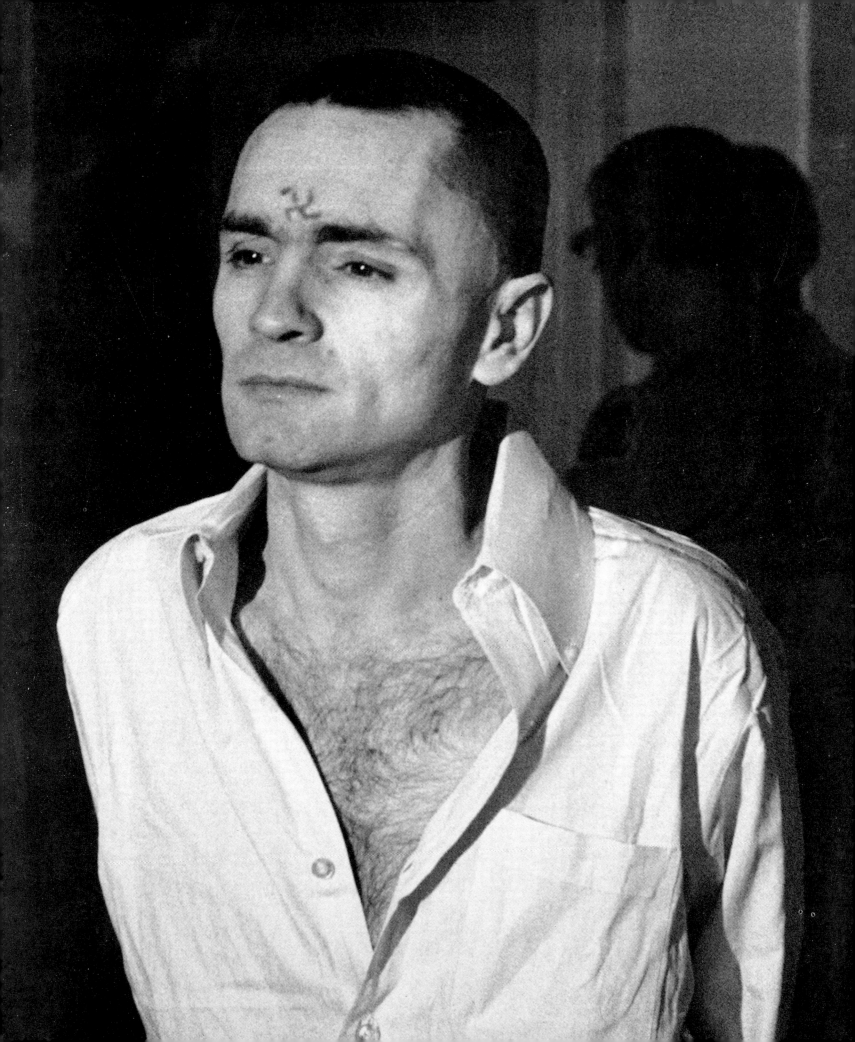

Recent British statistics show that the age category of maximum convictions for indictable crimes is 14 to 17. While U.S. statistics place this age slightly higher, those statistics are based on fingerprints submitted by local police departments to the FBI, and American police departments seldom fingerprint young people.

Males aged 15 to 19 have the highest arrest rates for automobile theft and burglary. Homicides and assaults are committed by persons who are much older, on the average. Females generally commit crimes at later ages than do males. Yet, sex offenses, narcotic drug offenses, crimes against families and children, driving while intoxicated, homicide, and forgery appear earlier in the lives of women than in the lives of men.

The type of crime most frequently committed by persons of various ages varies from one place to another. In some areas of Chicago, for example, delinquent boys between 12 and 13 years of age commit burglaries, while in other areas, delinquent boys of those ages commit petty larcenies or engage in gang violence. In rural areas, offenders of any specified age are likely to be convicted of crimes different from those committed by urbanites.

Juvenile delinquency is probably related in some manner to adult criminal behavior, but the juvenile delinquent of today is not the adult criminal of tomorrow. Although many juveniles commit delinquencies, not all of them develop into adult criminals.

IDENTIFYING THE MOST COMMON VICTIMS

In 1983, there were an estimated 40 million victimizations, ranging from stolen cars to murder. In 1982, approximately 3.2 percent of the nation's population (about seven million Americans) were victims of rape, robbery, or assault. Nearly one of every 12 males 16 to 19 years of age is the victim of a violent crime each year. Between 1984 and 1988, the murder rate for African-American men between 15 and 24 rose by 6.8 percent. In an especially disturbing trend, the murder rate for African-Americans between the ages of 15 and 19 nearly doubled in the same period.

Males, mostly those under 21 and over 51 years of age, are most frequently victimized. In the age group of 60 and over, the largest group of sufferers are females. Since women live longer, perhaps older women have a greater chance of being victimized.

Interpersonal relationships of the victims are of prime importance. Married persons of both sexes are more often victims than persons of any other marital status. Also, divorced individuals are less often victims of violent crimes than those who are only separated. In the age group of victims 60 and older, the spouse seems to be the major target of violent crimes. It is the only age group where almost half of the violent crimes are committed against the spouse.

CRIMES OF THE 20TH CENTURY

The previous pages have provided a brief insight into the history and status of several topics that are equally important to criminals, victims, and law enforcement officials. Keeping these facts in mind while pondering the over 150 crimes examined in this publication, it becomes obvious that the efforts of law enforcement officials to stay on the trail of criminals from 1900 to the present have been truly herculean. The descriptions of the cases that follow in *Crimes of the 20th Century* will surely attest to that fact.

1900–1909

THE CRIMES AND CRIMINALS THAT ATTRACTED PUBLIC ATTENTION IN THE first ten years of the 20th century were, like the decade itself, alternately charming and dreadful. Through the swashbuckling exploits of outlaws Butch Cassidy and the Sundance Kid, we experienced the passing of the Old West. In the homicidal career of woman-killer Johann Otto Hoch, we gathered a foretaste of modern serial murder. Paralleling a trend in legitimate society, women criminals began to equal the achievements of their male counterparts. America witnessed the grisly deeds of mass-murderer Belle Gunness, the Lady Bluebeard of Indiana, and the masterful con job that Cassie Chadwick pulled on gullible bankers and financiers. Criminals such as these established a colorful, if sometimes horrifying, legacy befitting an era that incorporated Victorian Age gentility and the alienated attitudes of an increasingly industrialized world.

MAY AND EDDIE...AND AMERICAN EXPRESS

Handsome Eddie Guerin was one of England's most successful and elusive robbers before he met Chicago May Churchill. Soon after the two became lovers, Guerin found himself on Devil's Island. The bond between them was so strong that Churchill funded a major portion of his escape.

LOVERS CHICAGO MAY CHURCHILL AND EDDIE GUERIN PULLED ONE OF THE MOST DARING ROBBERIES EVER

Chicago May Churchill was alluring, well-read, and sophisticated. She was also an extremely bawdy drunk and a liar. Chicago May held court among the elite of the international underworld for two decades. When she met her equal in crime—Eddie Guerin—they fell in love and decided to rob the American Express office in Paris.

Chicago May was born in Ireland on November 25, 1876, as Beatrice Desmond. When she was 13, she ran away, boarded a ship, and arrived in New York. After making her way to her uncle's Midwestern farm, she met Dal Churchill, an outlaw who was riding through. They eloped when she was only 14. Dal taught her safecracking, cattle rustling, and pistol marksmanship. She served as a lookout when Dal robbed a bank. The couple even rode with the infamous Dalton gang. After about 18 months, Dal bungled a train robbery, got caught, and was lynched.

The 15-year-old widow then went to Chicago to advance her criminal abilities. May enjoyed working with a "panel man." Posing as a prostitute, she would lure a dupe to her room, where an accomplice would hide (behind a secret panel, hence the name). At the appropriate moment, the accomplice would overpower the john and take all his money. Chicago May then moved on to New York City, became bored, and returned to Europe in 1897 as the toast of the underworld. However, May was no longer satisfied with small jobs.

In 1900, Chicago May met Eddie Guerin, an American, in London and fell in love. Eddie, who had pulled off several impressive heists, plotted his boldest job yet. Along with two men, he planned to rob the

American Express office in Paris. Guerin discovered that one guard was a drunk who always went to sleep after his second round. After they overpowered the sleeping watchman, Europe's best safe man, Timothy Oats, blew the safe without arousing the neighborhood. Their haul was over $100,000 in cash and checks.

Getting away proved a bit harder. All trains, ports, and highways were closely watched. May and Eddie boarded a train, with May concealing the loot on her person. When a gendarme called to Eddie, May separated from him and escaped with the spoils. Meanwhile, Guerin received a life sentence on Devil's Island.

May used part of her booty plus money obtained from her pals in Chicago to effect an escape attempt. In a breakout that defied fiction, Eddie left Devil's Island, made his way to Cayenne, French Guiana, and after suffering untold hardships, reached England. France demanded his extradition, but England refused.

May feared that Guerin would demand his share of the American Express loot, all of which was spent. After she stoked her new boyfriend, hothead Charlie Smith, into a jealous rage, he took several shots at Guerin, who survived the attack. Smith got 15 years, and Chicago May received 10 years as an accessory, and was deported upon her release. She never regretted her life: ". . . better to be an eagle for a single day than a canary bird for a lifetime."

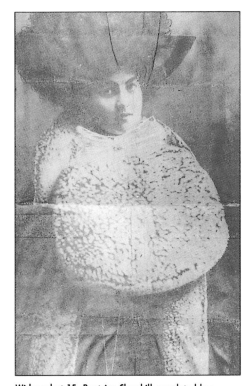

Widowed at 15, Beatrice Churchill completed her criminal education in the Windy City, where she began calling herself Chicago May. After the American Express robbery, she was torn between her loyalty to Eddie Guerin and her desire to live for the moment. She chose the latter when he took too long to escape from Devil's Island.

A CONSPIRACY OF MURDER

PERSONAL SECRETARY CHARLES JONES AND LAWYER ALBERT PATRICK CONSPIRED TO CHEAT A MILLIONAIRE

Multimillionaire William Marsh Rice had built himself an empire by speculating in oil and land, and by creating store and hotel chains. Through his will, Rice wanted to set up a nonprofit public works corporation. However, his personal manservant and a roguish lawyer had other ideas.

William Marsh Rice was a self-made man for whom the Land of Opportunity seemed tailor-made. In the rich territory of Texas in the early 1830s, he built himself an empire. Speculating in oil and land, creating store and hotel chains, he was a much-admired multimillionaire by the turn of the century. As he lived out his final days in luxury in New York City, he intended to return his wealth to the land that had blessed him—Texas. Through his will, he wanted to set up a nonprofit public works corporation called the Rice Institute.

Albert Patrick was a roguish lawyer employed by relatives of Rice's late wife in an effort to free up some of Mr. Rice's fortune for themselves. During this pursuit, Patrick endeared himself to Charles Jones, the personal secretary and manservant of the aging Rice. Patrick initially sought Jones's help in winning the lawsuit. However, when he discerned Jones's willingness to engage in some deceit, Patrick forgot about his clients. Jones gave Patrick access to all of Rice's personal papers, checks, will, and other legal documents. From March to September of 1900, they built a paper trail suggesting that Patrick had become Rice's lawyer and friend. A new will was written (leaving 90 percent of his fortune to Patrick), as were a power of attorney and checks totaling $250,000.

Jones persuaded Rice to switch to a new physician, Walter Curry. Dr. Curry had no part in the conspiracy, but the aged doctor's failing eyesight and faulty memory made him the ideal dupe. Jones began to give mercury tablets to Rice, which created digestive trouble that Dr. Curry began to treat. On September 23, 1900, on Patrick's instructions, Jones administered a lethal dose of chloroform to the sleeping

Rice. Waiting long enough for the telltale odor to subside, Jones called the physician. Dr. Curry signed the death certificate, which read "Cause of death—old age and a weak heart; immediate causes— indigestion followed by collacratal diarrhoea with mental worry."

Patrick sent Rice's body for cremation. If he'd waited until that was completed, there would have been only Dr. Curry's certificate for evidence. However, he was too eager and immediately presented the Swenson banking house with a forged check for $25,000. Patrick misspelled his name on the check to cover up the fact that he made it out to himself. This prompted the bankers' initial suspicion. Although the bankers did not doubt the check's authenticity, they decided to check with Mr. Rice before handing out such a sum to a stranger. When they called Rice's residence, Charles Jones was obliged to tell them that Rice was dead and about to be cremated. The alarmed bankers called the police and district attorney. The cremation was stayed and an autopsy ordered, which showed the deadly gas in Rice's lungs.

When he was first arrested, Charles Jones tried to kill himself. Jones had committed the murder, and the district attorney could hang him for that. However, Jones was granted limited immunity in exchange for testifying against the person that the authorities felt was primarily responsible for Rice's death—Patrick. The sensational month-long trial featured charges and countercharges. Medical experts attacked each other's opinions, and hand-writing specialists likewise feuded. Patrick was found guilty of first-degree murder on March 26, 1902, and sentenced to die in the electric chair. However, he fought on legally for ten years. On November 28, 1912, he was pardoned by departing New York Governor John Dix, an act that outraged the public.

Today, Rice University—endowed by Mr. Rice's millions—is one of the finest institutions of higher learning in the South.

JONES BEGAN TO GIVE MERCURY TABLETS TO RICE, WHICH CREATED DIGESTIVE TROUBLE THAT DR. CURRY BEGAN TO TREAT.

A KIDNAPPER AND AN ADVENTURER

PAT CROWE KIDNAPPED A MILLIONAIRE'S SON, GOT HIS RANSOM, AND THEN RETURNED TO TAUNT HIS PREY

Revenge drove failed cattleman Pat Crowe to kidnap the 15-year-old son, pictured above with his sisters, of meat-packing tycoon Edward A. Cudahy. Later acquitted of the crime, Crowe for years sent his victim an annual reminder of the terrifying episode in the form of a Christmas card.

Edward A. Cudahy was the millionaire owner of a meat-packing empire in Omaha, Nebraska. As the director of this powerful concern, he was able to control beef prices to a large extent. In doing so, Cudahy's actions often had the effect of ruining small cattle ranchers whom he had never met. Of course, they knew who he was. Pat Crowe was one of those struggling young ranchers whose business was devastated one year when the price of beef fell too low. In order to survive, Crowe tried bank robbing and other illegal pursuits. And he always intended to get his revenge on Cudahy.

On December 18, 1900, Pat Crowe kidnapped 15-year-old Edward Cudahy, Jr., from the family's Omaha mansion. Crowe demanded $25,000 in gold pieces from the elder Cudahy in a letter that concluded: "Mr. Cudahy, you are up against it, there is only one way out. Give up the coin. Money we want, and money we will get. If you don't give it up, the next man will, for he will see we mean business, and you can lead your boy around blind for the rest of your days and all you will have is the damn copper's sympathy."

Crowe insisted that Cudahy deliver the ransom. The gold sacks weighed over a hundred pounds. Cudahy put them in a buggy, affixed a red lantern, and drove out of town. When he saw a white lantern tied to a tree, Cudahy unloaded the gold and headed back to town. Shortly after he arrived home, his son rang the front door. Police then searched for Pat Crowe, but to no avail.

Crowe had escaped to South Africa. In the ensuing five years, his many adventures included organizing and fighting with a Boer commando unit. In 1906, Crowe returned to the United States and gave back the ransom. Crowe went to trial but was acquitted—mostly because the jury sympathized with him. For years afterward, Crowe sent Christmas cards to his former kidnap victim.

Adam Worth was perhaps Britain's greatest thief, often called the "Napoleon of Crime." Scotland Yard estimated that Worth had stolen over one million pounds sterling during his lifetime. He was never caught nor jailed. Adam Worth was clever and daring. He planned his jobs well and executed them with precision. During the many thefts attributed to him, nobody was ever killed or seriously injured.

Worth's most famous theft occurred on May 25, 1876, when he lifted Thomas Gainsborough's well-known painting "The Duchess of Devonshire" from Agnew's art gallery. When a member of his gang was jailed on an unrelated matter, he showed extraordinary loyalty by offering to trade the Gainsborough for his colleague. Before the deal was completed, however, the authorities were forced to release the man on a technicality. Worth quietly transported the painting out of England to the United States, where it remained for 25 years.

Various other robberies were credited to Adam Worth. During the 1880s, these included the theft of uncut diamonds from mailbags in South Africa and the heist of government securities from mail trains in France. Worth once flooded the Turkish economy with counterfeit notes and nearly toppled a corrupt Ottoman regime (1889). He also set up legitimate businesses to fence and/or launder his stolen properties.

After a lifetime of successful escapades, Adam Worth found himself in Chicago, free, but sickly. Worth pined for England, which had warrants out for his arrest. In 1901, Worth contacted the venerable detective, Alan Pinkerton, who knew Worth well—he'd been trying to capture Worth for years. Pinkerton helped Worth negotiate a settlement with the British authorities: He would return the Gainsborough painting in exchange for an undisclosed amount of money and an amnesty that would allow Worth to live out his remaining years in England. Adam Worth returned home in triumph. He had beaten the system and became an antihero of sorts. In 1907, Adam Worth died in London's infamous East End.

THE MASTER THIEF'S REDEMPTION

AFTER A QUARTER CENTURY OF CRIMINAL MASTERY, ADAM WORTH EXCHANGED HIS GREATEST TRIUMPH FOR AMNESTY

Adam Worth's crowning achievement was the theft of Thomas Gainsborough's "The Duchess of Devonshire" from a London art gallery in 1876. A quarter century later, old and homesick, he returned the painting so that he could live out his few remaining years in London.

THE ANARCHIST ASSASSIN

WHEN LEON CZOLGOSZ SHOT PRESIDENT MCKINLEY, HE PROFOUNDLY CHANGED HISTORY AND SPECTACULARLY FAILED IN HIS MISSION

Leon Czolgosz, shown above, was the second presidential assassin to be executed in the United States. On June 30, 1882, Charles Guiteau was hanged after slaying James A. Garfield. The first presidential assassin, John Wilkes Booth, Abraham Lincoln's killer, was apparently killed in the process of being apprehended.

Leon Czolgosz (pronounced CHOL gosh) was the son of Polish immigrants who worked on a small farm in Ohio. Leon was a moody, introspective child. He was prone to pondering, but rarely produced any great thoughts. He was restless and forever searching for something to believe in. At the age of 20, in 1893, he was laid off from his job at a wire factory during a strike. This event had a profound effect on him, as he never got another job. Czolgosz stayed on his parents' farm, reading and learning about many radical philosophies, but gravitating towards the anarchists.

In 1900, when Leon read of the exploits of Gaetano Bresci (see the accompanying sidebar), he was galvanized. He kept the clipping about the assassination of the king of Italy, and read it over and over. He started telling everyone that somebody should shoot an American president. He made trips to Chicago and Cleveland to hear speeches by the well-known anarchist Emma Goldman and to meet other anarchists. In Chicago, the anarchists he met were suspicious of him. On September 1, 1901, the anarchist newspaper *Free Society* printed a warning about this oddly behaved Polish visitor, stating that he might have been an agent provocateur or spy. This warning might have goaded Leon Czolgosz into trying to prove his credentials.

Five days later, on September 6, Leon was standing in line at the Pan American Exposition in Buffalo, New York, waiting to shake hands with President William McKinley. Czolgosz had a white handkerchief wrapped around his right hand, as if it were injured. When Leon got up to the president, McKinley reached for Czolgosz's free left hand. Czolgosz swatted the president's arm away and fired his pistol twice. One bullet hit one of the president's buttons and bounced off. The other bullet struck President McKinley on the left side of his belly and came out through the back. The action of the gun set Leon's handkerchief aflame. As police and soldiers pounced on Czolgosz, he mumbled, "I done my duty."

An artist's rendering of the McKinley assassination at the Pan-American Exposition in Buffalo, New York, on September 6, 1901. McKinley was the third U.S. president in a 36-year-period to be slain while in office. Since his death, only one other U.S. president, John F. Kennedy, has been assassinated.

THE ASSASSIN'S INSPIRATION

Leon Czolgosz was inspired to shoot President McKinley because of a similar assassination in Italy a year before. Gaetano Bresci was an Italian weaver from Paterson, New Jersey, which was a hotbed of anarchist political sentiment. Many people there talked openly about assassinating government leaders. King Humbert I of Italy was an obvious choice because most anarchistic Italian immigrants considered the monarchy to be even worse than elected governments. Bresci saved up his money for the trip back to Italy as if it were a long-sought vacation. On July 29, 1900, Bresci shot the king as he was handing out prizes to athletes. Bresci's hometown gang in Paterson was ecstatic. They sent Bresci a congratulatory telegram in his cell. There were many others across Italy who stepped up to applaud Bresci's actions as well. But the government was not amused. Bresci got life imprisonment—not a very appetizing prospect for an anarchist. After a few months in jail, Gaetano Bresci killed himself.

President McKinley lingered for eight days before dying of gangrene of the pancreas. With hindsight, we can say that McKinley's doctors ill-served him. He should have lived and recovered from that wound.

If Leon Czolgosz thought he was going to become a national hero like Bresci did in Italy, he had the wrong country. Even anarchists condemned his deed and tried to dissociate from him. For most Americans, Leon Czolgosz's deed succeeded only in cementing a distrust of foreigners and their new ideas. In a sense, the Red scare of the 1920s that cost Sacco and Vanzetti their lives can be traced back to him. Even more ironically, the line of succession that put Theodore Roosevelt in the White House meant that Czolgosz had replaced a relatively inactive and ineffective president with a dynamic and expansionist one. Czolgosz's last words before going to the electric chair were, "I am not sorry."

AN INHERITANCE OF GREED

THERESE HUMBERT PARLAYED A PHONY INHERITANCE INTO A FANTASTIC FRAUD

GIVEN THE PROMINENT STANDING OF THERESE'S FATHER-IN-LAW, NO ONE DOUBTED THE GREAT WEALTH LOCKED AWAY IN HER SAFE. IT HAS NEVER BEEN DETERMINED WHETHER MONSIEUR HUMBERT WAS A CONSPIRATOR IN HIS DAUGHTER-IN-LAW'S HOAX OR AN UNWITTING PAWN. HE DIED WITHOUT REVEALING HIS ROLE.

Therese Humbert was born about 1860 of humble parentage in France. She worked hard to become respectable. When she married Frederic Humbert, her father-in-law was France's Minister of Justice.

Therese then began to relate a remarkable story. Hearing an old man gasping in the next compartment on a train, she climbed along the outside footboard to reach him while the train was moving. Then Therese comforted the poor man, who happened to be Robert Henry Crawford, an aging American millionaire. Soon after, Mr. Crawford died, and Therese received a copy of a will stating that Crawford had left his entire fortune—over $6 million—to her. As the news spread, a second will surfaced. It divided Crawford's millions equally among his two nephews and Therese's sister Maria. This will named Therese as executor. (Both wills were forgeries from Therese's imagination.)

It was announced that an agreement had been forged between the fictional Crawford boys and the Humberts. It stated that the deeds and securities constituting the inheritance would be locked in Therese's safe until all legal conflicts could be resolved.

Therese wanted to die with the matter still undecided. She tried hard enough. There were suits and countersuits, judgments and appeals. No one, not even the lawyers who thought they'd been hired from abroad by the Crawford boys, suspected that the whole affair was a sham. Numerous eager creditors were delighted to lend huge sums to Madame Humbert for the assurance of a hefty interest payment to come. In this fashion, the Humberts received over $9 million of credit.

When several skeptical articles were printed in the newspaper *Le Matin,* the creditors began to demand their money. A judge ordered that the infamous safe be opened; its contents were worthless. On December 15, 1902, Therese and her husband were sentenced to five years in prison for fraud. She left prison in September 1906, and lived the rest of her life in poverty.

THE LOVER IN THE ATTIC

OTTO SANDHUBER TOOK FULL ADVANTAGE OF FRED OESTERREICH AND EVENTUALLY KILLED HIM IN HIS OWN HOME

In 1903, Walburga "Dolly" Oesterreich, 36, lived unhappily with her husband, Frederick, who owned a sewing machine factory. Fred preferred the bottle to his wife. Yet, his drinking made him jealous. He hired detectives to track her so she could have no lovers, but Dolly kept searching for a way out. One day, Fred sent one of his workers—17-year-old Otto Sandhuber—to his house to repair his wife's sewing machine. Dolly took a strong liking to the young man.

Knowing that the detectives prevented a liaison outside her home, Dolly persuaded Otto to move into the attic of her Los Angeles home. It seemed foolhardy, but Dolly figured she could fool her husband long enough to think of something else. Otto had no family ties, and he fancied a life of luxury, with love as his only chore. So he agreed to the arrangement. Somehow, on it went for *17 years!*

In August 1922, Frederick came home unexpectedly. Otto was still downstairs. Without seeing Otto, Frederick began a violent argument with Dolly. Suddenly, Otto entered the room holding a gun and shot Fred four times. Dolly reported the shooting, telling the police that a burglar had broken in and surprised her husband. The police were not overly suspicious. Dolly called her lawyer and asked him to evict her "brother" who had been living in the attic. The lawyer performed as asked, finding Sandhuber pleasant and willing to vacate. Before he left, Otto confessed to the lawyer, walked out, and disappeared.

Wasting no time, Dolly immediately took up with her lawyer. They stayed together romantically for seven years. In 1929, the lawyer panicked, imagining that Dolly was going to have him killed. He told his story to the police, who found Sandhuber. Otto had married during those seven years, and had two children and a steady job. Sandhuber was tried for manslaughter, but the statute of limitations had run out. The case was dropped. Dolly enjoyed some minor celebrity around Los Angeles in the early 1930s, but soon faded from view.

"HONEY, IT'S JUST MICE"

It is hard to imagine how Otto Sandhuber could have escaped discovery by Dolly Oesterreich's husband, Frederick, but Otto remained undetected for 17 years. He did it by hiding in the attic whenever Frederick was home. Otto would slip down to raid the icebox at night, and he had free reign of the house during the day. If Frederick complained of noises in the attic, Dolly would dismiss it as mice. If he bellowed about missing booze or cigars, Dolly would say that he had drunk too much the night before to remember how much alcohol or tobacco there was.

A HERO TURNED BAD

Tom Horn was an ex-Pinkerton man and former Indian scout who turned to killing for hire. Evidently, he changed his ways when he grew convinced that his heroic reputation would allow him, literally, to get away with murder.

GREED CHANGED TOM HORN FROM AN HONEST LAWMAN TO A COLD-BLOODED KILLER

Tom Horn seemed destined to be a hero. His skills and bravery marked him as a force for good in the wild West. Then, he transformed himself into a greedy, unscrupulous gun-for-hire, eradicating all the goodwill his heroic younger days had earned him.

Tom Horn was born in Memphis, Missouri, in 1861. Stories about local legend Jesse James roused 14-year-old Horn to leave home to join the pony express. He traveled to California and prospected for gold without much luck. There he met Indian scout Al Sieber, who taught him a lot about the Apaches. When the U.S. Army in Arizona called for Indian scouts, Al and Tom went to join up. General Nelson Miles was attempting to contain the Apaches who, led by the famous warrior Geronimo, were looting ranches.

By August 1886, the army had trapped Geronimo's men in the mountains near Sonora, Mexico. Tom's tracking skill had kept the army on clever Geronimo's path, which earned him the Apaches' respect. The cornered Apaches signaled that they would negotiate with Horn. The brave youngster strode into Geronimo's camp alone and resolved the details of their surrender. Tom headed for California again, this time to try ranching. Horn was good at the work, but found it boring.

Seeking excitement, in 1889, Horn joined the Pinkerton Agency, which was the closest thing to a national police force. Though a private company, Pinkerton was often hired by railroads to catch train robbers or by ranchers to investigate cattle rustling. Posted in Wyoming, Horn mainly tracked rustlers. His most famous pursuit was the single-handed capture of a train robber named Peg Leg Watson. Tom approached Watson's cabin and walked straight to the door. Awestruck by Horn's bravery, Watson did not shoot. This amazing arrest sealed Horn's fame as a legendary lawman.

Tom Horn quit Pinkerton in the mid-1890s. Instead of settling down, he worked as a tracker for cattle associations in Wyoming. Trackers were supposed to stop rustling, but in truth most acted as hired killers for cattle barons, settling old grudges and driving out farmers and sheep ranchers.

Horn knew the reputation of trackers, and he did little to improve it. He became greedy and charged a premium for his skills. Horn would kill anyone if the price was right. And he stopped taking chances. He would lie in ambush for his prey, shooting from afar with a long rifle.

In 1902, Horn crossed over the West's line of decency. He had been hired to kill Kels Nickell, a sheep farmer whose death was desired by several cattlemen. Horn set up an ambush for a distant rifle shot and waited. However, at that distance Horn could not discern between the farmer and his 14-year-old son, Willie Nickell, whom Horn shot and killed.

Most people knew that Horn had killed the boy, but their beliefs were no good in court. U.S. Marshal Joe Lefors contrived to get Horn drunk and obtain a confession. After a few drinks, Horn admitted to killing the boy. However, he didn't know that witnesses in the next room were listening in and writing down his confession.

After being convicted of murdering the youth, Horn was sentenced to hang. In jail, Horn wrote his autobiography and shaved off the large mustache that was his trademark. On November 20, 1903, Horn was hanged from a rope that he braided himself.

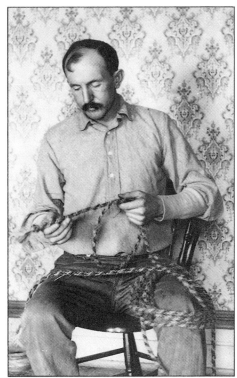

Tom Horn was photographed braiding the noose that was used to hang him for mistakenly slaying the 14-year-old son of sheep farmer Kels Nickell. Prior to mounting the gallows, Horn shaved off his trademark mustache and jotted down a shamelessly glorified account of his life.

THE CARNEGIE ESTATE

MASTER CON-WOMAN CASSIE CHADWICK BILKED MILLIONS BY PRETENDING TO BE A MILLIONAIRE'S ILLEGITIMATE DAUGHTER

Con-woman Cassie Chadwick, shown above, had bilked banks of millions while posing as the illegitimate daughter of multimillionaire Andrew Carnegie. Born Elizabeth Bigley, the swindler began her career as a teenager when she had cards printed up that read: "Miss Bigley—Heiress to $15,000."

Cassie Chadwick began life as Elizabeth Bigley on a poor farm in Canada in the late 1850s. By her seventeenth birthday, she had left home and moved to Toronto. Even at an early age she had a gift for pulling off a con. She soon trekked south to the richer United States. In her early days, she used her beauty—plus fraud and blackmail—to bilk dozens of businessmen out of thousands of dollars. It was estimated that in the early 1880s she was making up to $1,000 a week riding in Pullman cars and swindling the male travelers. This brilliant decade was capped by a three-year stint in prison. By the time she got out, her good looks were gone. She worked for some time in prostitution, but realized that sort of work was all downhill. So Cassie met and married Dr. Leroy Chadwick of Cleveland, Ohio. She quickly left him, but her newly acquired name and respectable background put her back in business.

In 1896, Cassie checked into a ritzy hotel in New York City. When she inadvertently collided with an attorney from Ohio named Dillon, she asked him to accompany her to her father's house. He agreed, and was astounded to watch Cassie enter the mansion of Andrew Carnegie, the nation's richest man. Mr. Dillon waited outside in the carriage while Cassie bluffed her way past the butler into the main hall. She spent 25 minutes explaining to servants that she had made a mistake. When Cassie finally reentered the foyer, Mr. Dillon saw her turn and wave to an old man far off across the long hall. He assumed it was old Andrew Carnegie himself. As Dillon helped Mrs. Chadwick get back into the carriage, he saw that she was holding a promissory note for two million dollars, signed by Andrew Carnegie. In the carriage ride back to the hotel, Cassie explained to the astounded lawyer that she was Mr. Carnegie's illegitimate daughter—his sole heir. She claimed to be holding another seven million dollars in promissory notes back in Cleveland, and further, that her father's entire $400 million fortune would fall to her when Carnegie died. Although she made Mr. Dillon promise to keep it a secret, Cassie knew that he would tell half of Cleveland.

Sure enough, when she returned to Cleveland, Cassie was treated like royalty. Her credit was good everywhere. Bankers were falling all over each other to offer her loans. Cassie pretended to be ignorant of business matters as banker after banker privately arranged huge loans at outrageous interest rates. The interest rates were so high that Cassie knew they were illegal. These bankers figured that the Carnegie estate would make good on the loans irregardless of the interest rates once Cassie Chadwick was named the heir. Cassie herself realized that the best mark to con is a crook who can't complain too loudly.

Cassie Chadwick's entire con relied on one crucial element. She figured that no one would dare to embarrass a big tycoon like Andrew Carnegie by asking him point blank if he had an illegitimate daughter. She was right. None of the many bankers encamped at her door bothered to check out the truth of the rumors.

Cassie Chadwick's scheme worked for over eight years. In November 1904, she sought and received a $190,000 loan from a Boston bank. Unlike the others, they investigated. The prim New England bankers were not impressed by rumors or reputations; they wanted assets. Carnegie found out about the swindle and issued a statement denying that he even knew Chadwick. The Boston bankers heard this, and they called in their loan. When Cassie couldn't pay it back, the news quickly swept all over Ohio. The president of one Ohio bank had loaned her so much of his bank's money that it was forced to close. Other businesses failed as well. It was estimated that Cassie Chadwick had swindled as much as $10 million to $20 million. Cassie had lived extremely well off that money, and she met her fate bravely. She received ten years in jail for fraud. Her years of high living were ill preparation for time in jail; her health deteriorated, and she died in prison in 1907.

Reputed to be the wealthiest man in the country, Andrew Carnegie was Cassie Chadwick's choice to be her "father" for the purpose of her con. The daring bluff made her appear to be his sole heir until the longtime bachelor found out about the scheme and blew the whistle.

TRUNK MURDERS: A BRITISH TRADITION

WHEN ARTHUR DEVEUREUX SEALED HIS FAMILY IN A STEAMER TRUNK, HE UNWITTINGLY LAUNCHED A THOUSAND PLOT LINES.

JANUARY 1905

The hacked up body in the steamer trunk seems to be a staple of classic British mystery fiction. However, fiction stole the idea from its stranger cousin, truth. England experienced a rash of trunk murders starting with a Mr. Crossman sealing a Mrs. Simpson in a tin case in 1902. It continued sporadically until 1927.

The most spectacular, well-conceived murder was committed by Arthur Deveureux in 1905. Deveureux, a 24-year-old chemist's assistant, was trapped in a loveless marriage. He felt he'd be better off without his wife, Beatrice, and his twin infant sons, leaving him with Stanley, his six-year-old son whom he adored. So Deveureux schemed to kill the others. He rented the flat under his own when the tenants left. Deveureux then obtained a huge tin trunk and stored it in the extra flat, away from his wife's view. Shortly thereafter, on January 29, he brought home a flask containing morphine. Deveureux coaxed his wife to drink most of the morphine, perhaps by telling her it was cough medicine. He then poisoned the twins. By the next daybreak, both his wife and the twins had died. Deveureux deposited his newly departed loved ones in the trunk and had a furniture van deliver it to a warehouse in Harrow, a borough in Greater London. Then he and his beloved Stanley relocated to another London address.

Arthur's mother-in-law, Mrs. Gregory, had never liked him. She had even warned her child against marrying Deveureux. When she lost contact with her daughter, Mrs. Gregory feared the worst. Discussions with her daughter's neighbors helped her learn about the furniture van. She was able to track it to the warehouse, where she found the trunk. Mrs. Gregory convinced the authorities to open it, confirming her worst fears. When the newspapers reported on the terrible discovery, Arthur and his son fled again. They were easy to locate, however. How many chemist's assistants traveling with one child could there have been? Scotland Yard found him in Coventry, England, a week later. Arthur Deveureux was hanged on August 15, 1905.

THE MARRYING KIND

JOHANN OTTO HOCH WAS OLD CHICAGO'S PLUCKY BLUEBEARD

Most people considered Johann Otto Hoch a mild-mannered meat packer. However, he had another vocation—he was a wife-murderer. He married 24 women over 14 years, solely for their money. The lucky ones he abandoned; the unlucky ones he murdered.

Born John Schmidt in Germany in 1862, Hoch emigrated to Chicago in the 1880s. Like many German immigrants in the windy city, he worked in the meat-packing industry. It was tough, unpleasant work; certainly no way to get ahead. In 1892, he began to place advertisements in lonely hearts columns as a man who, " . . . wishes acquaintance of widow . . . object matrimony." He graded each respondent for economic value, pursuing the most promising. After whirlwind courtships, he normally endeavored to gain control of his beloved's assets. Hoch never remained long. After taking control of his spouse's valuables, he either would disappear or poison his new wife.

Hoch's last two wives were Marie Walcker and her sister, Amelia. When Marie died within a month of the wedding, Hoch proposed to Amelia. When she criticized him about a period of mourning, Hoch told her, "The dead are for the dead, the living for the living." Amelia and Hoch were married, and within days, he vanished with all her money. The puzzled, grieving, angry newlywed went to the police. The death of Marie within a month and the abandonment of Amelia were coincidences too great for the police to ignore.

In January 1905, the police were able to piece together a pattern of dead and/or defrauded women. Word went out to be on the lookout for Hoch. A New York landlady named Katherine Kimmerle complained that her new tenant, one Henry Bartels, looked like Hoch and had proposed marriage to her. After being arrested, Hoch denied all and even claimed that they had the wrong Hoch. Among his possessions was a fountain pen containing arsenic, traces of which were found in the exhumed Marie Walcker. Johann Otto Hoch was found guilty in Chicago and hanged on February 23, 1906.

AFTER TAKING CONTROL OF HIS SPOUSE'S VALUABLES, HE WOULD EITHER DISAPPEAR OR POISON HIS NEW WIFE.

BLOODSHED IN THE UPPER CRUST

Stanford White, shown above, was slain by Harry Thaw to avenge his wife's dubious honor. A notorious womanizer and world-famous architect, White ironically met his death while watching a musical satire on the roof of Madison Square Garden, one of his creations. The old Garden has long since been razed.

MILLIONAIRE HARRY THAW SHOT A FAMED ARCHITECT OVER A CHORUS GIRL, SHATTERING THE CORE OF NEW YORK HIGH SOCIETY.

The killing of Stanford White by Harry Thaw was no mystery. It occurred in front of a packed house at the opening of a new musical at Madison Square Garden. However, the history and psychology that drove Thaw to pull that trigger opened a Pandora's box of greed, debauchery, and moral hypocrisy that changed New York's elite forever. It was a time of inestimable wealth conspicuously displayed. While money-rich railroad barons and oil tycoons tried to buy their way into respectability, the poor had to endure bitter poverty and hardship. One night's society dinner tab might cost more than a year's wages for ten miners. These contrasts were hidden behind lush velvet curtains. Stanford White's murder ripped down those curtains.

In 1872, Harry Kendall Thaw was born into a family who made their fortune in Pennsylvania railroads and the rich coal mines of that state. Thaw received a good education, but his bizarre lifestyle did not please his father. Since the family fortune was already made, Harry wanted only to spend it. On his death, Harry's father cut his allowance to $2,000 a year in hopes of forcing Harry to be constructive. However, the will let his mother control the trust fund, so she raised Harry's yearly allowance to $80,000. This significant sum went toward Harry's cocaine addiction and toward women for engaging in sadistic sexual activities. He treated the girls brutally with exotic whips, and it took a lot of money to keep them quiet. Although he was suspicious and possessive, Harry was also a napoleonic playboy who liked to chase after the Broadway chorus girls in New York City. He was not alone in this pursuit: Chasing after Broadway show girls was considered the thing to do by the philanderers of the upper class. Harry was not good at this game, however. Though he had plenty of money to lavish, his reputation preceded him. All the girls knew that Harry Thaw was trouble. And they could afford to ignore him—all the men chasing them were rich.

Evelyn Nesbit burst onto the Broadway scene in 1900 at the tender age of 16. She was a dazzling beauty who had started as an artist's model at age 14. She was tremendously successful at this: All the best illustrators had her pose for them, even Charles Dana Gibson, creator of the Gibson Girl. Evelyn's mother was loath to expose her daughter to high society's bad influences, but they were direly poor and Evelyn's beauty was the only asset they had. Her Broadway debut was in a long-running show called *Floradora*. It was said that the *Floradora* chorus girls were the most beautiful and the most sought after. It was predicted that every one would marry a millionaire. Evelyn was initially protected from this sort of attention, but the rich admirers were like a pack of dogs. There were too many dinner invitations and too many diamonds and bouquets of flowers sent backstage to resist for long. The most ardent of Evelyn's admirers was the architect Stanford White. Though he was careful to cultivate Mrs. Nesbit's trust, he seduced Evelyn and took her as his mistress. She would later say that he raped her the first time, but this claim was rather dubious. (It would, however, prove crucial in the mind of Harry Thaw.)

Stanford White was a brilliant architect and a leading social force in New York City. He was its number one citizen: the first to join a committee for one cause or another, and the first to design and build monuments to the city's greatness. White designed City Hall and the arch in Washington Park. He built and personally furnished the homes of New York's elite. White had a special feel for the incredible energy that was surging through the city at that time. People looked up to and respected White. He knew, more than most, how to spend the incredible wealth that was accumulating along Fifth Avenue. And New York's elite was happy to follow his lead. White's conception of the good life included sumptuous dinner parties and sexual feasts. Stanford White was no

WHITE'S CONCEPTION OF THE GOOD LIFE INCLUDED SUMPTUOUS DINNER PARTIES AND SEXUAL FEASTS.

pervert; he treated women respectfully and well. But he assumed, as all of New York's elite assumed, that he was allowed to have a larger appetite than most people. He cultivated the company of beautiful women. By all accounts, he was good-natured and generous with them. Evelyn Nesbit was certainly much richer for having known him, which she readily acknowledged. He paid for her apartments, her medical bills, clothes, and so forth. He taught her about the world; how to use the money that would be lavished upon her. "Stanny" taught her everything.

Evelyn's beauty became an obsession with Harry Thaw, who was determined to have her. She had heard all the warnings about Harry Thaw, and he was easy enough to resist when there were other men about. But Evelyn craved attention as badly as Harry craved cocaine. Whenever she found herself without a better offer, she would go out with Harry. His persistence drove them closer and closer. Though Stanford White had much affection for Evelyn, he never pretended to be obsessed. He had a wife and family, and other mistresses as well. When Stanford White went off on business one season, Evelyn accepted Harry Thaw's invitation to tour Europe with him. Evelyn's mother went along to chaperon, but Mrs. Nesbit and Harry Thaw did not get along very well. After a few months in Paris, Mrs. Nesbit returned to America, leaving her 18-year-old daughter to fend for herself. Isolated in Europe with no money of her own, Evelyn's only defense was the power of obsession she held over Harry. She skillfully fended off his requests for marriage. One night, she used as an excuse the fact that Stanford White had "ruined" her. This answer seemed to both satisfy and excite Harry. He began to refer to White as "that beast," jealous of a past that wasn't his. A few nights later, Harry used a whip to make Evelyn confess about her seduction by White. Harry alternately wept and became aroused as Evelyn spun her tale. She embellished and even lied as she saw fit because this Scheherazade-like ritual was her only way of controlling Harry.

Harry Thaw, pictured above, was put on trial for killing Stanford White. The jury understandably found it difficult to believe the somber and even scholarly-looking Thaw could have been sane when he committed all the brutal sadistic acts that prosecution witnesses chillingly recounted.

Thaw's devotion grew stronger and stronger, and eventually they were married on April 4, 1905, when Evelyn was 20. They settled down to a quiet life in the family mansion in Pittsburgh. Away from the gay life of New York, Evelyn became bored. Harry would occasionally slip away for several days for coked-out binges at some of the few brothels that still allowed him to come back. In 1906, Harry took his bride back to New York for a few weeks of fun. While they were dining in a fancy restaurant one evening, Stanford White walked by. No words were spoken, but a rage swelled up in Harry's face. The next evening, June 25, the Thaws attended the opening night of *Mam'zelle Champagne,* a musical satire playing on the rooftop garden of Madison Square Garden (a building designed by Stanford White). Several rows in front of them, White sat with some friends. Harry excused himself from his table, walked up to White, and shot him three times. Thaw surrendered immediately, telling reporters that he'd saved his wife's honor. He was happy to tell the press his side of the story.

New York's tabloid press was not part of the elite. The papers eagerly reported on the comings and goings of their "betters," but the media felt no loyalty to high society's point of view. Regular folks bought the newspaper, and that's who the editors purported to speak for. So it was that Stanford White was transformed instantaneously in death from a leading light of the city into a lecherous, sex-crazed egomaniac. The newspapers had Harry Thaw's words to quote, and the editorialists could expound their own. And there was no one to speak for Stanford White. His family and friends retreated into a dignified silence. Suddenly the ethics of the rich were questioned. Adding to this were some disturbing allegations about Thaw himself that started creeping forth. If Harry Thaw wasn't a moral crusader in his execution of Stanford White, if Harry Thaw was in fact a sadist and a coke fiend, then where was the moral right of this story? These questions abounded as Harry went to trial.

HARRY WOULD OCCASIONALLY SLIP AWAY FOR SEVERAL DAYS FOR COKED-OUT BINGES AT SOME OF THE FEW BROTHELS THAT STILL ALLOWED HIM TO COME BACK.

Evelyn Nesbit Thaw was a former *Floradora* chorus girl who became known as "The Girl in the Red Velvet Swing." This nickname referred to the swing hanging from the ceiling in the tower of Madison Square Garden, where she alleged Stanford White had first ravished her.

Thaw assumed that his money would get him off. People of his class simply didn't go to prison. His money did buy the best lawyers and special treatment in his cell (he ate catered meals). The defense felt that the trial hinged on Evelyn's testimony; her words could acquit or indict him. So the Thaw family treated her very well during this period. The first trial ended in a hung jury. At the second trial a year later, Thaw pleaded temporary insanity and won. The Thaw money bought Harry a comfortable lifestyle in an asylum, but they refused to give Evelyn a dime more. Evelyn returned to the stage, more popular than ever. Everyone wanted to see the girl that the big fuss had been about. She toured the country, selling out the nation's biggest arenas. When Evelyn tried to play Pittsburgh, which the Thaws considered their own, an injunction was filed. The Thaws lost.

When Harry Thaw was declared sane in 1915, his first act was to divorce his wife. Afterward, Harry would periodically cause some trouble, but he always bought his way out. Thaw still saw Evelyn on occasion, but she never trusted him. Harry died in 1947. When Evelyn's career faded with her beauty, she settled into a semi-obscurity, running speakeasies in New York and Atlantic City.

As for Stanford White, until recently, he had barely been a footnote in New York City's history. Most of his buildings have come down to make way for bigger ones.

KING FOR A DAY

HUMBLE SHOEMAKER WILHELM VOIGHT LIVED OUT HIS FANTASY OF POWER AS A PRUSSIAN CAPTAIN

Wilhelm Voight had never received his fair share of respect. He was a lowly shoemaker in the highly stratified society of Kaiser Wilhelm's pre-World War I Germany. And Voight had spent nearly half of his 50-plus years in Germany's super-strict prisons. On October 16, 1906, Wilhelm was in the town of Tegel. He had recently emerged from jail and was harboring fantasies of revenge. Then he saw the shiny, ornate uniform of a Prussian Army Captain in the window of a second-hand shop. He purchased the whole uniform—including the iron-spiked helmet.

When he changed into the uniform, an immediate transformation came over Voight. There was respect in the eyes of passersby. He now met their gazes proudly, instead of staring down to the ground. Growing more drunk with his power by the minute, Voight stepped in front of a passing troop of soldiers. Growling orders, he commandeered the troop for his own mission.

"Captain" Voight told the sergeant in charge that he had urgent business in nearby Kopenick, and he needed the troop. No German questioned authority wielded with bravado. Hence, the soldiers marched behind the captain for 20 miles. After the soldiers arrived in Kopenick, they were ordered to take charge of the town. Guards were posted at the town hall, and the mayor was arrested. The city's cash box was brought forth and Captain Voight accepted custody of it. Three vehicles were confiscated to transport the mayor to Berlin for questioning. The troop and the imprisoned mayor crowded into two of the cars. Captain Voight alone occupied the third car. The caravan quickly left for Berlin. When the first two cars arrived at the Berlin Police Station, the soldiers brought in their prisoner and waited for further orders. And they waited and waited. The third car never arrived.

A nationwide manhunt began for the imposter who made off with 4,000 marks from the coffers of Kopenick and embarrassed the German Army. Even the Kaiser was said to be laughing out loud. The hapless Voight was caught within a few days.

A FOLK HERO WAS BORN

Officially, Wilhelm Voight was a scoundrel, sentenced to four years of hard labor after his capture. Unofficially, he became a national hero. There were praises, toasts, and offers of marriage from admiring maids. Even his prison term was cut short—to 20 months. Although the German Army was not amused, Wilhelm Voight lived out the rest of his days as a respected hero of the common folk. He often appeared at music halls, local fairs, and circuses in his second-hand uniform, billed as the "Captain of Kopenick."

SUFFER THE CHILDREN

MADWOMAN JEANNE WEBER
KEPT HER HANDS ON THE
THROATS OF FRANCE'S
CHILDREN

Jeanne Weber was born in France in 1875, the daughter of a poor Normandy fisherman. Having no interest in her family's coastal fishing life, she sought work as a maidservant in 1889. Jeanne worked hard, but she ultimately decided that domestic service was not for her. She gave it up and started to travel about France, working odd jobs here and there. By 1893, she had settled in Paris, eventually meeting and marrying Marcel Weber. Despite the hardship of life in the Paris slums, their marriage was relatively happy. The couple had three children.

Both Marcel and Jeanne Weber drank heavily, using alcohol to forget their troubles. Suddenly, both of Jeanne Weber's small daughters died. Then the heartbroken woman drank even more than before. When two small boys for whom she was caring died soon afterward, no one said anything about the matter. After all, infant mortality in the slums of Paris was high. However, there was more concern about an incident that occurred shortly thereafter. Jeanne was looking after the two daughters of Pierre Weber, one of Marcel's brothers. A neighbor noticed one of the girls, Georgette, apparently having a fit while sitting on her aunt Jeanne's lap. The concerned neighbor questioned Jeanne and was told that everything was fine. Satisfied, the neighbor left. However, an hour later, Jeanne reported that the fit had recurred and the child was dead. After only nine days, Suzanne, Pierre's other daughter, was found dead, with a scarf gently draped about her neck. Seeing strange marks on the necks of both children, the doctor refused to sign Suzanne's death certificate. He was overruled by the police and their official surgeon. They were convinced that the deaths were from natural causes.

The curious incidents continued. Yet another niece died after three choking episodes, the first two of which were fortunately interrupted by a visitor. Marcel Weber, Jeanne's own son (aged seven), died next. Then Maurice Weber, a nephew, was left with Jeanne while his mother went shopping. When his mother returned earlier than expected, she found her son blue-faced and choking. He was rushed to the hospital, where he was revived. This time the police were called in. The infants' corpses were exhumed, but by now no throat marks were discernable. Jeanne was defended by a top lawyer who obtained an acquittal. The case was helped by the stubbornness of the official surgeon, who refused to go back on his original opinion.

Once free, Jeanne Weber left her husband and his now-quite-hostile family. She apparently disappeared—only to emerge again on April 16, 1907. At that time, nine-year-old Auguste Bavouzet died of strangulation at his home in central France. His sister, who disliked their new housekeeper Madame Moulinet, checked her belongings. In Madame's bag, Auguste's sister found damning letters and press clippings—Madame Moulinet was in reality Jeanne Weber. Again, Jeanne was tried and once more acquitted.

Afterward, a Madame Bouchery and her alleged husband checked into an inn in northern France. The woman asked the innkeeper if Marcel, his seven-year-old son, could stay in her room overnight. Madame Bouchery wanted some company while her husband was away at work. Obligingly, the kindly innkeeper gave his approval. Later, the child's screams brought his father running. Unfortunately, the boy's frantic father did not arrive in time. The police appeared, and Madame Bouchery was searched. This proved that she was Jeanne Weber. Madame Bouchery had recently been fired from a children's home where she had been found strangling a youngster who was ill.

In 1908, Jeanne Weber was declared insane and sent to an asylum. The madwoman died a most appropriate death in 1910, foaming at the mouth, when she strangled herself.

WHEN TWO SMALL BOYS FOR WHOM JEANNE WEBER WAS CARING DIED, NO ONE SAID ANYTHING ABOUT THE MATTER. AFTER ALL, INFANT MORTALITY IN THE SLUMS OF PARIS WAS HIGH.

THE WILD BUNCH

BUTCH CASSIDY AND HIS
OUTLAW PALS CLOSED THE
CHAPTER ON THE WILD WEST
WITH A BIG BANG

**THESE MEN WERE
NOT BORN OUTLAWS
(THOUGH MANY
SHOWED A VERY
NATURAL APTITUDE);
THEY WERE CREATED
BY THE TIMES.**

1908

The famous "Wild Bunch." Seated, from left to right, are the Sundance Kid, Ben Kilpatrick, and Butch Cassidy. Standing, from left to right, are Bill Carver and Kid Curry.

They were the most notorious, most brazen, and most successful of the gangs in the West after the Civil War. Known as the Wild Bunch, this loose combination of thieves gravitated together to combine their considerable skills. This gang was lead by Butch Cassidy (Robert Leroy Parker) and the Sundance Kid (Harry Longbaugh). It consisted of an alternating lineup of associates, sidekicks, and ne'er-do-wells. They included Kid Curry (Harvey Logan), George "Flat Nose" Curry, Bill Carver, Ben Kilpatrick (the Tall Texan), O. C. Hanks, Frank "Peg Leg" Elliot, "Laughing Sam" Carey, and many others. These men were not born outlaws (though many showed a very natural aptitude); they were created by the times.

They were cowboys in cattle country. It was the only life they had ever known. Two years after Wyoming experienced a drought, the beef market disintegrated. The winter of 1886–87 devastated herds all across the plains. Cowboys who had never done anything in their lives except punch cattle were suddenly out of work. Rather than starve like the herds or learn a new occupation, many took to cattle rustling. After all, the remaining beef was now very valuable. When the beef market returned to strength in the late 1880s, cattle rustling was no longer as profitable. Many of the outlaws refused to go back to the quiet, unassuming life of the cowboy after experiencing the money and excitement of cattle rustling. A great number of the outlaws took to raids and robberies. They found that if they swarmed down in large enough numbers, they could easily overwhelm a small-town bank, cattleman's association, or even a railroad. The outlaws also discovered some natural formations that made excellent hideouts. Two of the best-known were Hole-in-the-Wall, Wyoming, and Robber's Roost, Utah. These places were easily fortified gorges with single, narrow entrances. Outlaws lived there freely, beyond the reach of the law. These gathering places also made excellent crime colleges and employment agencies. Outlaws learned criminal techniques from each other and recruited new members. Out of these exchanges came a single, loose conglomeration of the best (or worst) outlaws. They were called the Wild Bunch.

Butch Cassidy was born Robert Leroy Parker in Circleville, Utah, in 1866. He grew up on a small farm among honest, hard-working folk. However, young Parker's hero was a neighbor named Mike Cassidy, who had been a hard-living outlaw in the 1850s. The old pro taught the boy how to shoot and filled him with romantic lore about the outlaw life. Out of respect, the young man took Cassidy's name as his own. He acquired the nickname Butch because his only legitimate job was as a butcher. Butch Cassidy was calm and easy-going. His company was much sought after by rival gangs. Hot tempers often cost lives and fouled up jobs. An unshakable, level-headed man who was also a dead shot was a valuable commodity. Butch robbed his first train in 1887. He hit his first bank two years later. In 1894, he served

THE JAMES/YOUNGER GANG

During the Civil War, loosely organized groups of marauders, such as Quantrill's Raiders, were authorized by the Confederacy to loot and pillage Union towns in the Arkansas, Missouri, and Kansas territories. Most of these bands were basically outlaws, except that after feeding and equipping themselves, they sent all surpluses to the Confederate Army. When the war ended, the Northerners in these territories were reluctant to grant official soldier status (and thus, immunity) to the marauders. They wanted to treat them as criminals. Among those trapped between official government immunity and the wrath of Northern townsfolk were Frank James and his younger brother Jesse, both ex-farmers. The James brothers tried to return to their simple farm life, but found themselves harassed and pursued. Frank joined forces with his neighbor, cousin, and former Quantrill mate, Cole Younger, and his brothers to continue their marauding ways. While Frank was initially in charge, Jesse James eventually rose to the lead because of his superior tactical planning. Between 1866 and 1882, the James/Younger gang were known to have pulled off over a dozen bank, stagecoach, train, and paymaster holdups. They've been credited with many more besides. The gang always found welcome hideouts among the many resentful Southern farmers in the territories who regarded the outlaws as heroes. The Younger brothers were severely wounded and captured after a shootout following an attempted bank robbery in Northfield, Minnesota. On April 3, 1882, Jesse James was infamously shot in the back by Robert Ford, a bribed associate. Frank James turned himself in six months later. However, two separate juries refused to convict him. They were outraged over the government collusion in the murder of his brother. Unlike Jesse James, Cole Younger made it to the 20th century, dying in 1916.

Robert Leroy Parker, aka Butch Cassidy. Americans have always loved stories of legendary bad men who mend their ways and disappear somewhere to live out their lives in quiet anonymity. Cassidy may have been one of the rare outlaws who built this grand myth into a reality.

a two-year prison term for cattle rustling. It was there that Butch first heard about Hole-in-the-Wall. On his release, he went straight there. Butch soon formed a gang that included Kid Curry and Flat Nose Curry. In 1899, they took the Union Pacific's *Overland Flyer.* They used so much dynamite that they practically blew up the entire railcar. This little job put the famous Pinkerton detective agency on their trail. It also caused four states to place $1,000 bounties on all their heads. However, the gang retreated safely to Hole-in-the-Wall.

Around 1900, Butch Cassidy met the Sundance Kid. They immediately became best friends. Sundance was the deadliest shot in the whole Wild Bunch. No one ever tangled with him, and he always proved himself very useful on jobs. He became Butch's second in command, though no one enforced rank too strictly. Pinkerton agent Charlie Siringo had worked his way into the gang, posing as an outlaw. He was able to thwart many of the planned train robberies by notifying authorities in advance. Luckily, none of the Wild Bunch ever found out. In 1901, they stopped a *Great Northern Flyer* and escaped with over $40,000. This time, a 100-man posse chased them. But the Wild Bunch was simply better at the game than the authorities. They escaped and fled to Fort Worth, Texas—hiding out in a lavish whorehouse. Butch and Sundance were beginning to feel the heat. They realized that it was only going to get harder to get away in a West that was rapidly becoming domesticated.

The Wild Bunch split up. Kid Curry took over the gang, which continued to hold up banks and trains in the northern states for a few years. He was caught in Knoxville, Tennessee, in 1902, but he shot his way out of jail a few months later. After one last train robbery, he died in a shootout in the Colorado Rockies in 1903. George "Flat Nose" Curry was killed in a chase following an attempted arrest for cattle rustling. In a macabre scene, the local residents of Castle Gate, Utah, cut hunks of skin from the dead outlaw as souvenirs. Pieces of

Butch Cassidy, born Robert Leroy Parker, worshipped neighbor Mike Cassidy, a former outlaw. The old pro taught young Parker how to shoot and romanticized the outlaw life. Out of respect, the young man took Cassidy's name. His nickname Butch came from his only legitimate job, which was as a butcher.

THE DOOLIN/DALTON GANG

Perhaps by coincidence, there is a direct connection between two of the most famous outlaw gangs of the Wild West. The aunt of Cole Younger and his brothers raised an outlaw brood of her own: the four Dalton brothers. Grat, Emmett, Bob, and Bill Dalton were the wildcats of a family of 15. Emmett, Bob, and Grat started out as sheriff's deputies. However, they kept forgetting which side of the law they were on. They eventually became wanted for murder and stealing horses. After forming a gang, the four brothers robbed their first train in 1891, quickly gaining notoriety and attention. For the next four years, they ranged across California, Texas, Oklahoma, and Kansas. They left behind a trail of broken banks and dead lawmen, citizens, and outlaws. Among the recruits who replenished their ranks was one Bill Doolin. He rose to a leadership position with Bill Dalton when younger brothers Bob and Grat were killed in Coffeyville, Kansas. Emmett was wounded and captured that day as well. The Doolin/Dalton Gang kept up their criminal activities for another two years. However, the public pressure for their arrest was too great. Posses eventually tracked down and killed the entire gang.

him survive today in western museums. Ben Kilpatrick, the Tall Texan, was picked up in St. Louis for the Great Northern job and served ten years in jail. On his release in 1911, he immediately held up a train. He was killed by a tough-minded railroad guard.

And what became of Butch and Sundance? With Etta Place, a very pretty schoolteacher and housewife, they sailed to Argentina by steamship from the port of New York. Despite the language barrier, Butch and Sundance easily held up banks and rich mining payrolls. Etta usually acted as a lookout. In 1907, Sundance took Etta back to the United States. After accompanying her to Denver, he then returned to Bolivia to rejoin Butch. They continued to pillage the countryside, but afterward the facts become blurred. It is rumored—and widely believed—that the duo were surrounded and killed by a force of the Bolivian Army in 1908. Some also speculate that Butch Cassidy escaped that ambush and returned to America, where he lived under an assumed name in Nevada until 1937.

THE LADY BLUEBEARD OF LAPORTE, INDIANA

BELLE GUNNESS LURED UNAWARE BEAUS TO HER FARM, WHERE THEY BECAME PERMANENT GUESTS

Belle Gunness, perhaps the first and certainly the most famous American female serial killer, is shown with her three children. One theory is that she disappeared into obscurity without her children, electing to kill them because they knew too much and had already shown loose tongues.

In 1904, when her second husband, Peter Gunness, died, Belle Gunness was left with three children and a hog farm near LaPorte, Indiana. A falling meat grinder struck Peter, who had been a butcher, in the head and killed him. Some gossip arose when one of the children blurted out at school, "My momma killed my poppa . . . ." Despite the coroner's doubts, nothing was done about it.

After her mourning had ended, Belle promoted her handyman, Ray Lamphere, to be her lover. Ray was a weak man and an alcoholic. He generally did whatever Belle told him to do. Belle then began to place advertisements in lonely hearts columns. From time to time, new gentlemen callers would appear at the farm. Belle would escort them about LaPorte like a new beau, and Ray would disappear like a whipped dog. However, none of these callers ever stayed for very long. They would disappear as suddenly as they appeared.

In 1908, Belle received a reply to her lonely heart ads from Andrew Helgelien of South Dakota. Taken with her romantic literary style and her pleas to meet him, he set up a meeting. As an afterthought, she asked if he could bring $1,000 to help her pay her mortgage. The townsfolk promptly noticed Belle's new beau, but he soon vanished like all the rest. Then Belle went to Sheriff Smutzer to complain that her handyman threatened to burn down the farm if she didn't quit seeing her suitors. She had fired Ray Lamphere, but he was in love and he kept hanging around.

Shortly thereafter, on April 28, 1908, a fire totally destroyed Belle's farmhouse. Four bodies were found: Belle's three children and the decapitated body of a woman believed to be Belle. The coroner assumed that the poor woman's head had been cut off by a wooden support that had fallen. Amazingly, he decided to overlook the fact that the corpse weighed 150 pounds, while Belle was a solid woman of 280. The sheriff arrested Ray Lamphere on the charges of arson

Nine bodies were unearthed from this section of the Gunness farm in LaPorte, Indiana, and 14 in all were found on Belle's property. After they viewed the grisly discovery, the investigators suspected that Belle had killed even more victims.

and murder. When Ray snapped out of a drunken stupor, he loudly professed his innocence. Meanwhile, Asle Helgelien popped up to inquire what had become of his brother Andrew.

The coroner had ordered the workmen to keep digging for the missing head. Though they never found it, 14 other corpses, including the missing Helgelien brother, turned up. The bodies had been cut up by someone who knew how to butcher. Then the pieces were packaged and hidden in the ground under the house. A police investigation later revealed that Belle might have taken as much as $30,000 from these men, collectively. A more intense search of the ruins turned up several gold rings and Belle's plate for her false teeth. That seemed to satisfy most people that the headless corpse was indeed Belle. They didn't care that the body was "missing" 130 pounds.

Ray Lamphere was convicted of arson. Still claiming that he was innocent, he died in jail. He maintained that Belle had killed a prostitute from nearby Chicago by giving her poison and beheading her. According to Ray, Belle then ripped out her own dental plate for evidence and fled to Chicago with her booty. Some LaPorte residents did claim to have seen her in Chicago on their outings to that city. However, no definite proof of this was ever found.

Belle's lover and handyman, Ray Lamphere, died in prison of tuberculosis, still maintaining that he had been nothing more than her dupe.

Unlike most of the lady Bluebeard's victims, Andrew Helgelien had a brother who knew where he had gone and who came looking for him. Unfortunately for Andrew, his brother arrived too late.

1910–1919

CRIMINAL ENDEAVOR IN THE CENTURY'S SECOND DECADE WAS OVER-shadowed by World War I. Indeed the war, which lasted from 1914 to 1918, might itself be regarded as the decade's greatest crime. One of its innumerable victims was Mata Hari, who was executed for espionage. This decade also saw acts of grisly murder—as Dr. Hawley Crippen, Harry Seddon, George Smith, and Louis Voison demonstrated. In France, Paris was terrorized by a daring gang called "the Motor Bandits," and a supposedly patriotic Italian swiped the *Mona Lisa* out of the Louvre. In Chicago, Illinois, the Everleigh sisters erected the best little bordello in the Midwest—or anywhere else. Chicago was also the setting for the 1919 Black Sox scandal. Meanwhile, Georgia provided the venue for the lynching of Leo Frank. And in California, convicted murderer Robert Stroud transformed himself into "the Birdman of Alcatraz."

THE FIRST MODERN MURDER MYSTERY

THE CASE OF DR. CRIPPEN ELECTRIFIED ENGLAND WITH ADULTERY, POISON, AND AN INTERNATIONAL MANHUNT

In England, the name Crippen is synonymous with murder. True, the case of the mild-mannered quasi-doctor who killed his overbearing wife for the love of his mistress certainly has its interesting facets. However, it is hard to understand how this particular murder and investigation so riveted the attention of the nation that had produced Sherlock Holmes and Jack the Ripper. Perhaps the British people were drawn to Crippen's story because it signaled that the times were changing. To be sure, the case brought forward sophisticated new methods of international investigation.

Hawley Harvey Crippen was an American who worked in the United States as an eye and ear specialist. The degree of his medical prowess is questionable—there were no professional standards for doctors in America at that time. In 1885, he found faintly disreputable employment with a patent medicine company.

Crippen's personal life seems to have been as precarious as his professional one: His second wife was a star-struck woman named Kunigunde Mackamotzki (wisely, she changed her name to Cora) who felt she was destined to become a great singer. To that end, she used the stage name Belle Elmore. In reality, Cora Crippen was a domineering, ostentatious woman who dwarfed her husband in size and personality. The short Crippen, with his bulging eyes and scrawny mustache, seemed all the more meek standing next to his hulking Cora.

The couple moved to London in 1900. Crippen's professional qualifications proved inadequate for Britain's stricter laws concerning medical practice at the time. He was obliged to take a job managing the London branch of the patent medicine company that he had moved to London in order to escape. Cora kept at her singing, expanding to music hall performances.

The couple lived at 39 Hilltop Crescent in North London. By 1907, Crippen completely hated his wife and her ideas of middle-class respect-

Wife-killer Hawley Harvey Crippen looked every bit the beleaguered and henpecked husband that he was. The police would almost undoubtedly have accepted his story that his wife had died after she had left him to care for a sick American relative had he not panicked and fled England.

Born Kunigunde Mackamotzki, Cora Crippen adopted the name of Belle Elmore when she began to seriously pursue a singing career. Most historians believe that Crippen was compelled to murder her by her extravagance and, even more, her insufferable artist friends who were constantly underfoot at the Crippen residence.

ability. He was fed up with her self-conscious devotion to opera and with the braggarts who encouraged her. He especially hated that neither his wife nor her friends had the slightest idea of how vulgar they were.

The Crippens' marriage was a sham as well. Cora took a lover, an American entertainer named Bruce Miller. Because Cora imagined that her domination of her husband had stripped him of all will to defy her, Bruce stayed openly at the Crippen household when he visited London.

But Hawley Harvey Crippen had a few surprises of his own. He had fallen madly in love with his young bookkeeper, Ethel Le Neve, a quiet, lovely, and most demure woman of 24. He began a romantic relationship with Ethel, and as their affair continued, Crippen began to hatch fantastic schemes. Finally, in 1910, he decided to kill his wife. He obtained five grams of hyoscine, a hypnotic nerve depressant. In early February, he invited several of Cora's theatrical friends over for dinner. As the last of them was leaving, Crippen poisoned his wife and then cleared away the dishes.

Crippen obtained £80 by pawning his wife's jewelry and some of her clothes. The rest of his wife's wardrobe he gave to Ethel. He informed the Music Hall Ladies Guild that Cora had fallen ill and could neither attend nor contribute to their cause. He started stepping out with Ethel, who wore fine clothes that friends knew belonged to Cora.

Rumors and suspicions finally brought the police to Crippen's door with official inquiries. The doctor informed them that his wife had returned to the United States to care for a sick relative, fallen ill herself, and died in California. The police were satisfied, and the investigation might have been dropped right there. However, Crippen's nerve subsequently broke, and he panicked and ran. When the police discovered that Crippen and Ethel had left England for Rotterdam, The Netherlands, warrants were issued for their arrest. In addition, Interpol (the International Criminal Police Organization) was informed. The police also started digging in Crippen's basement at Hilltop Crescent for clues. In the cellar, they found assorted pieces of human flesh. There were parts of a buttock, pieces of skin and muscle, and internal organs. Although the remains were inconclusive as to the victim's sex, the scar tissue showed that the victim had previously undergone abdominal surgery. These surgical scars matched Cora Crippen's medical history. The international search for Crippen and Le Neve intensified.

Aboard the SS *Montrose*, sailing from Rotterdam to Canada, Captain Kendall noticed that two of his passengers—a Mr. Robinson and his son—were oddly affectionate toward one another. They also looked very much like photos of Crippen and Le Neve that were splashed across the newspapers. Kendall radioed Scotland Yard from the middle of the Atlantic. The authorities were waiting at the dock as the ship pulled into Canadian waters on July 31. The press was waiting, too. Photos of Crippen's dramatic arrest and Ethel Le Neve's peculiar impersonation of a young boy made front-page news worldwide. Upon their arrest, Crippen muttered, "I'm glad it's all over, this business is too nerve-wracking."

With such a sensational arrest, a highly charged trial was assured. The doctor was the first of the two lovers to be put before a jury. His five-day trial opened on October 18, 1910. From the start, it was clear that Crippen had given up all chance of acquittal. Though apparently indifferent to his own fate, he was determined to put forth the innocence of his beloved Ethel, and swore in open court that she knew nothing of Cora's murder.

Crippen was found guilty and sentenced to death. While awaiting execution, he was much relieved to learn that a jury had acquitted Ethel of any wrongdoing. Dr. Crippen was hanged on November 23, 1910. His last request was that he be buried with a photograph of Ethel.

Ethel Le Neve in the male garb she wore aboard the SS *Montrose*. Along with her ladylike table manners, what gave her masquerade away to Captain Kendall, the ship's commander, was the fact that her trousers could not be buttoned because of her female proportions, and the trousers had to be held together by safety pins.

THE EVERLEIGH CLUB

SISTERS ADA AND MINNA EVERLEIGH CREATED THE FINEST BROTHEL IN AMERICA—SOME SAY THE FINEST EVER

Ada and Minna Everleigh were born into an aristocratic Southern family near Louisville, Kentucky in 1876 and 1878, respectively. Though their mother died early, their father—a lawyer—made sure that the girls were properly educated in literature, art, style, and etiquette. The sisters married two brothers in 1897, but each sister divorced within a year (claiming physical violence). Ada and Minna faced uncertain futures. Left a worthy inheritance by their father, they were determined to invest it in a business they could run themselves.

Nobody knows the leap of imagination or logic that led these proper ladies to turn to bordello management. Possibly, it was a sort of feminism, for their brief marriages left them with a harsh view of that institution. (Neither sister remarried or had any significant lovers.) Once the sisters decided to manage a bordello, they were determined to run the classiest, most expensive place and cater only to refined clientele.

In 1898, anticipating the Trans-Mississippi Exposition, Ada and Minna leased a bordello in Omaha, Nebraska. They redecorated it, hired new girls, raised prices, and operated it throughout the Exposition. They made good money, but business declined steeply after the Exposition closed. The regular gentlemen of Omaha refused to pay ten dollars for a girl. The sisters decided that they needed to be in a town that had a permanent supply of high rollers. In the winter of 1899, the Everleigh sisters bought the lease to one of the largest brothels in Chicago, at 2131–3 South Dearborn, for $55,000. They fired all the girls, hired new prostitutes, and redecorated the entire house. They rechristened the place the Everleigh Club and opened their doors on February 1, 1900.

Chicago had never seen anything like it. Under the management of the business-smart sisters, the Everleigh Club was the most notorious, most luxurious, and most consistently profitable bordello in the

United States; probably the rest of the world, as well. Visitors from Europe marveled at its splendor, saying it eclipsed anything in Paris. No house in New York, San Francisco, or even the celebrated French Quarter of New Orleans could compare.

The Everleigh Club's operating budget was enormous: The annual overhead tipped $75,000, covering such expenses as servants, music (supplied by three orchestras plus piano players), cooks (15 to 25 full-time gourmet chefs), and $15,000 a year in protection money to Chicago's corrupt ward bosses (see the sidebar). In return for their protection money, the sisters were never harassed or raided. If the costs of operating the club were huge, the profits were even bigger. They totaled between $1,000 and $5,000 a night, every night, from opening night in 1900 to the last evening of operation in 1911. The club's specialty was private parties. A host booked a room, and his guests were served an excellent meal and plied with all the alcohol and female companionship they desired. The host received separate itemized bills for the food, liquor, and girls.

The club closed in late 1911 because of growing pressure from civic reform groups. The voluntary closing was delicately negotiated with the police (who were loath to make any demands because they'd received generous bribes from the sisters). Ada and Minna retired, at the ages of 35 and 33, respectively, with a million dollars in cash and $200,000 worth of jewelry. They also amassed $150,000 worth of exquisite furniture, books, paintings, rugs, statues, and nearly 50 brass beds inlaid with marble. The sisters auctioned off one of the brothel's deluxe features: the 20 gold-plated spittoons that were distributed around the club.

Following retirement, Ada and Minna Everleigh moved to New York City, assumed their original family name of Lester, and spent the rest of their lives as wealthy socialites—giving money to charities and sponsoring poetry readings.

THE LEVEE

Chicago is a city divided into wards. The First Ward is the biggest and contains the downtown Loop district. In 1900, the First Ward was also the most corrupt. Ward bosses "Bath House" John Coughlin and Mike "Hinky Dink" Kenna ran the ward on the greased-palm system. Merchants had to pay bribes to receive essential city services. Criminals had to pay bribes to avoid arrest. The policy was "anything goes," as long as the ward bosses got their cut.

Out of this inspired stewardship grew the Levee, a specified 16-block district within the First Ward where vice ran rampant and unchecked. Levee combined the lawless aspects of a wild West town with the efficient planning of urban organized crime. Within the safety of its borders ranged thieves, muggers, streetwalkers, pimps, dope fiends and peddlers, pickpockets, panderers, and degenerates.

The Everleigh Club was located within the Levee for political expediency. Ada and Minna Everleigh worked hard to avoid conflicts, but they refused to associate with their riffraff neighbors. The sisters wouldn't allow their girls or their servants to visit the saloons, casinos, or other brothels that surrounded them. And the club's wealthier clientele generally avoided the rest of the Levee, too.

Many inhabitants of the Levee resented the Everleigh sisters' attitude and the club's high prices, but too much money was to be made on all sides for the feud to affect anybody's business. When Carter Harrison was elected mayor in 1910, he battled a corrupt police force and the ward bosses, to close down the Levee. The civic-minded reformers thought a new, better era lay ahead for Chicago, but that was before Prohibition and Al Capone arrived . . . .

THE MAN WHO STOLE THE *MONA LISA*

Vincenzo Perrugia hardly looked like the perpetrator of one of the 20th century's most cunning and extraordinary crimes. He was an unsuccessful painter himself.

VINCENZO PERRUGIA SUCCESSFULLY MADE OFF WITH THE WORLD'S MOST FAMOUS PAINTING

Sometime between five o'clock in the afternoon on August 20, 1911, and noon on the 22nd, Leonardo da Vinci's internationally famous masterpiece, the *Mona Lisa,* was stolen from its permanent place in the Salon Carre Gallery of France's National Museum of the Louvre in Paris.

On August 21, the gallery was closed to the general public. Officials had assumed that, for reasons of security, the painting had been temporarily moved. It was a bad assumption. The theft was not discovered until noon of the following day. Soon the museum was swarming with gendarmes, but by then the trail had grown cold. An investigation turned up the discarded frame, but nothing else. Officials at the Louvre and in the French government were fired for their colossal incompetence. The Sûreté (France's "criminal" police, somewhat similar to England's Scotland Yard or America's FBI) rounded up potential radicals, including the poet Apollinaire and the painter Picasso. However, the Sûreté could pin the crime upon no one. Louvre employees were grilled again and again; even spiritualists were consulted. There were no leads.

Two years later, on November 30, 1913, an Italian art dealer named Alfredo Geri was contacted by someone who simply signed himself as "Leonard" about the possibility of Geri buying the *Mona Lisa.* Although the letter bore a Paris postmark, Geri suspected a hoax. Nonetheless, he set up a meeting between Leonard, himself, and the director of the Uffizi Gallery in Florence. On December 10, at the specified rendezvous, the dealer and the gallery director met the mysterious Leonard, who asked for $100,000 in exchange for the masterpiece. Leonard took the other two men to his hotel. When he did indeed produce the genuine item, Geri and the Uffizi director went straight to the police.

Leonard was arrested. Under questioning, the thief revealed that his real name was Vincenzo Perrugia. Although an unsuccessful painter who was filled with a love of the visual arts, Perrugia was forced to support himself as a carpenter and handyman. He claimed that his motive for the robbery was purely patriotic: As an Italian, he felt that this Italian masterpiece did not belong in a French museum, but on Italian soil. That may have sounded noble, but Perrugia's argument had little legal or moral basis. The painting had been sold to the Louvre quite legally, and Perrugia's demand for $100,000 rather sullied the purity of his nationalism. However, the emotional climate of Italy at the time was such that Perrugia's sentiments made the thief a national hero. Although legal officials refused to bow to the wishes of the people and set him free, the fact that Perrugia was being tried in Italy rather than in France put the odds considerably in his favor.

The trial showed the French police to be imbeciles. Perrugia had a criminal record in Paris and had been employed by the Louvre. He had even been interviewed several times about the burglary. The police had considered him quite a helpful witness and thus had not bothered to take his fingerprints—fingerprints that might have shown up on the painting's discarded frame. Perrugia was found guilty, nonetheless, but received a sentence of only a year and 15 days. This was later shortened to seven months. After serving his reduced sentence, Perrugia left prison and slipped back into obscurity.

OFFICIALS HAD ASSUMED THAT, FOR REASONS OF SECURITY, THE PAINTING HAD BEEN TEMPORARILY MOVED. IT WAS A BAD ASSUMPTION.

THE LANDLORD'S FLYPAPER

FREDERICK HENRY SEDDON POISONED A TRUSTING LODGER FOR ALL HER WORLDLY POSSESSIONS

Frederick Seddon might never have come under suspicion of murdering his lodger. Mrs. Barrow might have gone unmissed by relatives if Seddon had simply given her a decent burial and sent her nearest kin proper notification of her death.

Englishman Frederick Henry Seddon held a respectable middle-class job as a mid-level bureaucrat for an insurance company. He lived in an upright suburb of London with his wife, five children, and his elderly father. Seddon's salary was barely adequate for such a large household, and in 1910, he took in a middle-aged lodger, Mrs. Eliza M. Barrow.

On September 1, 1911, Mrs. Barrow was stricken with vomiting and diarrhea. Doctors could do nothing and within two weeks Mrs. Barrow was dead. Showing little sympathy, Seddon buried her in a pauper's grave and didn't bother to inform any of her kin.

When a cousin of Mrs. Barrow, Frank Vonderahe, dropped by some months later, Seddon rudely informed him that Mrs. Barrow was dead. Furthermore, Vonderahe was told that Seddon was the executor and beneficiary of Mrs. Barrow's will, and that grieving cousins were not welcome. Such gruff treatment led Mr. Vonderahe to the police. He succeeded in getting his cousin's body exhumed. Examiners found that the body contained strong traces of arsenic, which Seddon had probably obtained by soaking ordinary flypaper in brandy and water. (A demonstration of this technique proved most interesting at Seddon's trial—especially to would-be murderers—and led to changes in the design of flypaper.)

In March 1912, the trial commenced, charging Seddon and his wife with murder. Frederick Seddon was shown to be an obsessively greedy and emotionally callous man. Mrs. Barrow had turned over to him all of her assets in exchange for a weekly, lifetime annuity of three pounds, five shillings. Seddon, in possession of his lodger's money and disinclined to pay any of it back to her, killed her as promptly as he could.

The jury found Seddon guilty. Mrs. Seddon came off as meek and uninformed, and was acquitted of any wrongdoing. Frederick Seddon was hanged on April 18, 1912.

THE MOTOR BANDITS OF PARIS

JULES BONNOT AND HIS GANG UTILIZED MOTORCARS TO ESCAPE THE POLICE

In 1912, Paris was terrorized by the Motor Bandits gang, bank robbers led by an ex-racing driver named Jules Joseph Bonnot. The Motor Bandits committed a series of daring robberies in which they showed no more regard for themselves than they did for their victims. Bonnot used his racing skills to pilot the gang's escape vehicle away from any pursuer. The Motor Bandits soon gained nationwide notoriety.

In March 1912, Bonnot and two other gangsters surprised famous sportsman Marquis de Rouge and his chauffeur in the forest. They were shot dead, stripped of their goatskin driving coats, and dumped in a ditch. The Bandits abandoned their fast De Dion-Bouton automobile for the Marquis' vehicle and drove to Chantilly. There they ran into the local bank, spraying bullets everywhere. Outside, passersby were held at gunpoint as Bonnot wheeled the car to the bank and took his allies away. They netted 80,000 francs. The Sûreté (France's "criminal" police—somewhat similar to England's Scotland Yard or America's FBI) was criticized for letting the Bandits act so brazenly.

After raiding a gun shop near the historic fortress of Vincennes, they moved on, but their greatest successes were behind them. François Callemin was the first gangster to be captured, after a savage police ambush. One member wrote to the Sûreté that he might be caught, but promised to take some policemen with him when he died.

In March 1913, 200 police and troops—tipped off about the location of the Bandits' hideout—surrounded a house in Choisy-le-Roi. After a vicious shootout, the attackers dynamited the hideout. Inside, they found Bonnot, who had four serious wounds. He spat one final word: "Bastards!" By his side, police found his last testament, written in his own blood: "I am famous now. My fame has spread throughout the world. For my part, I could have done without this sort of glory. I have tried to lead my own kind of life and I have a right to live." But then, so did the victims of the Motor Bandits.

AFTER SEVERAL DARING ROBBERIES BY THE MOTOR BANDITS, FRENCH PRIME MINISTER POINCARÉ STATED THAT THEY MUST BE CAUGHT "BY WHATEVER MEANS AND AT WHATEVER COST." TEN THOUSAND POSTERS PUT THE GANG MEMBERS' FACES ON DISPLAY ACROSS FRANCE. WHILE THE AUTHORITIES PRESSED THEIR SEARCH, THE BANDITS BUILT A FORMIDABLE ARSENAL BY ROBBING GUNSMITHS SO THEY COULD CONTINUE THEIR VIOLENT ACTIVITIES.

HATRED AND INJUSTICE IN GEORGIA

WHEN LEO FRANK WAS ACCUSED OF THE RAPE AND MURDER OF LITTLE MARY PHAGAN, ANTI-SEMITISM AND CIVIL WAR RESENTMENTS CLOUDED THE AIR

Leo Frank was the victim of what was probably one of the worst miscarriages of justice in American history. He was Jewish, and at that time in American history, in Atlanta, his heritage was his undoing.

April 26, 1913, was Confederate Memorial Day in Atlanta. The factories were closed so the workers could attend the annual parade. Leo Frank, a Northern Jew who had come to Atlanta to manage his uncle's pencil factory, didn't celebrate the holiday. So he used the time to catch up on paperwork in his office. At noon, a 14-year-old factory worker named Mary Phagan came to collect her week's wages. Mary was a pretty girl, but Leo Frank did not really know her, or most of his employees. He gave the girl her pay—a modest $1.20. Mary left Frank's office and he never saw her again.

The next day, Leo Frank was arrested for the rape and murder of Mary Phagan. A night watchman had found her body in the pencil factory's cellar. Mary evidently had struggled for her life and honor. Her battered and broken body was filthy with coal dust. The killer apparently hoped that police would believe that Mary could have composed a letter to her mother while in the throes of a violent attack. Mary's killer had left behind two illiterate letters addressed to "Mum" that described her murderer as "a long, tall, sleam, black negro . . . that long tall black negro did [it] by his slef."

When it became clear that Leo Frank had been the last person to see Mary alive, he was immediately suspected and jailed as the primary suspect in the killing. Jail was probably the safest place for him, because a wave of hysteria rushed forth from the depths of the city. Frank was slandered as a filthy, perverted Jew who swept down from New York City to defile and degrade Southern women.

Southern folklore about Jews had never been very kind. Frank became the innocent victim of years of ignorance and hate. There were other factors as well. Most Atlantans remembered 50 years of ill treatment by the conquering North. Atlanta had been burned to the ground by Northern troops. Many once-proud people still existed in a poverty brought on by the war. They were ashamed that their daughters had to work in factories for pennies a day. They were angry that most factories seemed to be owned by Northern "carpetbaggers." As a Northern Jew who ran the factory that Mary Phagan worked and died in, Frank bore the burden of these resentments.

Frank's trial quickly got out of hand. Onlookers cheered the fiery speeches of the prosecutor, who rode the trial into the governor's chair. Frank's defense lawyers were jeered by the spectators. Although Leo Frank was prohibited by law from testifying in his own behalf, he spoke informally. He did so with such quiet dignity and heartfelt conviction that the judge nearly declared a mistrial. But mob rule quickly reasserted itself. The guilty verdict was nearly automatic. When it was pronounced, America watched in horror.

Efforts were made to save Leo Frank. The appeal even went to the U.S. Supreme Court. To that lofty body's shame, the lower court's verdict was upheld on June 22, 1915. Two justices dissented.

Georgia Governor Slaton knew Frank was innocent. He also knew he couldn't pardon him—Slaton would commit political suicide by intervening at all. Slaton did commute Frank's sentence from death to life imprisonment—perhaps feeling that reason might prevail in the calmer years ahead. It didn't. Two months later, a mob broke into the state prison, captured Frank, and carried him to Atlanta. He was lynched on a tree near Mary Phagan's house.

Years later, in 1971, an eyewitness came forward to testify to Leo Frank's innocence. A fellow worker of Mary's, he had seen her raped by Jim Conley, the factory's African-American janitor. The witness said he'd told the story to the police at the time, and that they'd warned him to get out of town. He obeyed, thus sealing the fate of Leo Frank.

Mary Phagan became a symbol of the Southern girls who were forced by war-inflicted poverty to work in factories for Northern carpetbaggers. Her rape and murder brought forth resentment that had been festering since the end of the Civil War.

THE BRIDES IN THE BATH MURDERER

WIFE MURDERER GEORGE JOSEPH SMITH FOUND THE BATHTUB A MOST USEFUL IMPLEMENT

George Joseph Smith, the Brides in the Bath murderer, had a special talent for getting married. He called himself Henry Williams when he married Beatrice Mundy, his first known victim.

George Joseph Smith was not a brilliant businessman. After several years, he had worked himself up from junk shop proprietor to antique dealer, but knew he could never get rich that way. He seemed to drift from one southern English coastal town to the next. However, he discovered that he had a true talent for one thing: getting married. In 1898, he wed Caroline Thornhill, but the union failed. Although she had left him by 1900, they were never divorced. Undaunted, Smith remarried in 1910. Calling himself Henry Williams, he married Beatrice Mundy. This time he'd learned to pick a woman with substantial assets. The new Mrs. Williams was 33, well-educated, and had £2,500 in her bank account. As footloose as he was greedy, Smith deserted Beatrice later in 1910, encountered her by chance two years later, and romanced her all over again.

In July 1912, Smith arranged for the installation of a new bathtub. Not long after, he told his doctor that his wife was having fits. Before the doctor could arrive, Beatrice had died. The doctor examined her naked body in the filled bath and pronounced "death by misadventure." In his bereavement, Smith was heard to play "Nearer My God to Thee" on his harmonium.

Still bitten by the marrying bug, Smith proceeded to audition a number of new bridal prospects, finally choosing Alice Burnham of Bristol. She had £500 in her bank account and, like her predecessor, an unfortunate propensity for misadventure in her bathtub. Although at least one neighbor was unconvinced of Smith's innocence in the death, he remained free and unsuspected by the police.

On December 17, 1914, using the name John Lloyd, Smith married Margaret Elizabeth Lofty. On the very next day, Margaret Elizabeth went to a watery death in her bath. The coroner brought in another verdict of misadventure, and the bereaved husband pocketed £700. This death, however, was front-page news that brought forth people who remembered what had happened to Beatrice Mundy and Alice Burnham. On the testimony of Alice Burnham's father and landlady, Smith was arrested.

George Joseph Smith was first charged with bigamy. After further investigation, murder was added to the charge. Smith was defended by Edward Marshall Hall, a very good barrister who could do nothing to refute damning forensic evidence. It was the simple but elegant testimony of Scotland Yard's Bernard Spilsbury that sealed Smith's fate. Spilsbury said that each of the women was too tall to have simply slipped under the water. Force had to have been applied. A courtroom demonstration of Smith's probable method of murder nearly resulted in the drowning death of the woman who had agreed to participate in the reenactment. This dramatic moment is what convinced the jury of Smith's guilt. Later, as the jury received final instructions from the judge, Smith leapt to his feet and shouted, "I am not a murderer, though I may be a bit peculiar!" By that time, few in the courtroom were inclined to disagree.

George Joseph Smith was hanged on Friday the 13th in August 1915. After his death, yet another bride turned up, a living one named Edith Pegler, who had married Smith in 1908. She told the authorities that her husband would disappear at intervals, but would return to her at times that coincided with the aftermath of each "misadventure." So clever was the smooth-talking Smith that Edith had been unaware of his deadly avocation during their marriage.

SCOTLAND YARD SAID THAT EACH OF THE WOMEN WAS TOO TALL TO HAVE SIMPLY SLIPPED UNDER THE WATER.

THE BIRDMAN OF ALCATRAZ

This picture of Robert Stroud, taken in the year before his death, shows that the hardened killer who had been imprisoned for more than 50 years now had the appearance of a benevolent old man. Richard English, an attorney who represented Stroud in a legal move to gain freedom, took the picture hoping it would help to obtain presidential clemency for Stroud.

PRISON LIFE CHANGED ROUGHHOUSE MURDERER ROBERT STROUD INTO A REMARKABLE ORNITHOLOGICAL RESEARCHER

Robert Stroud was born in 1887 in the Pacific Northwest. Before he was 20, he had drifted farther north, to seek his fortune in the boomtowns of Alaska. "Pimp" is perhaps too fancy a word to describe the trade Stroud chose for himself in the rough wilds of that territory. It was a tough life that hardened Stroud and made him bitter. In January 1909, he shot and killed a "client," a bartender who refused to pay Stroud's girl, Kitty O'Brien, her ten-dollar fee. Stroud lacked the cash needed to buy his way out of a manslaughter conviction and was sentenced to 12 years' imprisonment. He was sent to McNeil Island in Puget Sound and was later transferred to Leavenworth Federal Prison in Kansas.

Prison life did not agree with Stroud. It made him even more hateful of mankind than before. He was disliked and feared by the other prisoners. On March 26, 1916, with barely more than four years to go on his sentence, he knifed and killed a guard with whom he had been feuding. Whether out of brazenness, stupidity, or both, Stroud committed the deed in the mess hall in front of the entire prison population. He was tried, convicted, and sentenced to death, with his hanging scheduled for April 1920. However, Stroud's mother interceded on his behalf with the ailing President Woodrow Wilson, whose wife saw to it that Stroud's death sentence was commuted to life in solitary confinement.

Even before Stroud's sentence was commuted, he had begun to cool off. With his anger strangely subsided, he was able to rehabilitate himself. He took the first step toward lasting fame in the summer of 1920, when he began caring for birds. By 1925, he was raising canaries and working through his mother to sell them commercially. His scientific study of bird pathology was in full swing by 1930. In August 1936, Stroud was visited in his cell by FBI director J. Edgar Hoover. Apparently impressed by Stroud's enterprise, the famous lawman purchased a canary for his own mother.

In 1942, Robert Stroud was transferred to Alcatraz, the foreboding, fortresslike federal penitentiary with which he would forever be associated. Stroud was not allowed to keep birds at Alcatraz, but his research continued. In 1943, his massive volume *Digest of Bird Diseases* was published, and was hailed worldwide as the most authoritative book ever written on the subject.

In 1946, Alcatraz was rocked by a bloody riot. Thirty years earlier, Stroud would have been one of the leading perpetrators. However, this time he stayed in his cell and calmly urged others to do likewise. He sheltered a wounded prisoner and interceded on the prisoners' behalf to end the riot after the violence had run its course. But despite his levelheaded behavior, Stroud sympathized with the rioters. He spent most of his remaining years fighting against the harsh penal philosophy then in fashion, and against Alcatraz in particular. He felt that Alcatraz represented everything that was wrong with the American prison system. Stroud was convinced that to simply lock a man up with no hope for the future and to give him nothing constructive to do in the present simply made that man angrier and more bitter than before. Stroud campaigned hard for the closure of Alcatraz, and he lived just long enough to see it happen. He died in Leavenworth on November 21, 1963—eight months after the Federal Bureau of Prisons shut down Alcatraz.

Stroud's mother, Mrs. Elizabeth Stroud, saved him from the gallows in 1920 and later helped him sell his canaries commercially.

THE MYTH OF MATA HARI

Gertrude Zelle was not a raving beauty. Nevertheless, when she performed her erotic dances as a backdrop to spiritual lectures, she generated a certain excitement among the male members of her audience. Dubbing herself Mata Hari was the touch that made hers the featured performance.

HOW GERTRUDE ZELLE SPUN AN ILLUSION OF INTRIGUE THAT BECAME REAL

There are two stories of Mata Hari—the fantasy and the reality. The fantasy was created by the woman herself and spun wildly out of control after her foolish martyrdom. The reality existed behind closed bedroom doors and military conferences. It may have been even harder to discern than the illusion.

Mata Hari began life as Margaretha Geertruida MacLeod, daughter of a middle-class Dutch family in the colonial Dutch East Indies. Although also known as Gertrude Zelle, she would later claim that she was "Lady MacLeod," the Indian-born daughter of an English lord. She claimed also that Mata Hari was her Hindu name, meaning "Eye of the Dawn." The quasi-pornographic dances for which she became renowned in Paris were, she insisted, religious rituals to the Hindu god Siva.

Mata Hari became the toast of Parisian high society when she brought this balderdash to town. Most people probably knew it was bunk, but there was something about the theatrical pretension of *la belle époque* ("the good old days," pre-1914 France) that preferred hypocrisy to truth. While common prostitutes couldn't possibly be invited to society parties, "Lady MacLeod" was always welcome. And while proper audiences couldn't openly enjoy the performance of an erotic dance, Mata Hari's "religious reenactments," accompanied by a spiritual lecture, could be excused on the grounds of cultural uplift. By any standard, though, Mata Hari's act was pure titillation, and her admirers ate it up.

Gertrude was able to parlay her fame into high-class prostitution with an upper-class clientele, as well. She had affairs with many of the most important men in Europe. Though not a tremendously alluring woman, she brought a fierce conviction to her fantasies and enchanted the men to whom she attached herself.

When war broke out in Europe in August 1914, the mood of French high society changed completely: Gaiety and laughter were forgotten beneath the kind of fevered patriotism that typically accompanies the beginning of a war. Though a political neutral who was allowed to travel from Paris to Berlin undisturbed, Gertrude got caught up in the aggressive mood of war. Always adaptable, she decided to maintain her lifestyle by spinning a fantasy that she was an espionage agent for the Germans. She began to cultivate the company of high-ranking German officers. She even asked a few of them for espionage assignments. But there is no evidence that the Germans ever took Mata Hari seriously, or ever used her as a spy. Then again, secrecy is the lifeblood of espionage, and one may choose to believe that Mata Hari simply did her job so well that no trace of her activities was left behind.

Mata Hari crisscrossed the capitals of Europe for two years. Perhaps she was operating as a spy, but certainly she was in personal contact with high-level German officers as well as French aristocrats and politicians. Afterward, in August 1916, she decided to offer her services to the French intelligence. Mata Hari presented Captain Georges Ladoux with her outrageous plan to seduce Crown Prince Wilhelm of Germany and steal secrets from him that would end the war. She added, humbly, that this service should be worth about a million francs. Ladoux immediately began to investigate his visitor and her contacts.

While Mata Hari had never met the Crown Prince, she did start sending Ladoux low-level information obtained from Arnold Kalle, the German military attaché in Madrid. Whether she was working with Kalle or spying on him has never been determined.

THOUGH NOT A TREMENDOUSLY ALLURING WOMAN, SHE BROUGHT A FIERCE CONVICTION TO HER FANTASIES AND ENCHANTED THE MEN TO WHOM SHE ATTACHED HERSELF.

Mata Hari was so ostentatious and flaunted her sexual favors so brazenly that many believed her tales of political double cross and deceit.

When she next arrived in Paris, in January 1917, Gertrude Zelle was arrested and taken to Saint-Lazare Prison. She waited there for six months while the French army decided what to do with her. Finally, in late July, she was court-martialed. Whatever harm her schemes may have caused, she certainly had cause for complaint about her rights: That a foreign national should be subjected to a closed military trial instead of a civil trial was absurd. But such improprieties often happen in the fever of war. Worse, the only authorities to whom Gertrude might have complained were the very people who were intent upon hanging her for espionage.

The French government was never able to conclusively prove its charge that Gertrude Zelle/Mata Hari spied against France for Germany. The prosecution's main evidence consisted of payments given to Gertrude by high-ranking German officers. Gertrude's very sensible defense was that as a courtesan (high-class whore), she quite naturally accepted money from the men with whom she slept.

Apparently unimpressed by the economic realities of the life of a working girl, the court found Mata Hari guilty and sentenced her to death by firing squad. On October 15, 1917, she went to her death in a manner that, according to most accounts, provided a great moment of drama. While those around her wept, Mata Hari remained calm and collected. Perhaps her serenity came from a belief that her death would transform the lies of her life into an enduring myth. At the last, Mata Hari refused a blindfold and blew a kiss to the firing squad.

"BLODIE BELGIAM"

LOUIS VOISON'S DEADLY GAME OF WARTIME PASSION ATTRACTED AN UNINVITED PLAYER—SCOTLAND YARD

On November 2, 1917, a London street sweeper found a bundle by the road. Inside were the trunk and arms of a woman, wrapped in a bloodstained bedsheet along with brown butcher's paper that had "Blodie Belgiam" scrawled on it. Legs were found in a nearby parcel. The head and hands were missing.

Scotland Yard traced the laundry mark on the bedsheet and deduced the victim's identity: Emilienne Gerard, a Frenchwoman missing since an October 31 air raid. Neighbors had thought nothing unusual of her disappearance; married to a French soldier, she often traveled to the continent to see him. Besides, she often stayed with a lover in town. Her lover was also French, Louis Voison. Scotland Yard believed the body parts were severed by an expert. As Voison was a butcher, the Yard questioned him further.

The investigators asked Voison to write "Bloody Belgium." He hesitated, but then agreed. The semiliterate butcher spelled the phrase as "Blodie Belgiam." They had him repeat the process five times; each time the spelling was the same. A search of Voison's kitchen/workroom turned up the victim's missing head and hands.

Though Emilienne Gerard's skull had been smashed, it did not kill her. There had also been an attempt to strangle her. This brutality contrasted to the sure-handed deftness with which Voison had dismembered Emilienne's body. Police deduced that there was an accomplice and quickly found Berthe Roche, who claimed to be another Voison lover.

The October 31 air raid had been particularly ferocious. Most Londoners sought shelter in the subways, but Emilienne Gerard preferred her lover's cellar, where she could wait in a passionate embrace. However, she found a very jealous woman in the cellar. Berthe attacked Emilienne with a poker. Voison, forced to choose between them, selected Berthe. Voison was hanged; Berthe Roche was sentenced to seven years.

WAS IT A POLITICAL KILLING?

At the time of the brutal murder and dismemberment of Emilienne Gerard, Great Britain was engaged in World War I. London was suffering through constant German nighttime air raids as a result of Belgium's loss of neutrality. Many Londoners, on edge from the frightful attacks, blamed the Belgians for not resisting harder. Because of the words "Blodie Belgiam" written on the piece of brown butcher's paper found with the body, speculation began that the killing was somehow politically motivated. However, this line of thought threw off Scotland Yard for only a short while, and it was quickly dismissed.

THE BLACK SOX

Many observers believe that "Shoeless Joe" Jackson, the most famous member of the Black Sox, was one of the best pure hitters in baseball history—as good as Ty Cobb or Babe Ruth.

THE GREAT BASEBALL TEAM THAT THREW AWAY GLORY FOR A FEW EXTRA DOLLARS

The 1919 Chicago White Sox were a special baseball team. They had a sense of destiny about them—in the same way that the 1927 New York Yankees and the 1969 New York Mets later would. The Sox had everything: an invaluable combination of youth and experience, good pitching, an excellent infield, clutch hitting, and a fighting spirit. Betting men said the Sox were a cinch to sweep the World Series. But one betting man bet otherwise, and thus began the story of one of the worst scandals in baseball history.

That fateful betting man was Arnold Rothstein, a scheming high-roller from Manhattan who liked to gamble on sporting events. But in 1919, he wasn't interested in betting on the World Series—the odds favored the White Sox too heavily. Rothstein's attitude changed when a small-time hood and ex-boxer named Abe Attell approached him with a remarkable revelation: Five, possibly seven, White Sox starters would be amenable to bribes. As it turned out, the real number was eight: Joseph Jefferson "Shoeless Joe" Jackson, Charles "Swede" Risberg, Oscar "Happy" Felsch, Arnold "Chick" Gandil, George "Buck" Weaver, Fred McMullin, Eddie Cicotte, and Claude "Lefty" Williams. Many historians are convinced that, through emissaries, Rothstein made a deal to pay these players a total of $70,000 to throw the first two games of the series. Rothstein would bet heavily on the rival Cincinnati Reds and make a killing. Plenty of time would remain in the best-of-nine series for the White Sox to come back and win overall, and no one would be the wiser. At least, that was the plan.

In reality, everything went wrong. First, the deal was never negotiated in good faith. Rothstein's flunkies decided to help themselves to some of the $70,000 as middlemen, and so never reported their

Eddie Cicotte won 29 games in 1919. He was promised a bonus by White Sox owner Charlie Comiskey if he won 30 games and was then benched after his 29th win.

BETTING MEN SAID THE SOX WERE A CINCH TO SWEEP THE WORLD SERIES. BUT ONE BETTING MAN BET OTHERWISE, AND THUS BEGAN THE STORY OF ONE OF THE WORST SCANDALS IN BASEBALL HISTORY.

"Shoeless Joe" Jackson went to his grave maintaining that he had given his all in the 1919 World Series. It's true that in the eight-game clash, Jackson led all participants in hitting, and he fielded flawlessly.

boss's full offer to the players. Second, the demands kept changing: From throwing the first two games only, the ante went up to throwing four of the first six (leaving the Sox players no margin for error in the deciding games). Finally, once the players had thrown the first game, the hoods figured they had them over a barrel and refused to pay the agreed-upon amount. The eight players were supposed to receive $15,000 per man—each actually received less than $3,000.

It is inconceivable in today's era of big baseball money that anyone would throw the World Series for less than $3,000, but times were very different in October 1919. The average baseball player earned about $3,000 a year—more than the average working man, but not much more. A star player might command $10,000, even $12,000. Good money for the day, but far short of real wealth.

Baseball's pay scale was particularly apparent to the eight Sox, who played for a tight-fisted owner named Charlie Comiskey. While things were frugal throughout the league, the quality of life was especially shabby in Comiskey's domain. His players were denied bonuses despite their winning season, and Comiskey announced that he was deducting travel expenses from their World Series pay (technically illegal, but since the money flowed through Comiskey, he could get away with it). The Sox players knew that they were the best in baseball *and* the most poorly paid. They saw Rothstein's bribe as the bonus that had been denied them.

When the money was slow to arrive, the eight threw two more games on faith. Then they wised up and played hard to win the series. In the final five games, every player gave everything he had (some observers claimed that Lefty Williams's pitching in his final start was suspect), but it was too late—the Reds beat the White Sox five games to three. Baseball experts couldn't account for the lackluster performances in those first few contests. Rumors began to spread.

The allegations flew throughout the off-season, persisted through the following year's spring training, and on into the 1920 season. When Chicago newspaper reporters dug up the facts, a grand jury was convened to get to the truth. America was mortified that the national pastime had been sullied by gambling and bribery. The country's feelings of shock and betrayal were summed up by a widely quoted newspaper account (of doubtful authenticity) of a young ball fan who sadly looked up at his hero, Shoeless Joe Jackson, and tearfully pleaded, "Say it ain't so, Joe. Say it ain't so."

Baseball owners rallied around Charlie Comiskey to protect themselves and the game. They thwarted the grand jury, and even let Arnold Rothstein off the hook to avoid his damning testimony. Privately, the baseball owners vowed that they would handle the problem themselves. They appointed Judge Kenesaw Mountain Landis as the first commissioner of baseball and gave him broad powers to oversee the conduct of the game. All of the White Sox who took money were banned from baseball for life. Strict rules were put in place about players gambling or even fraternizing with gamblers. These reforms restored the public's confidence in baseball, but the price was the 1919 White Sox. There could be no mercy, no extenuating circumstances for them. Cut short were the brilliant careers of eight players who were the core of one of baseball's greatest teams. The game recovered, but would never be quite the same. And Arnold Rothstein? The man who allegedly fixed the World Series was ambushed and fatally shot in a New York City hotel in 1928. The murder was never solved.

CUT SHORT WERE THE BRILLIANT CAREERS OF EIGHT PLAYERS WHO WERE THE CORE OF ONE OF BASEBALL'S GREATEST TEAMS. THE GAME OF BASEBALL RECOVERED, BUT IT WOULD NEVER BE QUITE THE SAME.

1920–1929

IN THE 1920S, A KIND OF FRENZIED SELF-INDULGENCE PREVAILED AS people sought to put the horrors of World War I behind them. In Chicago, the pursuit of good times led to the violent rise of gangster Al Capone, whose career culminated in the infamous St. Valentine's Day Massacre. White-collar crime found representation in the person of con man Charles Ponzi, inventor of the pyramid scheme. Rampant anticommunist sentiment contributed to the executions of Sacco and Vanzetti, even as it provided a springboard to the career of master spy Sidney Reilly. In addition, the decade featured the rousing exploits of Western desperado Henry Starr, as well numerous passion crimes and serial murders like those committed by such creatures as Earle Nelson and genius-killers Leopold and Loeb.

SACCO AND VANZETTI

WITH JUSTICE AVERTING HER EYES, THE CASES OF NICOLA SACCO AND BARTOLOMEO VANZETTI MOVED TO AN INESCAPABLE CONCLUSION

The tragedy of Nicola Sacco and Bartolomeo Vanzetti eventually became a notorious legal case among fair-minded Americans, but not before it was too late for the accused. The prejudice that led to their deaths was as powerful as it was inevitable. The unprecedented wave of immigration into the United States in the 50 years prior to 1920 combined with Americans' general disgust at having to send young men to fight and die in a "European War." These two factors led to a widespread distrust of foreigners. Also, Americans had an irrational fear of radical political ideas. Anarchists had been in thorough disrepute since Leon Czolgosz shot and mortally wounded President McKinley in 1901. The recent Bolshevik revolution in Russia scared many Americans, as well. There was a general fear that "Reds," which meant practically anyone foreign, were out to destroy the American way of life. The Sacco-Vanzetti case got caught up in this hysteria and came to symbolize it. Thus, only their deaths, however irrational, could dissipate this hysteria.

It all started with a vicious robbery in South Braintree, Massachusetts, on April 15, 1920. Two men outside the Slater & Morrill Shoe Factory attacked paymaster Frederick Parmenter and a guard named Berardelli as they approached with the payroll. Both employees were killed in the assault. The attackers grabbed the payroll—$15,776.51—and hopped into a Buick touring car that carried three accomplices. One of the three stood on the car's running board, firing wildly at the factory and passersby. As the car careened through South Braintree, the man on the running board continued to shoot the gun wildly, shouting at pedestrians in unaccented English.

The job of rounding up suspects for this terrible murder/robbery fell to Chief Michael E. Stewart of the Braintree Police. Stewart was a man who subscribed wholeheartedly to the theory that Reds were out to destroy and subvert the United States. If he needed suspects for this robbery, he consulted his list of known Reds.

In April 1927, Bartolomeo Vanzetti, left, and Nicola Sacco, right, boarded a bus at the Dedham, Massachusetts, jail to go to the courthouse where Judge Webster Thayer sentenced them to death in the electric chair. Despite worldwide pleas for clemency, they were executed four months later.

Bartolomeo Vanzetti arriving at the courthouse shortly before he received the death sentence in April 1927. Vanzetti, a wandering fish peddler, was an Italian immigrant.

Near the top of Chief Stewart's list was Ferucio Coacci, a former Slater & Morrill employee. Coacci had been deported, but Chief Stewart carried his investigation to Coacci's former residence. There, the chief found a man named Mike Boda, whom he questioned intensely about the robbery. Although Boda professed ignorance, Stewart was convinced he had found a new prime suspect. He ordered Boda watched. Before surveillance could be set up, however, a frightened Boda left town. Because Boda had left his Overland automobile behind, police set up a surveillance unit on the car, figuring that Boda would eventually come back for it.

On May 5, Boda returned with two friends—foreigners. Alerted by phone, Chief Stewart ordered the arrest of all three. Boda left in the car and thus eluded the police. The other two men were simply walking at a leisurely pace toward a trolley line when they were picked up. These men were Nicola Sacco, a local shoemaker (who never worked at Slater & Morrill), and Bartolomeo Vanzetti, a wandering fish peddler. Before police and the state of Massachusetts began to manufacture evidence against them, official suspicion hinged on one thing: Sacco and Vanzetti had been seen driving with Boda in a car similar to the one used in the robbery.

As far as Chief Stewart and the police were concerned, this flimsy thread of evidence told only part of the story. What really nailed the pair was that the authorities didn't care for their brand of politics. Undeniably, Sacco and Vanzetti were anarchists—they idealistically believed in a future without governments or leaders. Their principal anarchist activity consisted of passing out leaflets. This is what they had been doing with Mike Boda when caught. Sacco and Vanzetti were Italian immigrants who had never bothered to learn English well or to apply for American citizenship. Each man was carrying a revolver when apprehended. They explained that they were often attacked because of their political beliefs; the pistols were simply to defend themselves when they passed out leaflets.

Sacco and Vanzetti thought they had been picked up for anarchist activity, and had no idea they were being interrogated for armed robbery and murder. This assumption led to a certain arrogance on their part in their initial conversations with the police. Ignorant of the gravity of the crime being investigated, the pair fancied themselves political martyrs.

While none of the money or any physical evidence that might have linked the pair to the crime was ever found, Sacco and Vanzetti were formally charged with armed robbery and murder. The police chief's statement to the press at the time charges were made summed up the prevailing attitude: "In my own mind, I believe that the men who committed that atrocious crime knew no God and had no regard for human life. Anarchists fit the bill and Sacco and Vanzetti were anarchists."

Once the trial began, the petty prejudices of Chief Stewart seemed inconsequential next to the colossal animosity of Judge Webster Thayer. Unsympathetic from the bench, he privately referred to the defendants by several derogatory names. The evidence presented was confused: The prosecution seemed to argue that Sacco and Vanzetti were four of the five assailants involved. Sacco was first identified as the primary assailant who shot the guard and paymaster. Later, he was tagged as the mad gunman on the running board who shouted at everyone in unaccented English. Vanzetti was initially fingered as the second man outside the gate who collected the money, and then later identified as the driver of the getaway car. Judge Thayer cut through all the confusion as he gave final instructions to the jury. He made it clear that the jurors, if they loved America, would protect the nation from men like Sacco and Vanzetti. There seemed little doubt that Thayer would not be satisfied with anything less than a guilty verdict. The jury did not disappoint the judge: Sacco and Vanzetti were indeed convicted of armed robbery and murder.

Nicola Sacco arriving at the courthouse where he would later be sentenced to death. Like Vanzetti, Sacco was an Italian immigrant who had never learned English well.

JUDGE THAYER MADE IT CLEAR THAT THE JURORS, IF THEY LOVED AMERICA, WOULD PROTECT THE NATION FROM MEN LIKE SACCO AND VANZETTI.

Later, Judge Thayer remarked to cronies, "Did you see what I did to those anarchist bastards?"

As the case went through appeals and legal briefs, it began to attract the attention of fair-minded citizens. The Algonquin Round Table (a circle of writers including Robert Benchley, Dorothy Parker, Heywood Broun, John Dos Passos, and Edna St. Vincent Millay) were early converts and did much to popularize the cause. The stumbling block in all appeals, however, was Judge Thayer, who staunchly refused to reverse himself. In July 1927, Thayer finally overruled all appeals and sentenced Sacco and Vanzetti to the electric chair. This was his last official act before retiring. By this time, sufficient public outrage over Thayer's handling of the case existed to bring the governor of Massachusetts, Alvan Fuller, into the affair.

Fuller appointed a blue-ribbon panel to review the case and Thayer's decision. The panel was empowered to uphold or rescind the verdict as they saw fit. On this panel were many of the most prominent citizens of Massachusetts, including the president of Harvard. During the month in which the panel met, the executions were postponed. The panel, however, was less concerned with the lives of Sacco and Vanzetti than it was with preserving the sanctity of the Massachusetts judicial system. Not surprisingly, then, their decision was not to reverse a legally obtained verdict. The executions were rescheduled for August 23, 1927.

Sacco and Vanzetti's final days were steeped in anticipation. The press of the entire world focused sharply on the public protests and on the failed appeals to out-of-session U.S. Supreme Court justices. On that fatal day, a Monday, Boston resembled an armed camp. For the only time in its history, the Common was closed to orators. Edna St. Vincent Millay led a protest march through the city. Riot squads armed with tear gas roamed the streets. Their instructions were to break up any groups of 20 or more. At midnight on that day, Nicola Sacco and Bartolomeo Vanzetti stoically walked to their deaths.

THE PONZI SCHEME

CON MAN CHARLES PONZI BILKED BIG BUCKS BUILDING PAPER PYRAMIDS

On August 2, 1920, the Boston *Globe* published an exposé of famed financier Charles Ponzi, whose high return on investments had previously been the marvel of Boston. Mr. Ponzi's near-miraculous financial achievements were not the product of keen investment acumen, but rather the smoke screen of a highly ingenious con scheme he had invented: the Pyramid Game. Today, such cons are often called the Ponzi Scheme, in his honor.

Charles Ponzi was born in Parma, Italy, in 1878. He came to America around 1893 and had been a fruit peddler, dishwasher, waiter, and convicted forger before hitting upon his infamous plan. In Boston, in early 1919, Ponzi announced that his Financial Exchange Company could give anyone a 50-percent return on investments in 45 days, or double the investor's money in six months. The investment supposedly involved the purchase of International Postal Reply coupons in countries where the exchange rate was low. Ponzi claimed that the coupons, a kind of international postage, would then be sold at face value in countries with a higher exchange rate; it was ostensibly an early, primitive form of the investment technique now known as arbitrage.

In the first month of operation, Ponzi had 15 customers who invested a total of $870. Within six months he had persuaded some 20,000 investors to give him nearly ten million dollars. The secret of the scam was that he paid off early investors with new investors' monies, thereby gaining credibility—and more investors. At the height of the ploy, 16 clerks were employed to keep track of a daily cash inflow of $250,000. The cash boxes filled so quickly that Ponzi had to stuff bills into desk drawers and wastebaskets just to keep them out of the way.

From his meager beginnings as a fruit peddler, Charles Ponzi rose to become an apparent financial wizard. The bottom fell out of his simple, but nonetheless ingenious, scheme when the Boston Globe revealed that it was merely a "Pyramid Game."

THE CASH BOXES FILLED SO QUICKLY THAT PONZI HAD TO STUFF BILLS INTO DESK DRAWERS AND WASTEBASKETS JUST TO KEEP THEM OUT OF THE WAY.

With his new-found wealth, Ponzi purchased large tracts of prime Boston real estate. He bought a splendid mansion and a Locomobile limousine. He acquired a controlling interest in the Hanover Stock Company and bought out the brokerage firm of J. P. Poole, where he had worked as a translator only three years before. People cheered him in the streets as a local hero. Boston's Italian-American community, especially, took him to its bosom.

When the Boston *Globe* exposé was published, a run on the exchange for refunds burst Ponzi's bubble. The truth was that an exponentially expanding scheme of the sort devised by Ponzi could have only lasted just so long anyway. By the time the fraud was discovered, most of the investors' money was gone; a full 25 percent of it would never be paid back.

Charles Ponzi was sentenced to four years in the federal prison in Plymouth, Massachusetts. Upon his release in 1925, he was indicted by the state of Massachusetts for larceny. While those charges were being appealed, Ponzi moved to Florida and sold swampland (once a scam artist, always a scam artist). Before the state of Florida could indict him, he fled to Texas. In 1934, he was deported to Italy.

Before the outbreak of World War II, Ponzi went to Brazil to work for an Italian airline company. However, the company was closed down during the war. His sights suddenly lowered, Ponzi tried unsuccessfully to run a hot dog stand, and then made a modest living teaching English and French. In 1949, at the age of 71, Charles Ponzi died a pauper in a charity hospital in Rio de Janeiro. No trace of his former glory remained.

THE LAST OF THE BADMEN

WESTERN OUTLAW TRADITION PRODUCED HENRY STARR, THE NEVER-SAY-DIE DESPERADO

Henry Starr was the grandson of Tom Starr, who was a Native American outlaw in the Cherokee Nation (portions of which later became Oklahoma when the state joined the Union in 1907). Starr was also the son of George "Hop" Starr, the brother of Sam Starr, and a nephew of Belle Starr—all of whom were well-known outlaws, horse thieves, grifters, and bootleggers. Henry was born in Fort Gibson in 1873. He attended a Native American school for several years, and then took a job as a cowboy.

In 1891, he began to experience petty harassment and arrests due to his notorious lineage. After a series of minor scrapes and court appearances, Henry Starr got fed up with white justice. He reasoned that if he was going to be treated like an outlaw, he might as well become the best outlaw anybody ever saw.

Starr formed a small gang in 1892 and began robbing banks. This put Deputy Marshall Floyd Wilson on his trail. When Wilson came upon Starr in a clearing at Wolf Creek, Starr fired first. Wilson returned his fire, but the lawman's rifle jammed. Starr rode up on the helpless lawman and put him away at point-blank range. After Starr and his gang robbed several more banks, they then settled down at Colorado Springs to celebrate their successes. Detectives caught up with Starr there, and they arrested him as he was eating a steak dinner.

Starr was put on trial before "hanging judge" Isaac Parker and quickly found guilty. The first verdict was set aside when the trial record clearly revealed Parker's tampering with the jury. Before Starr's second trial in 1895, the outlaw was instrumental in quelling the prison break of Cherokee Bill and saving several lives. Nevertheless, Starr was found guilty at his second trial. Although he received prison time, he was spared the noose.

A drawing of Henry Starr, the Cherokee who began robbing banks in 1892 and continued until he was finally stopped 29 years later by a bank stockholder's bullet. A nephew of the fabled Belle Starr, he boasted with his dying breath that he had "robbed more banks than any man in America."

STARR BECAME THE FIRST AMERICAN THIEF TO USE AN AUTOMOBILE FOR HIS GETAWAYS.

While many observers regarded Henry Starr as simply a vicious murderer, many others were inclined to view him as heroic, the embodiment of the noble savage oppressed by white tyranny. The Cherokee Council successfully petitioned President Theodore Roosevelt for his pardon, and Starr was released.

Henry settled near Tulsa, Oklahoma, married, and worked at farming until Arkansas attempted to extradite him on an old robbery charge. He took flight and joined up with Kid Wilson, a just-paroled member of his old gang. After a few years of successful bank jobs, Starr was caught again in 1908 and served five years in prison for robbing the bank in Amity, Colorado. Starr returned to his chosen profession in 1913. He quickly stirred up more notoriety when he became the first American thief to use an automobile for his getaways.

Between September 1914 and January 1915, Starr and an accomplice robbed 14 Oklahoma banks. In March 1915, he and a gang of six others knocked off the State Bank of Stroud, Oklahoma. A 17-year-old boy in a nearby butcher shop wounded Starr with a rifle as the group was retreating. Starr was caught shortly thereafter, and spent another four years in the Oklahoma State Penitentiary.

Paroled again in 1919, Starr wrote his memoirs for serialization in the Wichita *Eagle.* He even portrayed himself in a silent movie western, *A Debtor to the Law.* However, Starr was penniless when he borrowed 20 dollars to buy a double-action .45-caliber revolver that he would use in his last bank robbery.

On February 18, 1921, Henry Starr and three companions strode into the People's National Bank in Harrison, Arkansas. As Starr prodded the cashier to open a safe, bank stockholder W. J. Meyers picked up a rifle hidden in an alcove and shot Starr. Starr's wound was fatal. As he lay dying, Starr's final statement was the boast that he had "robbed more banks than any man in America." His grand total—estimated at 48—is a record that still stands today.

A VERY BRITISH MURDER

MAJOR HERBERT ARMSTRONG CUT HIS DOMINEERING WIFE DOWN TO SIZE

Noted author and essayist George Orwell once wrote that the case of Major Herbert Rowse Armstrong had that unique feature of "strangulating respectability" that made the famous British murder cases of the 1920s and 1930s so captivating. The British seem to take an extra keen interest in murder when the most unlikely of suspects is proved to have lashed out in uncharacteristic violence.

Major Herbert Rowse Armstrong was a solicitor in the small town of Hay-on-Wye on the Wales-England border. Because he was the sort of retired British Army officer whose vanity would not allow him to accept a demotion to the rank of "Mister," he insisted that everyone address him as "Major." He was married to a woman named Katherine, who could not have been more different from him. Large and domineering in contrast to her small, mild-mannered husband, Mrs. Armstrong never hesitated to order Herbert about. She told him in public not to forget that it was his bath night. In an impatient mood, she would pull him off the tennis court in the middle of a match. She would tell him when he was drinking too much, and drove him to smoke in secret in his own house. It was a relationship not unlike that between Dr. Crippen and his wife Cora, whose case the major had no doubt carefully read and absorbed.

Outwardly, Armstrong was a quietly respectful man who suffered his wife's humiliations in silence. But behind the closed doors of their home, the major was doing something about Katherine's bullying—he was slowly poisoning her to death. On February 22, 1921, after a week of violent stomach trouble, Katherine Armstrong died. The local physician had been in attendance throughout and pronounced the cause of death as heart disease. The major mourned,

Major Herbert Rowse Armstrong got rid of his domineering wife with one of the largest doses of arsenic poisoning ever recorded.

BEHIND THE CLOSED DOORS OF THEIR HOME, MAJOR ARMSTRONG WAS DOING SOMETHING ABOUT KATHERINE'S BULLYING.

then departed for a long holiday that was characterized by his new-found penchant for chasing the ladies.

Home again in Hay-on-Wye, Armstrong refused to blend back into the woodwork. He started a feud with the town's only other solicitor, Oswald Martin (of whose business Armstrong was known be jealous). On the pretext of patching up their differences, he invited Martin to an afternoon tea at his home. The get-together was outwardly festive, and Armstrong was the model of propriety. He even buttered a scone for Martin before handing it to him.

At his own house later, Martin fell violently ill. Although he recovered, the illness was so severe as to attract the attention of Martin's father-in-law, a chemist who recalled Mr. Armstrong having bought a huge quantity of arsenic.

Martin's physician, a Dr. Hincks, suggested that an analysis of Martin's urine might be illuminating. It was: The test showed that the unlucky solicitor had indeed been poisoned with arsenic. Hincks and Martin went to the authorities with their suspicions. The police began a slow, methodical investigation of Major Armstrong, and began to build a case against him. In the meantime, Martin had been politely (and wisely) refusing Armstrong's entreaties to return for tea.

Finally, on December 31, 1921, Major Armstrong was arrested for the attempted murder of Oswald Martin. The charge prompted the exhumation of the body of Katherine Armstrong, and an autopsy revealed that Katherine had suffered one of the most massive doses of arsenic poisoning ever recorded. (The effects of arsenic appear as violent stomach troubles. Normal general practitioners cannot be faulted for failing to discover its presence if they are not looking for it.) Herbert Armstrong was charged with his wife's murder on January 19, 1922. He was tried, found guilty, and hanged at Gloucester Jail on May 31, 1922.

LIGHTS! CAMERA! MURDER!

HOLLYWOOD SHUDDERED WHEN FAMED DIRECTOR WILLIAM DESMOND TAYLOR WAS FOUND MURDERED IN HIS HOME; THE SCRIPT CALLED FOR A MASSIVE COVER-UP

William Desmond Taylor's previously undisclosed past was nearly as mysterious as his murder. The more that was unearthed about him, the murkier his life became.

As every newspaper editor knew in 1922, the next best circulation booster to a bizarre murder was a Hollywood scandal. Thus it was with enthusiasm that the press discovered that William Desmond Taylor, the famous and well-respected movie director, was found murdered in his Hollywood bungalow on February 2, 1922. Reporters quickly descended, dished out as much gossip and innuendos as their papers' readers could swallow, and stayed long enough to ruin the careers of several famous actresses. But they were too late. By the time they had arrived, the truth had already gone with the wind.

Taylor was barely dead before phones were ringing all over Hollywood. People in the know wanted certain facts of the killing hushed up. By the time the police arrived, studio executives were already burning papers in the bungalow's fireplace; the houseboy was in the kitchen washing evidence from the dishes; and (it was rumored) comedy star Mabel Normand was searching the place for her love letters. Several unidentified people were there—some were rumored to be drug dealers. In the confusion, an unidentified doctor appeared and examined the body. He pronounced Taylor dead from a stomach hemorrhage. However, when the coroner's men lifted the body, they discovered blood on the floor and a bullet hole in Taylor's back.

The police had been lax because one of the studios—Paramount—had told them that the whole matter was a sensitive one. Hollywood in 1922 was very much a company town, and the movie studios controlled the police. In this case, the police accepted Paramount's word that nothing was amiss. By the time the police realized that they'd been hoodwinked by the studio bosses, it was too late to seal off the crime scene or properly collect crucial evidence.

The exact facts that Paramount wanted to cover up have never been determined. It *was* known that William Desmond Taylor was the studio's star director and its greatest creative talent. And it was common knowledge that Taylor worked with Paramount's biggest stars: Mabel Normand and young, pretty Mary Miles Minter, the 15-year-old budding actress who seemed to have a promising future as a leading lady. Indeed, women figured prominently in Taylor's life. It was rumored that a large assemblage of pornographic photos was found in the bungalow, along with a collection of lingerie that had been tagged with dates and initials, as if they were gaming trophies. Love letters were also found—not from Mabel Normand, but from young Mary Minter. The letters allegedly confirmed that the 54-year-old Taylor had been carrying on a torrid affair with the underage Minter. Investigation into the director's life revealed several unknown facets: The highly respected William Desmond Taylor was actually William Deane Tanner, husband of retired actress Ethel May Harrison and co-owner of a posh New York antique store. Between the time of his New

Hollywood rumor said comedy star Mabel Normand, a close friend of Taylor's, was a morphine addict. It was speculated that, by trying to help Normand with her addiction, Taylor got into trouble with the drug-dealing underworld.

York society life and his Hollywood celebrity life, he had been a time-keeper for the Yukon Gold Company in Alaska; a night clerk at the Inter Ocean Hotel in Cheyenne, Wyoming; a gold prospector in Colorado; and an acclaimed theatrical performer in San Francisco.

As intriguing as Taylor's past was, it couldn't compete with the list of suspects in his murder. Charlotte Selby, Mary Miles Minter's dominating mother, had threatened to kill Taylor if he didn't end his affair with her daughter. Taylor's close friend Mabel Normand, a gifted but fading star, was rumored to be hopelessly addicted to morphine. There is speculation that Taylor's efforts to save Normand from her addiction got him into trouble with drug-dealing underworld figures. One of Taylor's ex-employees had stolen from him and possibly tried to blackmail him to avoid prosecution. Also, the director's houseboy had recently been arrested for soliciting young men in a park. Taylor was to have testified on the houseboy's behalf the day he was murdered. No author of mystery fiction could come up with such intriguing characters, clues, rumors, and leads.

Most of the rumors that swirled around the front pages in the days following February 2 were generated by Paramount Pictures. Since the rumors had the effect of defaming the studio's former star director, and of ruining the careers of Normand and Minter, one might wonder about what greater secret the studio was trying so hard to cover up. Many writers and amateur investigators have attempted to solve this mystery. Some speculate that Taylor had committed criminal acts in a previous life; others believe that the director was a homosexual in a Hollywood that was loath to deal with one more scandal. There is a wealth of evidence to study—newspaper accounts, police reports, eyewitness testimony. In the end, there is too much evidence and too little fact. That William Desmond Taylor was a man with a mysterious past is a certainty, but the people who knew the truth about his life and death are dead and gone.

Mary Miles Minter, the teenage budding starlet whose love letters were found in Taylor's bungalow. Her domineering mother had threatened to kill Taylor if he didn't end his affair with the girl.

MONSIEUR BLUEBEARD

Landru charmed nearly 300 women and married at least ten. His last fiancée remained infatuated with him even after his murders were uncovered.

COLD-BLOODED HENRI LANDRU MADE MARRIAGE AND MURDER HIS OCCUPATION

Henri Landru was a lover of women—283 of them by his count. Of these, he married and murdered ten. In France—the land of love—he was dubbed "Bluebeard," after the fairy-tale character. Though abhorred for his deeds, Henri Landru was secretly admired throughout France for his prowess as a seducer and lover. We look back through the gauze of history at yellowing photographs of a diminutive, balding, full-bearded man in his fifties, and ask, "How?"

There is nothing in the photographs, in the voluminous trial record, or in the testimony of surviving lovers to tell us what wiles and charms this man Landru possessed. Though the jury needed only an hour and a half to find him guilty on nearly all counts, they were sufficiently charmed by him to recommend leniency.

Henri Landru was born in Paris in 1869. Although his parents were honest and forthright, Henri seems to have preferred the irregular life from the very beginning. Prior to his spree of murder, he had been convicted seven times for fraud. In 1891, he took a second cousin, Mlle. Remy, as his mistress. The young mademoiselle gave birth to a child. Landru then married the girl in 1893, and they subsequently had a second child. Landru drifted from job to job and from scheme to scheme. His wife patiently waited for him through his prison terms; they had four children in all. Landru's retired father, distressed by his son, was apparently less understanding than Landru's wife, and he committed suicide in 1912.

The outbreak of world war in 1914 presented Henri Landru with his greatest opportunity for fraud and deceit: He would prey upon vulnerable war widows. By placing matrimonial ads in newspapers, he collected replies from interested women.

By maintaining two apartments in Paris and a pair of country villas, and by employing a plethora of fake names, Landru was able to juggle several prospective brides and mistresses at once. Once he married a mark, Landru would assume all her accounts and property. He would either sell her furniture or store it at one of his villas. A small outdoor stove on the property of one villa was used by Landru to burn the bodies of his victims.

Between 1914 and 1919, Landru sifted through what he claimed were hundreds of applicants to finally marry and murder ten women. They were: Anna Colomb, Celestine Buisson, Jeanne Cruchet (her 18-year-old son disappeared with her), Thérèse Laborde-Line, Madame Heon, Desirée Guillin, Andreé Babelay, Louise Jaume, Anne-Marie Pascal, and Marie-Thérèse Marchadier (whose three dogs also vanished).

Like earlier wife killers Johann Hoch and George Joseph Smith, Henri Landru was finally caught by the persistence of his victims' relatives. When the sisters of Anna Colomb and Celestine Buisson lost contact with them, they reported the matter to the police. Unfortunately, the only name the sisters could report was the false one that Landru had been using at the time.

Still, by April 10, 1919, careful police work had determined that the missing women were connected to a single individual who used a variety of aliases. A warrant was issued for that person in the names of the various aliases. By an odd stroke of luck, the sister of Celestine Buisson saw the man she knew as Mr. Dupont on the streets of Paris with another woman, just two days after reporting her sister's disappearance. She followed the couple into a china shop and observed as they ordered a set of dinnerware. Celestine Buisson's sister, Mlle. Lacoste, reported this find to the Paris police. The police were thus able to track down the couple via an address left at the china shop.

"WIDOWER WITH TWO CHILDREN, AGED FORTY-THREE, WITH COMFORTABLE INCOME, AFFECTIONATE, SERIOUS, AND MOVING IN GOOD SOCIETY, DESIRES TO MEET WIDOW WITH A VIEW TO MATRIMONY."

At 76 Rue de Rochechouart, the police encountered Henri Landru with a new mistress, Fernande Segret, to whom he was engaged. When confronted with charges, he denied everything, but he was observed trying to dispose of a small black notebook. It contained meticulous records of all expenses and assets related to his marriage and murder schemes.

The notebook alone was sufficient evidence to convict Landru for all ten murders, and it suggested his involvement in many others. Landru spent two years in jail while French justice untangled the whole sordid story.

Landru's belated trial was front-page news around the world. As the presiding judge laid out the facts in a precise and orderly fashion, Landru sat, bewildered by it all. When asked to clarify points or give testimony, Landru gave deadpan, sarcastic answers that suggested he regarded the whole affair as a trivial joke. His persistent cry throughout the trial was, "Produce your bodies!" He repeatedly insisted that all ten women had merely left him of their own free will and would perhaps show up at the trial to exonerate him. They never did.

Much anticipated was the testimony of Fernande Segret, the sole surviving fiancée. The judge questioned her carefully about Landru's sexual habits, looking perhaps for some evidence of perversity that might have tarnished Landru's Bluebeard aura. But Mlle. Segret would only say that he was a most tender and considerate lover. She revealed that she remained infatuated with the man despite what she now knew about him. In the end, Mlle. Segret's testimony was hardly necessary to convict Landru—the evidence against him was overwhelming.

Henri Landru walked briskly to the guillotine on February 25, 1922. He was unrepentant and in good humor, saying of the executioner, "I must not keep this gentleman waiting." He didn't.

Henri Landru, the French Bluebeard, being led to the guillotine in February 1922. He was found guilty after an overwhelming mass of circumstantial evidence was produced against him at his trial. He denied to the end ever having killed anyone.

THE PASTOR AND THE CHOIRGIRL

WHEN ILLICIT LOVERS REVEREND EDWARD WHEELER HALL AND ELEANOR MILLS WERE FOUND DEAD, SOLVING THEIR MURDER BECAME A TABLOID OBSESSION

On September 17, 1922, the bodies of a man and a woman were found in an apple orchard in the back roads outside New Brunswick, New Jersey. The dead man lay perfectly composed in a dark blue suit and clerical collar. His Panama hat had been carefully placed over his head, as if to avoid the heat. Next to him, wrapped in the crook of his arm, lay the woman, dressed in a bright blue and red polka-dot dress. Her legs were crossed, and her skirt was pulled as far down below the knee as the material would allow. Her face was demurely covered by a scarf. A serene setting, but beneath the hat and scarf were bullet holes from a .32 caliber pistol.

The man had been shot once through the brain. The woman had been shot three times in the face, and her throat was slashed. About the bodies were strewn several torrid love letters that had apparently been exchanged by the victims. Finally, and most macabre of all, a personal calling card had been propped up against the dead man's feet. The card identified him as Reverend Edward Wheeler Hall, pastor of the wealthiest, most respected Episcopalian church in New Brunswick. The woman, though not conveniently identified by the killer, turned out to be Mrs. Eleanor Mills, wife of the church's janitor and one of the leading voices in the congregation's choir. Reverend Hall was 41; Mrs. Mills was 34. The love letters revealed that their affair had been going on for several years without anyone having the slightest suspicion: quite a feat for someone with the small-town prominence of Reverend Hall.

In contrast with the after-the-fact delicacy of the murder scene, it appeared that a great deal of passion and vengeance had been vented by the killer: Closer examination of Mrs. Mills's throat revealed that the former singer's tongue, larynx, and windpipe had been cut out.

The New Brunswick police were ill-prepared to investigate such a crime. No autopsies were ever performed. No detailed search of the

Reverend Hall's wife, Mrs. Frances Stevens Hall, was socially prominent in New Brunswick.

Willie Stevens, the walrus-mustached brother of Mrs. Hall, was made out to be a buffoon by the press.

Henry Stevens, the other brother of Mrs. Hall, was known for his gentlemanly ways and for being an expert shot.

crime scene was ever made. The police forgot to cordon off the scene from the public, so within days the orchard was so overrun with curious onlookers and souvenir hunters that any investigation was impossible. In the absence of an official investigation, reporters from New York City—engaged at that time in an anything-goes circulation war—were only too happy to fill the void.

Reporters swarmed New Brunswick. They interviewed Mr. Mills, a small, retiring man who seemed confused by the whole, horrible situation. The reporters questioned the Mills's teenage daughter, a jazz-baby flapper who craved notoriety and proved herself to be willing to say anything.

Mrs. Hall, the reverend's widow, made herself unavailable for comment. However, her half-witted brother, Willie Stevens—who collected bugs and hung around the fire department—was good for tantalizing copy. Mrs. Hall was a wealthy socialite, a plain, plump-faced woman eight years her husband's senior. Her standing in the New Brunswick community was unquestioned. When she let it be known among her friends that she wanted the circus to be over, a grand jury (composed mainly of prominent New Brunswickers and close friends of Mrs. Hall) was quickly convened.

The grand jury heard what little evidence there was, but refused to even call Mrs. Hall to testify. The grand jury then closed the case, pronouncing it unsolved. The police were happy to let the matter drop, and the reporters had no avenues left to pursue. Mrs. Hall herself promptly sailed to Europe for an extended vacation. However unsatisfactorily, the matter seemed to have been settled.

Four years later, in the midst of another New York circulation war that sent newspaper reporters in search of sensational material, the New York *Mirror* decided to stir the ashes of the Hall-Mills case. Much evidence had been lost to souvenir hunters, but the papers knew that a persistent investigator with an expense account might pry something loose. And that's exactly what happened. The *Mirror* came into possession of the calling card that had been left at the feet of Reverend Hall's corpse, and had it tested for fingerprints. The prints on the card were those of Mrs. Hall's half-witted brother, Willie Stevens. Because of this evidence (and a threat of adverse publicity), the governor of New Jersey reopened the case. Four people were arrested and charged with murder: Mrs. Hall; Willie Stevens; another brother, Henry Stevens (an aristocratic gentleman who was an expert shot); and a cousin, Wall Street financier Henry Carpender.

The trial was dubbed "The Trial of the Century," and was emphatically covered by every newspaper in the country. Nearly 100 reporters, including Damon Runyon, jammed the little courthouse daily. It was estimated that over 12 million words per day were filed with the country's newspapers during the trial's 22-day run.

The case of the prosecution hinged on three points: The love letters, which established a deep and lasting love between the two victims; the fingerprint evidence, which placed Willie Stevens at the scene of the crime; and the testimony of Mrs. Jane Gibson, an eyewitness who lived next to the orchard. She claimed to have heard arguing voices and gunshots on the day of the murders, and to have seen Mrs. Hall's Dodge sedan parked nearby. This impressive testimony was made all the more compelling because Mrs. Gibson—dying of cancer—literally delivered her remarks from a deathbed that was hauled into the courtroom. Nevertheless, members of the local jury regarded Mrs. Gibson as something of a buffoon, and they resented the intrusion of the newspapermen and the seeming arrogance of the upstate state's attorney who prosecuted the case. The jury deliberated for six hours and brought back verdicts of not guilty for all four defendants. So it is that the murder of Reverend Hall and the younger woman who loved him remains unsolved.

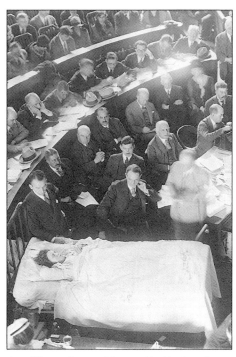

Jane Gibson, who raised hogs and had backward, countrified ways, was dubbed "the Pig Woman." Dying of cancer, she was brought from the hospital to testify in court, literally, from her deathbed.

DON'T DOUBLE-DARE HER

After her acquittal, the vindicated Mrs. Hall filed a three-million-dollar libel suit against the New York *Mirror*, which had been convicting her twice daily on their front pages for six months. Embarrassingly, during the trial, the managing editor of the New York *Mirror* had dared Mrs. Hall in print to sue his paper. When she took him up on his challenge, the *Mirror* was forced to settle out of court for a reputedly large amount.

THE INDECENT LOVERS

THE BOLDNESS OF FREDERICK BYWATERS'S LOVE AFFAIR WITH THE MARRIED EDITH THOMPSON WAS DEEMED EVEN MORE SHOCKING THAN THE MURDER OF EDITH'S HUSBAND

Frederick Bywaters, the 20-year-old steamship steward who went to the gallows maintaining that Edith Thompson knew nothing of his intention to kill her husband.

Notions of morality, as much as the letter of the law, decided the fate of the man and woman who were involved in one of England's most notorious murder cases. Edith Thompson, 28, worked as a manager and bookkeeper for a London firm of wholesale milliners. Her husband, Percy, 32, was a shipping clerk. They lived a quiet life in the suburb of Ilford, Essex, in England. Restless and imaginative, Edith wanted more than a ho-hum job and a boring marriage. In her dreams, she lived a rich fantasy life that made her drab existence even more unbearable.

In the summer of 1921, the Thompsons vacationed on the Isle of Wight with Avis Graydon, Edith's sister. Avis brought along a new boyfriend, a young steamship steward named Frederick Bywaters. The Thompsons quickly settled into their usual routine of arguing, and Avis and Frederick didn't hit it off too well, either. But Edith found the 20-year-old Bywaters very attractive.

Following the group's return from vacation, Bywaters joined the Thompsons as a lodger. After a violent quarrel with Percy Thompson, Frederick left—sailing with his ship to the Far East. While he was away, Edith started sending him a series of passionate love letters, accompanied by newspaper clippings of recent poison murders. Edith claimed to have tried to kill her husband in just this way. She also told her lover that she had aborted his child. Her letters gushed with romance-novel prose and wild flights of fancy. Read once by a lover and discarded, they were harmless enough; but as evidence in a trial, the letters proved both damning and damned embarrassing.

In September 1922, Bywaters docked in England again. On October 4, as the Thompsons walked home from an evening at the theater in London, a man leaped from the darkness and stabbed Percy Thompson to death. When actually confronted with one of her fantasies come to life, Edith was horrified. She screamed loudly and tried to stop the attack. When the police arrived, Mrs. Thompson could only describe the attacker as a "stranger." However, an inquisitive neighbor soon alerted the police to the affair between Mrs. Thompson and her young lodger.

Thompson and Bywaters were arrested separately; neither one knew that the other had been picked up. When they met in the hallway of the police station, Edith cried out, "Oh God, why did he do it?" Bywaters admitted the crime in his statement, taking all the blame and attempting manfully to shield his paramour. The love letters left the jury no room for doubt about a relationship between the two.

The prosecution's hostile summation stressed the violation of sexual morality that the case represented. The judge, Mr. Justice Shearman, was even more vehemently disgusted with the lovers than the prosecutor. Mr. Shearman described the whole affair as a "squalid and rather indecent case of lust and adultery." So it was that the members of the jury went to their deliberations, half believing that the moral tone of the nation hung on their decision.

Despite no clear evidence of collusion on Edith Thompson's part, both she and Bywaters were found guilty of first-degree murder. Bywaters never denied his guilt, and cried out loudly that Edith had taken no part in the crime. Public opinion was split on the young woman's fate. Many people viewed Edith as a shameless corrupter of morality, but many others petitioned for her life. In the end, the authorities were unmoved. Edith Thompson and Frederick Bywaters were hanged at the same moment, at sites a quarter-mile apart, on January 9, 1923. Bywaters went to the gallows stoically, but Edith—the young woman who was undone by morbid fantasy—collapsed in her cell and had to be carried to her death.

WHILE BYWATERS WAS AWAY, EDITH STARTED SENDING HIM A SERIES OF PASSIONATE LOVE LETTERS, ACCOMPANIED BY NEWSPAPER CLIPPINGS OF RECENT POISON MURDERS.

THE BATTERED BRIDE

BEAUTIFUL MARIE-MARGUERITE LAURENT MARRIED AN EGYPTIAN PRINCE, BUT KILLED HIM BECAUSE HE PLAYED TOO ROUGH

Marie-Marguerite Laurent, the Paris divorcée who married Prince Ali Kamel Fahmy Bey, found that she had to pay for a life of luxury with painful, abnormal sex.

Marie-Marguerite Laurent was an exotic Parisienne divorcée who lived with and eventually married Egyptian Prince Ali Kamel Fahmy Bey, a man ten years her junior. Marie-Marguerite was undoubtedly attracted by his considerable wealth, but found that the luxury he could provide came with a heavy price: Mme. Fahmy was forced to endure her husband's vicious and abnormal sexual desires.

Prince Fahmy, the son of a rich engineer, became infatuated with Mme. Laurent in Paris in May 1922. Fahmy actively pursued the French beauty and, in Deauville, France, persuaded her to become his mistress. The couple lived in Egypt and Paris, and it was in the French capital that Fahmy convinced Marie-Marguerite to become his bride, and a Moslem. They were married in civil and religious ceremonies, and they eventually settled in Cairo.

In July 1923, the couple went to London. On the night of July 9, they made public the fact that their marriage was troubled. The couple had an explosive quarrel in the restaurant of the exclusive Savoy Hotel. When the Savoy bandleader attempted to calm the situation by inviting Mme. Fahmy to request a tune, she replied, "I don't want any music. My husband has threatened to kill me tonight."

The eruption was caused by their disagreements over where Marie-Marguerite's surgery would be performed. Fahmy demanded London; she preferred Paris. The reason for the surgery? Fahmy's rough brand of sex, which had torn his wife's body.

The argument continued, intensifying after the couple returned to their Savoy suite. Alone with his wife, Fahmy reportedly offered Marie-Marguerite money, a bribe to get her to submit again to his desire for abnormal sex. She refused. He spat in her face. She burst out of the suite into the hallway; the prince chased after her. He clutched her by the neck and cut off her breath. Somehow she broke loose and returned to their suite.

Distraught, Marie-Marguerite grabbed the Browning .32 pistol Fahmy had given to her. As the prince resumed the brawl, his wife struggled with the gun's loading mechanism. The prince wouldn't let up and in a moment three shots rang out. Prince Fahmy collapsed onto the floor, dead.

The London papers made hay of the story, filling their pages with irresistible accounts of money, sex, and murder. The publicity led England's brilliant defense lawyer Sir Edward Marshall Hall—a man whose courtroom skill rivaled Clarence Darrow's—to accept Mme. Fahmy as a client.

In the celebrated trial that began on September 10, 1923, in London's Central Criminal Court, Hall put on a theatrical performance. He recreated the shooting scene by assuming the role of Fahmy. Hall assumed a low, pantherlike crouch and stealthily approached Mme. Fahmy in the manner in which a predator prepares to spring upon its next meal. The brilliant attorney claimed that Marie-Marguerite, in a trance induced by fright, had been unaware that the pistol in her hand had discharged three shots.

To counter the prosecution's claim that Mme. Fahmy had intentionally loaded the pistol, Hall presented an arms specialist who testified that the Browning reloaded automatically and would do so even in the hands of an inexperienced user.

So confident was Hall of his client's acquittal that he had Marie-Marguerite take the stand in her own defense. She gave a firsthand account of the killing, and supported the scenario put forth by her astute lawyer. Her testimony and Hall's convincing defense won Mme. Fahmy a complete exoneration. Whether or not a man's murder had gone unpunished was quickly forgotten in the acclaim given Edward Marshall Hall, who was hailed as the world's greatest lawyer.

THE LONDON PAPERS MADE HAY OF THE STORY, FILLING THEIR PAGES WITH IRRESISTIBLE ACCOUNTS OF MONEY, SEX, AND MURDER.

GENIUSES AT PLAY

NATHANIEL LEOPOLD AND RICHARD LOEB WERE SUPER-INTELLIGENT MISFITS WHO TOYED WITH MURDER AS AN INTELLECTUAL PUZZLE

Bobby Franks, the 14-year-old distant cousin of Richard Loeb, was selected out of desperation, killed clumsily, and then disposed of so ineptly that his body was found within hours of the crime. Just ten days after the supposedly "perfect" murder was committed, police had the two killers in custody.

Nathaniel Leopold and Richard Loeb were pals who lived in the chic Chicago neighborhood of Hyde Park. The sons of millionaires, each had a genius-level IQ and, by their respective ages of 19 and 18, had graduated from prestigious universities. In the spring of 1924, the young men were looking for something to pique their interest. They decided to commit "the perfect crime."

Because of their intelligence, each had felt superior to most other people. They gravitated towards each other in a bond of egoism. Leopold subscribed to the philosopher Nietzsche's theory of the "super-man," whom he felt they personified. By pulling off the perfect crime, they would prove once and for all their superiority. Leopold and Loeb predetermined that they would kidnap and kill one of the other young sons of millionaires that lived in their neighborhood. They would collect the ransom and use it for a summer holiday in Europe.

On the ordained day, May 21, 1924, they waited outside the local prep school in a rented car, planning to select a boy at random. Bobby Franks, Loeb's 14-year-old distant cousin, came by on his way to tennis practice. Bobby knew and looked up to the older boys. When invited, he happily got into the car. He sat in the front seat beside Nathan Leopold, who was driving. After a few blocks, Richard Loeb picked up a heavy chisel in the back seat and jabbed it into the back of Bobby Franks's skull. The boy bled to death in the car within 15 minutes. They drove the body to a marshland on the far south edge of the city where Nathan Leopold often went bird-watching. Then they stripped Bobby naked, poured acid on his face, and stuffed his body into a drainpipe. They drove back to Loeb's home and played cards until midnight. At that point, they phoned in their first ransom notice to Bobby's parents.

The body of Bobby Franks was found by a workman the very next day. This untimely event screwed up the geniuses' elaborate

Nathan Leopold, left, and Richard Loeb share a laugh during testimony at their 1924 murder trial.

THE BODY OF BOBBY FRANKS WAS FOUND BY A WORKMAN THE VERY NEXT DAY. THIS UNTIMELY EVENT SCREWED UP THE GENIUSES' ELABORATE RANSOM PLANS, AND WAS THE BEGINNING OF THEIR UNDOING.

ransom plans, and was the beginning of their undoing. A thorough police search of the area turned up a pair of spectacles of unique design. The eyeglasses belonged to Nathan Leopold, and the police traced them to him within eight days. Under interrogation, Nathan offered the plausible explanation that he'd lost that pair of glasses on a bird-watching expedition a few days earlier. When the police found some inconsistencies in the youths' testimony, they brought the villainous intellectuals back for a more intensive interrogation on May 31. Richard Loeb was the first to crack under the strain. Both

Clarence Darrow, the greatest defense attorney of his day. His representation of "the Thrill Killers" was nothing less than a work of art. At their trial, Darrow depicted the two as sane but hopelessly twisted to save them from the death penalty.

Nathan Leopold, hat in hand, leaving Statesville Penitentiary in Illinois in 1958, paroled after serving 33½ years of his sentence.

prodigies gave the police a full confession, most of which got leaked to a demanding Chicago press corps. The papers dubbed them the "Thrill Kill Killers," and ran coupons for readers to write in for a chance to be the executioner of Leopold and Loeb.

In this rising tide of public fury at the self-proclaimed supermen, the parents of Leopold and Loeb felt they needed special help to prevent a lynching, even in a large city like Chicago. Prosecutors and policemen were more likely to play politics than dispense justice. The parents hired wily criminal attorney Clarence Darrow, who promised them that he would spare their sons from the gallows.

Darrow set about trying to refashion the public's perception of these two super-brats. He tried to cast the two lads as mentally brilliant but emotionally stunted. At the trial, Darrow dwelt on their upbringing: their socialite, millionaire parents who were never around; their isolation; and especially, the development of their warped value systems. Much of this testimony centered on the new science of Freudian psychology and sexual deviations.

The newspapers and the public ate up Darrow's Freudian strategy—it turned their morning paper into some kind of secret sex manual. Throughout the lengthy trial there was no jury because the young men pleaded guilty. While the judge was not much impressed with Darrow's contention, he realized that it had lowered the public's temper about vigilante justice. He gave each defendant life plus 99 years—they were spared from the death sentence.

In prison, Richard Loeb was knifed to death by a fellow prisoner in 1936. Reportedly, it was self-defense against Loeb's homosexual advances. Nathan Leopold was a model prisoner. He was paroled in 1958, when luminaries such as Carl Sandburg spoke in his behalf. On his release, Leopold moved to Puerto Rico and lived quietly until his death in 1971.

REILLY, ACE OF SPIES

SIDNEY REILLY, BRITAIN'S GREATEST PRE-WWII SPY, WAS A SELF-STYLED ECCENTRIC WHO CHARTED HIS OWN COURSE

Sidney Reilly was the most flamboyant, insubordinate, and uncontrollable British agent ever. For all his cavalier behavior, Reilly always came through on his assignments—often in spectacular fashion.

Sidney Reilly, born of mixed parentage in Russia in 1874, spoke Russian, English, French, and German fluently. A true native of no country, he chose England as his home. He never felt accepted there, however; the snobbish disdain held by the aristocratic British Foreign Office for his mongrel past was always apparent. But Reilly's Russian background gave him excellent cover to move freely through a part of the world from which England vitally needed information.

In 1906, he traveled the far eastern coast of Russia to work for an Asian company. Connections he made there with high Japanese officials got him recalled to Petrograd (now Leningrad) to assist in negotiating the return of Russian POWs captured in the 1904–1905 Russo-Japanese War. Afterward, he became involved in shipbuilding, and was instrumental in securing contracts for German shipyards to rebuild the Russian navy. These activities moved Reilly ever higher into the realms of power. Along the way, he amassed an enormous personal fortune.

Sometime around 1908, Reilly began spying for the British in earnest. He reported on the strength of the rebuilding Imperial Russian Army. He reported on oil reserves in Turkey and Persia, both of which were under Russian influence. He was well placed within Russia when World War I broke out in 1914.

In 1917, Reilly sent back firsthand accounts of the collapse of the Czar's regime and the rise of Bolshevism. His middle-class business background confirmed him as powerful and useful, but not so close to the aristocracy as to be compromised. He easily established good relations with the new Soviet government and had free access to Leon Trotsky's office in the Soviet Foreign Ministry.

HAVING WITNESSED THE DANGEROUS FANATICISM OF THE BOLSHEVIKS, REILLY WAS DETERMINED TO STOP THEM.

Having witnessed the dangerous fanaticism of the Bolsheviks, Reilly was determined to stop them. While in the Soviet Union he organized a plot to seize Bolshevik leaders Lenin and Trotsky and take over the government. The plot failed, and Reilly had to flee the country in 1919. Back in Britain, Reilly tried to warn every high official to whom he had access against normal relations with the Soviet government.

Reilly's hatred of Bolshevism bordered on fanaticism. His last known act of espionage, the affair of the Zinovyev (or Zinoviev) letter, aimed at furthering his own political viewpoint within England. In the first political election in England after the first world war, power threatened to shift from the ruling Conservative Party to the more liberal Labour Party. This was disturbing to Reilly: While the Conservatives were staunchly anti-Communist, the Labour Party was leaning toward normal relations with the new Soviet government.

The Labour Party seemed to be headed toward an easy election in 1924. Four days before the voting, British newspapers printed a letter purportedly written by Zinovyev, head of the Soviet Comintern (which drafted Socialist policies and managed its parties' actions) to the British Communist Party. The letter urged British Communists to overthrow the British government, and implied a collusion with the Labour Party. An outraged British public went to the polls and swung the Conservatives back into power. This letter, supposedly a forgery concocted by Reilly, shattered a proposed Anglo-Russian trade treaty and soured relations between the two countries for years.

Reilly continued his anti-Soviet efforts, working with small groups of White Russians in Finland. He slipped over the border into Russia sometime in early 1925 on behalf of these efforts and was never seen again. Rumors that he was caught, tried, and executed as a spy have never been confirmed.

"MOMSIE WANT LOVER BOY TO MURDER HUSBAND"

RUTH SNYDER WAS A DOMINATING ADULTERESS WHO CONVINCED MILD-MANNERED JUDD GRAY TO HELP HER BRUTALLY SLAY HER HUSBAND

While the Ruth Snyder/Judd Gray case was not the most outrageous crime ever committed (a woman and her lover conspiring to kill her husband might have seemed commonplace by 1927), the public's imagination was caught by the donkeylike stupidity of the perpetrators. This excessively violent crime seemed emblematic of the times, the Roaring Twenties. The murderers seemed to generate equal measures of sympathy and disgust; the writer Damon Runyon dubbed the case "the Dumb-Bell Murder."

Ruth Snyder enjoyed what most would consider an ideal middle-class existence: She had been married for ten years to an outgoing man, Albert Snyder, who worked as art editor of *Motor Boating* magazine. She had a lovely little daughter, Lorraine, and the family lived in a large frame house in Queens, New York. But all this was not enough to satisfy Ruth Snyder.

Albert was a big, outdoorsy type who took his job and hobby (boating) seriously. Since Ruth, who was ten years his junior, did not share his passion for boating, the couple grew apart. Albert remained busy, loving, and faithful; he never noticed anything amiss. However, by 1925, Ruth Snyder was sneaking into New York City to hang out in speakeasies and look for affairs.

When Ruth Snyder met Judd Gray, a mild-mannered, small-statured corset salesman, she found what she'd been looking for: a pliable, willing slave. From the very beginning of her affair with Gray, Ruth barked orders and Judd Gray carried them out. It was an intense, sexually explosive relationship that satisfied the needs of both parties. For propriety's sake, Ruth Snyder would take her daugh-

Outwardly a middle-class matron, Ruth Snyder was carrying on a torrid love affair and plotted to eliminate her husband.

Judd Gray, under the influence of domineering Ruth Snyder, staged a burglary and killed Ruth's husband. The two lovers were sentenced to death.

ter into the city with her and leave the girl in the lobby of the Waldorf-Astoria while she cavorted with her lover in a room upstairs. As the lovers romped, the devoted Judd would call Ruth "Queen" and "Momsie"; Ruth dubbed Judd her "Baby," her "Lover Boy."

This banal, unimaginative affair went on for 18 months while the lovers conspired to get rid of Ruth's husband. Beginning in late 1926, Albert Snyder experienced a number of "accidents" that were potentially fatal—his car slipped off the jack and nearly fell on him; he was nearly asphyxiated by carbon monoxide in his own garage; the gas tap was left on inside the house and nearly killed him. With the luck of a cat, Albert Snyder survived these and other mishaps. Ruth knew that her husband's days were numbered, though, and took out insurance policies on his life amounting to $96,000. One way or another, she was determined to collect.

Finally, Ruth enlisted Judd to stage a phony burglary so he could murder her husband on Sunday, March 20, 1927. Armed with a heavy window-sash weight as a bludgeon, plus piano wire and chloroform, Judd waited in a closet for Albert and Ruth to retire. After Ruth crept from her bed to briefly snuggle with Gray and assure him that Albert had fallen asleep, Gray entered the bedroom and bashed Albert on the skull. Whether Albert's muscular frame was especially strong or Judd's blow was pathetically weak, the first impact simply awakened the sleeping man. Albert began to struggle with Judd, who panicked and cried out to Ruth for help. Ruth took the weight and did the deed herself, splattering herself with her husband's blood. For good measure, or perhaps just out of vengeful resentment, she topped off the job with chloroform and strangulation with the piano wire.

The main task accomplished, the killers upended some furniture and hid Ruth's jewelry and fur coat in order to make the crime look like robbery. Gray tied up Ruth and headed back to his hotel, planning to go to work as usual on Monday morning.

The police were wise to the clumsy charade from the start, and their suspicions were only confirmed when, embarrassingly enough for Ruth Snyder, her "stolen" jewels were discovered hidden beneath her mattress. Ruth quickly wilted under questioning and the police soon had Judd Gray in custody, as well. By keeping the two separated and claiming to each that the other had already confessed, the interrogators extracted full confessions from both killers.

The trial was heavily covered in the press. Ruth Snyder became hysterical at one point and Judd Gray painted himself as a helpless victim of a much stronger woman. However, in general, the proceedings were routine as such things go. Both Gray and Snyder were found guilty and sentenced to die in the electric chair, on January 22 and 28, 1928, respectively.

Thomas Howard, a reporter for the New York *Daily News*, strapped a small camera to his ankle and snapped a sensational photo of Ruth Snyder in the electric chair, at the precise moment her body stiffened from the voltage that coursed through it. The photo ran on the newspaper's front page and became one of the most famous tabloid images of the period. Gaudy and ugly, the photo seemed an apt souvenir of the crime itself.

RUTH KNEW THAT HER HUSBAND'S DAYS WERE NUMBERED, AND TOOK OUT INSURANCE POLICIES ON HIS LIFE AMOUNTING TO $96,000. ONE WAY OR ANOTHER, SHE WAS DETERMINED TO COLLECT.

THE GORILLA MURDERER

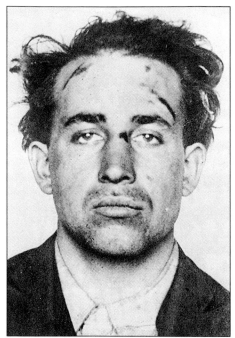

Bible-quoting Earle Nelson was perhaps the most prolific pre–World War II serial killer in North America. His murders failed to create an epidemic of panic because he spread them over two countries and many different states.

EARLE LEONARD NELSON RAMPAGED ACROSS NORTH AMERICA LIKE A HURRICANE

Earle Leonard Nelson was born in 1897 in Philadelphia, Pennsylvania. Orphaned early in life, he was brought up by his Aunt Lillian, a strict woman of obsessive religious fervor. She reared Earle by the Good Book; it was her intention that her nephew join the ministry when he grew up. All went well for a time. Young Earle read his Bible every day, and his manners were impeccable; he was just the sort of ingratiating child that most other children hate.

Everything changed when Earle was involved in a streetcar accident. His skull was cracked, and he very nearly died. Shortly thereafter, he began to manifest strange obsessions. He was caught peeping at his cousin as she undressed, and Aunt Lillian was horrified to have to reprimand Earle for "unclean habits."

In 1917, at the age of 21, Nelson was arrested for attempting to rape the daughter of a next-door neighbor. While serving two years in jail, he attempted to escape several times. Although prison authorities knew that the book had not been closed on Earle Nelson, he was released in late 1919 in accordance with his sentencing. In an apparent turnabout, Earle changed his name to Roger Wilson, met and married a schoolteacher, and seemed to settle down completely. Nothing was heard from (or known about) him for seven years. While his marriage didn't last very long (the wife blamed Earle's "intense sexual jealousy"), there were no psychotic incidents.

Then, in early 1926, Earle Leonard Nelson just exploded. From one end of the country to the other, he began raping and strangling women. He was called "the Gorilla Murderer" because of his large, throttling hands and the savage fury he possessed as he squeezed the life out of his victims.

Nelson's method and choice of victims remained quite consistent. Posing as a Bible salesman, he would take lodgings in a boarding house. In short order, he would rape and strangle the landlady. Between February 1926 and June 1927, Nelson murdered 22 women across the United States and Canada.

On June 1, 1927, Nelson raped and killed two sisters; he abducted a blind flower girl on June 3, killing her five days later. He murdered another woman the very next day. This spurt of violent activity called forth a continent-wide manhunt that put real pressure on Nelson, who did not kill again. In November 1927, he was spotted in the village of Wakopa, Canada. An entire army of police, Mounties, and regular army encircled and captured him.

Nelson was taken to Winnipeg, Canada, for trial. The savage killer remained mute and impassive throughout the proceedings. He displayed none of the violence that had typified his rampage, and many questions about the crimes and his motivations went unanswered. While standing on the gallows following his conviction, however, Nelson broke his silence and asked for forgiveness from his many victims and from God for his damned soul. The Gorilla Murderer was hanged on January 13, 1928.

NELSON WAS CALLED "THE GORILLA MURDERER" BECAUSE OF HIS LARGE, THROTTLING HANDS AND THE SAVAGE FURY HE POSSESSED AS HE SQUEEZED THE LIFE OUT OF HIS VICTIMS.

THE ST. VALENTINE'S DAY MASSACRE

AL CAPONE'S MOBSTERS DISPATCHED A RIVAL GANG IN A MEMORABLE FASHION THAT WILL LIVE IN INFAMY

The wholesale massacre of his gang ended George "Bugs" Moran's reign as an underworld chieftain. His prestige gone, he became a bank robber and spent the bulk of his declining years in prison.

In the late 1920s, Al Capone and his gang controlled bootleg liquor sales on Chicago's South Side. But they had rivals for the business on the North Side, where an Irish-American gangster named George "Bugs" Moran held control. The two factions had been warring over turf throughout the decade. Many men from both sides had been killed. In early 1929, Al Capone became determined to be done with this rivalry once and for all. He met with his underlings, approved an audacious plan, then left for a vacation/alibi in Florida, where he would wait for good news.

On February 14, 1929, at 10:30 A.M., a black Cadillac touring car pulled up in front of the S.M.C. Cartage Company garage at 2122 North Clark Street. Locals who happened to glance at the scene assumed they were witnessing a typical Chicago-style event: a police roust and arrest of suspected gang members. The black Cadillac was the type used by Chicago police detectives, and S.M.C. Cartage was known to be the hangout of Bugs Moran's gang. Sure enough, three uniformed policemen and two in plain clothes got of the car and stormed into the garage.

One of the locals who witnessed this scene was Bugs Moran himself. Late to meet his boys after a cup of coffee at a nearby café, he had time to turn on his heel as soon as he saw the Cadillac pull up. Moran quickly ducked into a nearby drugstore. He'd been arrested many times and was accustomed to the whole rigmarole—one that he was in no mood for on that particular morning. In a few minutes, Moran heard a harsh series of shots ring out.

The "cops" had rounded up the mobsters inside the garage, lined them up facing a brick wall, and shot them all to death with sawed-off shotguns and Thompson submachine guns. It wasn't a police raid—it was a hit by Al Capone. Six of Bugs Moran's top men, the core of his organization, and a hapless optometrist who liked to hang out with them, lay dead: Adam Heyer, Albert Weinshank, John May,

James Clark, brothers Pete and Frank Gusenberg, and Dr. Reinhardt Schwimmer. Later, a thoroughly shaken Bugs Moran had only one comment for the police and the press: "Only Capone kills like that!"

The city of Chicago had endured gangland wars for ten years. The average citizen never seemed to get too upset about one mobster killing another, and the police seemed to take the same attitude. But this killing, quickly dubbed "the St. Valentine's Day Massacre," signaled a dramatic rise in the level and intensity of the violence. Who knew what horrors might visit the streets of the city in the future? The public was outraged.

Despite intense public pressure, the police were unable to pin the job on their chief suspects, Capone and his lieutenants. It was widely believed that the job was masterminded by "Machine Gun" Jack McGurn. He, however, produced Louise Rolfe, a woman who insisted that McGurn had been with her on the fateful morning; the press quickly dubbed Rolfe the "Blonde Alibi."

Through ballistics, the police did link one suspect to the crime: Fred R. "Killer" Burke, who fled to Michigan before the Chicago police could nab him. He committed a capital crime inside Michigan and allowed himself to be caught in order to avoid extradition to Chicago. Burke spent the rest of his life in a Michigan prison, and avoided police and mob punishment for his role in the Massacre.

This bloodbath put an end to the North Side mob. Bugs Moran eventually turned to bank robbery, and died in prison in the late 1950s. For Al Capone, the murders strengthened his grip on Chicago's bootlegging trade, but hastened his downfall. Federal investigators, intent upon bringing him to heel, nailed him in 1931 for income tax evasion. After serving eight years of an 11-year sentence, Capone retired to his Florida estate. He died there, his mind and body destroyed by syphilis, in 1947.

The Gusenberg brothers, Peter (left) and Frank, were among the seven victims of the St. Valentine's Day massacre. Frank lived for several hours after the shooting but upheld the criminal code to the bitter end, refusing to identify his killers.

1930–1939

BESET BY THE GREAT DEPRESSION, UNTOLD MILLIONS WORLDWIDE found the 1930s to be a woeful decade. In the United States, however, those years also gave rise to a Golden Age of crime. On the East Coast, flamboyant hoodlums like Legs Diamond and Owney Madden blasted their way to the top of the gangster underworld, while the Midwest and South served as the stomping grounds for tommy gun–toting bank robbers like John Dillinger, Baby Face Nelson, Pretty Boy Floyd, and Bonnie and Clyde. Lest we forget, the 1930s also brought good times for Ma Barker and bad times for Al Capone. In addition to some especially depraved serial killers and several headline-grabbing crimes of passion, the decade saw the occurrence of the crime that made the media take notice: the kidnapping-murder of the Lindbergh baby.

THE EMBODIMENT OF EVIL

BLACK-HEARTED CARL PANZRAM HATED ALL MANKIND, AND HIS LONG LIST OF EVIL DEEDS PROVED IT

Criminologists often speculate on what drives a man to commit criminal acts. There are as many different reasons as there are different degrees of criminality. There has never been a more likely candidate to represent the *n*th degree than Carl Panzram. He may not be the most famous criminal who ever lived, but never has there been anyone who acted with such fury and criminal intent as he did. Before he died, he left behind a remarkable listing of his crimes and misdeeds. The napoleonic boasting of Panzram's account may seem unbelievable, but enough of it has been proven true to lend credence to the rest.

> *In my lifetime I have murdered 21 human beings, I have committed thousands of burglaries, robberies, larcenies, arsons and last but not least I have committed sodomy on more than 1000 male human beings. For all these things I am not in the least bit sorry. . . .*

Carl Panzram was born in 1891 in Warren, Minnesota. His parents were Prussian immigrants. Amazingly, at the tender age of eight, he was arrested for being drunk and disorderly. At 11, he went on a robbery spree that landed him in reform school at age 12. Not what one could describe as a meek lad, young Panzram later burned down the reform school, causing over $100,000 in damages. He enjoyed that fiery act so much that he burned down a warehouse in St. Paul, Minnesota, just for a thrill in July 1905. Following another year-long stretch in reform school, he was discharged and began his adult life of crime. From that point, Panzram's whole existence became a wild excess of sins.

FROM THAT POINT, PANZRAM'S WHOLE EXISTENCE BECAME A WILD EXCESS OF SINS.

WHEN PANZRAM WAS DONE, HE FED THE BODIES TO THE CROCODILES.

Reform school had turned a potential criminal into a confirmed one. Institutional life seemed only to accentuate the monstrous side of his nature. Panzram joined the army while drunk and spent the next 37 months in military prison rather than be broken by regimental discipline. After his dishonorable discharge, Panzram traveled the world—leaving a trail of raped, murdered bodies behind him.

After a large heist, he rented a yacht and lured several sailors aboard with the promise of free liquor. He drugged them all and raped each in turn. Then he slit their throats, threw them overboard, and sailed away. He called it "a party." In Portuguese West Africa, he hired eight native carriers to help him hunt crocodiles. Instead, he killed them and committed sodomy on their corpses. When he was done, he fed the bodies to the crocodiles.

In 1928, Panzram was arrested for a series of burglaries in the Washington D.C./Baltimore area. (He was suspected of several murders, but he was not tried for them.) He was convicted of burglary and sentenced to 20 years in federal prison.

On his arrival at Leavenworth, Panzram informed everyone he saw that he would kill the first man who got in his way. True to his word, he crushed the skull of a civilian laundry superintendent named Robert Warnke. That little stunt put Panzram on Death Row, where, one suspects, he wanted to be. When opponents of capital punishment petitioned for a commutation of his death sentence, he sent them venomous letters. One note threatened, "I wish you all had one neck, and I had my hands on it."

Carl Panzram's final burst of fury was directed at the hangman. As he stood on the platform on September 5, 1930, he berated the executioner for his slowness, and urged him to hurry it up: "I could hang a dozen men while you're fooling around!" Given the chance, he might have.

THE DEAD BEAUTY ON THE BEACH

WHEN THE BODY OF 25-YEAR-OLD STARR FAITHFULL WASHED UP ON LONG ISLAND, IT SIGNALED THE END OF A LIFE OF SEXUAL OBSESSION

It will probably always remain a mystery whether young, beautiful Starr Faithfull committed suicide or was murdered.

On the morning of June 8, 1931, a Long Island beachcomber named Daniel Moriarity came across the drowned body of a young woman that had washed ashore near the town of Long Beach. A missing-person report subsequently enabled police to identify the deceased as Starr Faithfull. The report had been filed three days previously by her stepfather, Stanley Faithfull. An investigation into the cause of her death painted a sad picture of a troubled young woman who had spent most of her life in a vain search for inner peace.

Dr. George Jameson-Carr, the ship's surgeon who was pestered unmercifully for months by the ill-fated Starr Faithfull. When Jameson-Carr showed no signs of submitting to her amorous attentions, she wrote letters to him threatening suicide. After her death, he was quickly cleared of all suspicion.

Starr Faithfull's descent into unhappiness began as a child, when her parents allowed her to be used as a sexual toy by the ex-Mayor of Boston, Andrew Peters. She had been 11 years old at the time. Starr's parents had accepted hush money from Peters to keep his indiscretions under wraps, but Starr had gotten nothing out of the episode except a warped attitude toward sex. As she grew older she developed an insatiably promiscuous sex drive that was accompanied by alcohol and drug abuse. At one point her nymphomaniacal behavior landed her in a Boston mental hospital. On another occasion, she was found naked, beaten, and bloody in the bed of a midtown Boston hotel room with a male companion, one Joseph Collins, standing over her. Evidently she had incurred Collins' wrath after failing to consummate a sex-for-money deal.

Like so many pathologically promiscuous men and women, Starr used sex to fill a deep emotional void in her life. In the months before she died, her obsessive need for physical affection was focused on Dr. George Jameson-Carr, the ship's surgeon for the Cunard ocean liner *Franconia*. She actually stowed away aboard the outward-bound ship to be with Dr. Jameson-Carr, only to meet with utter rejection from the man, who wanted nothing to do with her. Although she refused to disembark, Starr was nevertheless placed aboard a tug that supposedly returned her to shore.

In any event, it was the tide, not a tugboat, that carried her ashore. Was she murdered, or had she committed suicide? There were murder suspects aplenty, but also three letters to Dr. Jameson-Carr, written just days before her death, that might have provided a clue to her fate. In one letter, she stated that "I am going now to end my worthless, disorderly bore of an existence . . . before I ruin anyone else's life as well." From this, one might well conclude that Starr Faithfull had died by her own hand.

THE VAMPIRE OF DÜSSELDORF

PETER KURTEN, GERMANY'S MOST FEARED SERIAL KILLER, HAD A BLAND PERSONALITY THAT DISGUISED A THOROUGHLY DEPRAVED SOUL

In the summer of 1929, fear gripped the city of Düsseldorf as a homicidal maniac stalked the streets. The killer seemed particularly fond of molesting, raping, and murdering little girls and young women. In one day—August 23, 1929—he killed two girls aged five and 14, and attempted to rape a 26-year-old woman. This fiend's identity was unknown, but the city's populace coined a name for him: The Vampire of Düsseldorf. The uncertainty and terror fostered by the killer were tearing apart the social fabric of this working-class city. Close friends stopped talking to each other, strangers were harassed, and children were driven to hysterics by worried parents.

On the night of May 14, 1930, a new arrival to the city, Maria Budlick, stepped off a train at the Düsseldorf station. Immediately, a man volunteered to show her the way to a women's hostel. Budlick balked when she realized that he might be the Vampire. The man became angry and began to argue with Budlick. At that point, a second man appeared and chased the first man off.

Kindly and middle-aged, this second man seemed harmless. When he invited Budlick to his apartment for dinner, she accepted. After eating, the man offered to escort her to the women's hostel. On the way, her supposed benefactor pulled her into a forest preserve and sexually assaulted her. The hapless woman struggled to no avail. She was on the verge of passing out when the man grabbed her by the throat and asked if she remembered where he lived. When she told him she didn't, he let her go.

Maria Budlick had lied. The next day she led the police to his apartment. They placed the man under surveillance. His name was Peter Kurten, and he knew that the police were watching him. Certain that the jig was just about up, he told his wife that he was the Vampire of Düsseldorf. On May 24, Kurten's wife reported this to the police, who picked him up that same day.

Peter Kurten's fiendish crimes paralyzed the city of Düsseldorf with fear. This kindly, harmless-looking man had lived a lifetime of depravity.

FORTUNATELY, KURTEN SPENT OVER 20 OF THE NEXT 30 YEARS IN PRISON. OTHERWISE, HIS BODY COUNT PROBABLY WOULD HAVE BEEN MUCH HIGHER.

Kurten cooperated fully, providing a complete account of his terrible deeds. His trial began on April 13, 1931. Thousands of spectators crowded into a converted gymnasium. They were amazed to discover that the Vampire of Düsseldorf was a bland 48-year-old man with polite manners and meticulous habits. He seemed incapable of violence.

Yet violence was indeed his specialty. This he revealed in detail during his trial. In a low, monotone voice, Kurten chronicled a life of depravity that began, predictably, with an unhappy, poverty-stricken childhood and an abusive, alcoholic father. At age nine, a neighbor introduced him to the grotesque pleasures of animal torture and bestiality. While still a child, he drowned a friend in the Rhine River. As a teenager, he became a prolific arsonist and raped and slaughtered sheep, goats, and pigs on a regular basis.

After his release from a two-year prison term for theft, he killed his first young girl during a sexual assault. Fortunately, Kurten spent over 20 of the next 30 years in prison on various robbery and assault charges. Otherwise, his body count probably would have been much higher. On May 25, 1913, he killed his first victim as the Vampire of Düsseldorf. More murders followed, as did numerous sexual assaults and other violent acts.

Besides these facts, his trial also revealed his quite literal taste for blood. Evidently, Kurten not only relished the act of murder; he also liked to drink the blood of his victims. But his murderous escapades were over. Kurten was convicted and sentenced to death for the murder of nine women and children, and the attempted murder of seven others. It is certain, however, that the number of his victims far exceeded that total. Peter Kurten was executed on July 2, 1931, at Klingelputz Prison in Cologne. He seemed to look forward to the event, a beheading. Perhaps the experience of his own death was the only possible climax for his gruesome blood lust.

RAPE AND REVENGE IN PARADISE

OPPOSING CRIMES OF PASSION IN HAWAII LED TO MISCARRIAGES OF JUSTICE— AND RACE RIOTS

In September 1931, United States Navy Lieutenant Thomas Massie, a 31-year-old career officer stationed at the Pearl Harbor naval base on Oahu, enjoyed an exalted position in Hawaii's high society. His elevated social standing owed a great deal to his marriage to the daughter of one of Hawaii's most prominent families, the Fortescues.

On September 9, 1931, Massie's wife, Thalia, went swimming alone on a beach some distance from the Navy compound where they lived. She was spotted by five Hawaiian youths, who resented her presence on "their" beach. A tradition of racial hostility and segregation between Islanders and white Navy personnel then bore bitter fruit. The youths seized the woman and allegedly gang-raped her.

Tales of her ordeal quickly made the rounds among service families, instigating a backlash of anti-Islander sentiment. The five youths were arrested and released on bail—causing that sentiment to intensify into violence. Simultaneously, it was rumored that Thalia Massie had willingly submitted to her own rape. Tensions between Navy personnel and the Islanders were heightened. Gang rape was bad enough, but even more dismaying to Navy officialdom was the possibility that a white woman (and a Navy officer's wife to boot) would gladly indulge in group sex with five Island boys. Naval authorities gave Lieutenant Massie an unofficial but clear go-ahead to "get this thing over with one way or another."

Knowing that his superiors backed him, Massie ordered two of his men, E. J. Lord and A. O. Jones, to pick up one of the offending youths, Joseph Kahahawai. Lord and Jones brought Kahahawai to Massie, who gave the youth a harsh grilling about the incident. Kahahawai bore up under this third-degree like a tough-guy punk in a gangster movie. He became defiant, admitting to the rape and even boasting about his role in it. Enraged, Massie impulsively shot Kahahawai dead with his service automatic.

Lt. Thomas Massie on the witness stand at his second degree murder trial admitted he held the gun that killed Joseph Kahahawai.

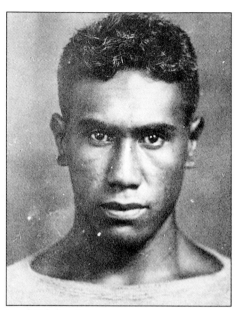

Joseph Kahahawai

Thalia Massie

The problem of disposing Kahahawai's lifeless body now presented itself. Massie's mother-in-law, Mrs. Granville Fortescue—who had witnessed the interrogation and murder—volunteered the use of her car. Kahahawai's body was transported to the countryside and unceremoniously dumped in a sugarcane field. Massie and his underlings did the honors; Mrs. Fortescue drove them in her car.

When Kahahawai's body was discovered, the authorities drew all the right conclusions. In due course, and despite some unconvincing alibis concocted by Mrs. Fortescue, the conspirators were indicted for their crime. At their trial, one of the defending attorneys was Clarence Darrow of "Scopes Monkey Trial" fame. Although he managed to get the charges against his defendants reduced to second-degree murder, he failed to win the support of the jury. The trial ended with a guilty verdict for all four defendants, who were sentenced to the maximum allowable penalty of ten years in prison.

Justice had been served—but only temporarily. Acting on direct orders from Hawaii's Governor Judd, the judge trying the case commuted each ten-year prison sentence to *one hour,* with time to be served in the dock of the court. The foursome sat in the courtroom for the allotted hour, then walked away scot-free. Outrage over this development inflamed the native community. Race riots exploded throughout Hawaii, and for two weeks violence and chaos ruled in the streets of Honolulu. Eventually the troubles subsided, but the harm to race relations in the Islands had been done. It would be many years before Navy personnel and Islanders could patch up their differences over the miscarriage of justice stemming from the alleged rape of Thalia Massie.

THE KING OF BATHTUB BOOZE

AL CAPONE WORKED HIS WAY FROM LOWLY STREET PUNK TO HEAD OF THE MOST NOTORIOUS CRIMINAL GANG IN AMERICA

Chicago was a city that was accustomed to being run by crooked politicians. These bosses took bribes and graft, and they consorted with criminals. From an ethical point of view, it was deplorable. But from a practical point of view, the setup maintained order. The criminals kowtowed to the bosses and never crossed the line that separated illegality from true public outrage. The bosses kept a lid on crime, making sure that nothing that might incur public wrath went unpunished.

The last of the great corrupt Chicago bosses was Big Jim Colosimo. Big Jim was outwardly a restaurateur (and owner of several brothels), but he had strong ties with the First Ward alderman who ran the profitable downtown vice joints. Big Jim was never an elected politician—his criminal ties were too explicit. However, he maintained the ward-boss style of leadership: sharing the wealth through payoffs, kickbacks, make-work jobs, and similar schemes. His style was conciliatory—he wanted to make everybody happy. Thus it was with some apprehension that he enlisted the help of his nephew, Johnny Torrio, a New York hood, to deal with some violent rivals.

Johnny Torrio, who belonged to New York's Five Points gang, did not shrink from violence. He eliminated his uncle's rivals and set about to streamline Big Jim's organization. As Torrio slowly worked himself into the operation, Colosimo steadily withdrew from his business enterprises to enjoy his wealth. He was happy to let his nephew take charge; he never noticed that fear and intimidation had replaced payola and conciliation as standard operating practice.

In 1919, Johnny Torrio imported a pal from his old gang in New York to be his bodyguard. The young man was a beefy, uncouth thug named Alphonse Capone. He was considered an accomplished killer, and bore a knife scar across his cheek that had earned him the nickname "Scarface." Torrio brought Capone in, offered him a quarter of Torrio's current take and half of all future business in exchange for one thing: Capone was to kill Colosimo.

When gangster Alphonse Capone was brought to Chicago from New York, he already had a reputation as an accomplished killer.

Killing Big Jim Colosimo, shown here with his wife, was Al Capone's first objective in Chicago. Once Big Jim was out of the way, Capone and Torrio were able to gain control of the city's bootlegging business.

When Al Capone carried out his assignment by knocking off Big Jim on March 21, 1920, Chicago was dragged into a new era of criminality. The lid was off. Basing themselves on Chicago's South Side, Johnny Torrio and Al Capone set out to gain control of the new bootlegging business that was springing up in response to Prohibition, the popular name for the 1919 Volstead Act that banned the sale of alcoholic beverages. High-minded persons in Washington, D.C., had decreed that Americans would not drink, but a significant proportion of the public did not agree. A vast new illegal market was opening up.

Of course, Torrio and Capone were not the only thugs with ambition. The pair had many rivals for control of the lucrative Chicago and Cook County markets. One thing was certain—the battles for dominance would be hard-fought. And they would be fought on the public streets of Chicago, with a horrified populace standing by as innocent onlookers—and sometimes as victims, too. As Capone shouldered his way to the top of the crime heap in Chicago, the death toll was staggering—some accounts put the number of his gangland victims at 500. There were many memorable hits, and attempts to kill Capone himself, along the way.

Rival bootlegger Dion O'Bannion, a North Side figure, was shot to death in his flower shop on November 4, 1924. This act prompted a retaliatory attempt on Capone's life: His car was raked with shotgun and machine gun bullets (Al was not in the car at the time). Capone paid $20,000 for an armor-plated automobile and went on with business as usual. Dion O'Bannion's successor, a cold-blooded killer named Earl "Hymie" Weiss, was assassinated by multiple gunmen as he stepped from his car in late November 1924; one of Weiss's companions died with him, and three others were seriously wounded.

The mayhem continued. During the spring and summer of 1925, three of the six Genna brothers who ran the Unione Sicilione, an underground association of bathtub gin stills, were found dead. This prompted the three surviving Gennas to sell out to Capone and return home to Sicily while retreat was still possible.

With these killings and the takeover of the supply source once controlled by the Gennas, Al Capone became the undisputed king of bathtub booze in Chicago. He also had 50 secret breweries to make beer, and a whole fleet of trucks to import bonded booze from Canada. But he still had not completed the consolidation of his power. His most spectacular rub out was the February 14, 1929, St. Valentine's Day Massacre (see the separate story) that wiped out the remnants of Dion O'Bannion's gang, by that time controlled by mobster George "Bugs" Moran.

Ironically, the Massacre was also the beginning of Capone's downfall. The public outcry over the brazenness of the act marshalled efforts to stop Capone, regardless of the difficulty. Elliot Ness of the Federal Treasury Department was assigned full-time to the task of finding a way to put Capone behind bars. He and his team pursued several avenues and were finally successful in amassing evidence that led to Capone's arrest and trial for income-tax evasion. Capone's defense—that he didn't know he had to declare profits from illegal enterprises—carried little weight in federal court.

On October 24, 1931, Al Capone was sentenced to 11 years in prison for tax evasion. He was sent first to the Atlanta Federal Penitentiary and later to Alcatraz. While serving his sentence, an untreated case of syphilis (contracted, some say, from Capone's liaison with a girl who worked at one of his brothels) ate away at his body and brain. He was released from prison on November 16, 1939, a physical and mental wreck. He spent his final years at his Palm Island, Florida, estate, increasingly insensible, under a doctor's care. Al Capone died on January 25, 1947, at the age of 48. He was buried in Chicago, the town that he had once held in the palm of his hand.

Johnny Torrio had a management style more intimidating than that of his uncle, Big Jim Colosimo.

THE RISE AND FALL OF LEGS DIAMOND

Legs Diamond had been shot at and wounded so many times without any permanent ill effects that he had begun to seem indestructible.

A SEEMINGLY IMMORTAL NEW YORK HOOD LIVED AND FINALLY DIED ON THE VIOLENT EDGE OF LIFE

Just prior to the beginning of World War I in 1914, John T. Noland, a small-time hood from Philadelphia, went to New York City with his brother Eddie seeking more opportunity—and money—in Gotham's flourishing criminal underworld. Born in 1896, John Noland was hardly more than a kid when he made his move, but he was nervy and tough—qualities that rapidly brought him to the attention of established racketeers. He soon acquired the nickname "Legs" for his ability to outrun pursuers after boosting parcels from the backs of traffic-snarled delivery trucks. He subsequently changed his last name to Diamond to reflect his flashy tastes.

When America entered the war, Legs Diamond was drafted into the army, and his budding criminal career was put on hold. But not for long. Legs went AWOL, got caught, and served two years in Leavenworth. It was the best thing that could have happened to a young man of his evil inclinations. In prison, Legs received a first-class criminal education under the tutelage of older cons. He also made connections that would prove useful on the outside. When he was released from prison in 1920, Legs went to work for one of the two biggest mob kingpins in New York City, "Little Augie" Orgen.

As luck would have it, Legs entered Little Augie's employ at a most opportune time for an aspiring mobster like himself. Little Augie was just then engaged in a violent turf war with his archrival, Nathan "Kid Dropper" Kaplan, and he needed all the soldiers he could get. In Legs Diamond he found a fearless infighter and a dead-shot gunman who positively reveled in street violence. It is certain that Legs performed numerous killings for Augie, although the final tally is unknown due to the tendency of potential witnesses to get themselves riddled with bullets or otherwise perforated. On August 28,

1923, Legs masterminded the killing of Kid Dropper outside a public courthouse in front of Kaplan's wife, henchmen, and dozens of policemen. A grateful Little Augie rewarded Legs with a large and profitable slice of the rackets.

With the big money now rolling in, Legs began to live it up in grand style. He hung out backstage at Broadway musicals, sponsored big parties for his pals, and opened his own restaurants and nightclubs. He cemented a reputation as a cocky charmer and a big spender. But his high profile also made him a better target for his gangland enemies. On October 15, 1927, Legs and Little Augie were strolling down Norfolk Street when they were blasted by gunfire from a passing taxicab. Little Augie was killed, but Legs escaped with minor arm and leg wounds.

After that incident, dodging hostile bullets became a commonplace activity for Legs. During the next few years, not all the bullets missed; none, however, killed him. His uncanny ability to survive numerous assassination attempts, as well as the wounds inflicted thereby, astounded both friends and foes alike, who came to think of him as immortal. It was just too bad for Legs that he couldn't keep tabs on his business interests with all that hot lead flying his way. Instead he spent a considerable amount of time and energy just trying to stay alive. Being thus preoccupied, Legs was unable to prevent his adversaries from muscling in on his rackets.

On December 7, 1931, Legs beat an indictment for the assault and torture of a pair of rival hoods. That night he celebrated his victory into the wee hours. Then, quite drunk, he took a cab to one of his secret hideouts in Albany, New York. Unfortunately for Legs, the secret was out. He was killed in bed by three gunmen who shot him five times in the head and torso. His murderers were never caught or named, although it is generally supposed that the notorious Dutch Schultz ordered the hit.

Local police supervised the removal of Legs Diamond's body from the rooming house in Albany, New York, where he was fatally shot.

THE KIDNAPPING OF THE LINDBERGH BABY

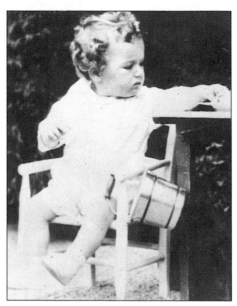

Nationwide grief and sympathy poured out when young Charles Augustus Lindbergh, Jr., was abducted on a raw late-winter night.

THE GUILT OR INNOCENCE OF BRUNO RICHARD HAUPTMANN WILL CONFOUND SCHOLARS FOR AGES, BUT THE DEPTH OF THE TRAGEDY WAS NEVER IN DOUBT

Many people believe that, more than any other event, the kidnapping of the Lindbergh baby deserves to be described as the "crime of the century." Other crimes have been more horrible, or deadlier, or more skillfully executed. But no crime more profoundly affected the lives of an entire nation. Charles A. Lindbergh was the greatest American hero of his time, a handsome, reserved aviator who achieved everlasting fame with his nonstop solo flight across the Atlantic in 1927. This extraordinary deed had made Lindbergh an object of public adulation to a degree previously unequaled in the annals of popular culture. Virtually overnight he became a legendary figure whose quiet courage and adventurous spirit moved Americans to regard him as the very embodiment of their national virtue. When his son and only child was kidnapped and subsequently murdered, their adulation was transformed into a heartfelt sense of shock and grief over the tragedy that had befallen their idol.

It all started on the night of March 1, 1932, at the Lindbergh country home outside Hopewell, New Jersey. At 9:00 P.M., Anne Morrow Lindbergh, wife of Charles Lindbergh, went up to the second floor nursery to check on their son, 20-month-old Charles Lindbergh, Jr. She found the child sleeping peacefully in his crib. At 9:50 P.M., the baby's nanny, Betty Gow, entered the nursery for a second check. This time the baby was missing. In his place a ransom note had been left on the windowsill, and an odd home-built ladder lay on the ground near the side of the house.

At first, the question of who should be responsible for investigating the crime sparked a bitter jurisdictional dispute between the

Hopewell police and the New Jersey state police. In the meantime, much important evidence was damaged or irretrievably lost. Once the investigation got underway, the police concentrated their efforts on a series of ransom notes the Lindberghs received from the unknown kidnapper. The police labored under an intense media scrutiny that went well beyond the bounds of good taste. Yet the media could claim with some justification that it was merely feeding the insatiable curiosity of the American people, who had reacted to the kidnapping as if a beloved family member had been abducted. A kind of hysteria was generated, one in which the police felt pressured to make an arrest. The newspapers tripped over each other to report every morsel of fact or rumor no matter how intrusive, hurtful, or just plain false. Lindbergh's meddling in the case presented a further hindrance to the police, as did the involvement of various individuals who thought they had a contribution to make. Among the latter were an heiress who offered to meet the kidnapper's ransom demands, and Chicago gangster Al Capone, who volunteered to help in any way he could—from his jail cell. Of more practical value were the efforts of the FBI, which was allowed to participate in the investigation after successfully lobbying Congress to pass the so-called Lindbergh Kidnapping Law.

Lengthy negotiations for a payout to the kidnapper were conducted by a certain Dr. John Condon, one of the many individuals who had made it their business to help Lindbergh. Dr. Condon met with a mysterious man in a cemetery who had enough information about the child to convince Lindbergh that he was genuine. On April 2, Lindbergh handed $50,000 in cash to Condon, who passed it on to the man. Condon was told where to pick up the child, but no one appeared at the given location. Lindbergh had been made the victim of a cruel, and expensive, hoax. But worse news was yet to come. On May 12, the badly decomposed body of Charles Lindbergh, Jr., was found in the woods not four miles from the family's New Jersey home.

Charles Lindbergh and his wife, Anne Morrow Lindbergh, in front of one of his planes shortly after their marriage. The most important American hero of his time, Lindbergh could not be refused by police when he insisted on an active role in the kidnapping investigation. His efforts hamstrung others who might have gotten better results.

Bruno Richard Hauptmann at New York City police headquarters in 1934. Scholars still disagree about whether Hauptmann was the Lindbergh baby's kidnapper-killer or an innocent man.

With the discovery of the child's body, the entire nation entered a period of mourning. In addition to grief, another powerful emotion emerged from the public psyche: rage. Across the land a clamor for vengeance was raised on the Lindberghs' behalf. But vengeance had to wait some two and one-half years, until German immigrant Bruno Richard Hauptmann paid for gas at a Bronx service station with one of the marked bills from the ransom payoff. The attendant notified authorities, who immediately arrested Hauptmann. A search of the traveling carpenter's premises turned up more of the Lindbergh ransom money. It seemed the murderer had been found.

Or had he? Whether Hauptmann was the kidnapper/murderer of the Lindbergh baby remains a topic of controversy. Many criminal justice scholars maintain that the police and the prosecuting attorneys manufactured evidence that implicated Hauptmann, while at the same time they withheld evidence that might have exonerated him. Moreover, it is known that many prosection witnesses lied on the stand or were coached about what to say. Yet legal malpractice does not an innocent man make, and there remains a strong possibility that Hauptmann was indeed the killer of Charles Lindbergh's son.

Innocent or guilty, Hauptmann was indicted for the crime. His 1935 trial was conducted openly, amidst heavy media coverage. A circus atmosphere prevailed in the courtroom, where radio broadcasters and newsreel cameramen were in constant and clamorous attendance. In the end, Hauptmann was found guilty and sentenced to die in the electric chair. Shortly before his scheduled execution, the Governor of New Jersey offered to commute his sentence to life imprisonment in exchange for an admission of guilt. Hauptmann refused, and was duly put to death on April 3, 1936. His willingness to die is as puzzling as the question of his guilt. Was this his way of punishing himself for a crime he had committed—or was it the last prideful act of an innocent man?

OWNEY THE KILLER

OWNEY MADDEN, A SOFT-SPOKEN ENGLISHMAN, WAS THE EMBODIMENT OF AN AMERICAN SUCCESS STORY WRITTEN IN BLOOD

Owen Vincent Madden—alternatively known as "Owney" and "Owney the Killer"—was a violent man in a violent era. His criminal career spanned several decades. During that time, he rose to the heights of public infamy through consistently harsh and murderous means. Yet despite adhering to a lifestyle that was hardly conducive to health and longevity, he somehow managed to die a natural death at the ripe old age of 73.

A native of Liverpool, England, Madden emigrated with his family to the United States in 1902, when he was 11 years old. What remained of his New York City childhood was marked by unruly behavior and constant scrapes with the law. The transition from a mere delinquent to a vicious thug was quickly made. His penchant for bloodshed and brutality was widely advertised on the streets, where he was tagged "the Little Banty Rooster Out of Hell." He committed his first murder before his 17th birthday, and had upped the body count to five by his 23rd year.

An oddly soft-spoken lad, Madden did his loudest talking with blackjacks, brass knuckles, and a piece of cast-iron pipe wrapped in newspaper. The frequent and unthinking use of such weapons commanded attention. It also thrust him into the leadership role of a rough-and-tumble group called the Gopher Gang.

As the boss of the Gopher Gang, Madden enjoyed a swift rise to prominence in the gangster underworld. Among those who regarded him as an equal were Lucky Luciano, Dutch Schultz, Frank Costello, Louis Lepke, Bugsy Siegel, and Meyer Lansky. The young Madden led

Owney Madden leaving a grand jury room after being grilled about his racketeering activities.

MADDEN HAD PLENTY OF ENEMIES TO KEEP HIM ON HIS TOES. HOWEVER, HE KNEW HOW TO DEAL WITH THEM.

a seemingly charmed life. Notwithstanding a rap sheet that listed 44 arrests beneath his name, he had avoided spending so much as a single day behind bars. And he just couldn't be killed. On November 6, 1912, 11 heavily armed gunmen from a gang known as the Hudson Dusters paid him a most unfriendly visit at New York City's Arbor Dance Hall. Shot five times by these would-be assassins, the 21-year-old Madden was rushed from the site to a nearby hospital, where he made a full recovery.

After his wounds had healed, Madden got right back in the swing of things by rubbing out a chap named Patsy Doyle. The reason for the unfortunate Mr. Doyle's premature demise was his desire to supersede Madden as the kingpin of the Gopher Gang. Madden's decidedly pitiless response to this challenge earned him a manslaughter conviction and a ten- to 20-year term in Sing Sing Prison.

Madden began serving his sentence in 1915 and was paroled eight years later in January 1923. Shortly after his release, he teamed with "Big Frenchy" DeMange in numerous bootlegging and speakeasy operations. Before Prohibition was repealed in 1933, Madden and his partner were brewing up to 300,000 gallons of illegal beer daily—and making a fortune in the process.

Of course, Madden's success was not without incident. He had plenty of enemies to keep him on his toes. However, he knew how to deal with them. Take "Mad Dog" Coll, for instance. In July 1932, a tommy gun cut down Mad Dog while he was in a phone booth, talking to Owney Madden. The gist of their conversation is not known. But it is certain that Madden knew how the conversation would end.

In 1935, Madden retired on the considerable proceeds of his then-defunct bootlegging trade to Hot Springs, Arkansas. He lived out the rest of his days in relative peace and quiet, finally dying on April 24, 1964—in, of all places, a hospital bed.

THE STAR-CROSSED STARLET

THE GUNSHOT THAT RANG OUT IN LIBBY HOLMAN'S HOUSE SIGNALED THE BEGINNING OF AN UNENDING STREAK OF BAD LUCK—AND DEATH

Libby Holman left her hometown, Cincinnati, Ohio, in 1924 to conquer Broadway. She wasn't the world's greatest actress or singer, but her energetic personality and erotic allure more than compensated for whatever she lacked in talent. She soon made a name for herself in Broadway musicals. Her sexual renditions of sad, soulful love songs earned her a reputation as a superb torch singer. As her popularity grew, so too did her legion of admirers.

Her greatest admirer was Zachary Smith Reynolds, a melancholy man almost seven years her junior and the heir to the Reynolds tobacco fortune. Two years after they met, Reynolds married Libby on November 26, 1931. Unfortunately, Libby's New York friends couldn't stand Reynolds, and the Reynolds clan was offended to have an actress in the family. Nonetheless, the couple was determined to make the marriage work. When Libby's theatrical commitments ended in the summer of 1932, the two settled down at Reynolda, the family's thousand-acre estate in North Carolina.

Libby found life on Reynolda luxurious but boring. Missing the bright Broadway cocktail parties, she began drinking too much. On July 5, 1932, during a party attended by Winston-Salem society, she got drunk early and left the party. After midnight, when most of her guests had gone home, Libby reappeared and went upstairs with Reynolds. A loud argument ensued, a gunshot rang out, and Libby began screaming. Servants and houseguests came running. They found Reynolds lying unconscious on his bedroom floor, bleeding from a bullet wound to the head. He died a few hours later in a Winston-Salem hospital.

Had Reynolds committed suicide, or had Libby murdered him? The media, scenting a scandal, fastened onto the incident with the tenacity of a pit bull terrier. The newspapers printed countless articles that implied that Libby had pulled the trigger. This made for good

Libby Holman married the heir to the Reynolds tobacco fortune, but she missed the gay parties and nightlife of New York.

Twenty-year-old Smith Reynolds died from a single bullet to the head. His family maintained for public consumption that the bullet was self-inflicted. Their private opinions were another matter.

copy and little else. No one knew what had really happened, not even Libby, who blamed her ignorance on memory loss due to extreme drunkenness. The cynics cried fake; they said Libby was merely acting out another role to avoid a murder indictment.

The Reynolds family bowed out early from the controversy. Reynolds, they said, had committed suicide, and that was that. Privately, many Reynolds family members had their doubts about Libby. But they chose not to press the matter, preferring to allow Reynolds to rest in peace. There would be no peace for Libby, however. It is probable that she was telling the truth about her amnesia; in the past, she had often suffered alcoholic blackouts. However, it still was possible that she had shot Reynolds in a drunken stupor. Maybe she had killed him, maybe not—she would never know for sure.

This uncertainty constantly tormented Libby. She had other concerns as well. In August, she revealed that she was pregnant with Reynolds's child. Then followed financial negotiations between Libby and her in-laws. Christopher Smith Reynolds was born on January 10, 1933. Two years later, the Reynolds estate bestowed $750,000 on Libby, and over six million dollars on the child.

Libby's inheritance bought her little happiness. Her return to the Broadway stage was a flop; a boyfriend, Phillips Holmes, died in a plane crash; her second husband, Rafe Holmes (brother of Phillips), died of a barbiturate overdose. In 1950, Libby's beloved son Christopher died in a mountain-climbing accident at age 17. In the years afterward, more close friends died or committed suicide. On June 18, 1971, Libby Holman, age 67, killed herself in her Rolls Royce. The cause of death: carbon monoxide poisoning.

THE MURDEROUS MAIDS OF LE MANS

CHRISTINE AND LÉA PAPIN WERE MODEL SERVANTS...UNTIL THEY SAVAGELY ATTACKED AND KILLED THEIR MISTRESSES

The Lancelin household in the French provincial town of Le Mans was the most ordinary of middle-class homes. René Lancelin, a retired attorney, lived quietly but well with his wife and daughter in the three-story townhouse. They had two servant girls, sisters Christine and Léa Papin, age 28 and 22, respectively. One evening the Lancelin house became the scene of a vicious battle between the classes.

On the evening of February 2, 1933, René Lancelin was to have had dinner with his wife and daughter at the house of his brother-in-law. After a day at his social club, Lancelin went home to collect the two women. He found the house dark and locked from the inside, and assumed that his wife and daughter had already left. But when he arrived at his brother-in-law's house, they were still missing. Lancelin returned to his townhouse, which was still dark—except for a candle in the servants quarters. Suspecting foul play, Lancelin summoned the police, who broke down the front door. They found the brutally beaten and mutilated bodies of Madame and Mademoiselle Lancelin on the first-floor landing. The police searched the house, and found the two servant girls in their quarters. The Papin sisters were freshly washed and dressed in nightgowns, lying in the same bed, shuddering as they waited for the authorities to find them.

The Papins admitted to killing and mutilating their mistresses. They were quite matter-of-fact about it, and never attached any great moral or social significance to their behavior. In their confession, they blamed the entire incident on a faulty electric iron.

It seems that the Lancelin women were petty, strict disciplinarians and were arrogant in their dealings with the Papins. As a result, the elder Papin sister, Christine, acquired a persecution complex. Days before the incident, Christine had had trouble with the electric iron, which would short out and thus shut off power to the entire house. The iron had twice been sent for repairs, yet it remained defective. That day, the iron shorted out again, and the power was shut off. When the Lancelin women returned home, Christine and Léa were waiting on the first-floor landing, anticipating punishment.

Christine later claimed that Madame Lancelin became angry over the power shutoff. When she perceived that Madame Lancelin was making a move as if to strike her, she snapped and attacked her employer. Léa followed suit on Mademoiselle Lancelin. The servant girls literally scratched out the eyes of the Lancelin women, and then beat them with a pewter teapot and a hammer. For the sisters' final attack, they hacked and stabbed at the Lancelin females with a kitchen knife. Their fury spent, the Papin girls withdrew to their quarters, leaving the walls spattered with blood and the two Lancelin women strewn in pieces across the landing and the stairs.

In court, the meek Papin girls seemed incapable of such carnage. Bewildered authorities labored to find some hidden explanation for their behavior. They discovered that the sisters were completely devoted to one another and had virtually no life outside their work. There were rumors of an incestuous lesbian relationship; there was also some suspicion, neither proven nor ever fully discounted, that Mademoiselle Lancelin had triggered the sisters' wrath by making sexual advances to one of them. Certainly, the Papin girls had an unusually close relationship. Separated from Léa in prison, Christine began to wither emotionally. Léa, in contrast, seemed to thrive on solitary confinement. It is thought that Léa, who was virtually mute throughout the trial, may have been mentally retarded.

Christine Papin was sentenced to life imprisonment. However, her increasingly irrational behavior soon got her a transfer to a psychiatric hospital. She died in 1937. Léa Papin was given a lesser sentence of ten years because it was felt that she had been unduly influenced by her sister. Léa Papin served her time quietly, and disappeared into obscurity upon her release.

IMPROVED WORKING CONDITIONS FOR FRENCH SERVANTS

After the trial, the memory of the crime Léa and Christine Papin had committed did not easily fade—particularly among the French upper class, where the notion of murderous servants was held in special dread. Terrified by the specter of a universal uprising by the lower class, well-to-do French citizens everywhere were moved to treat their servants more humanely—at least for a little while.

THE SWEDISH MATCH KING

IVAR KREUGER BUILT A FINANCIAL EMPIRE ON A FOUNDATION FLIMSIER THAN THE FIERY MATCHES THAT HELPED BUILD HIS FORTUNE

After World War I, phony Italian government bonds provided Swedish businessman Ivar Kreuger with the leverage necessary to amass a considerable fortune. He used his phony bonds as collateral for loans that were, in turn, utilized to acquire various companies. As Kreuger's holdings grew, so did his reputation as a financial wizard. In Sweden, he purchased all the companies that manufactured stick matches and matchboxes, and captured the majority share of the world's match market. He became known as "the Swedish Match King."

Kreuger expanded into the realm of international finance. He negotiated trade deals for the Swedish government, which rewarded him by investing money in his many enterprises. Unfortunately for Kreuger, these enterprises rested on flimsy foundations. His continued success depended on a constant influx of new loan money to pay off old loans. It also depended on secrecy. If the truth ever got out, the loans would stop coming in, and his empire would collapse.

Although Kreuger avoided this fate for quite some time, he inevitably ran out of nations and financial institutions willing to lend him money. By 1932, he owed $200 million. He approached New York financier J. P. Morgan for the money. Morgan made a verbal commitment, but put nothing in writing and ordered his operatives to investigate Kreuger.

When Kreuger found out about the investigation, he became despondent. Knowing he was doomed, he returned to France. Unbeknownst to him, he was followed by a private detective sent by Morgan to observe Kreuger for signs of suicidal behavior. After he arrived in France on March 12, 1933, Kreuger went to his Paris apartment. After scheduling a meeting with his French bankers for 10:00 the next morning, Kreuger died of a self-inflicted gunshot wound to the head. He used an antique dueling pistol that had belonged to Napoléon Bonaparte—purchased, no doubt, with his ill-gotten gains.

WHY THE ORIGINAL FAKE BONDS WEREN'T DETECTED

In the period of hyperinflation and financial collapse following World War I, the Italian government was forced to reorganize itself many times to stay afloat. In each instance, the government issued bonds to raise revenue. The bonds in each new issue guaranteed previous bonds as well. By the time Mussolini and the Fascists were in power, the situation had finally stabilized. But by then the Italian government had issued so many bonds that almost nobody could keep track of the real bonds, let alone the phony ones. And therein lies the heart of this tale.

BANK-ROBBING SWEETHEARTS

OUTLAW LOVERS BONNIE
PARKER AND CLYDE BARROW
RAGED ACROSS THE SOUTH

Bonnie pretends to get the drop on Clyde. They killed so many law enforcement officers that none of their pursuers wanted to take them alive.

On an early spring morning near Arcadia, Louisiana, six law officers trapped and ambushed the notorious bank-robbing couple Bonnie Parker and Clyde Barrow, who were betrayed by their own henchman, Henry Methvin. Local police and Texas Ranger Frank Hamer lay in wait at the road's edge, armed with machine guns, shotguns, and Browning automatic rifles. They fired more than 160 shots into the infamous couple's car. Bonnie died with a half-eaten sandwich in her mouth; Clyde was shoeless—he'd been driving in his socks.

The fatal shootout culminated months of intensive effort to apprehend the pair and their gang. During their two-year spree across the South during the Depression, Bonnie and Clyde were responsible for the deaths of 12 people and countless robberies, large and small. Bonnie Parker was high spirited and intelligent. Her lanky, cigar-chomping manner masked a quick-tempered, oversexed nature. She met Clyde Barrow at age 19, and immediately fell in love with the slow-witted, irritable petty thief. Barrow had already engaged in several scrapes with the law. Bonnie made her first criminal connection with him when she helped him escape by smuggling a gun into the Texas jail that held Clyde.

From April 1932 until their disgraceful end in Louisiana, Bonnie and Clyde tramped across the states of Texas, Oklahoma, Missouri, Arkansas, and Louisiana, robbing banks and gas stations, speeding away in a never-ending succession of stolen cars, and traveling with a shifting roster of gang members. The criminal lovers were generally incompetent at their craft—they once hit a gas station for six dollars—committing most of their murders needlessly in their haste to escape. Their sheer ruthlessness was part of their legend. They were involved in several remarkably bloody shootouts with police. Although they often got shot in the process, Bonnie and Clyde were incredibly lucky considering the odds they faced.

When news spread that Bonnie and Clyde had been killed on May 23, 1934, crowds gathered at the scene. They tore off parts of the car and hacked away locks of Bonnie's hair—they took whatever they could that had belonged to the famous pair. One determined souvenir hunter even tried to amputate Clyde's trigger finger. The death car itself sold at a 1973 auction for $175,000. When he heard of their death, bank-robbing pro John Dillinger remarked, "They were kill-crazy punks and clodhoppers, bad news to decent bank robbers. They gave us a bad name."

THE CRIMINAL LOVERS WERE GENERALLY INCOMPETENT AT THEIR CRAFT—THEY ONCE HIT A GAS STATION FOR SIX DOLLARS—COMMITTING MOST OF THEIR MURDERS NEEDLESSLY IN THEIR HASTE TO ESCAPE.

PUBLIC ENEMY NUMBER ONE

JOHN DILLINGER WAS THE BIGGEST, BADDEST, AND BEST BANK ROBBER TO RAGE ACROSS DEPRESSION-ERA AMERICA

John Dillinger was designated "Public Enemy Number One" when the FBI joined the search for him.

John Dillinger's career as a bank robber lasted scarcely more than a year. But in that brief time he became a bona fide American legend. His bank robberies were meticulously planned, boldly executed, and extremely lucrative. And the most memorable part was that he pulled them off with a swashbuckling flair that made him a hero to outlaws and law-abiding citizens alike.

Dillinger was born in 1903 in Indianapolis, Indiana. The son of a moderately successful grocer, he grew into a bright, athletic youth with a knack for getting in trouble. In 1923, he stole a car and then joined the Navy to avoid arrest. He deserted less than a year later and returned to Indiana, where he played semipro baseball and hung out in pool halls. When he and an acquaintance attempted to rob a local grocer, they bungled the effort and got caught. Dillinger threw himself on the court's mercy and got the book thrown at him in return. Entering prison in September 1924, Dillinger was destined to remain behind bars for nearly ten years.

In prison, Dillinger befriended several experienced bank robbers who taught him the intricacies of their trade. Dillinger and his new pals decided to form the best bank-robbing team ever. Paroled on May 22, 1933, Dillinger quickly went to work. Over the next three months he headed a gang that conducted a half-dozen bank holdups in Indiana and Ohio. The proceeds from these robberies were used to fund a mass prison break by his Michigan City buddies. This occurred on September 26. By then Dillinger—whom the authorities had recently captured in Dayton—was cooling his heels in a jail cell in Lima, Ohio. On October 12, the boys from Michigan City (Indiana) busted him out, killing the local sheriff in the process.

As a sign of things to come, the Dillinger gang grabbed the headlines with the Lima jail break. More spectacular incidents were soon to follow. Armed with tommy guns acquired in a raid on a police arsenal, the gang pulled off a series of profitable bank robberies in various midwestern towns before sneaking off to Arizona for the winter. In Tucson, they were apprehended after their hotel burned down and firemen uncovered their cache of loot and weapons. Dillinger was extradited back to Crown Point, Indiana; the others were sent to Ohio to stand trial for the murder of the sheriff in Lima.

But the jail hadn't been made that could hold John Dillinger—at least not in Crown Point. On March 3, 1934, Dillinger bluffed his way out of the slammer with a "gun" carved from a block of wood and blackened with shoe polish. Adding to Crown Point's embarrassment, Dillinger made his getaway in the sheriff's car. The newspapers went wild over this escapade, and further enhanced Dillinger's growing celebrity status.

Not content to rest on his laurels, Dillinger got busy recruiting yet another gang that included, among others, a murderous sociopath known as Baby Face Nelson. Although Dillinger didn't particularly like him, Nelson rather typified the character of the new gang, which was a decidedly trigger-happy bunch. The gang hit banks in South Dakota and Iowa before holing up in Minnesota. By that time the FBI had joined the hunt for Dillinger, who was designated "Public Enemy Number One." After narrowly missing an opportunity to capture the gang in Minnesota, federal agents tracked their quarry to the remote Little Bohemia Hunting Lodge near Manitowish Waters, Wisconsin. On April 22, 1934, a small army of G-men under the command of Melvin Purvis assaulted the lodge while Dillinger and his cohorts played cards in the bar. At the front of the lodge, the G-men quickly fired a massive amount of gunfire at what was mistakenly thought to be Dillinger's getaway car, wounding two innocent passengers and killing

ON MARCH 3, 1934, DILLINGER BLUFFED HIS WAY OUT OF THE SLAMMER WITH A "GUN" CARVED FROM A BLOCK OF WOOD AND BLACKENED WITH SHOE POLISH.

a third. In the meantime, the Dillinger gang made its escape out the back door.

The FBI's sorry performance in this episode shamed and angered all connected with the federal agency. Perhaps nobody felt more shame and anger than Melvin Purvis and FBI boss J. Edgar Hoover. Both men then exhibited a relentless, even desperate, determination to nab Dillinger and thereby restore the FBI's shattered prestige.

The manhunt for Dillinger led Purvis to Chicago and Martin Zarkovich, a cop from a nearby municipality. According to some accounts, Zarkovich told Purvis that he could produce Dillinger, but on one condition: the FBI had to kill the renegade bank robber on sight. Purvis supposedly agreed to this demand, against his desires, and a trap was set. The bait was a whorehouse-madam-turned-police-informant named Anna Sage, who also happened to be a sometime girlfriend of Dillinger. On the night of July 22, 1934, Anna Sage, wearing a bright orange dress as a signal to law enforcement officials, accompanied a man alleged to be John Dillinger to a movie at Chicago's Biograph Theatre. When the "Lady in Red" (so-called because Sage's orange dress looked red in the Biograph's neon marquee lights) emerged with her date from the theater, FBI agents waiting outside ordered them to halt. Sage's escort reached into his jacket as if for a gun, and made a break for the alley. He never made it; the FBI agents shot him dead. But had they in fact gunned down John Dillinger? Certain physical discrepancies between the corpse and what was known about John Dillinger seemed to indicate otherwise. One thing is known for sure: John Dillinger was never heard from again. And with such a mysterious end, he might have provided a fittingly mythical conclusion to his 14 months on the wild side of life.

The front of the Biograph Theatre in Chicago moments after the man assumed to be John Dillinger was slain by FBI agents when he tried to make a run for it. The movie that night was *Manhattan Melodrama,* a cops-and-robbers tale starring Clark Gable.

PRETTY BOY FLOYD

MADE A CRIMINAL BY HARD TIMES, BANK ROBBER CHARLES ARTHUR FLOYD WAS JUST A GOOD OL' OKIE BOY AT HEART

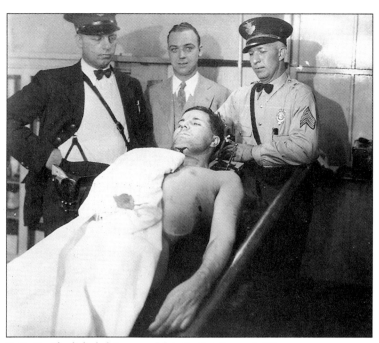

Pretty Boy Floyd's body lying on a slab in the East Liverpool, Ohio, morgue.

Charles Arthur Floyd was a typical farm boy from Oklahoma who dealt with the drought and economic depression of the 1920s and 1930s as best he could. Like so many Dust Bowl farmers, he made a valiant effort to eke an honest living out of the land, yet the land failed him just the same. When it did, he resorted to crime to make ends meet. A lot of Okies in similar straits didn't fault him for doing so. If Floyd had gone bad, they figured, it was only because his luck had gone bad first.

Floyd was born in Akins, Oklahoma, in 1901. In 1921, he settled down and married his 16-year-old sweetheart, Wilma Hargrove. He didn't stay settled for long. Unable to find work and incapable of supporting his beloved and then-pregnant wife, Floyd grew bitter, then desperate. In his desperation, he got himself a pistol and sped off to St. Louis, where he pulled off the armed robbery of a payroll truck. When Floyd returned home with the money, he and Wilma enjoyed a

FLOYD ACQUIRED THE "PRETTY BOY" MONIKER FROM A KANSAS CITY WHOREHOUSE MADAM WHO TOOK A LIKING TO HIM.

FBI agent Melvin Purvis led the group of agents who cornered Pretty Boy Floyd in 1934.

brief spell of good living. The law soon caught up with him, and he was eventually locked away for five years in a Missouri prison.

In 1929, he emerged from prison a hardened man with a keen disregard for the law and those who enforced it. After killing the man who had murdered his father, Floyd hightailed it to Kansas City, where he fell in with the local criminals. It was in Kansas City that he acquired the "Pretty Boy" moniker from a whorehouse madam who took a liking to him. From 1930–31, Floyd and a pair of hoodlums he had met in Kansas City robbed a string of banks in Ohio and Kentucky. In 1932, he shifted the scope of his activities to small-town banks in his native Oklahoma. Perhaps inevitably in a state where thousands of farmers had been foreclosed off their land, Floyd was regarded as a hero. Small wonder, then, that farmers everywhere were willing to shelter Floyd when he needed a place to hide. Floyd reciprocated by destroying whatever mortgages he could find when he robbed a bank.

On June 17, 1933, the Kansas City train station was the scene of a mob hit in which three men gunned down gangster Frank Nash and the four law enforcement officials who were guarding him. Among the five men killed in the so-called "Kansas City Massacre" was an FBI agent. Among those named as his killer was Pretty Boy Floyd.

The inevitable FBI manhunt was soon under way. After a few months spent on the run, Floyd was finally cornered in a field outside East Liverpool, Ohio, on October 22, 1934. Having vowed never to return to jail, Floyd refused arrest and was shot by a group of FBI agents led by the well-respected Melvin Purvis. By then, Floyd had killed at least ten men, several of them policemen. He had not, however, participated in the Kansas City Massacre—or so he would have Purvis believe. Speaking to Purvis with what was literally his dying breath, Floyd vehemently denied any involvement in that incident. He then passed away into the mists of criminal legend.

BABY FACE NELSON

THE 1930S' MOST INNOCENT-LOOKING BANK ROBBER WAS ALSO ITS MOST VICIOUS

The 1930s was the decade of the colorful bank robber. John Dillinger, Ma Barker and her boys, Pretty Boy Floyd, and Bonnie and Clyde were just a few of the larger-than-life figures who caught the public's imagination with their bold, if violent, exploits. George Nelson desperately wanted to join this illustrious criminal circle. He wanted to be a notorious bank robber—and so he was. He was also notoriously vicious. In fact, his viciousness was his trademark. It was what made him a big man in the world of crime.

Not surprisingly, Nelson was anything but a big man, at least in the physical sense. Born Lester Gillis in Chicago in 1908, Nelson never really grew up the way he must have wanted to; as an adult he stood five feet four inches and weighed a mere 133 pounds. Moreover, throughout the short span of his life, his features remained boyish and smooth. As if to compensate for his diminutive stature and innocent appearance, he developed a mean streak at an early age. In time, he changed his name to George Nelson, and let it be known that he wished to be addressed as "Big" George Nelson. Instead, everyone called him "Baby Face," a name he hated—and that few dared utter in his presence.

After an adolescence spent as a street punk, Nelson went to work for the Capone mob in the 1920s. In his job as a labor union rackets enforcer, he proved too wild and murderous even for the brutish Capone, who dropped him from the payroll in 1931. That same year he got caught robbing a jewelry store. A subsequent stint in Illinois' Joliet prison ended in a successful escape attempt. Free again, Nelson decided to become a bank robber. After recruiting a gang of like-minded villains, Baby Face Nelson began robbing banks throughout the Midwest.

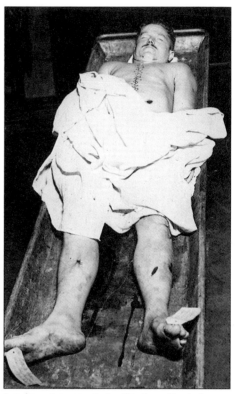

Baby Face Nelson's naked and bullet-ridden body was found beside a seldom-traveled country road. It had been dumped there by his wife and one of his crime partners after he was killed by FBI agents in a wild car chase through the Illinois countryside.

BABY FACE NELSON, THEN PUBLIC ENEMY NUMBER ONE AND PROUD OF IT, RESOLVED TO EMBARK ON A BANK-ROBBING SPREE THAT WOULD COMPLETELY ECLIPSE DILLINGER'S FAME.

In 1934, Nelson fulfilled a dream by joining up with John Dillinger after the latter's spectacular jail break in Crown Point, Indiana. Nelson idolized Dillinger even as he envied his fame. Dillinger soon discovered that his new partner was a trigger-happy psycho given to picking fights with fellow gang members and killing people for no good reason during bank robberies. He discovered as well that keeping this bloodthirsty runt in check was a full-time job. Dillinger, a pleasant and disciplined sort, quite naturally couldn't stand him.

When the FBI attacked the Little Bohemia Hunting Lodge in Wisconsin on April 22, 1934, Nelson ran off in one direction, the rest of the Dillinger gang in another. Nelson's escape was highlighted by a gun battle in which he shot and killed an FBI agent. In July, FBI agents gunned down Dillinger outside Chicago's Biograph Theatre. Baby Face Nelson, then Public Enemy Number One and proud of it, resolved to embark on a bank-robbing spree that would completely eclipse Dillinger's fame.

But it was not to be. On November 27, 1934, two FBI agents spotted Nelson, his wife, and a hood named John Paul Chase in a speeding car on country road near Fox River Grove, Illinois. The chase was soon on, with both cars careening down the road amidst a hail of bullets. Nelson finally turned on his pursuers outside the town of Barrington. A furious gun battle ensued, with the combatants using their parked cars for cover. Suddenly, Nelson jumped out from behind his car and began walking toward the G-men, his tommy gun blazing on full automatic. The two agents shot Nelson repeatedly, but failed to stop him. They paid for that failure with their lives. Nelson cut them both to pieces with tommy-gun bursts, but not before he had been hit by no less than 17 bullets. A few hours later, he too died. His wife and Chase dumped his naked body at the side of a nearby road, where the authorities found it the next day.

MA BARKER AND HER BOYS

MA BARKER AND HER BROOD GAVE A WHOLE NEW—AND VIOLENT—MEANING TO THE CONCEPT OF FAMILY TOGETHERNESS

Ma Barker was born Arizona Donnie Clark in 1872 in Springfield, Missouri. That being Jesse James country, young Miss Clark came to regard the notorious outlaw as a hero. In 1892, she married a farmer named George Barker—a short, shy man who was dominated by his wife. They had four sons: Herman (born 1894); Lloyd (born 1896); Arthur, also called "Doc" (born 1899); and Fred (born 1902). As teenagers, the boys were troublemakers who always enjoyed Ma's full support during their frequent scrapes with the law.

Eventually, all four Barker boys developed into criminals. Doc led the way by becoming an accomplished car thief and bank robber before age 20. In 1922, he was caught and charged with the murder of a Tulsa night watchman—a crime he did not commit. Nevertheless, he was found guilty and sent to the Oklahoma State Prison for life.

Meanwhile, Lloyd had gotten caught and convicted for holding up a post office, which netted him 25 years in Leavenworth. Fred, the youngest, was convicted of attempted murder and sent to the Kansas State Penitentiary for ten years. On September 19, 1927, Herman was cornered by police after robbing a bank in Newton, Kansas. Rather than surrender, he shot himself in the head and became the first Barker to die.

Herman's death caused Ma to become embittered toward the law. Ma walked out on her husband; her incarcerated sons then became her only concern. In 1931, after badgering the parole board for over three years, Ma secured Fred's release from the Kansas penitentiary. Fred returned home with his paroled cellmate Alvin "Old Creepy" Karpis, a nervy bank-robbing pro.

They went right to work. Operating out of St. Paul, Minnesota, the Barker gang made huge cash hauls in bank robberies around the West and Midwest. Ma, who did not participate in the robberies,

One of two known photos ever taken of Ma Barker. With her is her paramour, Arthur Dunlap.

MA, WHO DID NOT PARTICIPATE IN THE ROBBERIES, PLANNED EVERY JOB WITH PRECISION. SHE FREQUENTLY SCOUTED THE TARGETS DISGUISED AS A WIDOW WITH A SIZEABLE INHERITANCE TO DEPOSIT.

planned every job with precision. She frequently scouted the targets disguised as a widow with a sizeable inheritance to deposit. Unlike other outlaws, the gang wisely shunned the media limelight.

Doc was paroled from the Oklahoma prison in 1932, whereupon he promptly joined the gang. The Barker crime spree continued, with over three million dollars taken in between 1931 and 1935. Not all that loot came from bank robberies. A large portion—$300,000— was ransom paid for the release of millionaire beer-brewing mogul William A. Hamm, Jr. (kidnapped by the Barker gang in 1933), and a wealthy banker named Edward G. Bremer (kidnapped in 1934).

The Bremer kidnapping ultimately proved to be the gang's downfall. A fingerprint left by Doc Barker at the kidnapping site blew their cover, and in due course the FBI was hot on their trail. The gang scattered, and its members went into hiding. Fred Barker and Alvin Karpis underwent reconstructive surgery that left their features substantially unaltered and eminently recognizable. They later murdered their doctor, not for his lack of surgical skill, but because he had blabbed about his patients to a prostitute. On January 8, 1935, FBI agents grabbed Doc Barker in Chicago. A map in his apartment indicated that Ma Barker and her son Fred were holed up in the resort town of Oklawaha, Florida. On January 16, 1935, a task force of heavily armed G-men surrounded their cottage. An order to surrender was met from within by a burst of automatic gunfire. The ensuing gun battle lasted for 45 minutes. When it was over, both Ma and Fred Barker lay dead on the floor, their bodies riddled with bullets. The FBI agents found $10,000 in newly minted bills in Ma's pocketbook.

Some four years later, in 1939, Doc was shot dead by prison guards while attempting to escape from Alcatraz Prison. The lone remaining Barker boy, Lloyd, was paroled from Leavenworth in 1947 after spending 20 years behind bars. Two years later, his wife killed him during a violent quarrel. The Barker clan was no more.

ONLY THE DIM-WITTED SERVANT SURVIVED THE LOVE TRIANGLE

GEORGE STONER'S JOB AS A LIVE-IN STUD WAS AN ENVIABLE ONE . . . UNTIL MURDER ENTERED THE PICTURE

Early in 1935, 19-year-old George Percy Stoner answered a newspaper ad for a houseboy. A rather moronic lad, he soon found out that the job entailed getting in and out of Alma Rattenbury's bed regularly. Alma, a socially prominent resident of Bournemouth in England's Dorset County, had found marriage to retired architect Francis Mawson Rattenbury less than satisfying. And no wonder. At 66, Francis offered little to his vivacious 38-year-old wife. He drank himself into a stupor nightly while his wife made love with her houseboy.

Naturally, George Stoner did not object to this. He gave Alma his all, and she gave him plenty of expensive presents in return. On March 19, Alma took her lover on a four-day holiday to London's swanky Kensington Palace Hotel. Alma bought George an expensive wardrobe. George liked his new clothes and lifestyle. What he didn't like was Francis. His solution was brutally simple. Upon returning home on March 24, George battered Francis bloody and left him for dead.

George immediately heard from his conscience. Slipping into bed, he told Alma, "I'm in trouble." At this point, Francis groaned aloud; he wasn't dead. Alma and Irene Riggs (a friend who was staying in the house that night) rushed to the dying man's side. The police were summoned, but Francis died. Alma and George were charged with murder.

On May 31, George confessed and won an acquittal for Alma, and a sentence of death by hanging for himself. On June 3, a despondent Alma penned a note that stated, "I have quite made up my mind to finish things, should Stoner hang." The depressed and discouraged Mrs. Rattenbury then committed suicide.

Ironically, a few weeks after Alma's death, George recanted his confession and had his sentence commuted to life. It seems that Francis might have been murdered by Alma or Irene Riggs, or by both women. If so, Alma's suicide was a kind of poetic justice.

Alma Rattenbury advertised for a houseboy but found that she really wanted a lover. In George Stoner, she got a man half her age who was given to adolescent fits of jealousy.

THE GRANDFATHERLY GHOUL

A NICE OLD MAN ON THE OUTSIDE, ALBERT FISH WAS A MONSTER TO THE VERY CORE OF HIS PERVERTED SOUL

"There was no known perversion that he did not practice and practice frequently," wrote the prison psychiatrist who interviewed 66-year-old Albert Fish in 1934. The psychiatrist may have been exaggerating, but not by much. A housepainter and father of six children, Albert Fish also happened to be a multiple killer, child molester, and cannibal. This he revealed in a confession so shocking that even the prosecuting attorneys were loath to read it aloud in court.

Albert Fish started his career as a practicing degenerate rather late in life. In 1917, when he was 49 years old, his wife left him for another man. After that, Albert Fish's personality steadily deteriorated while his behavior became increasingly bizarre, and finally murderous. His victims were invariably children who were deceived into his clutches by his friendly manner and grandfatherly appearance. A vicious sadist who performed unspeakable tortures on those hapless innocents, Fish was also a masochist who induced his own offspring to beat him. When Albert Fish became bored with such cruelties, he sometimes amused himself by tendering obscene replies to lonely hearts advertisements, or by collecting press clippings on latter-day cannibals like Fritz Haarmann, otherwise known as "the Hanover Vampire."

In 1928, Fish indulged his taste for human flesh on a 12-year-old girl named Grace Budd. She was the daughter of parents who knew and trusted Fish. When Fish offered to take her to a party for children, they let him do so without any misgivings. Instead of a party, however, Fish took Grace to his cottage in Westchester county, New York. Stripping himself naked, Fish strangled the child, and then beheaded and dismembered her with a meat cleaver. He then cooked her body parts into a stew seasoned with onions and carrots. Incredibly, Fish consumed this grisly repast down to the last awful morsel. He then vanished, seemingly into thin air.

Albert Fish (right), looking like a tired old man, with an unidentified detective.

At first, Grace Budd's parents refused to believe that she was dead. Perhaps, they told themselves, she had simply run away from home. All hopes for her survival were hideously dashed some six months after her disappearance, when they surprisingly received a letter from Albert Fish wherein he explained exactly what he had done to their little girl.

Fish was apprehended and brought to trial soon thereafter. The jury discounted his insanity plea and sentenced him to death in the electric chair. He was executed at Sing Sing in New York on January 16, 1936. Fish reportedly faced death eagerly. In his final minutes, he remarked that this was "the supreme thrill, the only one I haven't tried." Two massive jolts of electricity were required to finish him off. To this day, he remains the oldest individual to have been put to death in the state of New York.

1940–1949

WORLD WAR II AND THE IMMEDIATE POST-WAR YEARS SERVED AS THE backdrop for many of the crimes committed in the 1940s. As England struggled through the Battle of Britain, there was murder among the decadent upper-crust British living in luxury in Kenya, untouched by the war. Back in London, a mutilating killer turned out to be an airman in the RAF. When the war ended, the extent of Hitler's thievery became apparent with the discovery of vast treasures hidden in Germany and Austria. The war came back to haunt America when ex-soldier and sharpshooter Howard Unruh went on a rampage, fatally shooting 13 people in his neighborhood. However, after the war, crime again resumed its relentless path of robberies, like those of safecracker Willie "the Actor" Sutton, and murders, such as the unsolved murder of "the Black Dahlia."

THE WHITE MAN'S LAW

THE BRITISH UPPER CLASS IN KENYA SEEMED TO HAVE THEIR OWN PECULIAR CODE OF BEHAVIOR

On the morning of January 24, 1941, the body of the Earl of Erroll was found in his car on a lonely country road. It was near his massive estate in Kenya Colony, part of British East Africa. A bullet had been fired through his head. There was no sign of a struggle, suggesting that he had been murdered by someone he knew. The local Kenyan authorities, in conjunction with the British military, took charge of the case. Due to the pressures of World War II, rationing was in effect. Because it hit the native population harder than the wealthy British colonists, relations between the two communities were tense. The importance of at least the appearance of even-handed justice in a case such as this was vital for morale.

When the motivation for the murder was considered, there appeared to be one very likely suspect: Sir Henry John Delves Broughton. The 39-year-old Lord Erroll had the reputation of a playboy, and he had been conducting a rather public affair with Broughton's wife for several months. It was widely rumored that Lady Broughton was seeking a divorce so that she and Lord Erroll could marry. The Broughton estate wasn't far from Erroll's, and Sir Henry was known to be very familiar with firearms.

All this made for delicious gossip, of course, but it was rather difficult to pursue in an official capacity. A thorough investigation would require frank interrogation and free access to premises that local Kenyan authorities would not be able to pursue because of Sir Henry's social rank and importance. This put the police in an impossible situation: They had to prove that white men were not above the law, yet for all practical purposes they were powerless to treat Sir Henry like an ordinary suspect.

Fortunately for the police, the world press became interested and raised a number of embarrassing questions. Newspaper accounts of the murder brought to light the unpleasant situations and indiscre-

Sir Henry John Delves Broughton, who was accused of the murder of his wife's lover, the Earl of Erroll.

THE POLICE WERE PUT IN AN IMPOSSIBLE SITUATION: THEY HAD TO PROVE THAT WHITE MEN WERE NOT ABOVE THE LAW, YET FOR ALL PRACTICAL PURPOSES THEY WERE POWERLESS TO TREAT SIR HENRY LIKE AN ORDINARY SUSPECT.

Lady Diana Broughton (left) made no secret of her affair with the Earl of Erroll (right). Rumors said she wanted to divorce her husband in order to marry Lord Erroll.

tions that the police would have been obliged to skirt. However, the press coverage was also highly inflammatory. It indicted not only the accused, Sir Henry, but all of Kenyan high society. At a time when the majority of the people in England were enduring nightly bombing raids and the deprivations of rationing, there was little sympathy for the privileged British nobility sitting out the war in distant Kenya in comfort. Not only were the lives of the Kenyan high society plush beyond ordinary British standards, these pampered few seemed to be engaging in a series of casual sexual affairs. The war-torn people back home were decidedly not amused.

Largely in an effort to appease the public, Broughton was eventually brought to trial for the murder of Lord Erroll. However, because there was virtually no physical evidence, the trial consisted mainly of Broughton's testimony. He denied responsibility, and was accordingly acquitted. In December 1942, however, he committed suicide from an overdose of barbiturates. The murder of Lord Erroll remains unsolved to this day.

A RIPPER IN WARTIME

A BRITISH AIRMAN TERRORIZED NERVOUS LONDON WITH A SERIES OF BLOODY ATTACKS

In the early hours of February 9, 1942, Evelyn Margaret Hamilton was found dead in a London air-raid shelter. The 40-year-old teacher had been strangled. The next evening another woman was found strangled in a Soho apartment building. This second victim, Mrs. Evelyn Oatley, had been mutilated with a razor blade or can opener. These attacks reminded Londoners of Jack the Ripper, who brutally slashed his female victims and terrorized London 54 years earlier.

On February 14, another victim, Mrs. Doris Jouannet, was choked to death with a stocking. Her body had also been slashed with a razor. Though apparently killed on the same day, the corpse of Mrs. Margaret Florence Lowe wasn't found until three days later, in her apartment. Several scratches were seen on her body. Still, the police lacked the evidence to find the killer.

The next night, February 15, Mrs. Heywood was accosted as she left a pub. She told the police a man tried to force himself on her and kiss her. When she refused, he began to strangle her. She was saved when a passerby intervened and the attacker ran off. This time, however, there was a clue: The strangler left behind a gas mask.

Later that same evening, someone broke into the home of Kathleen King and attempted to strangle her. Neighbors answered her cries for help, and the fiend escaped through a window. Once again he left a clue: the belt of a Royal Air Force cadet. Both the belt and the gas mask bore the same identification number.

Royal Air Force records revealed that the equipment was issued to Gordon Frederick Cummins. Scotland Yard was then able to link Cummins by physical evidence to the crimes. And many of the delays common to criminal proceedings for civilians could be bypassed. Military justice was often swift, especially during a war. In more lenient times, Cummins might have been given psychiatric care. But in time of war, that was a luxury. Cummins was hanged on June 25, 1942.

HITLER'S LOOT UNCOVERED

U.S. SOLDIERS DISCOVER BILLIONS IN NAZI LOOT—STASHED IN BANK VAULTS, SALT MINES, AND EVEN A HAYSTACK

PRECIOUS TREASURES ALSO LOCATED

Besides the vast amount of currency and bullion unearthed in the caches that once belonged to the Reichsbank, there were additional significant finds. For instance, in the Merkers salt mine, the U.S. troops uncovered rare cultural objects and priceless Jewish manuscripts that had been plundered from throughout the continent. The salt mine also yielded a sizable collection of art treasures. In addition, the second depository, located in Regensburg, yielded a solid gold tabernacle that had been pillaged from a Russian Orthodox church in Prague, Czechoslovakia. The recovery of such treasures was surely a boon to art lovers, historians, and religious figures around the world.

In April 1945, the 12th Corps of the United States Army made a startling discovery: A gigantic Nazi hoard was buried in Merkers, a small village in central Germany (between Frankfurt and Leipzig). This revelation occurred by accident when American military policemen walked by a mine entrance and overheard two women discussing the treasure.

The U.S. troops searched 2,100 feet down a salt mine that acted as a vault for the German Reichsbank. Germany's entire gold reserve—100 tons of gold bullion—was discovered, as were two billion U.S. dollars. Also found were a million French francs, 110,000 British pounds, and four million Norwegian kroner.

In June 1945, the 12th Corps located a second depository of even greater value. In Regensburg, a city in the southern German state of Bavaria, Lieutenant John J. Stack, Jr., and his men searched the cavernous subterranean vaults of the Reichsbank. There they found three billion dollars worth of Austrian securities, which constituted Austria's main national wealth. Enormous quantities of Bavarian securities were also found, with an estimated value of two billion dollars. About 2,200 pounds of silver bullion were recovered. The silver had been melted down from jewelry taken from concentration camp inmates. Lt. Stack unearthed $50,000 to $100,000 in gold and silver coins and $300,000 worth of gold bars. An Austrian haystack concealed another $50,000 in gold.

A military investigation established that the gestapo and Hitler's Elite Guard were responsible for the plundering. These Nazis made explicit arrangements with the president of the Reichsbank, Dr. Walter Funk, so that most of the stolen goods were sold through the bank—fenced, in effect—for a commission of 1.75 percent. With a total property value of untold billions, this was one of the largest heists ever.

AN OFFICER AND A GENTLEMAN... AND A MURDERER

A COOL BUT FOOLHARDY FORMER ROYAL AIR FORCE BOMBER PILOT MURDERED TWO YOUNG WOMEN

On June 21, 1946, soon after the war ended in Europe, a young woman's body was found in a room at London's Pembridge Court Hotel. The cause of death was suffocation, but the victim had been whipped and her erogenous areas had been badly mutilated.

The room had been rented to Mr. and Mrs. N.G.C. Heath five days earlier. Neville George Clevely Heath was a handsome, 29-year-old former flying officer. The victim was 32-year-old Margery Gardner, an extra in motion pictures. The evening before her body was discovered she had been seen drinking and dancing with Heath at the Panama Club. The police began searching for him.

In the meantime, Heath traveled around the English coast, ending up in Bournemouth. He checked in at the Tollard Royal Hotel under the name of Captain Rupert Brooke. That was a surprising alias to use: Brooke was a poet famous for his poems about World War I.

Meanwhile, a young visitor to the Bournemouth area disappeared. Miss Doreen Marshall had not returned to her room at the Norfolk Hotel for several days. When the manager of Heath's hotel mentioned that inquiries were being made about a woman with whom Heath had dined a few days earlier, Heath surprisingly promised to offer his assistance to the local police.

When he entered the Bournemouth police station on June 28, Heath had no idea that the police there had a complete description and photograph of him. They immediately arrested him on suspicion of murder. Heath remained cool and insisted he was Rupert Brooke. However, the police found Heath's whip and other paraphernalia. Within two days of Heath's being taken into custody, Doreen Marshall's body was found. She had also been violently assaulted.

During his trial, Heath entered a plea of insanity. It was rejected by the jury, which immediately returned a guilty verdict. Heath was executed on October 16, 1946.

A TROUBLED, BUT NONVIOLENT, PAST

During their investigation, the police discovered that Neville Heath, a former RAF officer, had been shot down in May 1944 while piloting a bomber. During his relatively short life, Heath had been in trouble repeatedly, but he had no record of violent crimes. Most of his offenses occurred while in the military. In fact, he had been commissioned as an officer on three separate occasions, only to be dishonorably discharged each time. However, the reason why Heath developed a violent personality remains a mystery.

THE BLACK DAHLIA

THE HORRIBLY MUTILATED BODY OF A BEAUTIFUL HOLLYWOOD HOPEFUL WAS FOUND INEXPLICABLY DUMPED IN A VACANT LOT

Few unsolved killings captured the public imagination as completely as that of Elizabeth Short. Shown here in one of her few nonblack outfits, she was nicknamed the Black Dahlia for her custom of dressing entirely in black.

The case of the Black Dahlia has haunted the people of Los Angeles since the day that the beautiful young victim was discovered dead. It has been the basis of some copycat killings and movie screenplays.

On January 15, 1947, the body of 22-year-old Elizabeth Short was found in a vacant lot on Norton Street in a suburb of Los Angeles. Her nude body had been completely severed—roughly cut through at its midsection. All the blood had been drained apparently before the body was moved from the murder site. The initials *BD* (for "Black Dahlia") had been carved into one thigh. Even more shocking, the autopsy revealed that Elizabeth had not yet died when some of the mutilation took place.

Elizabeth Short was one of the many beautiful young women who came to Hollywood with dreams of stardom—but never quite caught on. She got the nickname of Black Dahlia for her habit of dressing all in black: black dress, stockings, shoes, lingerie, and jewelry. Elizabeth worked on and off as a waitress, model, and movie extra, but eventually drifted into prostitution. She had retained her exceptional beauty, but lost her illusions.

The police had few leads to follow. A local newspaper received a message from the killer, made from cut-out words and letters, that read: "Here is (sic) Dahlia's belongings. Letter to follow." Included were some of Elizabeth's personal effects and a promise to turn himself in. A follow-up letter said only, "I've changed my mind. You would not give me a square deal. Dahlia killing justified."

Many people, male and female, confessed to the hideous crime, probably because of its sensational nature and their desire for publicity. However, their stories always conflicted with details known only to the police. Robert "Red" Manley, who became the prime suspect, was released for lack of evidence. He later committed suicide. The Black Dahlia case remains unsolved.

SAFECRACKER EXTRAORDINAIRE

WILLIE "THE ACTOR" SUTTON HAD DIFFICULTY FINDING A SUITABLE PRISON

Willie "the Actor" Sutton smiling wryly for the camera after his capture in March 1952. Thus ended a five-year nationwide manhunt.

Unlike the notorious John Dillinger and other bank robbers of the era, Willie Sutton chose to avoid gangs and violence. He preferred to work alone, or with a single partner. Rather than trying to intimidate bank employees, Sutton preferred, largely for reasons of his own safety, to disguise himself. He became famous for his false beards, plastic noses, fake limps, and odd mannerisms. Witnesses were completely at a loss to describe his true appearance. His fondness for disguise earned him the nickname "the Actor."

Sutton started robbing banks in the late 1920s. In 1930, he and a partner, Marcus Bassett, hit eight banks in four months, netting $214,000 (quite a sum of money at the time). The pair also stole $30,000 in precious stones before Bassett was picked up. Unfazed, Sutton continued on his own. In 1932, he was captured and sent to Sing Sing in upstate New York. Before the end of the year, Sutton pulled off the first of his many spectacular jailbreaks.

Having concluded that daytime bank robberies were too risky, Sutton turned to safecracking. That way he could rob the banks at night, when they were nice and quiet. He soon became one of the best in the business. It is estimated that he extracted cash and securities worth more than a million dollars from the 20-odd banks he robbed. However, after another successful string of heists, his luck turned sour. Thanks to information given to police by an informer, he was arrested in Philadelphia and sent to Eastern State Penitentiary in 1934. After 11 long years, Sutton escaped through a tunnel in 1945. He was quickly recaptured, however, and taken to Holmesburg Prison in Philadelphia. Sutton left that prison in a spectacular escape on February 9, 1947, when he scaled the walls like an acrobat.

Willie Sutton's fugitive status, plus the fact that he was suspected of several new robberies, landed him on the FBI's Ten Most Wanted List in 1951. This notoriety was a double-edged sword: It earned him folk-hero status among other crooks, but also put his picture in front of the general public. Before long, a New Yorker named Arnold Schuster spotted Sutton on the street and called the police. Willie was picked up shortly afterward, in early March 1952. Schuster basked in his moment of glory, and even gave interviews to television reporters. Unfortunately, among the millions of television viewers was Albert Anastasia, one of New York's crime bosses. Anastasia jumped up out of his seat and screamed, "I hate squealers!" Although he didn't know Willie Sutton, Anastasia reportedly ordered a hit on Schuster. On March 8, 1952, while he was out on the street, someone put a bullet in Arnold Schuster's head as a warning to "squealers." Sutton, in jail at the time, had a pretty good alibi, but he had a tough time convincing the authorities that he wasn't involved.

In 1969, Sutton got out of jail the hard way—by serving his full term. He lived out his final years with token celebrity status and died in 1982 at the age of 81.

Arnold Schuster paid dearly for his 15 minutes of fame: Little more than two weeks after he spotted Sutton and contacted the police, he was shot dead on the street.

THE MASTER FORGER

VAN MEEGEREN USED HIS SIGNIFICANT TALENT TO CREATE "NEW" WORKS BY A FAMOUS ARTIST

Dutch artist Hans van Meegeren stands beside the "masterpiece" he painted in imitation of Vermeer in order to prove that he had not traded with the Nazis during World War II.

Hans van Meegeren was destined to become well known in the art world. However, in the end, his notoriety was brought about by his forgeries rather than the artistic acclaim he sought but failed to achieve. Instead of obtaining the fame he desired by creating his own masterpieces, the gifted van Meegeren was reduced to doing simple portraits and restorations of the works of others.

At age 43, van Meegeren, bitter and disappointed, concocted a scheme to get revenge on those he blamed for his lack of success. He decided to copy the style of the great Dutch painter Jan Vermeer. Van Meegeren's objective was not to copy an existing work, but rather to create a new work in Vermeer's style that would be accepted as an authentic, previously undiscovered treasure.

This lofty goal required years of planning. To begin with, he had to use canvas of the correct age. Then he had to harden the paint artificially, for in nature it takes many years for the oils to lose elasticity. The most costly element was the blue oil paint. He had to crush

THE DEVELOPMENT OF AN ART FORGER

Born in Holland in 1889, Hans van Meegeren was still a youngster when his skill was first noticed. The rich artistic traditions of Holland guaranteed that his talent would be encouraged. He went on to art school and captured important awards there. Before long, he had a showing of his own work, and it was a resounding success. In short, he received praise from one and all, his work was popular, and his future seemed full of promise. But in time things began to change for young Hans. The critics lost interest in his work, his paintings stopped selling, and his career, which had once appeared so brilliant, began to fall apart. It was at that point that van Meegeren began to devise a plot to set things right.

semiprecious lapis lazuli stones, as was done in Vermeer's time, to get the correct shade of blue. All his efforts paid off, and his painting was sensational. He immediately began painting a second "Vermeer" that was even better. Van Meegeren had painted the second Vermeer to fit into a theoretical framework advanced by Dr. Bredius, a leading art historian and a special focus of van Meegeren's bitterness. After he inspected the second Vermeer, the art historian declared the "newly discovered" work genuine. If van Meegeren had ended his hoax here, he would have had his revenge. But the sums being offered for his forgeries led him to step from the artistic into the criminal world. He sold his two phony Vermeers and began painting more of them.

Unfortunately, one of his forgeries was obtained by the famous Nazi collector of art, Hermann Göring. Van Meegeren was implicated in the deal. It was a highly emotional issue—van Meegeren allegedly sold off the pride of Holland to a Nazi. Van Meegeren figured that his only defense was to admit that it was a forgery. In fact, he convinced the authorities that he was the artist by forging another painting. The art world was turned on its head by this, not to mention the reputation of Dr. Bredius. Through this harm to Dr. Bredius, van Meegeren gained some consolation, but at what cost to himself! In November 1947, van Meegeren was given a light sentence—only one year—but he died of natural causes before he could serve his term.

THE MAN ON DEATH ROW

CARYL CHESSMAN BATTLED AGAINST A HARSH PENALTY IN AN EFFORT TO ESCAPE THE GAS CHAMBER

Caryl Chessman was a classic example of a confirmed criminal who resisted rehabilitation. Nevertheless, his vigorous fight against a harsh punishment made many people reconsider their ideas about crime and what constitutes a fitting punishment.

Born in Los Angeles in 1921, Caryl Chessman was in trouble throughout his teens. At 16, he was sentenced to reform school. By the time he reached 26, he was already a four-time offender. In late 1947, he began to haunt the various lovers' lanes in the Hollywood hills. Chessman would sneak up on a parked car and shine a bright red light in the faces of the occupants to frighten and disorient them. Then, at gunpoint, he would rob the couple and force the woman to have sex with him. He became known as "the Red-light Bandit."

Eventually police encountered Chessman in a stolen car on January 23, 1948. Rather than surrender peacefully, he led them on a high-speed chase that resulted in the destruction of the automobile. On May 18, 1948, he was convicted of 17 of the 18 charges that had been brought against him, including robbery, rape, and grand-theft auto. Chessman certainly rated and probably expected a stiff punishment. But he was astonished to hear the judge utter the death penalty. This was perhaps the harshest sentence ever given for a case that did not involve murder or kidnapping.

Chessman decided to fight back. Through legal appeals and the court of public opinion, he struggled for his very existence. The legal process dragged on for 12 years. During that time, he completed his autobiography, *Cell 2455,* a best-seller. Many influential people got involved in the campaign to reduce his sentence. And even though he was personally opposed to capital punishment, California Governor Pat Brown refused to stay the execution. Caryl Chessman died in the gas chamber in San Quentin on May 2, 1960. Since that time, nobody in the United States has received the death penalty for less than a murder or kidnapping conviction.

Caryl Chessman at a press conference on April 30, 1960, two days before he was executed in the gas chamber at San Quentin.

THE DISSOLVING VAMPIRE

JOHN GEORGE HAIGH DRANK HIS VICTIMS' BLOOD AND THEN GAVE THEM AN ACIDIC VANISHING BATH

John George Haigh, the murderer who supposedly drank his victims' blood before giving them acid baths, in a police car transporting him to prison.

In 1949, con man John George Haigh moved to the Onslow Court Hotel in a trendy part of London. He posed as a self-employed engineer with his own factory. The hotel was occupied by well-off retirees with nest eggs in the bank. As he searched for a victim, he was kind and talkative to all his new neighbors. He found a candidate in Mrs. Olivia Durand-Deacon, a 69-year-old widow whose husband had left her £40,000.

Haigh and Mrs. Durand-Deacon became friends. She showed him her designs for a new product: plastic fingernails. Haigh told her that he could make prototypes at his factory. On February 18, 1949, Haigh and Mrs. Durand-Deacon traveled 30 miles to an industrial building, part of which he rented for "experiments." Once alone, Haigh killed the woman with a shot in the neck from a .38 revolver. According to his own account he then made an incision into an artery with a penknife, filled a glass with the fresh blood, and drank it. Haigh stripped the body and stuffed it into a 40-gallon drum designed to hold corrosive material. He then filled the drum with sulfuric acid. Experience had shown him just the right amount to use. The remains of Mrs. Durand-Deacon began to dissolve.

Haigh's scheme was to transfer Mrs. Durand-Deacon's assets to himself over a period of time through careful forgeries. In order for this plan to work, however, it was essential that her disappearance not be noticed quickly. If a relative or friend were to inquire later on, he could claim she was traveling on vacation. This was the method he had employed with five other victims over the past several years. However, this time a neighbor at the hotel noticed Mrs. Durand-Deacon's absence the day after the murder. Furthermore, this woman—Mrs. Constance Lane—had been told by Mrs. Durand-Deacon of her plan to visit Mr. Haigh's factory. Haigh claimed that she never showed up for the appointment and pretended to be concerned. By the next day, Mrs. Lane's apprehension was such that Haigh felt obliged to accompany her to the police and file a missing person's report.

At first, the police had no reason to doubt George Haigh's account. They began a simple, routine investigation. A check into Haigh's background alerted police to his criminal record. Within a few days, the police had found Haigh's "lab." The only evidence noticed there was a recently fired revolver and blood on the floor. Without a body, no case could be made. Yet at that point, the police were not well-enough informed to rake through the pile of acidic sludge that had recently been dumped out. They were, however, ready to question Mr. Haigh a little more intensely.

"Requested" to give further evidence, Haigh soon concluded that the jig was up. He began to volunteer evidence, and was quite a bit more helpful than the police expected. When he told them the part about drinking the victim's blood, the police began to sense that Haigh was laying the groundwork for an insanity defense. They analyzed the sulfuric sludge and found bone fragments and enough of Mrs. Durand-Deacon's bridgework to make a positive identification. The authorities then charged Haigh with murder.

Aware that Haigh would claim insanity, the prosecution kept a low profile on the case and made sure that every legal step was properly taken. With all these precautions, they were understandably horrified when the March 4, 1949, *London Daily Mirror* trumpeted: "VAMPIRE—A MAN HELD." Haigh had leaked his story to the press. The editor of the *Daily Mirror* was fined £10,000 and given three months in jail as punishment for pre-trial publicity and as a warning to other newspapers. The trial proceeded uneventfully. Though the defense claimed insanity and played up Haigh's blood-drinking, the jury was unmoved. It took them only 15 minutes to return a guilty verdict with the death penalty mandated.

HAIGH'S MISLEADING CRIMINAL RECORD

Before he moved to the Onslow Court Hotel in the fashionable South Kensington area of London, John George Haigh was a small-time thief and con man. However, he had a talent for forgery and a vivid, warped imagination. The 39-year-old schemer had already served three prison terms for fraud and robbery. However, unbeknownst to the authorities, Haigh's earlier escapades had often involved more than simple swindles or thefts; he had previously engaged in some of the sickest activities ever thought up by human beings.

"HE JUST... SORT OF... SNAPPED"

EX-GI HOWARD UNRUH SHOT 13 INNOCENT PEOPLE IN HIS NEIGHBORHOOD IN JUST 12 MINUTES

Armed with revolvers and machine guns, police moved in on the apartment where Howard Unruh was holed up. The dead man on the sidewalk is Maurice Cohen, who was slain as he left his drugstore, which is at the left center.

Outwardly, Howard Unruh was a likable young man. He had an excellent war record, was enrolled at a university, and attended Bible classes on the side. Nobody suspected that anything was bothering this troubled young ex-soldier. No one realized he had a serious problem, at least not until it was too late.

Unruh, born in 1921, volunteered for the Army in 1941. He served with distinction as a sharpshooter and tank gunner. When released from the army, he returned to his hometown, Camden, New Jersey, and enrolled in the state university to study pharmacy. Except for his Bible study classes, he showed little interest in social activities. He usually retreated to his room, reading his Bible and studying. But as time passed, he grew increasingly reclusive and moody. Unruh began compiling hate lists of neighbors, noting ways in which their behavior annoyed him. Some of the names even merited the notation "retal," meaning they were marked for retaliation.

Then his behavior grew more overtly troubled. His interest in weapons was reignited. He began collecting high-powered weapons and putting in long hours of target practice. He went so far as to erect a heavy fence around his backyard to protect his "secrets" and keep out intruders. Unruh labored long and hard to create an armor-plated gate for his fortress. It was an imposing gate, but since it rested on simple, exposed hinges, it must have proved to be an irresistible target for a neighborhood prank, because it was soon removed.

On September 5, 1949, when Unruh discovered his gate missing, he lost control of the delicate balance that had held his life together. He decided the time had come for "massive retal." His first target might have been his mother, but she noticed the crazed look in his eyes at breakfast, so she quickly left. She ran to a neighbor's house, but unfortunately, she did not call the police immediately. Meanwhile, Unruh armed himself with a 9mm Luger and another pistol, then

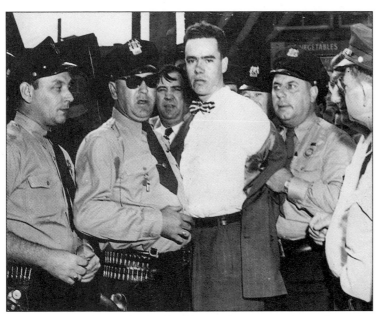

At last, Howard Unruh surrendered to the police. Unruh was never put on trial. Instead, he was sent straight to an insane asylum—for the rest of his life.

HIS PROWESS AS A MARKSMAN WAS SUCH THAT FEW WHO CAME INTO HIS SIGHTS WERE SPARED.

filled his pockets with ammunition. At 9:20 A.M., the crazed ex-GI walked out of his house and down the street, shooting randomly at everyone he saw. His prowess as a marksman was such that few who came into his sights were spared. Amazingly, 13 people were shot to death in only 12 minutes.

Unruh returned to his house and barricaded himself in his bedroom. As police arrived and surrounded the house, he answered a telephone call from a local newspaper. He talked to them calmly and rationally, but then tear gas came through the window and he hung up. Eventually he walked out of the house and surrendered to the police.

Howard Unruh never went to trial. The State of New Jersey sent him directly to the insane asylum—for life. He made only one statement at his commitment hearing: "I'd have killed a thousand if I'd had bullets enough."

1950–1959

CERTAINLY, THE COLD WAR, WHICH WAS THE MOST DOMINANT FACT OF life in the 1950s, provided its share of spying and espionage. The Rosenbergs sold secrets of the atomic bomb to the Soviet Union, and Donald Maclean—a high-ranking official in the British Embassy in Washington, D.C.—proved very useful to the Russians. The Cold War notwithstanding, many people think of the 1950s as a quiet and peaceful time, but various heinous crimes in those years contradicted that image. Perhaps in reaction to those "quiet" times, two teenagers, Charles Starkweather and Caril Ann Fugate, went on a killing spree, spreading terror across the Midwest. Meanwhile, quiet recluse Ed Gein of Wisconsin killed numerous women and indulged in cannibalism. And on a peaceful farm in Kansas, a family was killed in cold blood.

THE BRINKS ROBBERY

TONY PINO BECAME A FOLK HERO WHEN HE AND HIS GANG ROBBED THE "UNROBBABLE"

Anthony "Tony" Pino was a local Boston thief. Always a small-timer, he shied away from high-risk opportunities, preferring lightweight larcenies like shoplifting and unarmed stickups. He was constantly on the lookout for an easy score. In 1944, recently released from an involuntary vacation in jail, Pino discovered an easy mark in the most unlikely of locations: the Brinks Armored Car Company.

Brinks had apparently been coasting on its formidable reputation for security and had gotten lax in its safeguards. In fact—as Pino discovered—the Brinks building could be entered at night without sounding the alarm. With the utmost patience, Pino took six years to plan the greatest heist of his career.

At last, on January 18, 1950, Pino was ready. He'd gathered a gang of noteworthy Boston-area thieves to hold up the Brinks counting room at the end of the workday. Pino had timed everything precisely. Rather than try to blow the safe at night with the risk of noise and discovery, he opted to strike while the safe was still unlocked and the building in its most vulnerable state. By 6:45 that evening, all the guards and drivers, and most of the other employees, had left for the day. All that remained were a half-dozen supervisors, whose job it was to tally up the day's receipts and put the money in the vault. Pino and his pals made their move before the remaining employees had closed the vault. The operation worked flawlessly.

When the gang counted their haul in the safety of their hideout, they discovered that they'd netted $2,775,395.12, of which $1,218,211.29 was in cash. And only $98,000 of the cash were traceable new bills with sequential serial numbers. This was swell news for Pino and his gang, but bad news for Brinks; the company was thoroughly embarrassed. The FBI moved in on the case, and Bureau director J. Edgar Hoover regarded the robbery as a direct affront to him.

Tony Pino, the brains behind the Brinks robbery. A small-potatoes thief, he might have eluded police when he graduated to the big time but for the treachery of one of his gang. Authorities were grateful for the break, but a large section of the public would have preferred to see the Brinks robbers get away with it.

PINO PLAYED "CAT AND MOUSE" WITH BRINKS

Tony Pino was an extremely patient, cautious man. He waited six years before taking full advantage of his discovery about the lax Brinks security. He dreamed of a colossal score, but in the meantime, he worked his way up to it, studying the Brinks building unceasingly. He broke in night after night, just to wander around, eyeball the layout, and anticipate possible pitfalls.

One of Pino's minor preliminary triumphs was the successful theft of the keys that unlocked the backs of the Brinks armored trucks. When Brinks drivers took a coffee break in the middle of their rounds, Pino would sneak to the rear of a truck, open the door, and steal a bag or two of cash. He pilfered Brinks for a year or so in this manner, and none of the thefts were ever publicized; Pino guessed that Brinks had absorbed the loss in order to protect its reputation.

Handcuffed together, two of the Brinks robbers, "Jazz" Maffie (left) and Henry D. Baker, being escorted by a police officer to the Massachusetts State Prison.

Theories about the robbery were bandied about in bars and at dinner tables across the country. There were nightly jokes on TV shows. Because Pino and his cronies were well known to Boston police, he and most of the gang were regularly questioned, but to no avail. Time passed, and no arrests were made.

Law enforcement agencies soon found themselves staring at deadlines. The FBI had a three-year statute of limitations that cut off their involvement if no progress was made on a case. The state of Massachusetts had a six-year statute of limitations, after which the gang members could spend their loot with impunity.

Then, in 1954—four years after the heist—the gang members began to slip up. Two of the robbers were arrested in Pennsylvania for a robbery spree. Since the FBI knew them as possible suspects in the Brinks robbery, they were thoroughly questioned about that crime. Neither thief cracked under interrogation, but one, Joseph "Specs" O'Keefe, later found himself falling to pieces under the strain of the prison term he was serving for the Pennsylvania heists. He started making outrageous demands of the other gang members and threatened to squeal about the Brinks job.

On January 11, 1956, only six days before the statute of limitations would have closed the book on the case, O'Keefe confessed to authorities about the whole job. O'Keefe's foolish behavior was a remarkable break. Arrests were made, and charges were filed.

The public lined the courtroom and plaza steps to cheer the defendants at their trial in August 1956. Two of the gang members had died since the robbery but eight men were hauled into court: Tony Pino, Jimmy Faherty, Michael Geagan, Sandy Richardson, Joe McGinnis, Jimmy Costa, John Maffie, and Henry Baker. Each man was found guilty and received a life sentence. The money—nearly three million dollars—was never recovered.

ESPIONAGE WAS A FAMILY AFFAIR

NEW YORK COMMUNISTS JULIUS AND ETHEL ROSENBERG SOLD A-BOMB SECRETS TO THE SOVIETS

Born and raised in New York City, Julius Rosenberg and his wife Ethel were middle class, intelligent, and well educated. Julius took his degree in electrical engineering, and eventually put his training to practical use in the Army Signal Corps. Like many other bright, idealistic Americans who were attracted to Soviet ideology in the 1930s, the Rosenbergs developed their Communist sympathies while very young adults. Julius, for instance, was an active member of the Communist Party before 1940, when he was barely 20 years old. By 1950, the Rosenbergs had given the Communists far more than just moral support.

Ethel Rosenberg was very close to her brother and sister-in-law, David and Ruth Greenglass. During World War II, Sgt. David Greenglass was assigned to work as a foreman in a machine shop in Los Alamos, New Mexico, where the first atomic bomb was under development. He was kept in the dark as to the exact nature of his work, which was the manufacture of vital parts for the bomb. However, Julius, through his involvement in a Communist espionage ring, *did* know the nature of the project David was working on.

Julius also knew that David Greenglass could be very useful to the aims of the Soviet Union, and Julius was confident that he could exploit David. In 1944 or 1945, the Rosenbergs asked David Greenglass to give them secret information about the atomic bomb— information that would be passed on to the Soviet Union. The Rosenbergs explained to David that, following the war, international politics would be dominated by the mutually antagonistic United States and Soviet Union. If both powers had the atomic bomb, the Rosenbergs argued, the resulting balance of power would ensure world peace.

Although David at first refused to swallow Julius and Ethel's line, he ultimately relented, and fairly easily, too. David memorized vital, secret information and relayed it to his wife, Ruth. She memorized

Separated by a wire screen, Ethel and Julius Rosenberg head for jail after their conviction. Their guilt was never really at issue. However, many of their sympathizers found it hard to accept the notion of executing the parents of two young boys.

what she had been told and passed it on to the Rosenbergs. They relayed it to a man named Harry Gold, a Swiss who worked for the Communist espionage ring as a courier. Gold passed the information to Anatoly Yakovlev, Soviet vice consul in New York City. David Greenglass also turned over critical drawings of the bomb.

Discovery of the Rosenbergs' betrayal of the United States came in a roundabout way. The name of Dr. Klaus Fuchs was found in a file that listed names of Communist spies. Fuchs was a British physicist who had been designated by England to go to Los Alamos to help the United States build the bomb. When Fuchs's cover was blown in May 1950, the Rosenbergs' contact, Harry Gold, was implicated and taken into custody soon after. Well aware that a ripple effect would lead the authorities to them, the Rosenbergs tried to convince the Greenglasses to defect. They procured fake passports and money for both David and Ruth. The Greenglasses initially agreed, but at the last minute they refused to go.

The FBI arrested David and Ruth Greenglass, and found the incriminating passports and money. The Greenglasses agreed to testify against their relatives in exchange for immunity for Ruth and a lighter sentence for David. The Rosenbergs were arrested in July 1950 and tried in March of the following year.

Julius and Ethel had excellent legal counsel. They seemed to have ample funds, though the income from their jobs had never been substantial. On the witness stand, they repeatedly took the Fifth Amendment against self-incrimination. They denied ever passing secret information to any foreign power. David Greenglass (who would receive a 15-year sentence for his part in the espionage scheme) was the government's chief witness against the Rosenbergs. The public was aghast that Greenglass gave testimony guaranteed to send his sister to her death. Yet Ethel Rosenberg was no model sibling herself;

An outbreak of public demonstrations protested the Rosenberg's death sentence. At the railroad depot at Ossining, New York, the site of Sing Sing prison, actress Karen Morley is shown addressing a gathering of approximately 700 people.

she had preyed upon her brother's vulnerability by offering him large sums of cash at a time when he was in dire financial straits.

After a three-week trial in which the couple was found guilty under the Espionage Act of 1917, the judge pronounced sentence for a crime he termed worse than murder. Julius and Ethel Rosenberg were scheduled to be executed during the week of May 21, 1951.

The executions were delayed by numerous appeals, which were repeatedly rejected by the U.S. Supreme Court. Civil rights groups, some of which were found to have Communist ties, dedicated themselves to the Rosenbergs' cause. Rallies engineered by thousands of protesters filled stadiums. Sympathy for the plight of the Rosenbergs' two young sons was effectively played up by organized vigils and prayers. (Simultaneous prayer sessions for the thousands of American children who might have died had the Soviets acquired the atomic bomb went virtually unnoticed.) Petitions were circulated, and a fund-raising campaign was started. To raise money for the cost of the appeals, Ethel's love letters to Julius were bound and sold. One million dollars was raised.

Conversely, the Rosenberg case also inspired considerable public demonstrations *against* the couple. Many protesters displayed a frenzied hatred of the whole idea of espionage, and some used the case as an excuse for crude anti-Semitic outbursts.

A request for a stay of execution was denied three days before the death date, but another request was granted just 11 hours before the scheduled executions, on the grounds that the death penalty was permitted only if the jury recommended the punishment; the Rosenberg jury had not. Two appeals to President Dwight Eisenhower for clemency were denied. Finally, on June 19, 1953, Julius and Ethel Rosenberg were put to death in the electric chair at Sing Sing State Prison in Ossining, New York.

This drawing by cartoonist Hy Rosen appeared in the Albany *Times-Union*. Many political cartoonists, in keeping with the temper of the times, tilted hard to the right.

THE LATIN LONELY HEARTS KILLERS

RAYMOND MARTINEZ
FERNANDEZ STOLE HIS
VICTIMS' HEARTS, MONEY,
AND LIVES, ALL WITH THE
HELP OF HIS LOVING "SISTER"

Delphine Downing, a lonely young widow, became a victim of the Latin Lonely Hearts Killers.

Two years after the death of her husband, loneliness and the desire for a new start in life led 28-year-old Delphine Downing to look for a new spouse. She joined a lonely hearts club and began corresponding. Before long, she wrote to a charming 31-year-old man named Charles Martin. His letters awakened her hopes for a new husband and a father for her two-year-old daughter. In actuality, she was corresponding with Raymond Fernandez, and she was not his first pen pal.

Fernandez and a woman he introduced as his sister arrived for a visit at Downing's house near Grand Rapids, Michigan, on January 19, 1949. He was charming, and behaved lovingly toward Dowling's two-year-old daughter. But all was not as it seemed. He soon seduced the young woman. During the following weeks, he became her business agent and arranged for the sale of her properties. His "sister," Martha Beck, an obese and foul-tempered woman who was really his mistress and accomplice, became furious. She renewed pressure on Fernandez to carry out his original plan, which was for him to marry the unsuspecting widow.

In early March 1949, the mother and her child disappeared from sight. Concerned neighbors called the police. Following through on his suspicions, a deputy named Clarence Randle went to the house when Fernandez and Beck were out. There the police discovered a patch of fresh concrete in the cellar. Randle stated, "We dug until we found Mrs. Downing and her little daughter." When the conspirators returned, they were questioned about the bodies. Fernandez admitted that Mrs. Downing had been given sleeping pills and then shot in the head. Beck had drowned the little girl in a washtub.

Behind bars, Fernandez foolishly bragged that he made his living fleecing lonely women. Further investigation revealed that Mrs. Downing was not his first victim. In fact, the authorities came up with a list of over 20 suspected victims. For example, Jane Thompson had died mysteriously in October 1947 in La Línea, Spain, after a holiday with Fernandez. Back in New York, he first said she had been killed in a train crash. Later Fernandez claimed that she had died from a heart attack. Then he produced a will that gave him claim to Thompson's apartment, which was occupied by her mother. He moved in with her, and then had her evicted, making the apartment exclusively his.

In another scheme, Fernandez married Myrtle Young on August 14, 1948. The newlyweds settled in a boarding house in Chicago, but in no time at all, the couple became a trio. Martha Beck came along as Fernandez's protector, and she immediately took her place in the marital bed. Myrtle objected, so Beck fed her an overdose of barbiturates. Then Beck put Myrtle on a bus to her native Little Rock, Arkansas, where she died in a hospital.

New York was the site of yet another of the criminal couple's schemes. There the pair took $6,000 from a widow named Janet Fay. Once again, Fernandez promised marriage. And once again, it was Beck who made the decisive move: "I bashed her head in with a hammer," she admitted to police. Then Fernandez finished the job by strangling the widow with a scarf. Fernandez and Beck crammed the body into a trunk and buried it in the cellar of a rented house in New York City. Inexplicably, Fernandez confessed over the telephone to the New York district attorney.

After the killing of Delphine Downing and her daughter, Fernandez and Beck were held by the police in Michigan, which did not have the death penalty. New York, which allowed execution for murder, sought to have Fernandez and Beck moved to its jurisdiction for a trial for the slaying of Janet Fay. The evil duo attempted to remain in Michigan and evade the death penalty, but failed. New York tried and convicted them, and on March 8, 1951, Fernandez and Beck were executed in Sing Sing.

Martha Beck and Raymond Fernandez, right, congratulating their attorney, Herbert Rosenberg, after his summation at their murder trial. However, after the prosecution took its turn and the case went to the jury, they were both sentenced to death.

BRITISH PATRIOT TURNED SOVIET SUPERSPY

A LOVE OF COMMUNIST IDEOLOGY PROMPTED DONALD MACLEAN TO TURN HIS BACK ON HIS FAMILY AND HIS HOMELAND

David Maclean and his wife, Melinda, in Cairo two years before his disappearance.

Donald Maclean, who became one of the most notorious—and successful—Soviet spies, came paradoxically from a family of devout British patriots. His father, Sir Donald Maclean, was a respected Liberal Party member of Parliament who served with distinction.

Sir Donald Maclean's namesake seemed destined to follow in his illustrious father's footsteps. The younger Maclean was an outstanding scholar, but after his enrollment at Cambridge, he came under the influence of the Communist Party. Much to his family's chagrin, he trumpeted Communist causes for years and openly embraced Communist doctrines. One of Maclean's closest associates was Guy Burgess, who also had Communist leanings. Then, mysteriously, Maclean did a complete turnaround and denounced all things Communist. To all appearances, he had become an ardent patriot.

With his family's name and help, Maclean joined the British political scene and entered the diplomatic service. He moved rapidly up the diplomatic ladder. In time, he enjoyed the full trust of his superiors. In 1945, his outstanding work earned him the position of First Secretary of the British Embassy in Washington, D.C. He and his wife moved from their homeland to the U.S. capitol.

In his new position, Maclean saw every important message that came to the British Embassy. Some of these communications included detailed information on nuclear weapons: planning, stockpiling of vital raw materials, and information about completed nuclear projects. The data that crossed his desk was so highly classified that Maclean stored it in a special combination safe. An extremely conscientious worker, he took briefcases full of work home on weekends. Maclean received several awards and letters of recommendation for his devotion to duty. His security clearance was A1.

Though Maclean had the complete trust of his superiors, he nonetheless had habits that dismayed them. Married and an expectant father, he was reputed to be homosexual. People close to him knew he was a heavy drinker. For those two reasons, and because of a mysterious leak in British security, the FBI began to shadow Maclean. They did not suspect he was the leak, but they did fear that, when drunk, he might carelessly reveal information that had bearing on the security of the United States.

Through their surveillance the FBI linked Maclean to his old chum Guy Burgess, who by that time was suspected of being an unfriendly spy. FBI investigators found evidence that Maclean might be giving highly classified information to the Russians via Burgess.

This was indeed the case, and it was later discovered that, thanks to Maclean's treachery, the Russians gained at least two years' worth of atomic-research secrets.

Burgess had recruited Maclean into spying by inviting him to a stage-managed orgy. There, Burgess snapped compromising pictures of a drunken Maclean lying naked and oblivious in the arms of another man. When faced with his choices—spy or be exposed as a "degenerate"—Maclean's initial reluctance faded, and he entered fully into the conspiracy.

On May 28, 1951, Maclean was scheduled to be questioned by the FBI; only two highly placed Bureau officials knew this. Yet on Friday, May 25, on his 38th birthday, Maclean left his birthday party in the company of another man and was never seen again.

On the following Monday, Maclean's pregnant wife called the embassy to report him missing. It was determined that Maclean and Burgess had defected to Russia by way of Paris. Linked in ways perhaps unfathomable even to their friends, the pair disappeared behind the Iron Curtain. Apparently Maclean's love of Communist philosophy was stronger than his love of country or family. He made his choice, and turned his back on everything he had known.

ON HIS 38TH BIRTHDAY, MACLEAN LEFT HIS BIRTHDAY PARTY IN THE COMPANY OF ANOTHER MAN AND WAS NEVER SEEN AGAIN.

THE GREAT IMPOSTOR

SURGEON, MONK, PRISON WARDEN—UNTRAINED FRED DEMARA SUCCESSFULLY IMPERSONATED THEM ALL

Vancouver surgeon Dr. Joseph Cyr was baffled when this picture appeared in Canadian newspapers and the man in it was identified as Cyr. An investigation revealed that it was another daring imposture by Fred Demara.

Ferdinand Waldo Demara was born in Lawrence, Massachusetts, on December 12, 1921. No one remembered him as a particularly bright or astute child, and yet he had an aptitude for learning that would later blossom into near genius. In time, he excelled at numerous professions—but he used the identities and credentials of other men to enter those professions.

As a young man, Demara joined—and deserted—both the U.S. Army and Navy. He went on to a Catholic seminary, where he studied for the priesthood. He attached a false Ph.D. to his name to enter Illinois' De Paul University for the study of scholastic philosophy. Thus prepared, he turned to teaching. He taught at Gannon College in California and St. Martin's College in Washington state. At this point, the Navy finally caught up with him, and he spent a few years in jail to pay for his desertion. Demara's experiences while imprisoned sparked an interest in penology that he later pursued when he posed as a prison warden.

Once out of prison, Demara joined a Catholic teaching order in Maine, and posed quite successfully as a graduate physician and biologist. By the early 1940s, despite his unhappy experiences with the American military, Demara was determined to get in on World War II. Using the credentials of a Dr. Joseph C. Cyr, a Vancouver surgeon, Demara joined the Royal Canadian Navy. As ship's surgeon on a Canadian destroyer, Demara saw action in the waning months of the war. He became proficient at dispensing pills and setting broken arms. He liked practicing medicine so much that he maintained his charade through the gradual transformation from war to peace.

A few years later, however, the Korean War placed Demara and the Canadian Navy once more in the thick of battle action. During World War II, Demara had become expert at routine medical chores, but had never been called upon to perform surgery; wartime conditions in Korea truly tested his "skills." He removed a bullet from one man's heart and treated another's partially collapsed lung under primitive operating conditions and rough seas aboard his ship. Demara successfully performed these difficult operations after studying step-by-step instructions in medical textbooks.

Those exploits made the good doctor a hero, and heroes have always received publicity. When Demara's smiling picture appeared in the Canadian press, friends remarked to the real Dr. Cyr in Vancouver about the coincidence. Dr. Cyr was more interested in the fact that this hero doctor sported the exact same credentials as he. The real Dr. Cyr contacted the Canadian Navy, and Demara was exposed. When word of the fraud came out, Demara's fellow officers stood by him. They lavished praise on him as the finest ship's surgeon they'd ever seen, medical degree or not. Nevertheless, Demara alias Cyr was discharged from naval service on November 21, 1951.

Fred Demara continued to pop in and out of fake identities throughout the 1950s, and he became famous. Articles and books were written about him. His fame reached its apex in 1960. That year, *The Great Impostor,* a biographical movie starring Tony Curtis, was released, and Demara took a role (as a doctor) in a thriller called *The Hypnotic Eye.*

After a while, Demara stopped his impersonations, and slowly slipped into obscurity. At the height of his fame, though, the Great Impostor was unafraid to step forward and accept his notoriety and the public's fascinated praise. He used his celebrity as a forum from which to blast the notion of professional standing. Demara learned the hard way that his charades carried criminal penalties. Still, the notion of false identities and challenging professions must have intoxicated him, for he found the new professions difficult to resist. Demara died in West Anaheim, California, on June 7, 1982.

DEMARA SUCCESSFULLY PERFORMED DIFFICULT OPERATIONS AFTER STUDYING STEP-BY-STEP INSTRUCTIONS IN MEDICAL TEXTBOOKS.

THE FIEND OF RILLINGTON PLACE

JOHN CHRISTIE WAS A MILD-MANNERED NECROPHILIAC WHO EQUATED SEX WITH MURDER

John Reginald Christie's murder method was to lure women to his house, get them drunk, and then gas them. Once they were unconscious, he strangled them and finished off by raping their corpses.

John Reginald Christie was a "shy killer" who lurked behind a meek facade and escaped suspicion. Yet he murdered and raped eight women, including his wife, in 13 years.

Christie's sexual inadequacy found its release in violent murder and sex—in that order. Christie would strangle his victim to death and rape her dead body. Sometimes the murders were the unintended climax of a violent sexual act. Those victims who did survive the sex would be murdered anyway, to cover up his crimes.

On November 30, 1949, Timothy Evans, Christie's neighbor, came home and discovered that his wife and 14-month-old daughter had been strangled to death. Panicked, Evans fled London. A few days later, he walked into a police station in Wales and told the authorities about his wife and child. After an investigation, Evans was charged and tried for the murders.

Evans confessed to the murders during his trial, but he also blamed his neighbor, John Christie, for the deaths. The jury found Evans guilty, and he was hanged in 1950. Although some observers felt that Evans did kill his daughter, and perhaps his wife, others believed that Christie had terrified Evans into confessing to crimes that Christie himself had committed.

In December 1952, Christie's wife disappeared. During the next two months, Christie picked up and killed two prostitutes.

On March 24, 1953, another tenant in his building broke down a wall while renovating an apartment and found the decomposed bodies of three women. The authorities soon arrived, and when they dug up Christie's garden, more victims were uncovered. Mrs. Christie was discovered under the floorboards.

John Christie was arrested and tried. To convince the jurors he was insane, Christie divulged his diseased sexual inclinations. His insanity plea rejected, Christie was hanged on July 15, 1953.

THE KANSAS CITY KIDNAP-MURDER CAPER

HEARTLESS KIDNAPPERS CARL HALL AND BONNIE HEADY DECIDED THAT A SIX-YEAR-OLD RICH BOY MADE THE IDEAL VICTIM

Thanks to an astute business sense and plenty of hard work, Robert Cosgrove Greenlease had built a multimillion-dollar automobile business in Kansas City by about 1920. During his troubled first marriage, Greenlease and his wife adopted a boy, whom they named Paul Robert. At high-school age, Paul was enrolled in a military school. There, he met a fellow student named Carl Hall, who became intrigued with the elder Greenlease's wealth.

In 1939, a then-divorced Robert Greenlease married Virginia Pollack. They had two children, Virginia Sue in 1942, Robert "Bobby" Cosgrove, Jr., in 1947.

Carl Hall, the son of a prominent judge, had chosen lawlessness as a way of life. Following military school, he had lasted three months in college and had gone from there into the Marines, where he served poorly. His mother's death in 1944 left him $200,000, which he squandered. He married in 1946, but his drunkenness led to a divorce four years later.

In 1951, Hall netted the grand sum of $33 when he robbed several cabdrivers. He was sentenced to five years in prison and was paroled after 15 months. While incarcerated, Carl Hall bragged he was going to commit the perfect crime.

In May 1953, he met Bonnie Heady at a bar in St. Joseph, Missouri, and moved in with her. He outlined his plan to kidnap six-year-old Bobby Greenlease. Bonnie—a free-spirited divorcée, drunk, and intermittent hooker—listened attentively, and agreed to participate in the kidnapping plot. Hall told her he had decided in advance to kill the little boy in order to cover his tracks.

On September 10, Carl bought 50 pounds of quicklime; he would use it to dissolve the boy's buried body. On the 19th, he bought a .38 caliber handgun; on the 26th, a shovel. The very next day, Hall dug a grave.

The Greenlease kidnappers, Bonnie Heady and Carl Hall. They pulled off their brazen abduction scheme with almost shameless ease, but no sooner was the ransom collected than things began to fall apart. Less than three months after the kidnapping, they went to their deaths in Missouri's gas chamber.

Robert C. Greenlease, Jr., who was abducted from his Kansas City private school, Notre Dame de Sion. One of the kidnappers, posing as his aunt, convinced a teacher at the school that the boy's mother had suffered a heart attack and was urgently requesting to see him.

September 28, 1953, brought Hall and Heady to Kansas City. Bonnie took a cab to Notre Dame de Sion, Bobby's school, where she passed herself off as Bobby's aunt and said that the boy's mother had suffered a heart attack.

With Bobby in tow, Bonnie rejoined Hall. Then they drove to a field, and Hall shot Bobby behind his right ear.

The pair returned to Bonnie's house, where Hall placed the boy's body into the grave and covered it with lime. He then drove to Kansas City to mail a ransom note, and mailed a second one a day later, September 29, accompanied by Bobby's Jerusalem Cross.

The first note demanded $600,000 in small bills. Greenlease was warned against involving the police or trying any tricks. If he disobeyed, the note promised, death would come to the entire Greenlease family. An endless series of phone calls followed, in which Hall detailed the method of delivery of the ransom money.

At 12:30 A.M. on October 5, Hall picked up the money from the predesignated locale. He had promised to call the parents with instructions on how to retrieve Bobby. No call was ever made. Instead, the heartless kidnappers took off for St. Louis with their newly found wealth. When they arrived that same day, the pair drank continuously and hooked up with a variety of new "friends," one of whom told police that he had been with a man who threw around great sums of money. The next day, October 6, the police picked up Carl Hall, who admitted he had kidnapped Bobby Greenlease. A drunken Bonnie Heady was soon arrested. Each kidnapper confessed to the FBI on October 7, 1953.

A federal grand jury indicted Hall and Heady before the month was over. The pair pleaded guilty and were executed in Missouri's gas chamber on December 16, 1953. Fully half—$300,000—of the ransom money was never recovered.

THE MYSTERY WITHOUT AN END

THE MURDER OF DR. SAM SHEPPARD'S WIFE WAS JUST THE PRELUDE TO ONE OF THE MOST BIZARRE CASES IN OHIO HISTORY

On December 21, 1954, after 102 hours of deliberation, a jury in Cleveland, Ohio, found Dr. Samuel Sheppard guilty of bludgeoning to death his pregnant wife Marilyn with an unidentified weapon. However, rather than signifying the end of the landmark case that had electrified the nation, Sheppard's conviction for second-degree murder proved to be only the first chapter in a continuing melodrama.

Sentenced to life in prison by Judge Edward Blythin, the handsome 30-year-old osteopathic surgeon, who was called "Dr. Sam" by patients and colleagues, turned his back, perhaps intentionally, to the jury that had doubted his innocence. The convicted killer then stated, "I'd like to say, sir, that I am not guilty. I feel there has been proof presented to this court that has definitely proved that I couldn't have performed the act charged against me."

Sheppard's protestation was given little credence by anyone except his parents and two older brothers, Richard and Stephen, both of whom were also osteopathic surgeons. Even Judge Blythin was overheard to remark that Sheppard was "guilty as hell." In the following years, however, public sentiment changed and Sheppard came to be regarded as an innocent man who had been wrongly convicted.

The story began early on the morning of July 4, 1954, in a white frame house on the shore of Lake Erie in the quiet, affluent Cleveland suburb of Bay Village. While entertaining neighbors after a hard day of surgery, Sheppard fell asleep on the living room couch. Once the guests had departed, Marilyn Sheppard left her husband where he was and retired to the upstairs bedroom. There is only Sam Sheppard's version of what occurred during the ensuing five and a half hours. According to him, he was awakened in the night by his wife's scream. Rushing upstairs, he charged into their bedroom and was struck from behind while grappling with "a form" wearing a light-colored garment. Sheppard did not know whether he had battled one or two intruders.

Dr. Samuel Sheppard seemed to have had it all going for him. When his wife was murdered early on the morning of July 4, 1954, the popular and prominent Bay Village, Ohio, osteopathic surgeon was thought at first to be a co-victim of the crime. However, public opinion changed after some of the facts came to light.

Marilyn Sheppard was nearly unrecognizable after she was bludgeoned to death in her bed for reasons that have never been determined. Though her killing officially remains unsolved, most Cleveland police officials still privately believe that her husband killed her. However, her son holds a very different view.

In any case, he claimed to have discovered his wife's body when he regained consciousness. After determining that his seven-year-old son, Chip, asleep in the next room, was unharmed, Sheppard pursued the dimly visible, "bushy haired" form out of the house to the lakefront, where Sheppard was again knocked out during a struggle.

He came to lying partially in the water. At first, Sheppard thought he was "the victim of a bizarre dream." But when he again examined his wife, he realized that the night's events had been terrifyingly real. Marilyn Sheppard had been bludgeoned about the face and head; deep vertical lacerations scarred her forehead. Sheppard claimed he then called the first number that came to him—that of Bay Village mayor J. Spencer Houk, who lived three doors away. Both men later agreed that Sheppard said something like: "My God, Spence, get over here quick. I think they've killed Marilyn."

Houk and his wife dressed and rushed to the Sheppard house. After both went upstairs to view the murder scene, Houk called the police, an ambulance, and Sheppard's brother, Richard.

Sheppard was initially treated as a co-victim—he had a neck injury, purportedly from the beating he took. However, he soon was suspected of being the crime's perpetrator when the police could not find the murder weapon or any fingerprints in the house. The supposition was that Sheppard had used the long span of time before the police were summoned to dispose of the weapon, wipe away any incriminating evidence, and contrive his neck injury.

On July 16, an editorial in the *Cleveland Press,* the city's evening daily, attacked "the tragic mishandling of the Sheppard murder investigation." A banner headline four days later declared that Sheppard was "Getting Away With Murder." The following day, the Bay Village council voted to turn over the case to the Cleveland police. But by then it was already too late for a proper investigation.

Hopelessly out of their league, the Bay Village police had terribly mishandled the crime scene. In their amateurishness, they had even asked the high school football team to link hands and wade into Lake Erie on the remote chance that one of them might step on the murder weapon.

Meanwhile, the Cleveland police seemed interested only in unearthing evidence that implicated Sheppard. They found little until they learned that Sheppard had an affair with Susan Hayes, a former laboratory technician at Bay View Hospital, which was owned by Sheppard and his brothers. Now the police had a motive.

At the trial, Susan Hayes testified that Sheppard had promised to marry her if he were ever able to. The coroner, Samuel Gerber, stated that the missing murder weapon was a medical instrument, although he could not specify its exact nature. Sheppard added to his plight by being a stiff, arrogant witness. His fate, for the moment, was sealed.

During the years Sam Sheppard spent in the Ohio State Penitentiary, he was a model prisoner who volunteered for hazardous medical experiments. Fellow convicts believed he was the rare one among them who was as innocent as he claimed, but the courts denied his appeals for a new trial. Eventually, Perry Mason creator Erle Stanley Gardner became involved, writing of Sheppard's ordeal in his "The Court of Last Resort" column in *Argosy* magazine. Gardner cited Paul Leland Kirk, a criminalistics professor at the University of California, who gave the murder room and many trial exhibits their first, and probably only, thorough scientific examination.

Kirk discovered that the state had suppressed evidence found in the murder room of a blood type that belonged neither to Sheppard nor his wife. Kirk also found that the killer was probably left-handed—Sheppard was right-handed—and that Marilyn had been slain by many blows delivered over a long time with little force. It

THE STATE HAD SUPPRESSED EVIDENCE FOUND IN THE MURDER ROOM OF A BLOOD TYPE THAT BELONGED NEITHER TO SHEPPARD NOR HIS WIFE.

was surmised that the murderer might be a woman, perhaps the jealous wife of a man with whom Marilyn was having an affair.

In June 1965, Sheppard was granted a new trial but because the U.S. Supreme Court felt that his right to a fair trial had been violated by prejudicial news coverage. At the second trial, in late 1966, F. Lee Bailey acted as Sheppard's counsel. Lending Sheppard moral support was Ariane Tebbenjohanns, an attractive European divorcée. She had read of the case in a German magazine and begun a long-distance correspondence with Sheppard that culminated in their marriage.

Bailey promised to produce evidence that the real slayer was a woman—Mayor Houk's wife was the leading candidate. However, the high point of the trial was Coroner Gerber's contention that the murder weapon was a medical instrument. But he admitted that in 12 years, he never found an instrument that fit the bloody imprint left on a pillow near Marilyn Sheppard's savagely beaten body.

Found innocent, Sheppard had his medical license restored and moved back to Bay Village. Quickly, his new life fell apart. He was sued for divorce by Tebbenjohanns on the grounds of mental cruelty. Socked with two malpractice suits, Sheppard gave up medicine to become a professional wrestler. He then married the young daughter of his wrestling manager and joined a motorcycle gang. The bizarre story ended in 1970, when Sam Sheppard died of alcohol and drug abuse.

The Sheppard murder case remains officially open. In 1982, some old fireplace tongs that were initially thought to be the long-lost murder weapon were found buried in the yard of the house where Mayor Houk and his wife had lived at the time of the crime. During a June 1990 appearance on the *Larry King Show*, Sheppard's son maintained that authorities refuse to investigate an Ohio convict who is strongly suspected of his mother's murder.

Susan Hayes, the "other woman" in the case, is accompanied by a Cleveland detective as she heads into court to take the witness stand at the first-degree-murder trial of Sam Sheppard. Under oath, Hayes admitted to an affair with "Dr. Sam."

A BRAZEN WOMAN PAID THE ULTIMATE PENALTY

RUTH ELLIS LIVED A BAWDY LIFE AND BECAME THE LAST WOMAN TO HANG IN GREAT BRITAIN

By the prim social standards of the 1950s, Ruth Ellis had lived a pretty wild life. During World War II, at age 15, she started going to the dances with soldiers. In 1944, at 17, she had a child by a French-Canadian soldier. Determined to make it on her own, she worked as a waitress and then as a factory employee to support herself and her son. In 1950, she married a dentist named George Ellis. The marriage lasted less than a year, but for the sake of Ruth's son, the couple never divorced.

Rather than return to her meager-paying toil in the factory, Ruth chose the more lucrative and exciting career of nightclub hostess. Neither difficult nor wholly respectable, the job required Ruth to flirt heavily with patrons to get them to buy drinks. The club had strict rules against its girls having sex with customers. Ruth liked the job because it paid well. She liked hanging out in the loud, jazzy atmosphere of nightclubs. More importantly, she very much liked flirting with men. However, a "career" such as hers would win her little public sympathy when she needed it later on.

In 1953, Ruth began a tempestuous romance with race-car driver David Blakely. He came from a well-off family that considered his driving and his affair with Ruth Ellis as slumming. Blakely himself alternated between extreme affection and neglect in his feelings for Ruth, but he apparently didn't take the affair too seriously. Ruth, on the other hand, took the relationship *very* seriously. She considered Blakely the love of her life. While she had other lovers to occupy her while he was away, and though Blakely certainly had other lovers, as well, Ruth felt possessive about her man. She could not tolerate the other women in Blakely's life. Therefore, on April 10, 1955, she walked up to him outside the Magnolia public house in Hampstead, where he'd been with another woman, and shot him dead.

At her trial, Ruth's only defense was that she was jealous of Blakely's other affairs. Since there was voluminous testimony as to

Cool as ice throughout her trial for murdering her unfaithful lover, Ruth Ellis, shown here just prior to her arrest, stood absolutely still as she received the death sentence, and then she said only one word: "Thanks."

IN THE END, RUTH ELLIS'S SLACK MORALS CAUGHT UP WITH HER, FOR SHE WAS HANGED ON JULY 13, 1955— THE LAST WOMAN EVER TO BE HANGED IN GREAT BRITAIN.

Ruth Ellis, sometime model and nightclub hostess, with race-car driver David Blakely. Lovers for two years, the duo had progressed to an open relationship. When Blakely wanted to end even that limited involvement, Ellis gunned him down.

her own unfaithfulness, the argument did little to sway the jury. Indeed, the apparently wrathful jurors not only convicted Ruth, but mandated the death penalty.

The sentence surprised and shocked quite a few people in Great Britain because the country had for years been leaning toward abolition of the death penalty. Despite many petitions for the commuting of her sentence, the order stood. Many felt that Ruth's brazen past and her unrepentant attitude about her love affairs and the murder had clouded the issue; people who would otherwise have felt compassion for the defendant showed moral indignation instead. In the end, Ruth Ellis's slack morals caught up with her, for she was hanged on July 13, 1955—the last woman ever to be hanged in Great Britain.

THE MAD BOMBER

TIMID GEORGE METESKY TERRORIZED ALL OF NEW YORK CITY WITH HIS BOMB THREATS

George Metesky was a meek, mild-looking man with a grudge: He constantly complained that the New York City electrical utility, Consolidated Edison, had given him a disease. Calling himself "Fair Play" or "F.P.," he sent threatening notes to Consolidated Edison. Around 1940, he went a step further—he planted phony bombs around New York City and then called in bomb threats. To a war-bound country ever vigilant for spies and sabotage, this was no laughing matter. The first few bomb threats upset many people. However, like the boy who cried wolf, Metesky overplayed his hand; as threat after threat turned out to be false, the public lost interest. Eventually, Metesky lost interest, too. The bomb threats and letters to Con Ed stopped in 1941.

Ten years later, in 1951, Metesky began his campaign again. This time, his bombs weren't phony. New York was rocked by one explosion after another. Many people were injured but no one was killed—not even when Metesky's devices exploded in Grand Central Station, Radio City Music Hall, and Broadway theaters. Wiseacres quipped that Fair Play had taken ten years off to learn how to make a bomb. Police and bomb squads worked diligently to find the madman. No progress was made until Fair Play wrote to a newspaper claiming that Consolidated Edison had given him tuberculosis.

Alice Kelly, a bright, 25-year-old Con Ed employee, investigated. She went through company records and searched for a link to Fair Play's alleged tuberculosis. Eventually, she tracked down a file on Metesky, who had complained in 1931 that Con Ed had given him the disease. Kelly turned her information over to the police, who tracked Metesky to his home in Waterbury, Connecticut.

In January 1957, Metesky confessed to planting over 30 homemade bombs over 16 years. He was not arrested; instead, he was sent to the New York State Hospital for the Criminally Insane. The mad bomber's reign of terror was over.

George Metesky, right, smiling as Detective James Martin brings him to police headquarters. The smiling Metesky is holding up a New York newspaper that describes how he gave himself away. When asked about the bombings, Metesky said, "I'm sorry I injured people, but I'm glad I did it."

MURDER AND CANNIBALISM IN WISCONSIN

THE GRISLY DEEDS OF MAMA'S BOY ED GEIN SHOOK UP THE WORLD, AND MADE HIM THE ORIGINAL "PSYCHO"

Ed Gein, the 51-year-old recluse, as he arrives at the state crime laboratory in Madison, Wisconsin, for questioning in connection with the grotesque discoveries made at his run-down farm. The life led by Gein, which rhymes with "lean," was so solitary that until his arrest, no one had been inside his house in years.

Wisconsin-bred Ed Gein—lean, bony-faced, and marked by deep, unrevealing eyes—was a gentle man. With his plaid hunter's cap, he seemed the quintessential outdoorsman. And that's just what he was, a farmer with 160 acres outside Plainfield, Wisconsin. Gein (rhymes with *lean*) was born in 1906. Following the death of his alcoholic father in 1940, Gein worked the farm with his brother Henry; both lived with their mother. She was a domineering woman who kept a tight emotional grip on her sons. Ma Gein instilled in her boys a belief in the supposed evils of women and the sins of the flesh. She kept her boys pure, seeing that they worked God's land and brought forth its fruits without becoming befouled by the opposite sex.

Worry about her sons and farming their land pushed the family's stress factor to the breaking point. Son Henry exhausted himself fighting a fire one day and died. Mrs. Gein suffered a severe stroke in 1944, and died of a second, more serious attack in December 1945.

Then 39 and left alone, Ed withdrew from reality. His mind developed strange fantasies. He became a voracious reader of anatomical texts, and he developed a new interest in women. Then, without explanation, he sealed off all of the farmhouse except for his bedroom and the kitchen.

Because he qualified for a government subsidy, Gein was able to suspend all farm work. To earn extra money he did odd jobs (including baby-sitting) for Plainfield townsfolk and helped out other farmers.

Alone and independent, Ed Gein began to pursue a new vocation: grave robbing. He began exhuming the bodies of women buried in the remote areas of graveyards. Covered by the darkness, Gein dug up the corpses and dragged them to his farm. There, in a shed attached to the main house, Gein drew and quartered his prized trophies as if they were slaughterhouse cattle. Portions of the quartered corpses often wound up on his dinner table.

Gein carried on his macabre adventures until he tired of amusing himself with bodies of long-dead women. He turned to livelier game.

In early November 1957, Gein visited the Worden hardware store in Plainfield. Bernice Worden's son, Frank, co-owned the store with his mother. Gein frequently talked with Frank about hunting. The deer season was starting and Gein was very curious about Frank's hunting plans. When Frank said that he would go hunting on Saturday morning, November 16, Gein told Frank that he'd stop by the store that same day to buy some antifreeze.

When Frank returned to the store late Saturday, he surprisingly found the front door locked. Inside, he discovered a pool of blood on the floor. Alarmed by his mother's unexplained absence, he looked closer and found a sales slip in her handwriting made out to Gein for some antifreeze. Worden remembered Gein's earlier remark and called the sheriff to report his mother missing. Frank suggested that Gein be contacted immediately.

Gein was found at the home of Bob and Irene Hill, a friendly couple who often invited the quiet farmer to dinner. The group had finished eating and Ed was in his car by the time Officer Dan Chase and Deputy "Poke" Spees arrived. Chase asked Gein several questions; Gein's answers indicated that he knew Bernice Worden was dead. The lawman truly believed that Gein was involved, so he arrested Gein.

Meanwhile, Captain Lloyd Schoephoerster of nearby Green Lake County, along with Sheriff Arthur Schley, drove to Gein's farm. Inside the woodshed, they found Bernice Worden. Her body had been butchered like a deer. Bernice's severed head, found nearby, showed that she had been killed by a gunshot.

GEIN CARRIED ON HIS MACABRE ADVENTURES UNTIL HE TIRED OF AMUSING HIMSELF WITH BODIES OF LONG-DEAD WOMEN. HE TURNED TO LIVELIER GAME.

THE LEGACY OF ED GEIN

For Plainfield, Wisconsin, the horror of Ed Gein's crimes was something to be blocked out and forgotten. Indeed, so great was the community's antipathy that the Gein farm burned to the ground under mysterious circumstances not long after Gein's crimes were discovered. But to other observers, Gein became a source of fascination.

"Sick jokes" based on Gein's proclivities became common in schoolyards in Wisconsin and, later, across the nation. The Ed Gein "death car" was snatched up by promoters, and it toured fairs and carnivals for some years after the crimes. In Milwaukee, a writer named Robert Bloch followed the Gein case and was inspired to use it as a springboard for a novel entitled *Psycho.* The book, of course, became the basis for the famous 1960 movie thriller directed by Alfred Hitchcock. Like Gein, Bloch's central character, Norman Bates, was a tortured, murderous neurotic who had been unhealthily dominated by his mother. His mental illness was expressed via murder and an unorthodox sort of taxidermy.

Other films have been inspired by Gein's bizarre aberrations, most notably a very loose retelling in *The Texas Chainsaw Massacre,* and a more faithful interpretation in *Deranged.* Both of these 1974 movies included elements of cannibalism and grotesque taxidermy. It can be argued, too, that the Gein story inspired the whole crazy quilt of horror films of the late 1970s and early 1980s that dealt with rural nut cases who committed murder with a sick twist. Few will deny that Ed Gein has found a place in the dark side of the national consciousness.

A Wisconsin cop incredulously sifts through Ed Gein's junk-strewn kitchen. After his mother's death, Gein closed off all but two rooms of his farmhouse, and the kitchen became both his office and his sanctuary. From the female body parts they found there, investigators realized that Gein had used it for other purposes, too.

An expanded search uncovered the remains of Mary Hogan, a saloon keeper who had disappeared nearly three years before. The lawmen also found that Gein had used various parts from his female victims to "decorate" his house. As the grisly evidence was uncovered, investigators determined that 15 women had ended up as souvenirs in Gein's house of horrors.

Near Christmas 1957, the court found Gein criminally insane and sent him to Wisconsin's Central State Hospital for the Insane. Based on an expert conclusion ten years later that Gein could stand trial and defend himself, a petition was made for his release from the hospital. On January 16, 1968, the proceedings began before Judge Robert H. Gollmar. Gollmar ruled that Gein's "offense was first degree murder." Judge Gollmar ruled that Gein suffered from mental disease and that he should be returned to the Central State Hospital. Gein spent the remainder of his days there. He died of natural causes in 1984.

THE YOUNG THRILL-KILLERS

WITH HIS GIRLFRIEND IN TOW, GUN-CRAZY PUNK CHARLES STARKWEATHER EMBARKED ON A MURDER SPREE

Charles Starkweather was born poor, but he had grand plans. Though he worked as a garbageman in Lincoln, Nebraska, the 19-year-old idolized movie star James Dean and fancied himself standing up to authority in similar fashion. In one memorable month, Starkweather did just that.

On December 1, 1957, the little garbageman began a murder rampage. His first stop was a gas station, where he robbed the cashbox and then drove station attendant Robert Colvert to an isolated spot and killed him. Nearly two months passed before Starkweather killed again.

On January 28, 1958, Starkweather was at the home of his 14-year-old girlfriend, Caril Ann Fugate, waiting for her to arrive from school. With him was his constant companion, a .22 caliber rifle. Caril Ann's mother, Mrs. Velda Bartlett, disliked Starkweather and didn't want him hanging around her daughter. While Starkweather waited, the girl's mother expressed her opinion. When Starkweather told her to mind her own business, Mrs. Bartlett slapped him, and Starkweather slapped her back. Then Marion Bartlett, Caril Ann's stepfather, headed toward Starkweather, who fired his rifle. Mr. Bartlett was killed, and Starkweather proceeded to murder Caril Ann's mother. Caril Ann arrived home in time to see her boyfriend choke her stepsister, Betty Jean, to death with his rifle. Caril Ann thought fast and scribbled a note saying that the entire family had the flu and that everyone should stay away. She tacked the note to the front door of the house and made herself at home with Charles.

As if nothing had happened, the unabashed couple made sandwiches, watched TV, and necked on the sofa. The note kept anyone who was suspicious away at first, but the police were soon alerted.

Before the police arrived, Starkweather and Caril Ann had driven Charles's hot rod to parts unknown. When the carnage was discov-

Sheriff Merle Karnopp is attached to the belt chain worn by Charles Starkweather, right, as they enter the Lincoln, Nebraska, courthouse. After he was sentenced to death, Starkweather was asked to donate his eyes to an eye bank when he was executed. He replied, "Hell no! Nobody ever did anything for me."

ered, an alert went out across Nebraska, Kansas, South Dakota, and Wyoming to look out for Charles Starkweather.

The villainous couple stopped at the farm of August Meyer. Starkweather and Caril Ann left Meyer for dead. Next, they came across another teenaged couple. Seventeen-year-old Robert Jensen was shot; 16-year-old Carol King was shot after being raped.

Charles and Caril drove back into the Lincoln suburbs and selected a wealthy household at random. C. Lauer Ward, president of Capital Steel Works; his wife, Clara; and their maid, Lillian Fenci, were bound and gagged. The victims remained alive while Starkweather and Caril Ann helped themselves to food and other goodies. Eventually, however, Starkweather began to mutilate his victims with a knife. Finally, he ended their torment by killing them.

By that time, a 1,200-man posse, backed by a troop of the National Guard, was forming a dragnet for Starkweather and Caril Ann. In Douglas, Wyoming, the young lovers shot shoe salesman Merle Collison. When they tried to get away, their car wouldn't start. Starkweather asked a passerby, oil agent Joseph Sprinkle, for help. The alert Sprinkle grabbed Starkweather's rifle and held him at bay while the police were called. As Caril Ann eagerly surrendered herself (she had grown tired of the "adventure"), Starkweather managed to escape in Sprinkle's car. During the chase, he was grazed by a police bullet. His minor wound frightened him; he stopped the car and was captured. Starkweather's rampage had lasted 26 days.

Tried and convicted, Starkweather went to his death a boastfully proud killer. He died in the Nebraska electric chair on June 24, 1959.

Caril Ann Fugate denied any complicity in the crimes and swore that she was kidnapped. No one believed her. Although a minor, she was sentenced to life in prison. She continued to protest her innocence and was paroled in 1977.

To avoid prosecution, Caril Ann Fugate tried to pretend she had been Charles Starkweather's hostage throughout his homicidal rampage. For a while, Starkweather went along with her. However, when she put all the blame on him in court, he dropped the sham and recited all the ways in which she had been nearly as ruthless as he.

NIGHTMARE IN HOLLYWOOD

LANA TURNER'S DAUGHTER CHERYL CRANE FATALLY STABBED HER MOTHER'S HOODLUM LOVER

Back in 1935, Julia Jean Mildred Frances Turner was a 15-year-old student at Hollywood High School. In October, she cut class to go to the Top Hat Soda Shop. There she was discovered by a talent scout who liked her pretty face and shapely figure. Two years later, dressed in a form-fitting sweater and cast in a film called *They Won't Forget,* the young beauty (by then named Lana Turner) made an immediate impression on studio executives and the public.

Seldom acclaimed as an actress, Turner nevertheless won millions of fans and worked steadily throughout the 1940s and 1950s. She invested her money wisely and became wealthy. Her daughter Cheryl was born in 1943, when Turner had not yet reached the peak of her fame. But by Good Friday, 1958, Turner's good looks had begun to harden, and the quality of her films had slipped. However, neither the money nor the glamour had diminished, a fact that undoubtedly appealed to Johnny Stompanato.

Five years younger than Turner, Stompanato was an ex-Marine who had come to Hollywood from the Illinois farmlands. By about 1950, he had progressed from restaurant bouncer to bodyguard for mobster Mickey Cohen. Stompanato also dabbled in fraud, blackmail, and extortion. Stompanato impressed Lana Turner with his charm and good looks.

From the beginning of Stompanato's relationship with Turner, he was cordial and friendly to Cheryl. By the spring of 1958, the love affair had been going on for about a year. Turner had grown tired of Stompanato's sponging, and let him know she wanted him out of her life. Stompanato was in no mood to get off the gravy train. Bitter arguments raged frequently through the rooms and hallways of Turner's Beverly Hills home. Finally, on the evening of April 4, 1958, Stompanato's threats of physical violence against Turner became particularly vile and frightening. Fourteen-year-old Cheryl heard Stompanato scream and swear at her mother: "I'll get you if it takes

Cheryl Crane removes her dark glasses as she begins to testify in the $705,000 suit filed by the family of Johnny Stompanato, the lover of her mother, actress Lana Turner. The 14-year-old daughter of restaurateur Stephen Crane survived the tragic episode to become a successful restaurateur in her own right.

THE DARK SIDE OF GLAMOR

At 14, Cheryl Crane was a beautiful Hollywood princess, the daughter of restaurateur Stephen Crane and film star Lana Turner. Dark-eyed Cheryl Crane had all the luxuries and material possessions that rich and famous parents could give her. By the time she was 14, her parents had divorced, and she had lived with two stepfathers—millionaire playboy Bob Topping and, later, actor Lex Barker, who allegedly sexually abused her. Cheryl had been caught in the middle of the disintegration of her mother's marriage to Barker. Afterward, Cheryl had no choice but to observe as Turner went on to a stormy relationship with a grinning hoodlum named Johnny Stompanato. Simmering beneath Cheryl's glamourous life, though, was disaster. On April 4, 1958—Good Friday—the destinies of Cheryl Crane, Lana Turner, and Johnny Stompanato collided, with results that rocked the movie capital.

Johnny Stompanato and Lana Turner at a Hollywood nightclub. Turner's daughter, terrified when Stompanato threatened her mother with physical violence, felt compelled to intervene on her mother's behalf.

a day, a week, or a year. I'll cut you up . . . and if I can't do it myself, I'll find someone who can!"

Cheryl stumbled into the kitchen and picked up a butcher knife, intending to frighten Stompanato. The girl forced herself up the stairs to the hall outside her mother's bedroom. Turner opened the bedroom door and stepped into the hallway. Stompanato advanced on her from behind, his arm raised as if to strike her. Cheryl stepped forward and raised the knife. Stompanato kept coming and impaled himself on the blade. He fell backward, fatally wounded.

At the Beverly Hills police station shortly after the killing, Turner told police, "I didn't know what was happening. I thought [Cheryl] was just poking Johnny with her finger." With both of her parents by her side, Cheryl Crane told police, "I did it to protect mother. I thought he was going to get her."

After a thorough investigation, a coroner's jury voted ten to two for a verdict of justifiable homicide. Cheryl—who had a background of truancy and runaway attempts—would not be prosecuted. However, she was made a ward of the court until her 18th birthday. Custody was granted to her grandmother (Lana's mother).

Cheryl was soon packed off to a boarding school and then to an exclusive sanitarium for psychiatric treatment. She became a model in 1962 and subsequently went to work for her father, first as a hostess and then as an executive in his burgeoning restaurant operation.

In 1979, Cheryl moved to Hawaii with her longtime companion Joyce "Josh" LeRoy; the two of them prospered as real estate agents and restaurateurs. Today, Cheryl Crane and her friend live together quietly in San Francisco, where they garden, entertain, and look after their investments. The troubled Hollywood princess has written her own happy ending.

COLD-BLOODED KILLERS

DISAPPOINTED BY THE MONEY THAT WASN'T THERE, RICHARD HICKOCK AND PERRY SMITH SLAUGHTERED A KANSAS FARM FAMILY

The story of ex-convicts Richard Hickock and Perry Smith is one of greed, violence, and, most pointedly, stupidity. Both small-time thugs, neither Hickock nor Smith would likely have gone through with their plan individually. But like the killers Leopold and Loeb, each seemed to bring out the other's worst impulses. So it was that a pair of inconsequential hoodlums committed a crime that shocked the nation.

Thanks to remarks made by a former cellmate named Floyd Wells, Hickock and Smith were convinced that Herbert W. Clutter, a prosperous farmer in Holcomb, Kansas, kept substantial sums of cash at his home. Because Wells had once worked for Clutter, Hickock and Smith were quick to believe his story.

The dim-witted duo wasted little time, and began planning their big heist as soon as they could. Like every other crook, they were motivated by a dream of personal gain, but their dream was more unusual than most: The pair planned to use their booty to retire to an island off the coast of South America, where they hoped to dive for hidden treasure.

Shortly past midnight on November 15, 1959, the pair entered the Clutter home through an unlocked side door. They confronted Herbert Clutter in his bedroom and kept him at bay with a hunting knife. Floyd Wells had told Hickock and Smith that the Clutter cash was kept in a hidden safe. They demanded to be told the safe's whereabouts, but Clutter answered that the only money in the house was the $30 in his wallet.

Richard Hickock, shown above in his mug shot, and Perry Smith killed the Clutter family during a bungled robbery attempt. By the time Truman Capote had finished probing their motivations in his best-seller *In Cold Blood*, it became one of the best-remembered crimes of the 1950s.

On the day before his murder trial began, Perry Smith, right, confers with his defense attorney, center, and a psychiatrist from the Larned, Kansas, State Hospital. During the episode that led to the senseless slaughter of the Clutter family, Smith convinced Hickock to forget about raping 16-year-old Nancy Clutter.

Hickock and Smith didn't believe Clutter. The terrified farmer was forced to wake his wife, Bonnie, who burst into tears and said, "I don't have any money." The group then awakened the Clutter's 15-year-old son, Kenyon. Sixteen-year-old Nancy Clutter came to investigate the noise, and was promptly tied up. Hickock liked Nancy's looks and was on the verge of raping her when Smith told him to forget about the idea. Momentarily at a loss and unsure of what to do next, the pair concluded the break-in by using a shotgun and the knife to kill the entire Clutter family.

When the bodies were discovered the next day, a shock wave of anger and fear swept across the American heartland. No place, it seemed, was safe from senseless violence. The local public outcry was tremendous, and a large police investigation was organized in response to it.

When the imprisoned Floyd Wells heard about the murders, he contacted the authorities and told them what he knew. The two killers were subsequently tracked to Las Vegas and apprehended. Once separated, each informed on the other without hesitation.

The investigation and trial relating to this sensational, highly publicized case consumed nearly four years. In the end, Richard Hickock and Perry Smith were found guilty. They were hanged on April 14, 1965.

While the trial was underway, noted author Truman Capote became fascinated by the case and was able to interest *The New Yorker* in an article. Capote traveled to Kansas and interviewed the two condemned men extensively before their executions. His research produced the best-selling book *In Cold Blood,* which in turn inspired a well-received 1967 motion picture of the same title. Hickock and Smith had made their mark, but would be remembered only as two of the most savage and stupid criminals who ever lived.

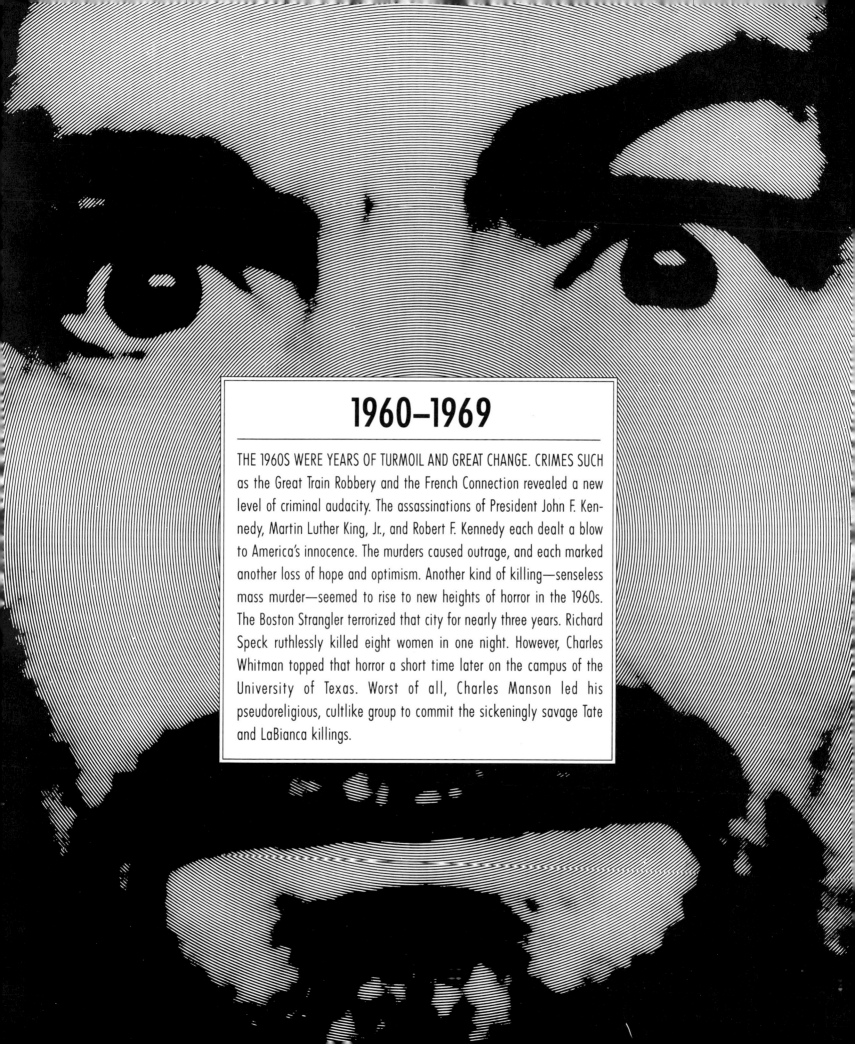

1960–1969

THE 1960S WERE YEARS OF TURMOIL AND GREAT CHANGE. CRIMES SUCH as the Great Train Robbery and the French Connection revealed a new level of criminal audacity. The assassinations of President John F. Kennedy, Martin Luther King, Jr., and Robert F. Kennedy each dealt a blow to America's innocence. The murders caused outrage, and each marked another loss of hope and optimism. Another kind of killing—senseless mass murder—seemed to rise to new heights of horror in the 1960s. The Boston Strangler terrorized that city for nearly three years. Richard Speck ruthlessly killed eight women in one night. However, Charles Whitman topped that horror a short time later on the campus of the University of Texas. Worst of all, Charles Manson led his pseudoreligious, cultlike group to commit the sickeningly savage Tate and LaBianca killings.

THE FRENCH CONNECTION

TWO NEW YORK CITY POLICE DETECTIVES RELAXED IN A BAR AFTER WORK, AN ACT THAT LED TO ONE OF THE BIGGEST DRUG BUSTS IN AMERICA

This now-famous investigation into narcotics traffic led to the confiscation of vast amounts of heroin as well as the arrest and conviction of several top Mafia-connected drug dealers. At the time of the bust in early 1962, it was the single most devastating blow to drug trafficking in the U.S.

The investigation began by accident. On October 7, 1961, New York City Police Detective First Grade Edward Egan, 32, and Detective Second Grade Salvatore "Sonny" Grosso, 30, went to the Copacabana nightclub to relax after a long, hard, successful drug bust. There, they recognized Pasculano "Patsy" Fuca, the nephew of middle-level Mafia boss Angie Tuminaro. Fuca was spending a lot more money than the detectives expected. Egan and Grosso decided to follow him.

Their observations revealed that Fuca was leading a double life. By day, he ran a small luncheonette in a low-rent district and drove an old car. After work, he switched to a new car and flashy clothes, and lived in a two-story brick house.

Posing as interns from the hospital across the street, the detectives infiltrated the luncheonette. A wiretap hinted of a large shipment of heroin due in the United States soon. The shipment's route was from Turkey to France to Canada to the U.S.

Fuca was kept under constant surveillance, as were his known contacts. One of those contacts was Jean Jehan, a French-Canadian dope dealer. The FBI worked closely with the New York City Police Department. As many as 300 officers played a role in the case.

Several details of the deal came out later. Two Frenchmen—François Scaglia and Jacques Angelvin—were involved. Scaglia provided the heroin; Angelvin was a well-known French television star who traveled widely. Angelvin had a 1960 Buick that he would bring to America with him. The heroin was transported to the U.S., hidden in a special place in the Buick. When cut (diluted with inert ingredients), the heroin would have had a street value of $32 million. A bill of lading for the shipment led Grosso to the Buick. When shipped over, the car weighed 12 pounds more than its return weight. By requesting an adjustment on his shipping bill, Angelvin had risked millions to save $33.

Unfortunately, the wily dealers eluded the police. The Buick disappeared, and some of the drugs hit the street. Enough evidence had been gathered, however, that the police could arrest Fuca at a relative's house. Other minor dealers were also arrested, including Tony Fuca, Patsy's brother. In the basement, the officers dug up illegal guns and 11 kilograms (approximately 24 pounds) of heroin, the largest single haul up to that time. The police traced about 40 kilograms (approximately 88 pounds) to a warehouse.

Tony Fuca was released on bail. Two weeks after his release, Tony went to the stash at the warehouse. He took some of the drugs to another drug dealer, who was also arrested. But one drug kingpin, Jean Jehan, escaped with half a million dollars in drug money.

Patsy Fuca was also released on bail. Less than a month later, he asked to be returned to the safety of the maximum security cell. His uncle, Angie Tuminaro, also preferred jail. Patsy Fuca pleaded guilty and was sentenced to 15 years in jail. Scaglia got 21 years. Angelvin received three to six years. Jehan was apprehended in France in 1967, but he was never extradited to the United States. Patsy Fuca apparently made a wise choice by staying in jail. His successor, Frank Tuminaro (Angie's brother), was killed execution-style only a few months after taking over Patsy's territory.

Both Egan and Grosso received death threats and word that there was a contract out on them. They had bodyguards throughout the trial, and they were never allowed to be together. Fortunately, their alleged contract killer died in a car crash.

IN THE BASEMENT, THE OFFICERS DUG UP ILLEGAL GUNS AND 11 KILOGRAMS (APPROXIMATELY 24 POUNDS) OF HEROIN, THE LARGEST SINGLE HAUL UP TO THAT TIME.

THE BOSTON STRANGLER

ALBERT DESALVO, A DERANGED SEX KILLER, TERRORIZED AN ENTIRE CITY FOR NEARLY THREE YEARS

Albert DeSalvo on his way to Middlesex County Court in Boston for a legal hearing. Had DeSalvo not chosen to boast that he was the Boston Strangler, the possibility is strong that he might never have been identified as such. Investigators, in many respects, were still at square one when DeSalvo came forth with his confession.

From June 1962 until the spring of 1965, Boston was a city under siege. An unknown, unseen maniac was raping and murdering its single women, although not necessarily in that order.

The killing started on June 14, 1962, when Mrs. Anna Slesers, a 55-year-old divorced seamstress, was discovered by her son lying nude on the floor outside her bathroom. Her housecoat was spread open, and she had been strangled with its cord. About two weeks later, 85-year-old Mary Mullen was found dead. However, her death was not at first attributed to the Strangler. Sixteen days after the initial murder, two female victims were discovered in nearby Brighton and Lynn townships. Mrs. Nina Nichols, a retired therapist age 68, and Miss Helen Blake, a registered nurse age 65, were both found dead, strangled with nylon stockings. Mrs. Nichols had been on the telephone when the doorbell rang, which was heard at the other end of the phone line. Mrs. Nichols excused herself, saying she would call right back; she never did. Eleven days later, a 60-year-old widow, Mrs. Margaret Davis, was found strangled—apparently by hand.

When 75-year-old Mrs. Ida Irga—a sweet little old lady who lived alone—turned up dead on August 19, Bostonians began to panic. Mrs. Irga had been sexually assaulted and left propped up in a lewd display, as if in preparation for discovery. Details of the assault were kept secret to aid in identifying the killer, but that simply made the rumor mill churn more wildly. About ten days later, Miss Jane Sullivan, another nurse in her sixties, was found dead in Dorchester. Evidence showed that Miss Sullivan, a big woman, put up a valiant fight. However, she had been strangled with a nylon stocking, and her death had occurred several days before she was found, perhaps on the day after that of Mrs. Irga.

At that point, the pattern seemed to gel. The killer was going after elderly single women, highly vulnerable victims. Half the women were involved in medicine. Senior citizens and nursing organizations braced themselves. Neighbors of elderly women kept a watchful vigil. After he remained inactive for over three months, the Strangler struck again on December 5, 1962. Confounding everyone, he did not pick an elderly woman. He chose Sophie Clark, a 21-year-old student who had two roommates. Boston's reputation as a college town meant that a staggering number of young women then felt much more open to attack. Sophie Clark could not have been more different from the previous victims. She was young, outgoing, active, and African-American. Still, she was attending a school of medical technology and lived only two blocks from the first victim. Before the year was out, the Boston Strangler would strike again, murdering Patricia Bissette, a 23-year-old secretary, on December 30.

It would be just over two months before the Strangler would slay another, savagely killing Mary Brown, age 69, on March 9, 1963. Then came the vicious murder of 23-year-old Beverly Samans on May 6, 1963. The death of Evelyn Corbin, a vivacious divorcée of 58, was shocking for its audacity. She was assaulted after returning from breakfast at her neighbor's down the hallway. The Strangler was waiting in Corbin's apartment when she arrived. By the time this same neighbor called less than an hour later, the Strangler had sexually abused and murdered Corbin. The next murder was even more shocking for its sense of timing. The day after the assassination of President John F. Kennedy, who was Boston's famous son, 23-year-old Joann Graff became another victim on November 23, 1963.

The killer's last murder was his most outrageous. Once again, he chose a college student, 19-year-old Mary Sullivan. On January 4, 1964, he broke into the apartment where she lived with two roommates. He raped her at knife-point, strangled her with his hands, and proceeded to "decorate" her body for the police, complete with a New Year card placed between her toes. The details were hard to keep out

BRILLIANT PSYCHO OR DERANGED FOOL?

The case of the Boston Strangler was as confusing as it was bizarre. While the specter of a sex-crazed killer drove the citizenry into a near panic, the killer, when finally caught, turned out to be more deviant than anyone could imagine. The police had been looking for a perverted genius—figuring that only a master criminal could elude them. And yet he turned out to be a very ordinary man whose lack of planning gave him the randomness that the police might overlook. Albert DeSalvo himself never knew when he would strike until the urge came over him.

DeSalvo was a married man with two children. He was deeply devoted to his wife, and most of his post-arrest efforts were aimed at sheltering her. He did not hate his mother; he simply pitied her for the abuse she had received from his father. DeSalvo offered as his sole motive an absolutely consuming sexual appetite. He had sex with his wife about five times a day (more on weekends) and sought outside relations to supplement these urges. DeSalvo reckoned that he had raped over 2,000 women in his lifetime. The police confirmed at least 300 in the Boston/New England area. He was found to have raped three different women in separate cities in a three-hour span.

of the press, no matter how cryptic the wording. The death of pretty, young Mary Sullivan was the last straw. The state of Massachusetts turned all the cases over to the state attorney general's office. Eventually, over 2,600 law enforcement agents became involved.

The murders had enough similarities to suggest a single killer. All the victims were women who were strangled—some by hand, most by nylon stockings. Each was attacked while alone in her apartment. All were left in a nude state and were sexually violated. There was no pattern to the sexual activity. Although the first victim had not been raped, evidence suggested that the killer had engaged in some type of solo sexual activity. The Strangler had raped and desecrated the bodies of Nina Nichols and Helen Blake. So the theory of a sadistic, woman-hating psychopath seemed to be valid.

The police had never found any evidence to describe the killer. No one ever seemed to see him. The lack of signs of forced entry was particularly disturbing because of all the media hysteria and official warnings to single women. The police began to resort to unusual sources for help, employing various clairvoyants and ESP sensitives. The most famous of these was Peter Hurkos. His description of the Strangler led the police to arrest a mentally disturbed shoe salesman who turned out to have nothing to do with the stranglings.

The police also turned to psychiatrists for help. A task force was put together that included autopsy examiners, gynecologists, and therapists specializing in treating sex criminals. They were ordered to create a character/personality sketch. They found that the killer had a consuming rage toward women and that he suffered from an Oedipus complex. These "experts" also deduced that the Strangler was impotent and that he violently hated all women.

In September 1964, nine months after the last strangling, a man attacked a young married coed in her apartment. He forced her onto

DeSalvo, captured after escaping from the hospital.

TERROR IN BOSTON

While he was on the loose, the Strangler wrought enormous social changes on Bostonians, especially on his target group—single women. Neighbors began to spy and inform upon each other. Strangers found themselves quite unwelcome. Yet despite an increasingly high public awareness, the killer continued to gain easy entry into the apartments of new victims.

Fear of the Boston Strangler became a generalized paranoia that struck out in all directions. A long-haired youth was arrested for tampering with parking meters, and several women claimed that he was the Boston Strangler. A music student was arrested in a movie theater for peeping at the open toes of women with a pocket flashlight. Sales of security locks and trained dogs skyrocketed. A woman opened her front door one day only to find a complete stranger standing there. She died of a heart attack. It turned out that the stranger was an encyclopedia salesman.

her bed, raped her, and immediately left. Using police mug shots, the woman identified Albert DeSalvo as her assailant.

DeSalvo had previously spent 11 months in jail for breaking and entering. He had been released in April 1962, just three months before Anna Slesers was killed. DeSalvo had been known as "the Measuring Man." He approached young women in their homes and offered them a chance to apply for high-paying modeling jobs. All they had to do was allow Mr. DeSalvo to take their physical measurements. Strange as this sounds, he was quite successful at it. Since this scheme would not go over with his elderly strangling victims, DeSalvo apparently posed as a repairman.

When DeSalvo was arrested for the September 1964 rape of the young married coed, he was sent to Bridgewater State Hospital. DeSalvo began to boast to other inmates. One inmate took him seriously and informed DeSalvo's lawyer, the young F. Lee Bailey. To test DeSalvo's veracity, Bailey obtained a list of confidential questions. When satisfied of DeSalvo's guilt, Bailey informed the police that his client was the Boston Strangler. Since the police had no concrete evidence, they were forced to agree to Bailey's terms. The police could not use the confessions against DeSalvo. They gave up the right to prosecute him for the murders in exchange for the certainty that the Boston Strangler was off the streets.

However, the police and psychiatrists just couldn't accept that DeSalvo was the real Boston Strangler. He didn't fit their profile. Nevertheless, DeSalvo's confessions held up, despite being heavily scrutinized. This dull, uneducated, ordinary man eluded capture simply because there was no rhyme nor reason to his attacks.

Albert DeSalvo was sentenced to life imprisonment for rape, but never stood trial for any of the murders. DeSalvo was stabbed to death in prison in 1973, allegedly over a drug deal.

During the mid-1960s, F. Lee Bailey, shown leaving a courthouse, was the most in-demand defense attorney in the country. In addition to Albert DeSalvo, the Boston Strangler, Bailey represented the impoverished Dr. Sam Sheppard at his second trial (for the murder of his wife) in return for the royalties to a book that Sheppard wrote about his tribulations.

THE MOBSTER WHO UNVEILED THE COSA NOSTRA

Known as the "Boss of Bosses," Vito Genovese arrives at a New York courthouse in handcuffs in 1959. Indicted on a narcotics conspiracy charge, the Mafia warlord drew a 15-year sentence in a federal prison in Atlanta. After Joe Valachi sang, Genovese gave him the Mafia's traditional "kiss of death."

MOBSTER JOSEPH VALACHI BROKE THE MAFIA'S CODE OF SILENCE AND LIFTED THE VEIL OFF THE CRIME SYNDICATE KNOWN AS THE COSA NOSTRA

Testifying in 1962 before a Senate subcommittee chaired by Senator John L. McClellan and through extensive interrogation by the Justice Department, Joseph Michael Valachi revealed for the first time the inner workings of the notorious Mafia "families." U.S. Attorney General Robert F. Kennedy called the testimony, which held a national TV audience spellbound, "the biggest intelligence breakthrough yet in combating organized crime and racketeering in the United States." The crime bosses put a $100,000 price on Valachi's head. Valachi became the most closely guarded inmate in the federal prison system.

Valachi was born September 22, 1904, in Manhattan's East Harlem, a neighborhood with a large population of Italian immigrants. He grew up in a tough, crime-ridden neighborhood. His alcoholic father operated a vegetable pushcart and had to pay a dollar a week in protection money to keep his cart from being wrecked.

By age 14, Joseph Valachi was a thief and a burglar. His early manhood was at a time when gang activity was rampant. Murder—especially the killing of rival mobsters—was routine. By the late 1920s and the 1930s, Joe Valachi was deeply involved in the gangland wars between crime lords that blazed across New York City. As a so-called "soldier," Valachi was a street muscleman and enforcer, a numbers runner, and a hit man who took part in an estimated 33 gangland killings. (Valachi admitted to only five murders during his talks with the Justice Department and the Senate subcommittee.)

Valachi first worked for Salvatore Maranzano, a New York City mobster who was trying to take over the operations of the other organized gangs. Maranzano himself administered the Cosa Nostra's blood oath of allegiance to young Valachi in a rural mansion. Valachi was thus bound forever to a deadly "honor" that required complete silence concerning the syndicate. The price of breaking the code of silence was death.

Valachi's first impression of Maranzano was that he looked like an ordinary businessman, but Maranzano's business approach was far from ordinary. Maranzano was in the midst of a war with another Mafia leader, Joe "the Boss" Masseria, for full control of New York's gangs and their rackets. As bodies fell and Maranzano's domination of the Italian underworld grew, two of Masseria's most trusted lieutenants—Charles "Lucky" Luciano and Vito Genovese—defected to Maranzano's side. The two ex-lieutenants set Masseria up for a hit. He was gunned down in a Coney Island restaurant.

Then unchallenged as the top man, Maranzano started organizing the modern crime syndicate that became known as the Cosa Nostra (literally, "our thing"). The crime lord called for a meeting at a large hall in the Bronx. Several hundred gang members who had fought each other attended the meeting. A new structure—five New York City "families" and other "families" in different major American cities—was formed. Lieutenants and other commanders were appointed to supervise the soldiers; territories and rackets were divided up. Valachi later referred to this finely tuned organization as a "second government" within the nation.

Valachi continued his violent duties throughout the years of the Great Depression, taking part in several hits. World War II opened up opportunities for a slew of new illegal operations, including the black-marketing of ration stamps and coupons that earned Valachi $100,000 a year. By the 1950s, the New York families were deeply involved in narcotics trafficking, which ultimately led to the downfall of Valachi and his boss, Vito Genovese.

After the testimony of "singing gangster" Joe Valachi before the Senate Investigations Subcommittee in Washington, D.C., this cartoon by Gib Crockett appeared in the *Washington Star.*

FINALLY, VALACHI AGAIN ENTERED THE PRISON POPULATION, CONVINCED HE WOULD DIE A MAFIA DEATH.

Fighting among the families developed into more bloodletting, with the top gangsters as targets. One of the bloodiest hits was the barbershop shooting death of Mafia chieftain Albert Anastasia. Genovese was responsible for hatching the Anastasia murder. In an attempt to alleviate the growing fears of the other family heads, Genovese called a nationwide meeting of the organization's leaders.

The meeting took place in a country house in a small town in upstate New York. The house—set deep within the woods—offered privacy, but alert state police spotted the conclave of crime's royalty. The police set up roadblocks to detain and grill the mobsters. Before the meeting was broken up, a primary item on the agenda had been the U.S. Bureau of Narcotics and the woe it was causing the Cosa Nostra. The gang chiefs talked about getting out of drug trafficking, with death as the penalty for any member who didn't keep such a covenant.

Within a year of that rural meeting, Vito Genovese was convicted in a drug conspiracy case. He received 15 years, which he began serving at the Atlanta federal penitentiary. Even behind bars, though, Genovese continued to run things, both inside and outside the prison's walls.

In June 1960, Joseph Valachi was sentenced to 15 years for a narcotics violation. He was also sent to the Atlanta prison. Prison life was nothing new to Valachi. During the 1920s, he had served two separate terms in New York's Sing Sing penitentiary, where he had been stabbed by another inmate.

In the Atlanta prison, Valachi found that some 90 ex-mobsters imprisoned there were under the thumb of Vito Genovese. They did his laundry, paid him respect, and made appointments to see the still-powerful crime boss. Genovese—who came out of his cell only twice a week—settled disputes and granted favors.

Valachi also learned he was in disfavor with his former boss. Genovese believed Valachi had informed drug agents about Genovese's narcotics operations. He invited Valachi to live in his cell. After this had been arranged, Genovese one day gave Valachi the Mafia's traditional "kiss of death"—an embrace that marks the recipient for execution. Valachi denied to Genovese that he had ever broken the code of silence, but he knew it was a futile plea. His denial would not lengthen his life span.

Valachi's gnawing fear for his life became an obsession. He even went so far as to have himself placed in solitary confinement. Finally, however, he again entered the prison population, convinced he would die a Mafia death. On the morning of June 22, 1962, Valachi, walking in the exercise yard, became enraged at the sight of another inmate who he believed had been assigned to kill him. Valachi grabbed an iron pipe from a construction site and beat the convict to death. The man had been mistaken for Joe DiPalermo, one of Genovese's inner circle. The murdered inmate was actually John Joseph Saupp, a forger, bank robber, and remarkable look-alike for DiPalermo.

After drawing a life sentence for the murder, Valachi became so overcome with fear that he agreed to tell the U.S. Justice Department all he knew about the most closely kept secrets of the Cosa Nostra. For months, he told his story in Washington, D.C. He was protected by as many as 200 federal marshals. Finally, as a protective measure, Valachi was moved to the La Tuna federal prison in El Paso, Texas.

The dreaded Cosa Nostra hit teams never got to Valachi, but a heart attack did. Joseph Valachi died on April 3, 1971, in prison at the age of 66. But he had outlived his former boss, Vito Genovese, who had died in prison in 1969 of a heart attack.

Joe Valachi testifying before the Senate.

VITO GENOVESE'S METHOD: MURDER

Vito Genovese, who ordered Joseph Valachi's execution, had a lifelong habit of initiating murders. Born in 1897 in Naples, Italy, Genovese was 16 when his family moved to New York City. He rose rapidly in the American Mafia. Wanting the top spot, Genovese gave the orders that resulted in the killings of Willie Moretti, Steve Franse, and Albert Anastasia. He also ordered the murder of Mafia chieftain Frank Costello. The hit failed but led to Costello's retirement.

It was said that Genovese had only one soft spot: Anna Petillo. Genovese had married her after arranging her husband's murder. Later, during divorce proceedings, she testified about his rackets—which enraged the Mob—but he refused to harm her.

In 1937, Genovese fled to Italy. He became closely involved with Benito Mussolini, furnishing drugs and arranging the hit of a longtime enemy in New York. He returned to the U.S. in 1944. In the late 1950s, Genovese landed in an Atlanta federal prison on a narcotics conviction.

"RELIGIOUS" MURDER, PERVERSION, AND THIEVERY

PROSTITUTE MAGDALENA SOLIS AND HER BROTHER ACCEPTED A PROPOSITION TO HELP FLEECE MEXICAN PEASANTS BY PROMISING THEM TREASURES

Early in 1963, two brothers, Mexicans Santos and Cayetano Hernandez, concocted a scheme to make a lot of easy money. They planned to take advantage of the faith that the peasants of the village of Yerba Buena had in the Inca gods of the mountains. The brothers wove fantasies designed to capture the people's desire for riches. Santos and Cayetano promised rewards of gems and gold to the villagers if they worshipped the Inca gods of the mountains and made sacrifices to the gods. The villagers' offerings would consist of the use of their bodies in sexual expressions that would open the door to riches.

The Hernandez brothers selected a cave in the mountains to hold their cultlike ceremonies, which included inducing the villagers to "donate" their possessions and monies. To help provide an atmosphere of ritualistic extravaganza, Santos and Cayetano convinced lesbian prostitute Magdalena Solis and her homosexual brother, Eleazor, to come to Yerba Buena to participate in the mountain cave rites.

In the center of the cultic service, a brazier of hot coals cast a subtle glow throughout the cave. Flash powder thrown on the embers brought forth a burst of clouds of smoke. As the smoke cleared, Magdalena and Eleazor "magically" appeared. The peasants, told by the Hernandez brothers that Eleazor was St. Francis of Assisi, immediately acknowledged him as this saint. This "miracle" caused a frenzied reaction among the peasants, who beat and hacked away at the mountainside.

In the midst of this spirited emotional rite, "High Priest" Santos Hernandez sexually "purified" a teenage girl, Celina Salvana. Magdalena Solis watched the intimacies between Santos and Celina, which stimulated her own desires for the girl. Santos then passed the young Celina to Magdalena. Meanwhile, Eleazor Solis and Cayetano Hernandez, who also preferred males, took advantage of the boys in the assemblage.

But one skeptical villager, Jesus Rubio, doubted the sanctity of the Hernandez brothers. Challenged, the brothers took Rubio into their confidence and paid him off with a share of the take.

As the rituals began to get out of control, the peasants started to complain that the promised Inca treasures were not appearing. In an effort to quell the peasant's objections, Magdalena preached the requirements of "sacrifice" that the gods demanded. She revealed that only by cleansing the cult disbelievers could the jewels of the gods be delivered. Two men who had refused to accept the word of the Inca gods were quickly beaten to death. The victims' blood was mixed with that of a chicken and drunk from a sacrificial bowl by the assemblage. During the following two months, six more disbelievers were killed in ongoing ritual gatherings. Many others fled in fright.

During this time, Celina craved Santos more and more, touching off a jealous rage in Magdalena, who had the girl bound to a sacrificial cross. In a "spiritual offering" of her own, Magdalena beat the teenage girl unconscious. The spellbound peasantry continued the pummeling until Celina was dead. A passing student, Sebastian Gurrero, witnessed the final frame of this ordeal: The worshipers piled brush around Celina's body and set it afire.

In terror, Gurrero rushed to the police station in the village of Villa Gran and reported what he had seen. Patrolman Luis Martinez reluctantly agreed to drive the boy back to Yerba Buena. They were never seen alive again; their mutilated bodies were discovered during the police follow-up.

Santos Hernandez was killed in a shoot-out with police, but Cayetano Hernandez disappeared. Jesus Rubio later confessed that he had killed Cayetano so he could be "High Priest." In June 1963, Magdalena Solis, Eleazor, and 12 cult members were tried, convicted, and sent to prison for 30 years.

IN A "SPIRITUAL OFFERING" OF HER OWN, MAGDALENA BEAT THE TEENAGE GIRL UNCONSCIOUS. THE SPELLBOUND PEASANTRY CONTINUED THE PUMMELING UNTIL CELINA WAS DEAD.

THE GREAT TRAIN ROBBERY

THE CLASSIC 1903 MOTION PICTURE BECAME REALITY IN ENGLAND 60 YEARS LATER, AND RESULTED IN PERHAPS THE GREATEST HEIST EVER

Ronald Biggs, one of the perpetrators of the Great Train Robbery. His carefully orchestrated escape from London's Wandsworth Prison in July 1965 made him a media hero and led to an erroneous impression that he was the leader of the bold heist. Later, the real mastermind was thought to be Bruce Reynolds.

After midnight on August 8, 1963, engineer Jack Mills, 58, and fireman David Whitby, 26, boarded their diesel engine train at Crewe, England. Mills pulled the train out and headed for London, carrying nothing unusual for this mail run. The second car carried "high value" cargo: 128 mailbags filled with money from Scottish banks.

The train breezed through Leighton Buzzard in Bedfordshire at 70 miles an hour. A half hour out of London, the dwarf signal ahead showed amber, telling the engineer to slow down. The succeeding light, "home signal," beamed red—a command to halt the train. Mills brought the train to a stop and directed Whitby to go to the signal box and find out how long the delay would be.

Whitby yelled back to Mills that the wires were cut. Returning to the engine, Whitby saw the figure of a man at the rear of the second car. "What's up, mate?" Whitby asked. The figure motioned Whitby forward to the edge of the railroad embankment. When he arrived, Whitby was pushed over the side of the embankment. He landed at the feet of two men who threatened to kill him if he cried out. Whitby was returned to the engine's cab. There, he found many masked men as well as Jack Mills, who was bleeding freely from his head. The thieves uncoupled all the cars behind the mail car.

Mills was ordered to drive to the bridge about a half mile ahead. The robbers smashed out the windows of the mail car. They passed the mailbags through the windows and loaded them onto a waiting truck. The thieves sped off to Leatherslade Farm, some 20 miles away. Two mail clerks ran to the village of Linslade and notified Scotland Yard.

Within five days, Scotland Yard and local police had uncovered the farm. Neighbors tipped off the authorities concerning the comings and goings of many strange men. It was also observed that the farmhouse windows had been draped with bunting to shut out any view inside. And a Mrs. Brooke told police that she had delivered the keys to the supposed buyers of the property. This and other bits of information led to the identity of some of the suspects. The robbers had also carelessly left fingerprints all over the farmhouse.

Another break occurred in Bournemouth. Two men had asked Ethel Clark, a policeman's widow, if they could rent a garage for their van. Clark became suspicious and called headquarters. Gerald Boal, 50, and Roger Cordrey, 41, were arrested when £141,000 in notes were found in their van. Another £300 in notes were recovered from Boal's house. A couple found yet another £101,000 in notes in Redland Wood, believed discarded by panicked robbers.

Brian Field, 29, and Leonard Field (not related), 31, participated in the heist and were arrested. Also taken into custody were Douglas Goody, 34; John Wheater, 42; and John Daly, 32. Robert Alfred Welch, 35; Roy James, 28; Thomas Wisbey, 34; James Hussey, 31; Charles Wilson, 31; and Ronald Arthur Biggs, 34, were also linked to the theft and arrested. Bruce Reynolds, the reputed leader, remained loose for four years before he was apprehended. Ronald Edwards and James White were not immediately caught, but they were later apprehended and convicted.

The trial started on January 24, 1964, in Buckinghamshire. All the defendants were convicted. Except for Wheater, who got only three years, the robbers were sentenced to 24 to 30 years.

The spotlight remains on Ronald Biggs, one of several men involved in the Great Train Robbery. After being tried and convicted, Biggs was sentenced to 30 years. While in Wandsworth Prison, London, Biggs brazenly leapt from the prison wall to the top of a waiting truck and escaped. He lived in Australia for several years and later moved to Brazil, where he apparently continues to beat extradition proceedings. Some two million pounds have never been recovered.

THE SECOND CAR CARRIED "HIGH VALUE" CARGO: 128 MAILBAGS FILLED WITH MONEY FROM SCOTTISH BANKS.

AMERICA LOSES ITS INNOCENCE

LEE HARVEY OSWALD APPARENTLY FIRED A POWERFUL RIFLE, AND THE PRESIDENCY OF JOHN F. KENNEDY CAME TO AN UNTIMELY END

One of the most dramatic moments ever to be televised live to an entire nation. As the camera watches, Jack Ruby steps forward and pumps a fatal bullet into the stomach of accused presidential assassin Lee Harvey Oswald.

Lee Harvey Oswald was born on October 18, 1939, in New Orleans, two months after his father died of a heart attack. As a child, Oswald was shy and awkward, described as unmannerly, opinionated, contrary, resentful, suspicious, and withdrawn. His mother, Marguerite, worked and had too many problems of her own to notice that her son was not well-adjusted. Lee Harvey Oswald felt he had no one to turn to, saying once, "I dislike everybody." He felt that his mother "never gave a damn about him" and that there was never anyone at home.

At age 13 in the Bronx, Oswald was ordered to appear at Children's Court on truancy charges; he spent three weeks in Youth House. A few days after his release, someone handed Oswald a "Save the Rosenbergs" pamphlet (part of a campaign for clemency for Julius and Ethel Rosenberg, who were on death row). This chance incident led Oswald into the study of Marxism and a growing interest in politics. He read a great deal, including Karl Marx's *Das Kapital* and George Orwell's *Animal Farm*. Although he had above-average intelligence, Oswald dropped out of school after the ninth grade at age 16. In 1956, he wrote to the Socialist Party of America, asking if there was a local branch of the youth league he could join.

When he reached 17, Oswald enlisted in the U.S. Marine Corps. He was court-martialed twice—once for challenging his sergeant to fight and once for the possession of a pistol. His fellow soldiers called him "Ozzie Rabbit," and he was not well-liked. From time to time, he expressed his belief in Communism, and in a letter to his brother Robert, Lee Harvey Oswald called America a "dying country." After serving two years, he was transferred to the inactive reserve at his own request. The reason was to care for his mother, who was ailing. But the young ex-Marine did not help her for long.

A short time later, Oswald defected to the Soviet Union, using funds from an unidentified source. Oswald gave up his American citi-

The scene just seconds before President John F. Kennedy was fatally shot. Beside Kennedy is his wife Jackie, holding her hat. Seated in front of the Kennedys are Texas Governor John Connally and his wife. Connally was seriously wounded.

zenship to work on radar installations for the Soviet Union. He married the daughter of a KGB colonel—19-year-old Marina Nikolalaevna Prusakova. Oswald applied for Soviet citizenship but was rejected; that led to an attempted suicide. After staying in the Soviet Union for two and a half years, Oswald returned to the United States with Marina and their baby daughter named June. The FBI—responsible for interviewing returning defectors—called Oswald in for questioning. The agent found him "insolent and tense." Unable to find suitable work and wandering from one job to another, Oswald eventually ended up in Dallas.

After a while, Oswald traveled to New Orleans. While there, he called constant attention to himself as a Castro supporter—he handed out pamphlets, gave speeches, wrote letters, and tried to organize Fair Play for Cuba Committee charters. Oswald then traveled to Mexico City, where he made an effort to return to the Soviet Union or to gain entry to Cuba. After that failed, he returned to Dallas and got a job at the Texas School Book Depository.

Oswald learned that President John F. Kennedy would be in Dallas on November 22, 1963, and that the motorcade would pass di-

OSWALD DEFECTED TO THE SOVIET UNION, USING FUNDS FROM AN UNIDENTIFIED SOURCE. HE GAVE UP HIS AMERICAN CITIZENSHIP TO WORK ON RADAR INSTALLATIONS FOR THE SOVIET UNION.

rectly beneath the windows of the Texas School Book Depository. Late on the morning of November 22, Oswald went to the sixth floor of the depository and took up a position at a window.

President and Mrs. Kennedy, Texas Governor John B. Connally, and Mrs. Connally were riding in an open car that moved into Oswald's rifle sight around 12:30 P.M. It is alleged that Oswald then squeezed the trigger. President Kennedy clutched his throat and fell forward. One bullet passed through Kennedy and hit Connally; it tore through his chest and embedded itself in his thigh. The victims were rushed to Parkland Memorial Hospital. President Kennedy was pronounced dead on arrival.

Oswald hid his rifle, and walked downstairs, where he was identified as an employee. He drank a soda, and then, as the building became flooded with law officials, walked out unnoticed. Oswald went home, changed his clothes, and went outside. When he was stopped by Dallas police officer J.D. Tippit, Oswald shot him four times.

Police later captured Oswald in a movie theater when his pistol misfired during a struggle with some detectives. Bullets taken from President Kennedy and Governor Connally matched those fired by Oswald's rifle. The bullets and a palm print on the rifle refuted Oswald's constant denials of the crime. While in police custody, Oswald was killed by Jack Ruby, the owner of a nightclub. Ruby shot Oswald in front of millions of television viewers and in the presence of 70 police officers. Sentenced to death for the murder, Ruby died in jail before being executed.

The Warren Commission investigated the assassination and in September 1964, it concluded that Oswald had acted alone. Many doubted those findings, and believed that Oswald acted as part of a conspiracy. The exact truth remains a puzzle to this day.

Despite warnings that there might be some trouble, President John F. Kennedy insisted on riding in an open car in the motorcade that cruised through the downtown streets of Dallas on November 22, 1963. He felt that the American public ought to be able to view its president, and both he and the nation paid dearly for it.

FRANK SINATRA, JR., IS KIDNAPPED

THREE KIDNAPPERS TRIED TO CASH IN ON THE SINATRA FORTUNE IN A BOLD EPISODE THAT ENDED WITHIN A FEW DAYS

Frank Sinatra, Jr., is reunited with his mother Nancy, right, and sister Tina. After a 54-hour ordeal, the kidnap victim was released unharmed near his mother's home. Within two days of his return to the family fold, the FBI had all three of the abductors in custody.

Frank Sinatra, Jr., 19, the singing son of the famous singer and actor, was kidnapped from his room at Harrah's Tahoe Casino in Lake Tahoe on Sunday night, December 8, 1963. Two men—one brandishing a gun—burst into Sinatra's room after knocking on the door and saying, "Room service." The kidnappers tied and gagged John Foss, Sinatra's friend and a trumpet player with the revamped Tommy Dorsey Orchestra that the younger Sinatra was appearing with nightly at the casino. The abductors then hustled the youthful singer outside into a raging snowstorm. Foss freed himself and sounded the alarm.

Frank Sinatra, Sr., waited beside a telephone in a Reno, Nevada hotel, as instructed by the FBI. He received three phone calls from the kidnappers during Monday and Tuesday. Frank, Sr., talked briefly to his son and agreed to deliver the ransom of $240,000 in small bills that was demanded.

From left to right, John Clyde Amsler, Barry Worthington Keenan, and John William Irwin leave a federal courtroom in Los Angeles following their conviction and sentencing for the kidnapping of Frank Sinatra, Jr. Amsler and Keenan abducted the teenage son of the famous crooner from a Lake Tahoe hotel room at gunpoint.

Relying on a friend who was the president of a Beverly Hills bank, Sinatra, Sr., arranged for the money to be prepared. Bank employees and FBI agents spent the night collecting, marking, and photographing the cash. During the third call, the famous showman was told to go to the Los Angeles home of the singer's former wife, Nancy, and wait.

In Los Angeles, Sinatra received another call starting him on a circuit of phone booths for progressive instructions and promising to free Frank, Jr., when the payoff was made. An FBI agent accompanied Frank, Sr., on these rounds. The agent was the final courier, dropping the satchel of money at a West Los Angeles site.

The abductors freed the younger Sinatra early on Wednesday, December 11, 54 hours after he had been snatched at the casino. Frank, Jr., was walking along a street near his mother's home when he hailed a passing private patrol guard. The guard concealed Frank, Jr., in the trunk of the car and drove to Nancy Sinatra's mansion. The kidnapping victim was kept hidden from the approximately 100 news representatives waiting there for developments.

The younger Sinatra had been held at a ramshackle residence in the San Fernando community of Canoga Park. Within two days of the release of Frank, Jr., the FBI arrested three men and charged them with the kidnapping: Barry Worthington Keenan, 23, who plotted the crime; John Clyde Amsler, 23; and John William Irwin, 42. All three men came from the Los Angeles area. Most of the ransom money was found buried in the backyard of the Canoga Park home.

In March 1964, a Los Angeles jury rejected a defense claim that the kidnapping had been a publicity hoax. The jury gave the three kidnappers long prison terms that were later reduced by the court.

BROTHEL OWNERS AND KILLERS

DELFINA AND MARIA DE JESUS GONZALES FORCED TEENAGE GIRLS INTO PROSTITUTION AND KILLED THE GIRLS WHEN THEY LOST THEIR LOOKS

In December 1963, Mexican police raided a ranch northwest of Mexico City near the city of León in the state of Guanajuato and literally unearthed a horror story. On the Rancho El Angel, the police found the buried remains of 80 girls, 11 men, and many newborn babies.

The ranch was a flourishing brothel where captive teenage girls forced into prostitution either died from extreme abuse or were killed when they lost their beauty. The male murder victims were migratory workers who had returned to Mexico from the United States. When the workers visited the brothel, they were given doped drinks and then slain for their season's wages. The babies had been unwanted infants born to the girls.

For weeks, police in western Mexico had been probing reports of girls who disappeared after they accepted jobs as maids. One 16-year-old, Maria Hernandez, dropped from sight after catching a bus to take the job. The description of the woman who offered the job to Maria led to the arrest of Josefina Gutierrez. Gutierrez admitted to enticing young girls for brothel owners Delfina and Maria de Jesus Gonzales. Gutierrez received up to $70 for each girl.

Investigators traced the Gonzales sisters to their ranch, which was way off the beaten path and could only be reached over a rocky trail. It was surrounded by a high fence, and the entrance was manned by an armed guard. Thirteen teenage girls were being held prisoner in various rooms. The once-pretty girls were now ravaged by sexual and drug abuse, torture, and forced prostitution.

The Gonzales sisters heard about the raid and went into hiding. They planned to flee to the U.S., but they were arrested before they could leave Mexico. Both women were convicted and received 40-year prison sentences. Other accomplices, including police involved in the corruption, also received long sentences. The Gonzales' fortune was given to victims and their relatives as compensation.

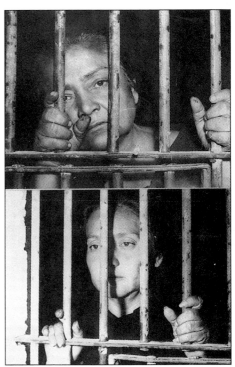

The Gonzalez sisters, Delfina, 52 (top), and Maria, 39 (bottom), behind bars in León, Mexico. Arrested before they could flee to the United States, the murderous siblings drew 40-year sentences.

VICTIM OF APATHY

WITH 38 PEOPLE WATCHING, EACH AFRAID TO GET INVOLVED, KITTY GENOVESE WAS STABBED TO DEATH

Because of the capital punishment laws, Winston Mosely, above, could not be executed for killing Kitty Genovese. While in prison, he severely injured himself with a jagged tin can so that he would be moved to a hospital. Once there, Mosely escaped to kill again after lulling his guards into thinking that he was semiconscious from all the blood he'd lost.

Kitty Genovese was born in 1935. Then her family moved from Brooklyn to New Canaan, Connecticut. After graduating from high school, she married. But Genovese was a lesbian, and the marriage was annulled after two months. In 1960, Genovese moved to New York City. She first worked in offices and then became a barmaid.

Just before 3 A.M. on March 13, 1964, Kitty climbed into her red Fiat and left Ev's 11th Hour Bar, where she worked. She drove home to Kew Gardens, a pleasant area. Kitty parked at a railroad station and began a short walk to her house. She didn't make it.

Kitty's screams woke a man in a seventh-floor apartment across the street. "Help me! Help me! Oh God, he's stabbed me!" Kitty cried. The onlooker saw her kneeling on the sidewalk and a smallish man in an overcoat standing over her. The witness yelled, "Let that girl alone." The assailant ran.

Neighbors rushed to their windows. They saw the victim stumble and hide herself inside an entryway. Then the assailant drove away in a car. Witnesses saw him return a short time later. While people watched from their safe homes, the attacker opened doors, searching for his victim. When he found her, he finished the job. At least 38 people witnessed the brutal slaying, which took 35 minutes. Nobody helped her. Someone finally called the police, but only after checking with a lawyer.

The police first looked for a lesbian connection. However, Winston Mosely, 29, was picked up for routine questioning about several local burglaries. Mosely stunned police when he confessed to stalking, raping, and murdering Kitty Genovese. The police also discovered he had murdered another woman two weeks earlier. Mosely was convicted and sentenced to the electric chair. (Because of the capital punishment laws at that time, this, in effect, meant a life sentence.) Mosely later escaped and killed again, but he was recaptured.

THE DOCTOR WITH A PRESCRIPTION FOR DEATH

DR. CARL COPPOLINO KILLED HIS WIFE AND ALLEGEDLY HIS MISTRESS' HUSBAND, BUT SCORNING HIS MISTRESS WAS HIS BIG MISTAKE

Carl Coppolino was born poor, but he was determined to become rich. He enrolled in Long Island Medical School, where he met and married fellow student Carmela Musetto, daughter of a wealthy doctor.

After he graduated in 1958, Carl became an anesthesiologist at Riverview Hospital in Red Bank, New Jersey. After admitting he wrote threatening letters to a nurse, Carl was dismissed from the hospital.

In 1962, Carl began a torrid affair with Marjorie Farber, the 48-year-old wife of neighbor William Farber, a retired colonel. On July 30, 1963, Colonel Farber died of suffocation. On Carl's instruction, Carmela completed the death certificate, which read "heart failure."

In 1965, the Coppolinos moved to Florida. Marjorie Farber followed them and bought the house next door. After he met Mary Gibson, a woman in her late thirties, Carl sought a divorce. Carmela refused. At 6 A.M. on August 28, Carl summoned Juliette Karow, a local doctor. He claimed his wife had died of a heart attack. Although suspicious, Dr. Karow accepted Carl's diagnosis and signed the death certificate. Soon afterward, Coppolino married Mary Gibson.

Spurned Marjorie Farber told Dr. Karow that Carl had murdered her husband and Carmela. Both bodies were exhumed in the subsequent investigation. The victims had apparently died from an injection of succinylcholine, a compound with effects similar to curare, which is used both as a muscle relaxant and in arrow poisons.

Attorney F. Lee Bailey defended Carl Coppolino against two first-degree murder charges. In September 1966, Carl was acquitted in New Jersey. But in April, 1967, he drew a life sentence upon conviction in Florida of second-degree murder.

A model prisoner for 12½ years, Carl Coppolino was paroled. Restricted from practicing medicine, he decided to write his story, *The Crime That Never Was,* in which he declared his innocence.

Carl Coppolino after being paroled in October 1979.

THE MURDERS ON THE MOORS

Ian Brady, above, and Myra Hindley obtained sexual pleasure by terrorizing and killing children. The pair lived together for several years but were only occasional lovers, if even that. To this day it is uncertain when they started their torturous murders or how many victims they claimed.

IAN BRADY AND MYRA HINDLEY COMMITTED CRIMES OF TORTURE AND MURDER SO ATROCIOUS THAT EVEN HARDENED POLICE VETERANS WERE SHOCKED

Ian Brady, 28, and Myra Hindley, 23, were living together in Hindley's grandmother's house in the quiet town of Hattersley, England. The modest home was surrounded by moors—large expanses of rolling, infertile land covered with stunted vegetation and marsh plants called sedges. To the people aware of the couple—no one, it seemed, really knew them—there seemed little to note. Brady and Hindley had one set of friends: a young couple living near them, David and Maureen Smith, who were Hindley's sister and brother-in-law.

On the night of October 6, 1965, Myra Hindley left her sister's house and headed for home; David Smith accompanied her. Reaching Hindley's house, they went into the kitchen for a glass of wine. David later remembered, "All of a sudden I heard a very loud scream, very loud. Just before it died out another one followed it. Then Myra shouted out, 'Come help him!' I didn't know what was coming. I just ran out of the kitchen and into the living room, and I just froze and stopped dead. My first thought was that Ian had hold of a life-size doll and was just waving it about. Then it dawned on me that it was not a rag doll." The "doll" was actually Edward Evans, 17. Brady struck him repeatedly with an ax—the autopsy showed 14 times. To make the hideous deed certain, Brady strangled his victim.

The murder had been a "demonstration" murder for David Smith. He had a long juvenile record of violence and drank heavily. To Brady and Hindley, David seemed a perfect candidate to recruit to help them in their crimes. David, in shock, helped the couple clean up the mess and prepare the body for burial. As they swabbed the blood from the walls and floor, Brady made sick jokes about the victim being a bleeder, a deadweight, and a brainy swine. When David Smith got home, he became very sick and vomited for hours. He told his wife what had happened, and at 6 A.M., they went to the police.

Thus was uncovered one of the ghastliest series of child murders in England's history. The graves of two missing children, Leslie Ann Downey, 10, and John Kilbride, 12, were found. Brady and Hindley were suspected in at least 11 other murders or disappearances. Brady and Hindley denied any guilt in the hideous crimes, but Brady helped convict himself by taking a picture of Myra on the moors. She was looking down at a disturbed patch of dirt. Officers located the spot and dug up the body of John Kilbride.

Leslie Ann Downey, who had been missing for ten months, had been subjected to unspeakable horrors worse than her brutal death. Leslie Ann had been stripped, photographed in pornographic poses, and subjected to sexual abuse. During her torment, the callous pair had made a recording of her screams and pleas. Brady and Hindley then added seasonal Christmas music to the tape. Police found the tape recording of the last hours of her brief life. Hardened police officers—who thought they had seen and heard everything—said the tape of the murder in progress carried the most heartbreaking sounds they had ever heard.

During the trial, Hindley sat without expression. She even listened to the tape of Leslie crying and begging for her life without any sign of remorse, though several jurors and spectators wept openly. Brady was more emotional. When Myra Hindley told the jury that the ghastly murders were totally Brady's scheme, he burst into obscenities. Brady and Hindley were both found guilty and sentenced to life in prison.

During the trial, Myra Hindley appeared to be cool, calm, and collected. Unlike many others in the courtroom, Hindley showed no emotion when she listened to the audiotape of ten-year-old Leslie Ann Downey pleading unsuccessfully for her life.

BORN TO RAISE HELL

Convicted of the mass murder of eight nurses on the south side of Chicago, Richard Speck sits in Peoria County Courthouse awaiting transportation to Cook County Prison. The brain-damaged alcoholic might have gotten away with his crime if he had not lost count of the number of women whom he held captive.

RICHARD SPECK ENTERED A CHICAGO TOWNHOUSE AND KILLED EIGHT STUDENT NURSES WHILE A NINTH STUDENT NURSE HID

Richard Franklin Speck had a tattoo on his left arm: "Born to Raise Hell." Certainly Speck's life was one of hell-raising; it culminated in the killing of eight young women. Born in Illinois in 1941, he worked as a hand on Great Lakes freighters, and achieved distinction as a drunk and a drug user. He habitually shuttled between Texas and Illinois, running up an arrest record of 37 busts for a variety of offenses. Psychologists believed that many of his crimes were committed without awareness due to his brain damage caused by repeated batterings to the head early in his life.

On the night of July 13–14, 1966, 25-year-old unemployed Richard Speck, unable to get a job on a ship bound for New Orleans, sauntered along east 100th Street on Chicago's South Side in a drunken stupor. He wandered to the door of the townhouse numbered 2319, across the street from Luella Public Elementary School. Speck knocked, and student nurse Corazon Amurao, 23, opened the door. He flashed a gun and a knife. As he pushed his way inside, Speck assured her, "I'm not going to hurt you."

Speck ordered her upstairs, where he found five more women—three in one bedroom, two in another. He commanded the student nurses to lie on the floor in one of the bedrooms. Then he ripped a bed sheet into strips, which he used to tie up each student. Speck again promised his prisoners that he would not harm them.

At 11:30 P.M., Gloria Davy, 22, returned home. Speck directed her upstairs to join the others. He bound her without delay. Suzanne Farris, 21, arrived after midnight with 20-year-old Mary Ann Jordan, a guest for the night. Speck also tied them up. He announced, "I need your money to go to New Orleans." He rifled through their purses, wallets, dressers, and any other place where money might be kept.

Apparently in a muddled state, Speck sat on the floor toying with his gun. He then untied Pamela Wilkening, 20, and took her to an adjacent bedroom. Speck plunged his knife into her left breast and strangled her. Mary Ann Jordan and Suzanne Farris were seized next and pushed into a third bedroom. He killed Jordan with stabs to her neck, breast, and eye. Farris tried to fight off the knife-wielding freight hand, but he overpowered her, driving the knife into her 18 times. After she collapsed, he strangled her. He then ripped off her underclothing and tore them to shreds.

Speck took time to wash his hands before returning to his march of murder. In sequence, he killed Nina Schmale, 23; Valentina Pasion, 23; Marlita Gargullo, 23; and Patricia Matusek, 20. All were stabbed, strangled, or both. During this sequence, Amurao hid herself under a bed. Speck had apparently lost count of the number of women in the townhouse, and he never found Amurao.

From her position under the bed, Amurao watched Speck pull off Gloria Davy's jeans before raping her. Speck then took his final victim downstairs, and sodomized and killed her. Amurao, frozen with fear, remained cowering under the bed for hours.

After he left the townhouse, Speck shuffled along skid row on Chicago's Madison Street, barhopping. He drank incessantly for three days and spent three dollars on a prostitute.

Corazon Amurao's detailed information led to Speck's arrest. He was tried in the spring of 1967. After deliberating for 49 minutes, the jury found Speck guilty of murder and sentenced him to death. When the U.S. Supreme Court abolished capital punishment, Speck escaped the electric chair. He was resentenced in 1972 to a series of life terms totaling hundreds of years.

Corazon Amurao, the 23-year-old student nurse originally from the Philippines who greeted Richard Speck at the door of the townhouse in which she lived. She alone survived the ensuing slaughter by rolling under a bed when Speck's back was turned.

DEATH FROM A TEXAS TOWER

CHARLES WHITMAN'S ANGER AND HOSTILITY BURST OUT IN A RAMPAGE OF KILLING ON THE UNIVERSITY OF TEXAS CAMPUS

Damaged emotionally by his early home-life and his parents' recent separation, Charles Whitman, a former altar boy, also was discovered to have a small brain tumor when his body was autopsied. The combined physiological and psychological traumas might have ignited a murderous rage that only death could still.

Shortly before noon on August 1, 1966, 25-year-old architecture student Charles Joseph Whitman dollied a footlocker containing weapons into the 300-foot-high tower of the main building on the University of Texas at Austin. Whitman took the elevator to the 27th floor. He then carried the load up three half-flights of stairs to the observation level. Whitman clubbed Edna Townsley, the 47-year-old receptionist, to death and dragged her behind a couch. A young unsuspecting couple came in from the outside walk, said hello, and left. While Whitman unpacked his footlocker, a family of six tourists interrupted him. Whitman blasted them with a shotgun, killing Mark Gabour and Margaret Lamport, and injuring two others. He blocked the door with furniture, took three rifles to the observation walkway, and began shooting with deadly accuracy, hitting victims up to 500 yards away. In 90 minutes, he killed ten more people, including one unborn child.

Three Austin police officers and a deputized civilian crawled over bodies on the stairway leading to the observation level. They forced their way into the reception room. The four men moved outside and crouched behind the parapet to avoid the heavy gunfire coming from police and civilians below. They came from two directions and trapped Whitman in a corner of the rectangular walkway. Backed up by Officer Jerry Day, 40-year-old civilian Allen Crum moved along the building's south side and fired a blind shot around the corner toward Whitman. Simultaneously, Officers Ramiro Martinez, 29, and Houston McCoy, 26, stepped out from the northeast corner and fired. Martinez's revolver shots missed. As Whitman swung his rifle around to fire at the officers, McCoy hit him with two shotgun blasts to the head and neck. Martinez then grabbed McCoy's shotgun, ran to Whitman's still-moving body, and fired at point-blank range. It was 1:24 P.M.

Whitman was identified from papers on his body. Police rushed to Whitman's home, looked for his wife, and then went to his mother's

A young woman puts a statue between herself and sniper Charles Whitman as a man lies wounded on the grass nearby. The photo was taken by UPI staffer Tom Lankes, one of the first members of the press on the scene.

apartment. Whitman had murdered both women the night before. The death toll was 15.

That an ordinary college student with ordinary friends could suddenly become a cold and methodical killer stunned the nation. Acquaintances knew Whitman as an all-American boy; an Eagle Scout at age 12; a former altar boy; and a Scoutmaster.

But Whitman was consumed with hatred for his father—a rigid disciplinarian who beat his children and wife. Whitman's mother had left his father a few months earlier; this seemed to revive Whitman's recurring battles with violent impulses. Whitman visited the school psychiatrist, mentioning these impulses and an urge to go "up on the tower with a deer rifle and start shooting people."

During an investigation, police found letters written by Whitman. They told of Whitman's hatred for his father and his love for his wife and mother. Whitman felt he could no longer control himself and did not want to leave his wife and mother to suffer the consequences of the horrible thing he had to do. In one note, Whitman had asked for an autopsy to determine if he had any mental disorders. A walnut-size tumor was discovered, but its effects are disputed.

WHITMAN BLOCKED THE DOOR WITH FURNITURE, TOOK THREE RIFLES TO THE OBSERVATION WALKWAY, AND BEGAN SHOOTING WITH DEADLY ACCURACY, HITTING VICTIMS UP TO 500 YARDS AWAY.

AN UNSOLVED SUBURBAN MURDER

AN UNKNOWN ASSAILANT BROKE INTO A MANSION AND MURDERED THE YOUNG DAUGHTER OF A FUTURE U.S. SENATOR

Valerie Percy, one of twin 21-year-old daughters of Charles Percy, then U.S. senatorial candidate from Illinois. Although her murder is still listed among the unsolved cases, Illinois state police now believe that she was slain during a bungled burglary attempt by Frederick Malchow, who died a year after the crime.

On Sunday, September 18, 1966, beautiful Valerie Percy was beaten and stabbed to death in her family's English-style lakeshore mansion in Kenilworth, Illinois, an exclusive Chicago suburb. She was one of the 21-year-old twin daughters of Charles H. Percy, Illinois candidate for the United States Senate. The killer entered the 17-room home after cutting a hole in the patio glass door. He stealthily climbed the staircase. The murderer bypassed two bedrooms where two of the younger Percy children slept and entered the large bedroom where Valerie was sleeping. It was about 5 A.M.

Loraine Percy, Valerie's stepmother, was awakened by the sound of breaking glass. She thought one of the children had knocked a glass of water off a bedside table. However, when she heard moaning from Valerie's bedroom, she went to investigate. When she opened Valerie's door, a shadowy figure bending over the bed shined a flashlight in Loraine Percy's eyes. Mrs. Percy screamed and ran down the hall to set off the burglar alarm. Her screams woke up Charles Percy. He dashed to his daughter's room, but the intruder had fled. Mr. Percy called the police and a neighborhood doctor, who found Valerie dead from her wounds.

Illinois state police believe the murderer was Frederick J. Malchow, 40, a member of a gang that specialized in burglarizing the homes of the wealthy. Malchow allegedly admitted to another burglar that he had killed Valerie Percy while trying to silence her when she sat up in bed.

Malchow died in 1967 when he plunged from a train trestle into a river near Norristown, Pennsylvania. He was trying to escape only minutes after his conviction for the rape and robbery of a Norristown woman. The burglar convicted with Malchow in the same case later told police of Malchow's confession. A lie detector test supported the convict's story, as did other evidence that was uncovered. However, this was not enough to officially declare the crime solved.

A MAN OF PEACE FALLS

IN THE EARLY EVENING HOURS OF APRIL 4, 1968, ONE SHOT RANG OUT, AND AMERICA'S GREATEST CIVIL RIGHTS LEADER DIED

Dr. Martin Luther King, Jr., was a staunch advocate of human rights. King made speeches, preached, and participated in sit-ins and peace marches. He fought for the rights of all people, not just African-Americans, in every peaceful way possible. King never used any form of violence and never allowed his followers to do so. In 1964, King won the Nobel Peace Prize.

On April 4, 1968, King went to Memphis to organize a march in support of striking city sanitation workers. While standing on the balcony of his motel room about 6 P.M., King was shot in the neck by a sniper's bullet. Dr. King died instantly.

Dr. King's senseless murder set off riots in cities across the nation. Rioters burned stores, overturned cars, smashed windows, and threw rocks. Within a week, 39 people had been killed.

The fatal shot had been fired from a hotel across the street. On the pavement outside the hotel, police found a rifle with fingerprints on it. They traced a 1966 Mustang with a Los Angeles sticker as well as underwear with an L.A. laundry mark to California. Within days, James Earl Ray was added to the FBI's Most Wanted List.

While on the run, Ray used several aliases and fake passports as he crisscrossed North America and Europe. Even after the FBI circulated his picture, Ray was difficult to identify. Just before assassinating King, Ray had undergone plastic surgery on his face. James Earl Ray was finally captured in London, England, on June 8, 1968. From April 4 to June 8, the FBI had used 3,014 agents, traveled 500,000 miles, and spent $1,400,000 to find Ray.

Ray pleaded guilty and was sentenced to 99 years. Many authorities believe that Ray was part of a conspiracy. Ray himself mentioned a vague figure known only as Raoul who allegedly gave him thousands of dollars. In 1977, Ray escaped from his Tennessee prison; he was captured 54 hours later.

James Earl Ray before he had plastic surgery in 1967.

One fateful bullet killed Dr. Martin Luther King, Jr.

YOUNG GIRL MURDERS TWO BOYS

TWO YOUNG BOYS DIED, AND THE AGE OF KILLER MARY FLORA BELL, WHO WAS TEN YEARS OLD, SHOCKED THE WORLD

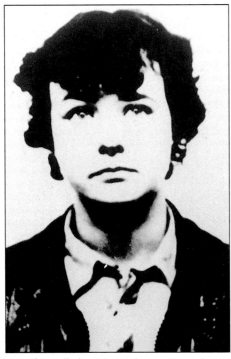

Mary Flora Bell, the pert prepubescent Newcastle, England, girl who was convicted in 1968 of killing two young boys. Highly intelligent, Mary made a lively and entertaining witness when she testified at her trial. She was freed when she was 22 after serving 11 years behind bars.

The trial of two young defendants charged with strangling two small boys began December 5, 1968, in Newcastle, England. The crime was hideous, but even more abhorrent were the ages of the accused killers: Mary Flora Bell was 11, and Norma Bell (no relation) was 13.

The Crown claimed the two girls had killed four-year-old Martin George Brown on May 25, 1968, and three-year-old Brian Howe on July 31, 1968. The slayings came amid a series of strange happenings. There were reports that Mary Flora Bell had tried to choke two young playmates. A day after Martin George Brown's murder, police found a crudely written note in a vandalized nursery school. The note included obscenities and said in part, ". . . we murder, watch out . . . ." Another note included a disturbing statement that "We did murder Martin Brown." On May 30, pretty, dark-haired Mary Bell, then only ten years old, went to the home of Brown's parents and asked with a smile to see him in his casket.

When questions began to arise concerning the death of Brian Howe, Mary Bell and Norma Bell accused each other of the murders. Norma Bell was acquitted in both cases. Mary Bell was convicted of choking both boys to death, as well as inflicting minor wounds on Howe with a scissors and razor blade. The final verdict was manslaughter, rather than murder. The jury ruled Mary had "diminished responsibility" at the time of the attacks.

Since there was no hospital available that met the requirements of England's Mental Health Act, the judge sentenced Mary to detention for life. She was confined in a correctional institution for boys. Although she was carefully segregated from the boys, there were still many problems. The lack of social services or mental institutions to accommodate the child shocked the world and brought a call for reform.

THE MIDEAST CONFLICT COMES HOME

DISGRUNTLED ARAB SIRHAN SIRHAN STOOD BEFORE PRESIDENTIAL CANDIDATE ROBERT F. KENNEDY IN LOS ANGELES AND FATALLY SHOT HIM

The assassin who killed Senator Robert F. Kennedy, brother of the late President John Kennedy, altered the course of American history. Robert Kennedy supported the Israeli cause. Sirhan Bishara Sirhan saw himself as a protector of the Palestinian people, as a soldier in a war, not as an assassin of a prospective president of the United States. Notebooks discovered in Sirhan's apartment specified that Kennedy had to die before June 5, 1968, the first anniversary of the beginning of the Arab-Israeli Six-Day War.

Just after midnight on June 5, Senator Kennedy had concluded a California primary victory speech during his campaign for the Democratic presidential nomination. Following a last-minute routing change, the Kennedy party headed through the hotel kitchen to a press conference in the hotel dining room.

Completely unaware, Kennedy walked straight into Sirhan's gun path. The killer fired his .22 caliber revolver. Two bullets entered Kennedy; one shattered his brain and ended his life. Five other people were also shot by Sirhan as he fired. Reacting instinctively, football star Rosey Grier, Olympic decathlon winner Rafer Johnson, and others jumped the assassin and wrestled him to the floor. Grier broke Sirhan's thumb while tearing the revolver from his hand.

In an unusual display of speed, the Los Angeles County Grand Jury indicted Sirhan on June 8, 1968, of first-degree murder, as well as five counts of assault with intent to kill. Sirhan pleaded not guilty. His trial was set for November 1, 1968, but legal actions delayed it until March 1969. The prosecution recounted Sirhan's hatred of Kennedy and Jews, and how Sirhan had stalked Kennedy that fateful night. Sirhan stated at the trial that he wanted to "blast" Kennedy because of his commitment to send 50 Phantom jets to Israel. The jury weighed the evidence and found Sirhan guilty of murder. He was sentenced to life in prison.

Sirhan Sirhan is held in a headlock under an upraised arm after shooting Robert F. Kennedy. The Arab fanatic was subdued within moments of the assassination by All-Pro tackle Rosey Grier, among others. Grier, in the foreground, broke Sirhan's thumb as he wrenched the gun from the assassin's grip.

BURIED ALIVE

KIDNAPPERS BURIED BARBARA
JANE MACKLE UNDERGROUND,
WITH ONLY A FEW BARE
NECESSITIES, AND SHE
SURVIVED THE 83-HOUR
ORDEAL

Barbara Jane Mackle, one year after her ordeal.

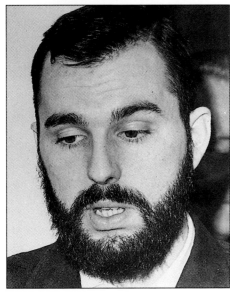

Gary Krist after being convicted of the kidnapping.

Barbara Jane Mackle grew up in Coral Gables, Florida. Wealthy but unspoiled, Barbara was a junior at Emory University in Atlanta. A bad case of the flu caused Barbara to check into a motel so her mother, who had arrived from Miami, could care for her. On December 17, 1968, two masked strangers burst into the motel room and kidnapped Barbara.

The kidnappers drove the sick 20-year-old woman to a lonely hillside near Atlanta. They buried her underground in a fiberglass and plywood capsule that measured two feet by two feet by eight feet. The coed had a breathing tube, jug of water, snacks, refuse bucket, fan, pump, and a light that quickly burned out. Her abductors told her there was enough power to provide fresh air for a week. If she overused the appliances, she would suffocate sooner. The criminals then returned to Miami to negotiate a ransom.

Condensation made the small capsule damp and cold. Unable to sit up or turn around, her body soon grew sore. To keep her sanity, Barbara prayed, sang, and imagined what her family was doing.

Barbara's parents contacted the FBI, and bank officers marked the $500,000 ransom money. The Mackles were horrified when local police—investigating a burglary—inadvertently appeared at the drop-off point for the ransom. Another ransom drop was made by 1952 Heisman Trophy winner Billy Vessels. When the kidnappers collected the cash, they phoned in Barbara's location. Racing against time, the FBI dug up the young woman. She was weak, but alive, after 83 hours without eating.

After a spectacular pursuit through Florida's swamps, the FBI captured Gary Krist and Ruth Eisemann-Shier. Krist, born in 1945 and of near-genius intelligence, had been in trouble most of his life. Eisemann-Shier, born in 1942, was shy and likable. Krist received a life sentence, and Eisemann-Shier got seven years in prison.

MURDER BY OMISSION, MURDER BY COMMISSION

DR. JOHN HILL WAS ACCUSED OF MURDERING HIS WIFE, JOAN ROBINSON HILL, BUT HE WAS SLAIN WHILE AWAITING TRIAL

John Hill, a prominent plastic surgeon, was Joan's third husband. They had married in 1958, but in the mid-1960s, Joan, a Houston socialite, learned about John's extramarital affairs. On March 17, 1969, Joan was stricken ill and taken to a hospital. On March 19, she died from a sudden heart failure.

Strangely, Joan's body was sent to a funeral home and partially embalmed before an autopsy could be performed. Joan's father, 70-year-old oil multimillionaire Ash Robinson, wanted his son-in-law charged with murder. Two grand juries didn't act, but a third indicted the 38-year-old Hill for "murder by omission," alleging that he purposely did not provide proper medical care for his ailing wife.

After Joan's death, Dr. Hill married Ann Kurth, his lover. Three months later, they divorced. At Hill's murder trial, Kurth stated that Hill had told her he killed Joan with an injection. This and other inadmissible statements caused a mistrial. In September 1972, before the state could retry Hill, a gunman shot and killed the doctor.

John Hill's family believed Ash Robinson, who was vengeful over the death of his only daughter, had commissioned Hill's death. Robinson denied it. Houston detectives arrested a 33-year-old Dallas hit man—Bobby Vandiver—for Hill's murder. Vandiver said a former Galveston brothel madam offered him $5,000 for the hit. Vandiver said he met the madam through his girlfriend, a 23-year-old prostitute. In April 1973, Vandiver and the madam were indicted for murder, with the prostitute as an accomplice.

Vandiver pleaded guilty in exchange for a lighter sentence and his testimony against the others. However, Vandiver escaped and was killed by police trying to capture him. The madam was convicted by the prostitute's testimony. Both women received prison terms. Ash Robinson, who won a wrongful death suit by John Hill's family, died of natural causes at age 87. He was never indicted.

HELTER SKELTER

CHARLES MANSON AND HIS "FAMILY" MASSACRED HOLLYWOOD'S "BEAUTIFUL PEOPLE" TO START A WAR OF AFRICAN-AMERICANS VERSUS WHITES

The son of a prostitute and an unknown father, Charles Manson began life as "No Name Maddox." Taking the name Manson when his mother married William Manson, he later claimed that his mother was an early "flower child." By the time he was in his teens, Manson was already considered to be extremely dangerous.

Born out of wedlock, Charles Manson was the illegitimate son of a 16-year-old girl named Kathleen Maddox who lived with a succession of men before marrying William Manson. As a child, Charles alternated his time between a very strict aunt and his promiscuous mother who let him do as he wished. At 12, he was sent to Gibault School for Boys. There he had "a tendency toward moodiness and a persecution complex." Charles ran home to his mother, who sent him back; he ran away again. He began to burglarize and was sent to juvenile centers, from which he ran away. Young Charles then started to steal cars. Manson committed his first armed robbery at age 13 before graduating to more serious crimes and further incarcerations. At the age of 17, when his aunt offered to supply him with a home and employment, his chances for leading a normal life looked good. Manson was due for a parole hearing. Instead he held a razor blade to another boy's throat and sodomized him. For that, Charles was sent to a federal reformatory.

Then Manson changed. He improved his work habits and education so much that in 1954, at the age of 19, he was granted parole to stay with his aunt and uncle. He joined his mother for a while, but in 1955 he married a 17-year-old girl. Although Manson took various jobs, he also stole cars, taking two or more across state lines. He drove one from Ohio to California where, accompanied by his pregnant wife, he was arrested. They ultimately got divorced.

In and out of jails for escalating offenses from robbery to procuring (prostitutes) to forgery, Manson had spent half his life in prison when he was finally released from jail in the late 1960s into a world of upheaval. Those were the days of LSD and heroin, of Flower Power and Stop the War, and of long-haired kids and nonstop sex. It was heaven to Manson.

By the age of 34, Manson had gathered together a group of drifters and hippies. Some of his "family" were misfits—young, middle-class girls who felt unwanted and craved love, freedom, and admiration. His family also included some ex-cons, bums, punks, and musicians. Manson made them feel important—part of an exciting mission.

These cultists worshipped Manson, viewing him as a mix of Jesus Christ and the devil. Often he played his guitar and sang. Under the guise of pseudoreligious rites, Manson led his group in free love, drug experimentation, and sexual perversions. As time went on, his followers also practiced guerrilla tactics.

After moving around awhile, he set up a commune at an old Hollywood filming location—the Spahn Ranch near Los Angeles. Various Hollywood personalities supplied money in the beginning so the Manson family could buy food and other necessities. At times, they raided garbage cans. One of the girls, Lynette "Squeaky" Fromme, was assigned to keep the elderly, half-blind owner of the ranch, George Spahn, happy.

Manson, who has a high IQ, believed a race war was imminent in which the African-Americans would conquer the whites. He called this war "Helter Skelter," and preached of it often to his followers, noting that it was also the title of a Beatles song. Manson's plan was to accelerate this war by murdering whites in such a way that the "pigs" (the establishment) would blame the African-Americans. Before the war's culmination, Manson and his family—comprised at its peak of more than 40 members—would escape to the hills.

In the summer of 1969, Manson started talking murder. Soon after, he shot an African-American drug dealer who had allegedly crossed him. The man recovered and didn't press charges.

Shortly thereafter, Manson sent cult members Bobby Beausoleil, Susan Atkins, and Mary Brunner to Gary Hinman's house. Supposedly

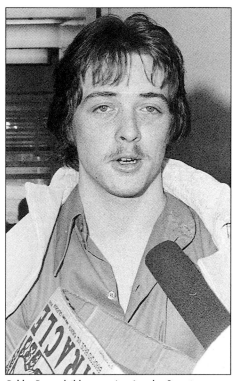

Bobby Beausoleil leaves a Los Angeles Superior courtroom in June 1970 after his plea for a new trial on charges of murdering Gary Hinman was rejected. Beausoleil had been arrested shortly after the Hinman slaying. Some Manson family members later claimed that the Tate murders were copycat versions of the Hinman crime.

AS HE UNLOADED HIS PISTOL INTO THE HAPLESS VICTIMS, WATSON KEPT SCREAMING, "I AM THE DEVIL AND I'VE COME TO DO THE DEVIL'S WORK!"

From left to right, Patricia Krenwinkel, Susan Atkins, and Leslie van Houten after being convicted of first-degree murder.

the purpose of their visit was to invite Hinman to join their family, but in reality it was to rob him of the $20,000 rumored to be in his possession. When Beausoleil called his leader to say he couldn't find the cash, Manson drove over and nearly cut off Hinman's ear with a sword. The gang made the victim sign over his cars before stabbing him, at Manson's orders, and leaving him to die. Beausoleil wrote "Political Piggy" in blood on the wall. He also drew a panther paw to make the police think the radical Black Panthers had committed the murder.

One week after Hinman was found, the police stopped Beausoleil, and seeing the transfer document to Hinman's car, they held him. The police also arrested family members Sandra Good and Mary Brunner for using stolen credit cards. Upset, Manson claimed it was time for Helter Skelter on August 9, 1969.

Charles "Tex" Watson, Patricia Krenwinkel, Susan Atkins, and Linda Kasabian—all part of the Manson family and high on hallucinogens—went to Cielo Drive in the hills above Hollywood. At the secluded home of film producer Roman Polanski, who was abroad, they murdered his pregnant wife Sharon Tate. In addition, they killed four others—Abigail Folger, coffee heiress; her lover, Voityck Frykowski, Polish writer and producer; Jay Sebring, noted hair stylist; and Steven Parent who had been visiting the mansion's caretaker. As he unloaded his pistol into the hapless victims, Watson kept screaming, "I am the devil and I've come to do the devil's work!" During the slaughter, the victims were stabbed, hanged, shot, and clubbed. Their blood was used to write slogans like "Pig" and "War" on the walls. The atrocities, according to Susan Atkins later, were copycat versions of Hinman's murder. Linda Kasabian, lookout for the killers, lost her nerve during the merciless massacre and later turned witness for the prosecution.

The murders caused panic in Hollywood. Manson was pleased. Within hours, he led the next slaughter himself. The Tate killers accompanied him; so did Clem Grogan and Leslie van Houten. As before, they were all high on drugs. The hideous scene of Cielo Drive was repeated at the home of Leno and Rosemary LaBianca. A fork was left in Leno's flesh and "War" was carved on his abdomen; "Helter Skelter" (misspelled), "Death to Pigs," and "Rise" were written in blood on the refrigerator and walls. After the murder, the group took showers, ate, and fed the victims' dogs.

Although Manson and 20 family members were arrested a few days later when the police raided the Spahn Ranch, it was for suspicion of car theft. No proof was found, and they were released.

In October, Bobby Beausoleil's girlfriend, who had quit the family once but returned, was taken to jail for the Hinman murder. She de-

Sharon Tate in 1965. When the beautiful film star begged to be spared for the sake of her unborn child, Susan Atkins said, "Look, bitch, I don't care . . . I have no mercy on you." Atkins, Patricia Krenwinkel, and Tex Watson then stabbed the actress 16 times, continuing long after she was already dead.

MANSON'S INFLUENCES

How could Charlie Manson—a little man of sparse schooling with a meager musical talent—control a group of mostly middle-class youngsters so much that they murdered many innocent people in the most gruesome, savage ways imaginable?

Manson apparently borrowed a number of teachings from Satanism. He claimed to be both Satan and Christ who had come together through "love."

Hitler, too, influenced Manson by precept and example. Manson saw himself as a similar leader who would shatter the future of African-Americans and save only his all-white "superior family." Like Hitler, Manson was a racist and sexist who was engrossed in the occult. Both men had "hypnotic" eyes and had others do their murdering. Manson and Hitler both believed killing for a cause was right. Both liked to have worshippers around. Hitler worried he had a Jewish ancestor; it's said that Manson feared his father was African-American. Fortunately, Manson's influence did not bring about the murder of millions of innocent people.

nied involvement but named the two women who were there—Susan Atkins and Mary Brunner. Although Atkins also denied the Hinman charge, she boasted to a cellmate, Virginia Graham, that she'd taken part in the Tate-LaBianca murders. At first, the woman thought she was crazy, hearing Atkins rave on about Charlie being "love, pure love" and how "it feels good when the knife goes in." But Graham told her friend Ronnie Howard, who occupied the same cell, about it. Hearing more, Graham realized the girl was telling the truth, but when she tried to tell lawmen, she was ignored. It was Howard, a former call girl, who finally reached someone who would listen, and the murder story reached the Los Angeles Police Chief.

As a result, Watson, Krenwinkel, Kasabian, and later Manson, Atkins, and van Houten were charged with the Tate-LaBianca slayings. Throughout the much-publicized trial, the women maintained Manson's innocence, shaving their heads in protest of his confinement. Not one showed remorse. Before long, all members of Manson's family involved in these murders, the Hinman slaying, and the killing of Donald "Shorty" Shea—a bit-part cowboy actor whose body was never found—were found guilty except for Linda Kasabian and Mary Brunner. In a separate trial, Bobby Beausoleil was given life imprisonment, as was Susan Atkins. Charles Manson and the others were sentenced to death. However, because the California Supreme Court abolished the death penalty in 1972, their sentences were altered to life imprisonment.

Manson boasted of having committed 35 murders. Although the exact number has never been established, Vincent Bugliosi, the prosecuting attorney, believed the amount may have even exceeded Manson's estimate.

ONE OF LABOR'S WORST SCANDALS

VIOLENCE WAS PART OF THE UNITED MINE WORKERS' HISTORY, BUT WHEN TONY BOYLE ORDERED JOSEPH YABLONSKI MURDERED, THE LAW INTERVENED

When John L. Lewis stepped down from the presidency of the American United Mine Workers Union, Joseph Albert Yablonski, who was close to Lewis, expected to replace him. Yablonski was disappointed; longtime member Tony Boyle was selected for the position.

Afterward, Yablonski was under the impression that Boyle had been embezzling funds from the union. Yablonski was further outraged when, after a West Virginia mine exploded in November 1968, Boyle praised the safety record of the mine's owners despite evidence to the contrary. Yablonski decided to challenge Boyle for the presidency of the union.

The United Mine Workers (UMW), in fighting to protect the rights of coal miners, had often used strong-arm tactics against anyone who didn't kowtow. By announcing his candidacy, Yablonski signed his death notice. When he lost to Boyle, Yablonski planned to go to court to contest what he felt was a dishonest election.

An investigation into the UMW's financial dealings was already underway. The entire affair made Boyle nervous. He decided Yablonski must die. Several people became involved in the conspiracy: Albert Pass, treasurer of the East Kentucky UMW branch, who was allegedly responsible for much of the union's violence; UMW representative William Prater, with whom Pass had already discussed murdering the head of a rival union; Silous Huddleston, president of a local union and supposedly one of the strong-arm boys; and Huddleston's son-in-law, Paul Gilly, who was talked into participating against his will. Gilly located Claude Vealey, a young burglar who, in

Former United Mine Workers Union president Tony Boyle (trenchcoat and hat) declines when newsmen invite him to comment following his conviction of ordering the 1969 murders of rival Joseph Yablonski and family. Federal investigators were amazed not so much by Boyle's involvement in the crime as by its incredible amateurishness.

turn, brought in James Phillips. Phillips was eventually replaced by Buddy Martin.

Gilly, Vealey, and Martin drove from Cleveland, Ohio, to Clarksville, Pennsylvania, on December 30, 1969. There they broke into Yablonski's house and shot him and his wife, Margaret, and daughter, Charlotte, as they lay in their beds. The killers then drove back through a snowstorm, and disposed of their guns by throwing them into a river.

The police learned that the three men, claiming to be out-of-work miners, had gone to Yablonski's home two weeks earlier. Apparently suspicious, their intended victim did not let them in and, in fact, copied down their car's license plate number. Police found this notation and located the name of the owner—Annette Huddleston Gilly. Her husband, Paul Gilly, was interviewed by the police.

Meanwhile, police heard that Claude Vealey was being loose-mouthed about the money that he had been paid. Vealey led the police to Buddy Martin and James Phillips, who explained the murder plan. Annette Huddleston Gilly, her husband, and her father were also arrested. Vealey confessed in an effort to bargain for his life, but Paul Gilly and Martin remained silent and drew death penalties.

Although the name Tony frequently appeared during the investigation, no connection was made to Tony Boyle until Annette Gilly talked. She showed investigators photos of Boyle with her father, thus revealing the identity of the "Tony" they kept hearing about. Later, another union leader, William Turnblazer, stated he had heard Boyle discussing the murder of Yablonski.

About to be arrested, Boyle made a vain suicide attempt. Prater, Pass, Turnblazer, and another union executive, Davis Brandenburg, were all found guilty. In 1974, Tony Boyle was given a life sentence for the murder of the Yablonskis.

Joseph "Jock" Yablonski challenged Tony Boyle for the presidency of the United Mine Workers Union, hoping to rid it of corruption. When he lost a tainted election, he contested it in court. Before the legal wheels could begin turning, union leaders secretly met to determine how to dispense their own justice.

1970–1979

AN EXTRAORDINARY NUMBER OF SERIAL KILLERS STALKED THE AMERI-
can scene during the so-called "Me Decade" of the 1970s. These insa-
tiably homicidal monsters included Ted Bundy, John Wayne Gacy, the
Hillside Strangler, Son of Sam, and Juan Corona. By far the most cata-
strophic crime of the decade was perpetrated by the Reverend Jim
Jones, whose "religious" exploits resulted in the deaths of 912 men,
women, and children. Less prolific but no less murderous were Green
Beret Dr. Jeffrey MacDonald and a death-obsessed ruffian named Gary
Gilmore. The 1970s also witnessed the kidnappings of rich kids Patty
Hearst and J. Paul Getty III, and the disappearance and presumed mur-
der of Teamster boss Jimmy Hoffa. On a gentler note, skyjacker D. B.
Cooper won lusting fame and public admiration for his larcenous and
possibly fatal hijacking of a Boeing 727 jetliner.

FAMILY MURDER

THE BRUTAL SLAYING OF
GREEN BERET CAPTAIN
JEFFREY MACDONALD'S WIFE
AND DAUGHTERS IS STILL AN
ENIGMA

Jeffrey MacDonald—doctor, Green Beret, murderer?

Colette, 26-year-old wife of Captain MacDonald.

FEBRUARY 1970

On the raw, rainy morning of February 17, 1970, military police at Fort Bragg, North Carolina, responded to a phone call from Captain Jeffrey MacDonald. They found a scene of carnage. In three separate bedrooms of the apartment were the bloody bodies of the captain's pregnant wife, Colette, 26, and their two daughters, five-year-old Kimberly and two-year-old Kristen. Captain MacDonald, 26, a Princeton-educated doctor from New York, was on the floor beside his wife, suffering from what were later revealed as only minor wounds.

The rooms showed few signs of a struggle. The word "pig" was scrawled in blood on the headboard of the bed in Colette's room. As medics attended him, MacDonald raved that a band of drug-crazed hippies had invaded the home, chanting "Acid is groovy, kill the pigs!"

Captain MacDonald said he was asleep on the living room couch when he was awakened by screaming. He fought with the intruders, who clubbed him and stabbed him in the chest. MacDonald described the frenzied attackers as three men accompanied by a woman with long, blonde hair who was wearing a floppy hat and carrying a candle.

Army investigators were skeptical of MacDonald's story. Six weeks later, with no break in the bizarre case, the Army announced that MacDonald himself was a suspect. However, a closed door hearing recommended that no charges be pursued against the captain. MacDonald applied for and received an honorable discharge.

In 1971, the Army's Criminal Investigation Division reopened the investigation. The FBI made extensive laboratory tests of bloodstains and other physical evidence. The agents again interrogated MacDonald. An informant offered a tip that a young woman in the hippie district of Fayetteville, North Carolina, matched MacDonald's description of the blonde. The woman and several of her men friends, all drug users, were questioned and discounted as suspects.

A June 1971 CID (Criminal Investigation Department) report to the Justice Department concluded that all evidence still pointed to the Green Beret doctor. The case remained at a stalemate until 1974, when the known facts were presented to a federal grand jury at Raleigh, North Carolina.

The grand jury heard 75 witnesses including MacDonald. On January 24, 1975, the grand jury indicted the doctor on three counts of murder. His trial took place in federal court in Raleigh. Federal prosecutors presented a strong circumstantial case based largely on the bloodstain evidence that showed untruths in MacDonald's story of what had happened. In August 1975, the jury found him guilty of second-degree murder in the deaths of Colette and Kimberly and first-degree murder in Kristen's killing, which the jury decided was calculated to cover up the other murders. Jeffrey MacDonald received three consecutive life sentences.

Acting on grounds that the long delay between the crime and the trial had denied the doctor's right to a speedy trial, the U.S. Fourth Circuit Court of Appeals in July 1980 set aside the trial verdict and ordered dismissal of the indictment. MacDonald was freed on bail, and he returned to California to resume his pre-trial lifestyle in a luxury condo, mixing with wealthy friends. However, his bubble burst in March 1983, when the U.S. Supreme Court reversed the appellate court action and ordered MacDonald back to prison to serve the sentences imposed at his trial. Two months earlier, the blonde hippie drug addict who had been a suspect died of natural causes.

In October 1990, MacDonald's attorneys filed a motion for a new trial, claiming that evidence in the FBI's possession had not been disclosed at the trial. The motion alleged that the evidence—black wool fibers and a blond wig strand found at the death scene—would verify MacDonald's story. The motion was pending at this writing.

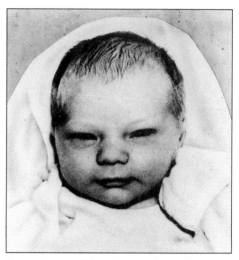

Younger daughter Kristen Jean, murdered at age two.

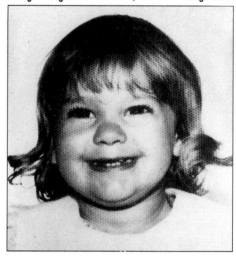

Older daughter Kimberly, killed at age five.

HARVEST OF MURDER

FARM-LABOR CONTRACTOR JUAN CORONA VICIOUSLY KILLED 25 DRIFTERS AND MIGRANT WORKERS

Convicted serial killer Juan Corona during a 1973 interview at the Vacaville Medical Facility in Vacaville, California. Corona drew 25 life sentences for killing 25 male vagrants and migrant workers, but many believe that he had at least one accomplice who went unpunished.

In the farming region around Yuba City, California, a mass grave of male corpses was discovered on May 19, 1971. The first body unearthed was that of transient Kenneth Whitacre. He had been stabbed to death and his head was mutilated by a machete. The authorities found gay literature in Whitacre's pocket and physical evidence of homosexual intercourse.

Four days later, on a nearby ranch, officers unearthed the mutilated body of an elderly man. By June 4, the bodies of 25 men ranging from age 40 to 68 had been found. Some corpses were naked; others partially clothed. The trousers of some had been left pulled around the victims' ankles. All of the bodies had been mutilated with a machete and bore evidence of homosexual encounters.

Found in two graves were bank deposit slips bearing the name Juan Corona. The 38-year-old Corona, a contractor supplying workers for seasonal fruit picking, had come from Mexico in the 1950s as a migrant laborer. Officers searched Corona's house and found blood-stained clothing and weapons, including a machete.

Corona, a schizophrenic, may have been involved in a 1970 Marysville, California, incident in which a severly beaten young Mexican man was discovered, alive, in the men's room of a cafe owned by Corona's homosexual half-brother, Natividad. The victim's head wounds were similar to those discovered on the 25 bodies unearthed in 1971.

Natividad had fled to Mexico after the young man recovered and successfully sued Natividad for assault. Juan remained in the United States and lived a seemingly normal life with a wife, children, and ordinary sexual tendencies.

At Corona's trial, the defense suggested that there were two killers and that neither of them was Corona. Nevertheless, the jury convicted Corona and sentenced him to 25 consecutive life sentences.

A DARING HIJACKING AND GETAWAY

AFTER HE COMMITTED THE FIRST SUCCESSFUL SKYJACKING OF AN AMERICAN AIRLINER, D. B. COOPER BECAME A NATIONAL LEGEND

On Thanksgiving Eve, 1971, a shy, polite, middle-aged man dressed in a business suit paid cash for a ticket on Northwest Airlines Flight 305 from Portland, Oregon, to Seattle. He told the ticket agent that his name was Dan Cooper. News reports later incorrectly identified the man as D. B. Cooper, an alias that held fast.

Shortly after takeoff, Cooper handed a flight attendant a note that he had a bomb. He showed her an odd device inside a case and calmly explained that he intended to blow up the Boeing 727 unless he was given $200,000 and two parachutes.

When the plane landed in Seattle, the hijacker's demands were met. Cooper allowed the passengers to leave the aircraft and ordered the crew to fly south to Reno. When the plane landed there, its rear bottom exit door was ajar, and Cooper was nowhere to be found.

Investigators believe Cooper bailed out somewhere over southwest Washington, into freezing darkness and dense clouds, with the $200,000. This theory was proven correct nine years later. Near Frenchman's Bar on the Washington side of the Columbia River, eight-year-old Brian Ingram found packets of tattered, water-soaked $20 bills, totaling nearly $6,000, embedded in sand. The serial numbers matched those of Cooper's ransom money.

Ralph Himmelsbach, assigned to the FBI's Portland office, investigated the hijacking for nine years until his 1980 retirement. He believes Cooper died in the jump. Others disagree—mostly because no trace of Cooper's body had ever been found.

Cooper's intrepid crime, the first of its kind, stunned the world and created a legend that continues to live on. The hijacking of Flight 305 on November 24, 1971, remains the only unsolved airliner hijacking in U.S. history. The true identity of D. B. Cooper, as well as whether or not he survived the jump, remains a mystery.

An artist's conception of skyjacker D. B. Cooper. This sketch is based on the recollections of the passengers and crew on the Boeing 727 hijacked on Thanksgiving Eve, 1971. Lacking fingerprints or any other tangible physical evidence, the FBI never identified the quiet middle-aged man who called himself "Dan Cooper."

MUTUAL FUND FRAUD

AN INGENIOUS SCHEME REPORTEDLY NETTED FUND MANAGER ROBERT VESCO A GREAT DEAL OF MONEY

Stockholders of Investors Overseas Services thought at first that Robert Vesco was their savior. But instead of helping the ailing mutual fund empire avoid bankruptcy, the slick financier siphoned off $224 million from the firm's coffers and fled to Costa Rica, chosen probably because it has no extradition agreement with the U.S.

In 1968, Investors Overseas Services (IOS), a financial services company based in Geneva, Switzerland, professed to have $2.1 billion in assets. However, by 1971, the firm's founder, Bernard Cornfeld, had mismanaged company finances and IOS was approaching bankruptcy. At that time, Robert Vesco, who had loaned IOS five million dollars, took over the company in order to "rescue" it—or so the stockholders thought. According to a December 1972 civil suit filed by the U.S. Securities and Exchange Commission (SEC), Vesco, instead of bringing salvation, drained most of the firm's remaining assets, reportedly at least $224 million.

A Vesco-controlled group used a minimum amount of money to hastily set up "shell" banks and corporations in Europe, Costa Rica, and the Bahamas. Starting in April 1972, Vesco and his group then allegedly looted three major mutual IOS funds. They simply transferred the assets of the three IOS funds to the banks and corporations that Vesco controlled, and sold nearly a quarter of a billion dollars worth of their newfound blue-chip stock. The SEC said that $99 million had simply vanished, while $125 million was stashed in banks controlled by Vesco in Luxembourg and the Bahamas.

During the time that the mutual fund fraud was going on, Vesco tried to conceal his part by pretending he was not involved in IOS. He resigned as its chairman, sold his stock, and bought it back through another dummy corporation that he owned.

By the time the SEC investigation had implicated Vesco, he had disappeared. The FBI searched for four years before locating him in Costa Rica. However, Costa Rica has no extradition agreement with the United States. In addition, when he arrived in Costa Rica, Vesco reportedly put $25 million into low-cost public housing, a water distribution system, and Costa Rica's nationalized banks. According to the latest information, Vesco was paying the Costa Rican government $100,000 a month for "rent."

LOST AN EAR TO ITALIAN KIDNAPPERS

BEING THE TEENAGE GRANDSON OF AN OIL BILLIONAIRE WAS A TICKET TO PERSONAL DISASTER FOR J. PAUL GETTY III

J. Paul Getty III with his mother, former actress Gail Harris Getty, as they arrive in a police car at Rome police headquarters on the night that his kidnappers released him. Behind the car, a photographer attempts to capture the teenage heir from an angle that will show his missing right ear.

Sixteen-year-old J. Paul Getty III was a red-haired and freckled teenager who dropped out of school in the ninth grade. He lived the life of a drifter in the bohemian section of Rome, Italy. Young Getty dabbled in painting and sold handmade jewelry to tourists. Not that he was the average Italian child of the streets. The carefree American youth was the grandson of U.S. oil billionaire J. Paul Getty, Sr.

On the night of June 10, 1973, the teenage Getty was last seen in central Rome's seamy Piazza Navona, known as a hippie habitat. A 20-year-old go-go dancer later told police that she watched the long-haired Getty walk away in anger after she rejected his invitation to go to a seaside resort. Two days later, Paul's mother, ex-actress Gail Harris Getty, who lived in a plush Rome apartment, received a phone call that said her son had been kidnapped. The caller demanded $17 million in ransom.

The tearful mother told reporters that her ex-husband, a wealthy man in his own right, and the boy's oil tycoon grandfather, both living

THE TEARFUL MOTHER TOLD REPORTERS THAT HER EX-HUSBAND, A WEALTHY MAN IN HIS OWN RIGHT, AND THE BOY'S OIL TYCOON GRANDFATHER REFUSED TO PAY THE RANSOM.

in Great Britain, refused to pay the ransom. The oil billionaire was quoted in the press as saying that if he paid ransom money for one of his grandchildren, he would eventually have to pay ransom for the other 14.

For five months there was no trace of the missing teenager. Rome's national police conducted an intensive search, but it was discontinued at the request of his family, who feared for his life. There were even rumors that the kidnapping was a hoax, or that the boy himself was involved.

When a Rome newspaper received a human ear and a lock of hair said to be young Getty's, the worst was feared. More mutilation was threatened if the ransom was not paid.

On the night of December 15, 1973, a truck driver spotted a boy standing in the rain along the superhighway between Naples and Sicily, desperately waving to motorists who didn't stop. Fearing a possible robbery, the trucker drove on past the lad and called the police. They picked up the soaked youth, who identified himself as J. Paul Getty III. His right ear was missing. He told the police that he had been held in various mountain hideouts during his captivity.

It was revealed that his father had paid $2.5 million in ransom after the ear was sent to the Rome newspaper. In time, eight members of the kidnap gang, who belonged to a Mafia branch called the Calabria, were arrested for the abduction. On July 28, 1976, six of the defendants were acquitted of any complicity in the kidnapping. (Five of them, however, were convicted of possession of and trafficking in narcotics.)

Found guilty of kidnapping Getty were Giuseppe la Manna, who was sentenced to 16 years in prison, and Antonio Manguso, who received an eight-year sentence.

THEY MADE HER A TERRORIST

PUBLIC SYMPATHY WAS WITH KIDNAPPING VICTIM PATTY HEARST—FOR A WHILE

Born in San Francisco in 1954, Patricia Hearst was the daughter of millionaire newspaper publisher Randolph Hearst. She was raised in an affluent world of large homes and country clubs. The Hearsts neither spoiled nor overindulged their five daughters. Mrs. Hearst was very strict and often cautioned the girls about kidnappers.

While attending a rigid private high school, Patty was repeatedly disciplined despite her attempts to follow the rules. When she complained, the Hearsts transferred Patty to a small day school for her junior year. She vindicated their faith by graduating from high school a year early.

At the second school, Patty fell in love with math instructor Steven Weed. A year later, when Weed won a fellowship at the University of California at Berkeley, Patty moved in with him and enrolled as a student there. Although Patty and Weed were engaged, they set no wedding date. Patty became disenchanted with Weed.

Patty's life changed completely on February 4, 1974, when four members of the Symbionese Liberation Army—an obscure terrorist organization—broke into her apartment, beat Weed, and kidnapped her. Threatening the gagged and blindfolded 20-year-old girl, the group drove her to a San Francisco house and locked her in a smelly closet.

For two months Patty stayed in the closet, bound and sightless. The blindfold, wet from her tears, irritated her skin. Having no appetite, she lost weight and her strength ebbed. For a long time, her only exercise came from her trips to the bathroom. She had no privacy. But worse than anything else was the constant political propaganda that the SLA members forced on her. Terrified for her life, nearly always kept in the closet, she wondered if her captors were right—that her country was involved in a revolution, that the FBI was composed of enemies who would kill her and blame the SLA, and that the rich

A photo of Patty Hearst, automatic weapon in hand, after she was designated a fugitive rather than a kidnapping victim. Arrested more than a year and a half after her abduction, she was later convicted of bank robbery and served 22 months of her seven-year sentence in prison.

were "pigs" who robbed "the people." Patty's only chance for life was to act as if she believed in her captors' cause.

The SLA forced Patty to make audiotapes that were sent to her parents. The first tape was accompanied by a message telling Randolph Hearst that he must finance and organize a Feed the People give-away. Hearst was told that Patty was in "protective custody." The paper that carried the message bore a logo of a seven-headed cobra. The multiple heads represented the SLA's diverse aims: self-determination, cooperative production, creativity, unity, faith, purpose, and collective responsibility. The group's motto was "Death to the Fascist insect that preys upon the life of the people."

Hearst was ordered to distribute $400 million worth of food to the needy. The kidnappers also demanded that two SLA members—Russell Jack Little and Michael Remiro—be released from Soledad Prison. The two had been incarcerated for the murder of a school superintendent who had committed "crimes against the people"—specifically, he had worked with the police to reduce juvenile crime. The SLA wrote to Hearst that Patty would remain captive until the SLA's "soldiers" were released.

Negotiations began, and very quickly, the story became the media event of the decade. The drama became more tense when it became apparent that Randolph Hearst could not meet the kidnappers' demands. Frantic, he started a two-million-dollar food distribution campaign. He put up half a million dollars himself; the rest came from the William Randolph Hearst Foundation. The SLA considered this amount "a few crumbs" tossed to the people.

Ten days after the food program began, the terrorists gave the exhausted Patty a chance to join them. Knowing that it meant her life, she agreed. When her blindfold was removed, she saw eight scruffy people. Though Americans, each had assumed a Swahili name.

Officers lead Russell Little (front) and Michael Remiro from the Contra Costa County courthouse. The two SLA members had been implicated in the execution slaying of Oakland School Superintendent Marcus Foster. When they were refused a nationally televised press conference, the SLA broke off negotiations for Patty Hearst's release.

Thirty-year-old escaped convict Donald DeFreeze—"General Field Marshal Cinque Mtume" ("Cin")—was the SLA's founder and leader. The others included "Cujo" (William Wolfe), "Gelina" (Angela Atwood), "Gabi" (Camilla Hall), "Zoya" (Patricia Soltysik), "Fahizah" (Nancy Ling Perry), and "Teko" and his wife "Yolanda" (William and Emily Harris). Patty was dubbed "Tanya."

By the time she had been released from the closet and indoctrinated in SLA technique and ideology, Patty was too immersed in the whole absurd experience to consider escaping. Her will to resist eliminated, she found herself an accomplice of her captors.

Patty's ultimate test was yet to come: She was expected to take part in a bank robbery on April 15, 1974. Ironically, the president of the target bank was the father of Patty's best friend. Surveillance-camera pictures taken during the robbery showed the rifle-toting Patty, apparently a willing participant albeit with three guns pointed at her. A warrant for her arrest was sworn out that day.

On May 17, 1974, the SLA hideout in Los Angeles was discovered and attacked by 150 police officers. Over 6,000 shots were exchanged, and the six members who were inside, including leader Donald DeFreeze, were killed. Fortunately, on that day, Patty was with William and Emily Harris. Although Patty despised the couple, she ran with them for 16 more months.

The FBI finally arrested Patty Hearst on September 18, 1975. She was convicted of bank robbery the following year and sentenced to a seven-year term, but President Jimmy Carter reduced her sentence. After 22 months in prison, she was freed.

Patty Hearst married a lawman (not Steven Weed) and became a society matron. In 1990, she spoofed herself by playing a conservative suburban mother in the movie comedy *Cry Baby*.

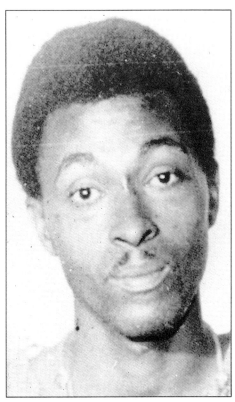

A 1969 police photo of Donald DeFreeze, founder and "General Field Marshal" of the Symbionese Liberation Army. DeFreeze called himself "Cinque," taking the name of the leader of a slave-ship revolt during the 1830s. DeFreeze's revolutionary outfit had its roots in the African-American prison population in California.

PYRAMIDING OILDRILL SCAM

ROBERT TRIPPET'S OIL
SWINDLE SHEARED $130
MILLION FROM 2,000
(MOSTLY) RICH AND
FAMOUS PEOPLE

Charming Oklahoma lawyer Robert S. Trippet organized Home-Stake Production Company, an oil- and gas-drilling corporation, in 1955. Trippet's Home-Stake Production Company went public in 1964, offering investors a nice tax shelter and massive profit returns, too.

Using the name of cousin Oscar Trippet—lawyer, civic leader, president of the Los Angeles Chamber of Commerce and Hollywood Bowl—Robert made important contacts in the California showbiz community. Trippet found no shortage of eager opportunists. The list of the duped included Candice Bergen, Jack Benny, Walter Matthau, Liza Minnelli, Andy Williams, Barbra Streisand, and hundreds more. Senators Ernest Hollings and Jacob Javits and Florida's Governor Claude Kirk were among the political powers who were taken in.

Robert Trippet's scheme followed the basic scam that pays early investors large profits or dividends from funds invested by later contributors. It was later charged that very little cash was actually used for drilling. In a dramatic hoax, Trippet's company camouflaged a vegetable farm by painting its irrigation pipes oil-field orange and erecting derricks to simulate actual pumping.

The tower tumbled in 1973, when a suit was filed by the Securities and Exchange Commission (SEC), and Trippet's company went bankrupt. A separate, criminal investigation ordered by the SEC stated on June 26, 1974, that of the reported intake of $130 million, $100 million had apparently vanished.

Criminal charges brought Robert Trippet before the federal court. Trippet changed his pleas of not guilty to nolo contendere (no contest), which U.S. District Court Judge Allen Barrow stated was identical to guilty. On December 21, 1976, he sentenced Trippet to pay $19,000 and ordered him to deposit $100,000 for restitution to widows and orphans who were cheated out of their money. Trippet never served time, but he was put on probation for three years.

THE MURDEROUS NOBLEMAN

THE BUNGLING LORD LUCAN MISTAKENLY KILLED HIS CHILDREN'S NANNY

About 9:45 P.M. on November 7, 1974, Lady Veronica Lucan burst into London's Plumber's Arms pub and hysterically cried, "Help me . . . he murdered the nanny." Her children's British nanny, Sandra Rivett, had been bludgeoned to death in the Lucan home. Lady Lucan had also been attacked, but she survived, and Lady Lucan was sped to St. George's Hospital. At the Lucan home, officers discovered a blood-stained, nine-inch lead pipe wrapped in tape.

The hospital doctors attended to Lady Lucan's scalp wounds and numerous cuts inside her mouth. On the next morning, she formally accused her husband, Richard John Bingham, 7th Earl of Lucan (Lord Lucan), 39, of murdering Mrs. Sandra Rivett and also attempting to murder her.

The accused was an indebted gambler, separated from his wife and family. He had lost his children in a custody case and became obsessed with a desire to regain them.

On the night of the attacks (nanny Sandra Rivett's night out), Lucan sneaked into the house and hid. He unscrewed the basement light bulb and waited for his wife to descend for her nightly tea in the basement breakfast room. Footsteps announced an approaching woman, whom Lucan viciously clubbed to death. As he doubled the body over and pressed it into a mailbag, he heard a call from the house upstairs: "Sandra . . . Sandra . . . ." Lucan immediately realized that he'd killed the nanny, not his wife, so he waited for her to enter the basement. He attacked, and Veronica fought back, tore at his private parts, and escaped to the pub. When police arrived at the house, Lord Lucan had vanished.

Lucan phoned his mother, imploring her to take the children. He drove to the English Channel, took his speedboat out, and scuttled it.

A coroner's inquest on June 16, 1975, concluded that Rivett's death was "murder by Lord Lucan." Lucan is still unaccounted for.

Richard John Bingham, the 7th Earl of Lucan, and his wife Veronica in 1964. Lord Lucan vanished in November 1974 after slaying a servant whom he mistook for his wife. Seven months after his disappearance, a coroner's jury named Lucan the killer *in absentia.*

WHITHER JIMMY?

WHEN FORMER TEAMSTER PRESIDENT JIMMY HOFFA MADE A QUICK EXIT, FOUL PLAY SEEMED EVIDENT

Jimmy Hoffa, right, seated at a table beside his bespectacled attorney, testifies before a packed house. At the time of his mysterious disappearance, the former Teamsters head was barred from engaging in union activities. However, it was thought that he still was pulling the strings from behind the scenes.

As president of the International Brotherhood of Teamsters for 19 years, James R. Hoffa ruled a union two million men strong. He could cripple a city by halting the transportation of trucked goods. Jimmy Hoffa's political power could elect judges and senators. He controlled a pension fund with reserves of $400 million. Much of his power came from reputed Mafia connections.

Jimmy Hoffa was born in Brazil, Indiana, in 1913. His father died when Jimmy was seven. Hoffa's family moved to Detroit in 1924. He quit school at 14. Hoffa organized unions for the Teamsters in the 1930s and became president of the Michigan Teamsters by 1942. In 1952, Hoffa was elected an international vice president of the Teamsters. Five years later, he became international president.

Law enforcement agencies, aware of Hoffa's underworld connections, worked unsuccessfully throughout the late 1950s and most of the 1960s to imprison him. In 1967, Hoffa was convicted of jury tampering, fraud, and conspiracy, and sentenced to 13 years in prison. Hoffa refused to give up the union presidency while in prison. He remained Teamster president until 1971, when President Nixon commuted Hoffa's sentence.

On July 30, 1975, Hoffa left home and headed to a suburban Detroit restaurant to meet Detroit racketeer Anthony Giacalone and Anthony Provenzano, a New Jersey Teamster official and former Mafia figure. Although Hoffa reached the restaurant, nothing else is known. One rumor stated that Hoffa left the restaurant's parking lot in a car, shouting, his hands tied behind him.

Another rumor said that Teamsters killed Hoffa, crammed him into an oil drum, and buried it in a garbage dump. Other stories placed Hoffa's body in swamps, in building cornerstones, even in an NFL football stadium. Nevertheless, Hoffa apparently was killed shortly after his disappearance. No suspects have been arrested.

THE SEWER GANG

ALBERT SPAGGIARI WAS THE BRAIN OF A FRENCH GANG THAT TUNNELED INTO A BANK VAULT AND NETTED TEN MILLION DOLLARS

When the vault door of the largest bank in Nice, France, wouldn't open in July 1976, officials used jackhammers to open the door, which had been welded shut from the inside. Astonished officials saw a stove, food, empty wine bottles, and chamber pots (which served as toilets). They also saw that ten million dollars was missing.

The vault, protected by 18 inches of reinforced concrete, had been entered by a narrow, 30-foot-long tunnel connected to a sewer.

A week before the crime, a policeman had spotted a suspicious car and occupants. The car contained some chisels made for hammering through reinforced concrete. The policeman had let the car go, but after hearing of the heist, he recalled the chisels and the driver's name, Daniel Michelucci.

On July 9, before the robbery, a villa that was supposed to be empty was reported to have people in it. The five inhabitants identified themselves and gave satisfactory explanations. One of the men was Michelucci.

The police tailed the five known members of "the Sewer Gang." Two men were caught trying to sell gold ingots whose numbers coincided with those stolen in Nice. The police then arrested 27 persons connected with the heist. One was Albert Spaggiari.

Spaggiari admitted he was "the brain." Two years before, he had rented a box in the vault and photographed the inside. He couldn't afford the necessary tools, so he went to the Marseilles (France) mob with his idea. They agreed to back him. It took two months to dig the tunnel. On Friday, July 17, when the bank closed for the weekend, they pierced the final 18 inches of reinforced concrete.

Then the thieves completed their history-making heist. And except for a policeman's excellent memory, the Sewer Gang might now be basking on the Riviera instead of being in jail.

Albert Spaggiari, leader of the Sewer Gang. He secretly took pictures of the interior of the largest bank in Nice, France. Then he and his gang dug a tunnel into the bank's vault. The bold robbery netted the gang ten million dollars, but none remained free long enough to enjoy their spoils.

ARROGANT KILLER DEMANDED THE DEATH PENALTY

GARY GILMORE'S EXECUTION MARKED THE RETURN OF CAPITAL PUNISHMENT IN AMERICA

Gary Gilmore moves through reporters before hearing Judge J. Robert Bullock set the date of his execution by firing squad. Gilmore told the judge that he wanted to stand and not wear a leather hood at his execution. However, his request was denied; Gilmore died strapped to a chair.

Gary Gilmore was born in Texas on December 4, 1940. He was raised in Portland, Oregon, where he earned a reputation as the kind of kid who was always in trouble. He hated his alcoholic father, but deeply loved his mother and younger brother. They loved him in return, but their affection could not keep him from going bad.

And Gilmore went bad with a vengeance. At age 12, he stole cars and burglarized houses along his paper route; at age 14, he stole firearms. Around that time, he was rebuffed in his attempt to join an adult criminal gang. Shortly thereafter, he was convicted of auto theft. There followed an 18-month term in a reformatory, where he further honed his already well-developed criminal instincts.

Following his release from the reformatory, Gilmore continued to get into trouble. Intelligent and artistically gifted (he had a genuine flair for painting and drawing), he nevertheless seemed incapable of turning his life around. By age 22, a robbery conviction had netted him a 15-year term in a federal prison, where psychiatrists labeled him a "classic sociopath" who presented a significant threat to society.

Gilmore was paroled in April 1976. He moved to Orem, Utah, where relatives provided him with a job and a place to live. He was soon drinking heavily and devouring pain killers. But neither alcohol nor drugs could calm his raging spirit. On the night of July 19, 1976, he drove to a local gas station armed with a .22 caliber pistol. There he confronted the attendant, a 24-year-old law student named Max Jensen, with a demand for money. Jensen gave him $150. Gilmore then ordered Jensen into the washroom, instructed him to kneel, and fired two bullets into his brain, killing him.

The next day Gilmore drove to Provo in search of his estranged girlfriend, Nicole Baker. Needing more money, he parked his car at a gas station and walked two blocks to a motel. The motel clerk on duty was Bennie Bushnell, age 25. After robbing Bushnell at gunpoint,

Gilmore forced the frightened young man to lie facedown on the floor and shot him in the back of the head.

Once outside, Gilmore accidentally shot himself in the hand as he threw his gun into a bush. When he returned to the gas station to pick up his car, the attendant saw Gilmore's bloody hand and notified the police. Gilmore was arrested a short time later. Tried and convicted on two counts of murder, he soon found himself back in prison, this time on Utah's death row.

Against his lawyers' advice, Gilmore appeared before the Utah Supreme Court, which was to hear his appeal. Instead of fighting for his life, however, Gilmore arrogantly informed the justices that he had been given a fair trial. Moreover, he insisted that his sentence be carried out as soon as possible. Four out of five judges ruled in his favor. Gilmore was then given a choice: execution by hanging or by firing squad. Gilmore chose the bullet over the rope. Yet he tried to hasten the hour of his death by twice overdosing on drugs after making a suicide pact with his girlfriend, Nicole. He recovered from both attempts, and it is quite probable that he didn't want to die in either instance.

Gilmore's impending execution became the focus of a media circus in which Gilmore himself was the star attraction. He relished the attention. Gilmore ensured his lasting fame by selling the rights to his story to journalist Lawrence Schiller. Author Norman Mailer also got involved, and his subsequent Pulitzer Prize–winning book about Gilmore, *The Executioner's Song,* was eventually made into a movie.

By that time Gary Gilmore was dead. His execution occurred on January 17, 1977. Gilmore was strapped to a chair in the compound of the Utah state prison and shot by four Salt Lake City policemen armed with rifles. It was the first execution in the United States in more than ten years.

GILMORE THEN ORDERED JENSEN INTO THE WASHROOM, INSTRUCTED HIM TO KNEEL, AND FIRED TWO BULLETS INTO HIS BRAIN, KILLING HIM.

THE MISSING CANDY HEIRESS

HELEN VOORHEES BRACH WAS DROPPED OFF AT THE AIRPORT ONE DAY AND NEVER SEEN AGAIN

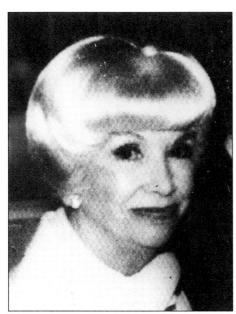

Candy heiress Helen Brach, shown wearing a wig. Fourteen years after her disappearance in February 1977, it remains a mystery as to whether she was murdered or whether she vanished of her own free will.

The third wife of candy magnate Frank Brach became one of America's richest women when he died in 1970 and left her $21 million. Helen Voorhees Brach had come a long way from the Ohio coal mines where her father had toiled. Following her husband's death, she lived as a wealthy recluse in Glenview, Illinois, a Chicago suburb. She did, however, spend time at her Florida condominium.

Following a New York visit, Helen Brach was met on February 17, 1977, at Chicago's O'Hare Airport by longtime Brach employee Jack Matlick. He drove her home, where she remained for four days. Authorities initially doubted that Matlick delivered the widow back to O'Hare on February 21 for a Fort Lauderdale flight. Brach had not purchased a ticket and she had not boarded any flight to Florida—at least not under her own name. Helen Brach had simply vanished.

An investigation revealed that Matlick had purchased a nine-pound meat grinder and had scoured Brach's Cadillac after returning from the airport on February 21. Bank records revealed that 11 forged checks, most made out to Matlick, were drawn on Brach's account.

When asked why he did not report Brach's disappearance for nearly two weeks, Matlick explained that he had informed Helen's brother, Charles Voorhees, who traveled to the Brach estate from Ohio. Together they burned Mrs. Brach's diaries. Were the two men in collusion? The authorities apparently did not think so, because neither man was prosecuted, despite Matlick failing two lie detector tests when he responded negatively to the question, "Do you know where Mrs. Brach is?" Charles Voorhees offered a reward of $250,000 for Brach's discovery. There were no takers.

On May 23, 1984, Helen Brach was declared legally dead. That freed the estate and gave Charles Voorhees $200,000. In late 1990, a headless body was exhumed in a Chicago suburb. Doubts remain about whether the body had belonged to Brach.

THE GREATEST MANHUNT IN NEW YORK CITY'S HISTORY

THE "SON OF SAM" WAS A PARANOID LONER WHO NURSED HIS HATRED FOR WOMEN INTO A DEADLY SHOOTING SPREE

David Richard Berkowitz was born out of wedlock in Brooklyn on June 1, 1953. His mother gave him up for adoption shortly thereafter. According to psychiatrists who examined him many years later, the trauma of this rejection fostered in Berkowitz the violent, bizarre behavior that would one day characterize his actions as the so-called "Son of Sam" killer.

As a child and teenager, Berkowitz was a prolific arsonist with above-average intelligence and desperately low self-esteem. A decent job with the U.S. Postal Service in the Bronx did nothing to improve his mental state. He became a loner, withdrawn and paranoid. In time, his low self-esteem mutated into an enduring hatred for women. In December 1975, Berkowitz's malice found expression in knife attacks against two separate women. Both victims survived.

Berkowitz then exchanged his knife for a powerful .44 caliber Bulldog revolver. On the night of July 29, 1976, he used this weapon to shoot Donna Lauria and Jody Valenti in a parked car. Lauria was killed, and Valenti was seriously wounded.

Berkowitz struck again on October 23, 1976. Attacking, as always, at night, he shot at Carl Denaro and Rosemary Keenan in a parked car in Flushing, New York. Denaro suffered a crippling wound to one of his fingers; Keenan was unhurt. On November 26, Berkowitz shot Donna DeMasi and Joanne Lomino on the front stoop of a house in Queens. Neither was killed, but DeMasi was paralyzed from her waist down.

By then, panic over the shootings gripped the metropolitan New York City area. The search for the elusive killer involved hundreds of police and detectives, and eventually led to the formation of a multiunit task force led by Deputy Inspector Timothy J. Dowd. The pursuit of the ".44-caliber killer", as he was initially called, became the greatest manhunt in the city's history.

David Berkowitz, "Son of Sam." Berkowitz supposedly took his name from Sam, a neighbor's dog that harbored his father's evil spirit. Nobody knows whether Berkowitz was insane or merely a clever actor.

AS A CHILD AND TEENAGER, BERKOWITZ WAS A PROLIFIC ARSONIST WITH ABOVE-AVERAGE INTELLIGENCE AND A DESPERATELY LOW SELF-ESTEEM.

On January 30, 1977, Berkowitz shot and killed Christine Freund in a parked car in New York's Ridgewood neighborhood. On March 8, he murdered Virginia Voskerian in Forest Hills. On April 17, his .44 claimed the lives of Alexander Esau and Valentina Suriani, both shot in the same parked car in the Bronx.

At the site of the Esau-Suriani killings, Berkowitz dropped off a letter in which he explained that his orders to kill had come from barking dogs that were actually demons. A certain dog named Sam was possessed by his father's evil spirit; hence, he signed the letter "Son of Sam." In subsequent letters to police and newspaper columnist Jimmy Breslin, the Son of Sam taunted his pursuers and warned of future attacks.

He was as good as his word. On June 26, 1977, he shot and wounded Salvatore Lupo and Judy Placido in a parked car in Queens. On July 31, he shot Stacy Moskowitz and Robert Violante in a parked car in Brooklyn. Moskowitz later died; Violante was partially blinded.

This last shooting led to a break in the case. A woman walking her dog near the crime scene saw policemen ticketing an illegally parked Ford Galaxy. A few minutes later she saw a man hurriedly drive off in the same car. She reported all this to the police, who traced the ticket to Berkowitz.

Berkowitz was arrested outside his Yonkers apartment building on August 10, 1977. He submitted amiably to the arresting officer, Inspector Dowd. "You finally got me," he told Dowd. "I guess this is the end of the trail." It certainly was. The prosecution had an air-tight case against David Berkowitz. He pleaded not guilty by reason of insanity, but the jury rejected that defense after psychiatrists testified that he was faking his disorder. The Son of Sam was ultimately sentenced to a total of 365 years at the Attica Correctional Facility in upstate New York, where he remains to this day.

DIAMONDS ARE NOT FOREVER

COMPUTER EXPERT STANLEY MARK RIFKIN ILLEGALLY TRANSFERRED BANK FUNDS TO HIS SWISS ACCOUNT AND USED THEM TO BUY SOVIET DIAMONDS

It was described by Associated Press in 1979 as the nation's largest bank theft. Stanley Mark Rifkin, a mild-mannered and smiling computer expert, was charged with the $10.2 million caper.

Rifkin had obtained a master's degree in computer science and was working toward a doctorate from the University of California. As an employee of a computer firm that did business with the Pacific Security Bank of Los Angeles, it was not considered unusual that the 32-year-old computer consultant visited the bank frequently.

On October 25, 1978, Rifkin lied in order to gain admission to the wire transmission room, where funds were transferred between banks by cable. Once he got inside the room, Rifkin managed to obtain the special coding used to make a transfer of funds.

Later that day, Rifkin called the transfer room from a pay telephone and impersonated a bank officer to order that $10.2 million be transferred to the Irving Trust Company in New York City.

From New York, the money was then transferred to the Zurich, Switzerland, bank account of the branch of the Soviet government that handles diamond exports. Two days later, Rifkin's broker bought over eight million dollars worth of diamonds from the Soviets.

After the transaction was completed, Rifkin used a phony passport to fly to Geneva, Switzerland, to pick up the diamonds. He was arrested by the FBI in November 1978, in Carlsbad, California. At the time, Rifkin had in his possession $12,000 in cash, and diamonds with a retail value of $13 million. While out on $200,000 bond, Rifkin allegedly planned to rip off another bank for $50 million and then flee the country. However, the plot was thwarted.

On March 26, 1979, Rifkin appeared in federal court in Los Angeles and pleaded guilty to two counts of grand-theft wire fraud. For these felonies, Rifkin was sentenced to serve eight years in prison.

Stanley Rifkin speaks to reporters after his release on $200,000 bail. The computer expert used his knowledge of wire transfers to pull off what was considered the largest bank theft in U.S. history.

SID VICIOUS: A PROPHETIC STAGE NAME

ALTHOUGH HE GREW UP AS A MEEK LAD, JOHN SIMON RITCHIE CHANGED FOR THE WORSE AFTER HE JOINED THE SEX PISTOLS

Sid Vicious and his girlfriend Nancy Spungen arrive at a London court in February 1978 to answer to drug charges. In October, Vicious was charged with killing Spungen.

John Simon Ritchie was nicknamed "Sid Vicious" in a joking way when he joined the English punk rock group called "the Sex Pistols." John Rotten, the lead guitarist and singer for the group, said he suggested the name because Ritchie really wasn't vicious. Time proved Rotten to be wrong and the nickname a valid one. For in October 1978, in New York City, Ritchie was charged with the stabbing death of his 20-year-old girlfriend, Nancy Laura Spungen. Four months later, Ritchie himself died from an apparent overdose of heroin.

Ritchie was a meek, extremely thin youth who had been the target of beatings by neighborhood gangs when growing up in London's tough East End. Ritchie met Rotten (real name John Lydon) in school. Within a short time after Ritchie left school at age 15, he joined the Sex Pistols. That notorious ensemble specialized in such acts as vomiting onstage, cutting themselves, and hurling insults at the audience.

The band developed a following but stirred up controversy in England. A hit tune of the Sex Pistols in the United States titled "God Save the Queen," which contained antiroyalist lyrics, was banned by English radio stations during Queen Elizabeth II's Jubilee year. When the Sex Pistols appeared on a TV show in England, their use of obscene language resulted in the cancellation of their first national tour.

Eventually, after working out visa problems, the group reached the United States, but that tour flopped as well. It was then that Rotten announced that the Sex Pistols was being disbanded, a move that greatly depressed Ritchie, who had joined the group as bass guitarist only nine months earlier.

Ritchie was accompanied in the U.S. by his girlfriend, Nancy Spungen, who became his manager for appearances at local clubs. Having grown up in a Philadelphia suburb, she got into the rock scene in New York in 1975. She moved to London two years later, where she met Ritchie. Friends revealed that both Ritchie and Nancy had become hooked on heroin and methadone, an artificial heroin substitute often used to treat heron addiction.

Nancy registered as Ritchie's wife when they moved into a Manhattan hotel, where they lived quietly until October 12, 1978. At 9:30 A.M. that day, Ritchie phoned the 911 emergency number to report, "Someone is hurt." When police arrived, they found Nancy Spungen, who was clad only in black underwear, stabbed to death in the bathroom.

Ritchie, who said he didn't remember what had happened, was charged with second-degree murder. Freed on bail, he made a suicide attempt on October 23 by cutting his wrists with a broken light bulb. He spent several weeks in a psychiatric hospital.

When he struck a man with a beer mug during a nightclub argument, Ritchie was jailed again. He was released on bail for this incident on February 1, 1979. Ritchie attended a party celebrating his freedom and capped off an evening of beer drinking with a shot of heroin. The deadly dose sent Ritchie into a seizure, but he apparently recovered in about an hour. When the party broke up at about two in the morning, Ritchie went to bed.

Shortly after noon the next day, Ritchie was found dead in his bed by his mother who went to check on him. Still asleep in the same bed was the musician's current girlfriend. A syringe and a spoon containing heroin residue were found nearby.

Ritchie's death at age 21 came at a time when the bizarre music that brought him temporary fame was evolving into the mainstream. His kind of music was also being replaced by more sedate groups that played music of the so-called "New Wave." Even Ritchie's old friend and mentor, John Rotten, had turned to performing under his given name, John Lydon.

FRIENDS REVEALED THAT BOTH RITCHIE AND NANCY HAD BECOME HOOKED ON HEROIN AND METHADONE, AN ARTIFICIAL HEROIN SUBSTITUTE OFTEN USED TO TREAT HEROIN ADDICTION.

THE JONESTOWN MASSACRE

IN A COMMUNAL ACT OF MURDER AND SUICIDE, REVEREND JIM JONES AND 912 CULT FOLLOWERS DIED IN GUYANA'S JUNGLE

The Reverend Jim Jones in January 1977. At the time, his People's Temple was located in San Francisco. Growing notoriety and media hostility drove Jones to move the Temple's headquarters to Guyana and build Jonestown with money contributed by loyal followers.

In the late 1950s, the Reverend Jim Jones, a charismatic man who professed to have healing powers, began his own ministry in Indianapolis, Indiana. Claiming to be affiliated with the Christian Church (Disciples of Christ), Jones soon commanded a group of devoted interracial followers that forged his "People's Temple."

Even in the early days of his ministry, Jones's mysterious power over others was tremendous. He easily drew people searching to discover themselves into his sect. Then he persuaded his newly found followers to turn all their money and worldly possessions over to the Temple in the name of God, with the hope that they would together build a better world.

Unaware that they were blindly serving a ranting and raving maniac, there was no question that Jones's followers meant well. They performed deeds time and again that benefited mankind. His followers were dedicated to integration and were concerned with all the things that they felt mattered in life. Working together, they fed the poor and sheltered the homeless.

Although his People's Temple ministry received a great deal of praise, Jones eventually became dissatisfied. He wanted more power, wealth, and recognition to feed his already bloated ego. Hoping to achieve those ends and build his ministry to a national level, he moved to Ukiah, California, in the mid-1960s. About 150 people followed him.

Despite Jones's secrecy-induced paranoia and unchecked obsessiveness, the People's Temple grew and prospered. By the early 1970s, the cult had established firm roots in Los Angeles and San Francisco. Jones's presentations of supposed healings continued to bring in new members, most of whom he quickly dominated by demanding total selflessness in return for his assurances of a better life and a better world.

Because Jones and his sect were so secretive, little information about their activities was shared with nonmembers. However, by the mid-1970s, members began to defect, and the stories they told generated serious questions about the People's Temple.

Defectors revealed that Jones's healings were dramatically staged and completely fraudulent. Reports of beatings, mysterious deaths, and deviant sexual practices within the cult also began to surface. Faced with increasing pressure from journalists and law enforcement organizations, Jones began looking for a way out.

He soon found what he believed would be his salvation in Guyana, a small former British colony on the northeast coast of South America. Much of the country, which is about the size of the state of Idaho, is undeveloped and difficult to reach; that appealed to Jones immensely. In 1975, he founded Jonestown in an outlying region of the country, and the majority of the People's Temple settlers moved to the remote site that same year.

Pressured by increasing speculation and investigations in the United States, Jones virtually shut down his San Francisco and Los Angeles operations in May 1977 after convincing nearly 1,000 members of his People's Temple to move to Jonestown. After wrapping up the loose ends, Jones left for Guyana in August 1977.

The Jonestown project cost the People's Temple "investors" an estimated five million dollars. However, it soon became a fully functional community, complete with generators for electricity, tractors for farming, and buildings to house livestock. Cult members also built classrooms in which to teach their children. Given a a less deranged leader, the community might have flourished.

However, over the next year, Jones's behavior changed dramatically for the worst. He became more domineering, and he began to

REPORTS OF BEATINGS, MYSTERIOUS DEATHS, AND DEVIANT SEXUAL PRACTICES WITHIN THE CULT ALSO BEGAN TO SURFACE.

Surrounded by the fallen bodies of those who drank of its contents, "the vat of death" sits on a walkway at the People's Temple in Jonestown. Cult members who escaped the mass suicide later revealed that some unwilling victims were forcibly injected with poison by armed guards.

subject cult members to more stringent discipline and regimentation, demanding total personal submission to his authority. Jones implemented programs that entailed psychological pressures and brainwashing, forced labor, and physical abuse that bordered on torture. In short, he had turned Jonestown into a concentration camp.

There was strong evidence to suggest that Jones began abusing drugs during his final year, and he might have developed a psychosis. In his sermons from the Jonestown pavilion, which were nothing more than emotional sessions he termed "white nights," Jones began to dishonor the Bible and deny the power of God. Instead of preaching the gospel, he dwelled on sex, revolution, defectors, external and internal enemies, and death and suicide. Some said that he began to hallucinate and that he eventually came to believe he was God.

Because of the extreme measures employed at Jonestown, there were, naturally, a number of defections. Viewing the defectors as traitors to his cause, Jones's anger soon turned to rage. Eventually, reports that members of the People's Temple were being held against their will reached the United States. Those reports were brought to the attention of a Northern California congressman.

On November 17, 1978, Representative Leo Ryan brought a group of American journalists and relatives of temple members to Jonestown to observe first-hand the conditions there. Although alarmed by what he saw, Ryan spent the night in Jonestown.

Tension was high the next morning, November 18, as Ryan and his delegation left for an airstrip seven miles away. Several Jonestown residents had declared that they wanted to return to the United States, but an angry Jones denied their right to leave. After declaring that a conspiracy was underway to destroy his organization, Jones sent a death squad to the airstrip.

Armed with automatic weapons, the death squad opened fire on Congressman Ryan, members of his staff, journalists, and relatives of cult members as they walked toward the waiting airplane. When the shooting was over, Ryan and four other people were dead. Ten others were seriously wounded.

Back at Jonestown, Jones assembled everyone at the pavilion and told them that their community would soon be attacked. He insisted that everyone had to "take the potion like they used to take in ancient Greece." It turned out that the potion consisted of a lethal mixture of grape Kool-Aid and potassium cyanide.

The potion was mixed in a large metal tub and placed in the pavilion. Jones, promising that they were "going to meet again in another place," ordered that infants go first. Volunteers used syringes to squirt the poison into the backs of the crying childrens' mouths.

Paper cups filled with the deadly drink were then passed out to the adults and older children. Those who resisted were injected as armed guards stood by, ready to shoot anyone who disobeyed Jones's orders. Everyone drank the potion, some enthusiastically. Most were dead within five minutes. A few lucky people managed to flee into the jungle and lived to tell about the tragedy.

Satisfied that he had brought his cult to "a gallant, glorious, screaming end," it is believed that Jones shot a close aide to death moments before taking his own life by firing a single bullet from a .38 caliber pistol into his brain. When it was over, 912 followers of the People's Temple cult and their leader lay dead. The bodies of men, women, and children covered the ground. Some were holding hands; some were clutching each other in a death embrace. It was a scene that shocked the world, created by a man who played God to show everyone that he was in control, even at the end.

A MAN IN CONTROL

The Reverend Jim Jones gained complete control over his followers because of their search to find themselves and their need to believe in something or someone. Members looked to him as a father figure, someone they could turn to when troubled, someone they could depend upon to satisfy their every need. With his powerful speaking voice and his overwhelming, charismatic sermons, his followers listened to him and they enthusiastically obeyed his every command. Sitting upon his thronelike chair, Jones constantly warned that, "Those who do not learn from the past are condemned to repeat it." By virtually isolating his followers in Guyana, separating them from family and friends, he created a social environment that had only one reality for its community to believe in: Jim Jones.

MASS MURDERER OF GREATER CHICAGO

THE FAT MAN IN THE BLACK OLDSMOBILE USED HIS SUBURBAN HOME AS A KILLING FIELD AND BURIAL GROUND

John Wayne Gacy after he was convicted of committing 33 murders. He had previously been photographed with then First Lady Rosalynn Carter. Gacy used the photograph to enhance his veneer of respectability.

Harwood Heights, Illinois, is a quiet Chicago suburb located northwest of the city. In the mid- to late-1970s, it became the unlikely setting for an overweight contractor named John Wayne Gacy to enact his monstrous perversions. From 1975 through 1978, in his innocuous ranch-style home, Gacy sexually assaulted, tortured, and murdered numerous boys and young men.

Gacy was born in Chicago on March 17, 1942. After an uneventful childhood, he attended business school, got married, and lived for a time in Iowa. Gacy managed a fried chicken business in Waterloo, where he became a respected community member. Nothing about him seemed abnormal. He seemed a kind and generous man. Then, at age 26, Gacy was arrested for sexually assaulting a young boy.

Gacy's trial disclosed that he had forced the handcuffed boy to have sex with him. Gacy had then paid his victim to keep quiet about the incident. But the youth testified against him anyway. In response, Gacy hired another young man to beat up the boy.

Gacy's wife divorced him after he was found guilty and sentenced to ten years in an Iowa prison. His good behavior won him an early parole in 1971, and he was placed on probation.

After he moved to Harwood Heights to begin a new life, Gacy remarried and started a construction business, which he ran out of his house. He had been out of prison less than a year when he was arrested for soliciting a juvenile male for sex. But the charges were dropped when his victim failed to appear in court.

Seeking recognition and status, Gacy involved himself in local politics and various community activities. As in Iowa, he impressed his associates as a generous and caring individual. Gacy frequently donated time and money to help people in need. Occasionally, he dressed up as a clown to entertain children at different social events.

It was all a facade. In fact, Gacy was an ill-tempered sort who quarreled frequently with his second wife and treated his construction company employees badly. In 1975, one employee, John Butkovich, vanished shortly after getting into an argument with Gacy. In 1976, Gacy's wife divorced him and left the house. Not long after that, Gacy employee Greg Godzik disappeared. Gacy himself was frequently seen behind the wheel of his black Oldsmobile, cruising a district of Chicago frequented by homosexual male prostitutes. Many young men from that district made the regrettable decision to go for a ride with Gacy. Most of them survived the encounter, but not without suffering some degree of physical harm. Gacy, they discovered, was a savage brute who liked to inflict pain. Nevertheless, they did not report him to the police.

After Gacy's divorce, neighbors began to see young men enter his Des Plaines residence at all hours of the day and night. They also noticed that he often worked late at night on the inside of his house, as if he was remodeling it.

In March 1978, 27-year-old Jeffrey Rignall checked into a Chicago-area hospital in a sadly abused state. Rignall told police that had been abducted by a fat man in a black Oldsmobile. The man had lured him into the car, then rendered him unconscious with a chloroform-soaked cloth. At the man's house, Rignall claimed to have been sexually assaulted and beaten with a whip. Since Rignall's memory had been fogged by chloroform, he could not pinpoint the location of the house,

Nonetheless, Rignall was determined to find his assailant. He began to stake out the known haunts of the cruising black Oldsmobile. When he finally spotted the vehicle, he copied down the license plate number and gave it to the police. Gacy was arrested and then released because the authorities lacked sufficient evidence.

Robert Piest, the 15-year-old youth whose disappearance at long last induced police to search the home of local contractor John Wayne Gacy. Piest's mother prodded the police to take action when her son failed to appear at her birthday party.

Until that time, Gacy had been lucky. But his luck changed on December 11, 1978. That was the day 15-year-old Robert Piest disappeared. Piest was last seen by his mother when she dropped him off at a Des Plaines pharmacy that Gacy was remodeling. The boy had gone inside the pharmacy to a discuss a job offer from Gacy. He never came home. The mother notified the police, and a warrant was obtained to search Gacy's house, which was permeated by a repugnant odor. Police searchers traced the smell to a crawlspace beneath the house, where they found the decomposing bodies of three young men. Gacy was promptly arrested, and he confessed to the sexual torture and murder of over 30 victims.

Investigators returned to Gacy's house and began to remove the floors. In the crawlspaces beneath the house, they discovered several bodies in shallow graves and long trenches. Many of the bodies had been covered with quicklime to hasten their decay. The house was razed, and more bodies were found. A total of 28 corpses were eventually unearthed. Gacy admitted to having dumped five additional bodies in the nearby Des Plaines River. He had used the river, he explained, when the crawlspaces became filled to capacity. In all, Gacy had murdered 33 victims.

Medical examiners later noted that many of the victims apparently had been strangled, while some had underwear stuffed in their mouths. The amount of physical evidence against Gacy was overwhelming. He went to trial in March 1980 and pleaded not guilty by reason of insanity. Nobody bought Gacy's insanity plea, and he was found guilty and sentenced to die in the electric chair.

The means of execution for condemned criminals in Illinois has changed since 1980. Lethal injection has replaced the electric chair. Until the execution of James Walker in September 1990, no execution had occurred in Illinois since 1962. John Wayne Gacy still awaits his fate on death row in an Illinois prison.

The body of 16-year-old William Carroll, Jr., was one of the 28 found beneath John Wayne Gacy's house. Billy Carroll, who had disappeared in 1976, was listed as missing for 2½ years before his parents learned his fate.

THE HILLSIDE STRANGLER

TWO COUSINS WENT ON A LOS ANGELES KILLING SPREE JUST FOR THE THRILL OF IT

Angelo Buono and Kenneth Bianchi were cousins, both natives of Rochester, New York. Buono, born in 1934, left Rochester early in life and moved to Glendale, California, near Los Angeles, where he started an upholstery business. Bianchi, born in 1949, left Rochester in 1975 at the age of 26. He, too, settled in Glendale, and moved in with his cousin for a time. Less than two years after Bianchi arrived in California, a murderer known as "the Hillside Strangler" began a string of vicious killings.

Between October 1977 and February 1978, ten Los Angeles–area girls and young women ranging in age from 12 to 28 were raped and murdered. With the exception of the final victims (who were found in the trunk of a car that had been pushed over a cliff), their bodies were discarded like rubbish along hillsides throughout the Los Angeles area.

Curiously, neither Buono nor Bianchi had a background of violent crime. One day, they decided to murder someone, and so they did. Perhaps they were motivated by some warped spirit of adventure. Maybe they merely wanted to experience the thrill of killing someone. In any event, they found homicide to their liking.

They agreed from the outset that working as a team would make the murders easier to commit. Buono often posed as a policeman to gain the trust of the intended victims, whereupon they were abducted and driven to his house. The hapless females were taken to a spare bedroom, appropriately dubbed "the torture chamber," and strapped into a chair. Then the victims were raped repeatedly, penetrated with various instruments, and finally strangled to death.

Each successive victim, it seemed, was subjected to even more unthinkable horrors than the previous one. One young woman was injected with a cleaning fluid, then gassed to death with a bag that had been placed over her head and connected to the oven with a hose.

Angelo Buono leaves court in October 1979 after pleading innocent to charges stemming from "the Hillside Strangler" murders. The Glendale resident was ultimately convicted of murdering nine women. Neither he nor his cousin Kenneth Bianchi had any previous history of violence.

Nabbed for the murders of two female students in Bellingham, Washington, Kenneth Bianchi revealed that he was also involved in "the Hillside Strangler" murders. Bianchi initially claimed that the evil half of his split personality was responsible for joining his cousin Angelo Buono in the slayings.

Another hapless victim was subjected to electric shock torture before being strangled.

Ten murders were committed in Los Angeles before the killings came to an abrupt halt in February 1978. Homicide detectives were convinced that the murders were the work of two men, but had no firm suspects and little in the way of evidence. Spurred on by harsh public criticism of their efforts, the police labored long and hard to solve the case. Privately, though, many investigators doubted that the killers would ever be caught.

Eleven months after the tenth murder, the baffled Los Angeles police got an unexpected break. On January 11, 1979, two female students in Bellingham, Washington, disappeared from the house they shared. Their bodies were found the next day in the trunk of one of their cars. This discovery prompted a friend of one victim to come forward. Recently, the friend said, the murdered girl had mentioned something about a "surveillance" job that a security guard had offered her. The guard's name was Kenneth Bianchi, and he had recently moved to Bellingham from Los Angeles.

Questioned by local police, Bianchi initially denied any involvement in the Bellingham murders. He changed his story when confronted with irrefutable evidence found at the murder scene, plus statements from witnesses. Astute lawmen quickly concluded that they had cracked California's Hillside Strangler case as well.

Hoping to cut a deal with the authorities, Bianchi implicated his cousin in the Hillside Strangler killings. Bianchi admitted to the murder of five Hillside Strangler victims, and testified against Angelo Buono. As a result, Buono was convicted of nine murders and sentenced to a life term without the possibility of parole. Bianchi was sentenced to life imprisonment in Washington State; he must serve a minimum term of 26⅔ years before his first parole hearing.

THE COED MURDERER

THEODORE "TED" BUNDY BLENDED INTELLIGENCE, WIT, AND GOOD LOOKS INTO MASS SEX MURDER

Ted Bundy was probably the most atypical serial killer ever. The illegitimate son of a mother who for years led him to believe she was his older sister, he had an otherwise uneventful childhood. When Bundy appeared in a Utah courtroom in 1975, it was unclear whether he was a vicious murderer or a victim of mistaken identity.

In January 1974, Sharon Clarke, a young woman living in Seattle, Washington, was beaten with a metal rod while asleep. Believed to have been Bundy's first victim, Clarke survived the assault. Four weeks later, Lynda Ann Healy, a University of Washington coed, vanished from her basement room in a group house. Although her bedsheets were heavily bloodstained, none of the other residents heard any sounds of a struggle the night she was abducted. Within less than five months, five other coeds at schools in Washington and northern Oregon had also disappeared without a trace. The last was Georgann Hawkins, who was seen by several students on the night of June 11, 1974. She had been walking down a well-lit alley behind fraternity and sorority houses on the University of Washington campus. Hawkins vanished only a few yards from the back doorstep of her sorority house. Her fate remains a mystery.

On July 14, 1974, two young women vanished from Lake Sammanish Park in Washington. One, Janice Ott, was seen accompanying a handsome young man to his Volkswagen. The man had his arm in a sling and called himself "Ted."

After the Lake Sammanish incident, the disappearances ceased in the Seattle area. However, that fall, the skeletal remains of the missing women were found in wilderness graves throughout the region. By that time the disappearances had shifted to Salt Lake City, where Bundy had enrolled in law school. Soon the crimes embraced neighboring Colorado. Bundy had already been suspected. Liz Kendall, a former girlfriend from Seattle, had told police that he might be the wanted "Ted."

Ted Bundy, "the Coed Murderer." In June 1977, Bundy escaped from an Aspen, Colorado, court during a pretrial hearing recess. He was captured soon after. Six months later, Bundy escaped again, this time from a Colorado jail. Before he was apprehended, three more murders had occurred.

Margaret Bowman, one of two Chi Omega victims.
Ninety minutes after killing two sorority sisters and
viciously assaulting two more, Bundy attacked
another girl a few blocks away. Later, as police sirens
wailed, he watched from the porch of his house, which
was two blocks from the Chi Omega sorority house.

Bundy was one of over 2,000 suspects until, on August 16, 1975, an off-duty patrolman in Salt Lake City arrested Bundy after he operated his Volkswagen in a suspicious manner. In the car, the patrolman found a ski mask, ice pick, crowbar, and other paraphernalia that contradicted Bundy's law student posture. Bundy was then identified by Carol DaRonch as the man who had tried to abduct her in November 1974. After being convicted of kidnapping DaRonch, he was extradited to Colorado to stand trial for the murder of Caryn Campbell. Bundy escaped twice during the pre-trial hearings. The second attempt was successful for nearly two months. By the time he was recaptured, he had slain Kimberley Leach, a junior high school student, and Lisa Levy and Margaret Bowman, members of the Chi Omega sorority at Florida State University in Tallahassee.

On July 23, 1979, Bundy was convicted of the Chi Omega murders largely because his teeth matched the bite marks left on Lisa Levy's buttocks. Although sentenced to be executed, Bundy maintained his innocence. Carole Ann Boone, one of many who believed Bundy, married him while he was on death row. To the embarrassment of Florida prison officials, she conceived a child with him during one of her routine visits.

Ted Bundy differed from most sex killers because he was very intelligent, good-looking, and amusing. His arm in a cast, Bundy played upon a woman's sympathy to entrap her. The frenzy that caused him to beat his victims unconscious and then rape and kill them was never explained. In his early twenties, Bundy had been rejected by a woman who strongly resembled the pretty coeds he murdered. Bundy asked his accusers why he would rape and kill women when he had all he could want. On January 24, 1989, Ted Bundy went to the electric chair with his question still unanswered.

THE MOST DARING FRENCH CRIMINAL EVER

ROBBER-MURDERER JACQUES MESRINE COMBINED BRUTALITY, ARROGANCE, AND BOLD ESCAPES TO BECOME FRANCE'S PUBLIC ENEMY NUMBER ONE

Born in Paris in 1937, Jacques Mesrine was a loner as a child. Jacques was expelled from two schools for playing hooky. As a teenager, he stole cars for joyrides. Married at 18, Mesrine soon became a father. At 19, he was drafted and sent to Algeria, where he received the Military Cross for bravery. After divorcing his wife, he returned home. Boredom set in, so he robbed a wealthy financier.

Paroled in 1963 after being sentenced for an aborted bank robbery, Mesrine went straight. He remarried, fathered a daughter, and studied architecture. Mesrine, a good architect, returned to crime after being laid off. Mesrine became known for his cool demeanor and quick thinking. During a jewelry shop holdup, for instance, he heard police coming and ran into the backyard to open the gate so they would think he'd fled; in actuality, he hid nearby.

In 1967, Mesrine tried to go straight again when his father financed a venture as an innkeeper. Bored again, he ran off with a woman named Jeanne Schneider. They robbed a Swiss hotel, moved to Canada, and became servants for Georges Deslauriers, an aged, crippled Montreal millionaire. The pair then kidnapped Deslauriers. Before a ransom was paid, the victim escaped.

After moving to Percé, Canada, the couple met Evelyne le Bouthillier, an elderly, wealthy widow who was found strangled the next day. Although Mesrine claimed he knew nothing of the murder, he and Schneider crossed the border into the United States. They were arrested, returned to Canada, and jailed. Mesrine overpowered a guard, and he and Schneider escaped, but they were soon recaptured. They were convicted and imprisoned for the kidnapping, but acquitted of the murder charges.

In 1968, Mesrine led prisoners in an escape from St. Vincent-de-Paul prison in Canada. After robbing a bank, he returned to the prison, intending to free more prisoners, but had to flee when police-

One of several disguises Jacques Mesrine had assumed during his reign as France's Public Enemy Number One. Mesrine had sworn never to be taken alive; the police had every reason to believe him. When they trapped him on November 2, 1979, without warning, the police showered his car with a hail of bullets.

WHEN A TELLER PUSHED AN ALARM DURING ONE BANK HOLDUP, MESRINE SAID, "DON'T WORRY, I LIKE TO WORK TO MUSIC."

men engaged him in a gun battle. While hiding in the woods, Mesrine killed two forest rangers in cold blood.

Following more bank robberies, Mesrine, then age 36, traveled to Venezuela with his beautiful 19-year-old mistress, Jocelyne Deraiche, and two pals. When Interpol began closing in, Mesrine and Deraiche fled to Madrid and then to France. There Mesrine assembled a top-flight gang and pulled many armed robberies. Captured again and brought to trial, Mesrine brandished a gun left for him in a courthouse lavatory, used the judge as a human shield, and escaped.

For the next decade, Mesrine mixed showy escapes with daring kidnappings and robberies. When a teller pushed an alarm during one bank holdup, Mesrine said, "Don't worry, I like to work to music." On another occasion, Mesrine posed as a juvenile officer, interrupted a shoplifting arrest, took charge of the 15-year-old perpetrator, and let the boy go once outside the store.

While imprisoned for more robberies, Mesrine wrote an autobiography, *L'Instinct de Mort* (The Killer Instinct). The manuscript was smuggled out of Paris's La Santé prison and published in 1977.

Three months later, Mesrine went to trial on murder charges. Soon after his conviction, he engineered his most spectacular prison escape when he and an accomplice overpowered guards, dressed in the guards' uniforms, and pulled guns from a ventilation shaft. Mesrine and his pal used a ladder to escape over a wall.

On November 2, 1979, Mesrine and girlfriend Sylvie Jeanjacquot, driving their BMW in Paris, suddenly found one truck behind their car and another in front of it. At a stop, the tarpaulin on the truck in front flipped back, revealing four police officers who opened fire. Mesrine was killed instantly, his body riddled with 18 bullets; his girlfriend was severely wounded, though she survived.

1980–1989

AN UNDERCURRENT OF MADNESS RAN THROUGH THE 1980S. SERIAL killers such as the Yorkshire Ripper and the Atlanta child killer terrorized their communities. James Oliver Huberty murdered 21 innocent people in a MacDonald's restaurant, and Laurie Dann entered an elementary school and shot into a crowd of children. Mark David Chapman gunned down former Beatle John Lennon, and John W. Hinckley, Jr., tried to assassinate President Reagan. It was a lunacy that seemed to have no bounds. Besides the decade's insanity, greed also ran awry in the 1980s. However, people didn't rob banks anymore; the new way to steal was through white-collar crime. Michael Milken, who paid $600 million in penalties, epitomized everything wrong with the selfishness of the 1980s. And did Charles Keating buy the influence of five U.S. senators, costing taxpayers billions of dollars?

THE SCARSDALE DIET DOCTOR MYSTERY

Jean Harris leaves court during her trial. Freed on bail during legal proceedings, the headmistress of an exclusive girls' school entertained hopes of remaining at liberty. Her hopes were dashed by a medical expert's testimony that established that her former paramour had not been shot accidentally.

THE DEATH OF RENOWNED DR. HERMAN TARNOWER BROUGHT UP THE UNBELIEVABLE QUESTION, "CAN A MAN BE ACCIDENTALLY SHOT THREE TIMES?"

On the night of March 10, 1980, Jean Harris, 56, felt that her life was no longer worth living. Her career as headmistress of the exclusive Madeira School was in jeopardy. She had expelled three students for smoking marijuana and had been called before the board of supervisors. Much worse, however, was her belief that her lover of 14 years, Dr. Herman Tarnower, a prominent physician and author of *The Scarsdale Medical Diet,* was leaving her for a younger rival.

Harris signed a new will, wrote a suicide note, and put a gun loaded with five shells in her purse. She wanted to say goodbye to Tarnower before she killed herself in the quiet garden at his home.

According to Harris's testimony at the subsequent trial, she entered Tarnower's bedroom where he was sleeping, and she became enraged at the sight of her rival's nightgown. When Harris threw a box of curlers through the window, Tarnower awakened and slapped her. Harris later testified that she took out the gun, put it to her head, and pulled the trigger. Tarnower grabbed the gun, it went off and shot him in the hand. He went to the bathroom to wash his slight wound while Harris got the gun again.

As Tarnower tried to buzz for the housekeeper, he allegedly struggled with Harris over the gun and it went off, hitting Tarnower again. Harris then tried to shoot herself in the head. The gun malfunctioned, but it did fire when she aimed it at the bed.

Harris could not reload the gun, so she later maintained that she smashed the weapon against the bathtub in anger. She also helped the bleeding doctor into bed and tried to call for help, but the phone did not work. Thinking the phone was out of order, Harris left the house to go to a nearby phone booth to call for help. When she returned, the housekeeper had called the police.

Harris was charged with second-degree murder. She had hoped that her story of attempted suicide and accidental death would be believed. However, the prosecution contended that Harris deliberately shot Tarnower. The first bullet went through his outstretched hand into his chest. Prosecutors contended that the second shot was also aimed deliberately and hit Tarnower in the shoulder. Harris and Tarnower struggled, and the gun fired a wild bullet out the window. Another shot went into the bed. When Tarnower tried to call the housekeeper, the prosecution claimed that Harris took dead aim and shot Tarnower in the arm. He then collapsed and died.

At first, it was thought that four bullets had struck the victim. Later it was determined that one bullet had caused two injuries—one when it entered Tarnower's hand and again when it went into his chest.

Damaging testimony came from a medical expert who said that palm tissue was found in the chest wound. This proved that Tarnower had held up his hand in a futile defense attempt. The medical expert also testified that the chest wound was cylindrical, not round. The bullet apparently was "tumbling" when it struck his chest, the way it behaves when it strikes an intervening object.

The prosecution also read to the jury a long, bitter letter Harris had sent to Tarnower on the very day he died. The letter was full of rage against Tarnower's new lover. It seemed to provide a motive for the killing.

On February 5, 1981, Jean Harris was convicted of second-degree murder and sentenced to a minimum of 15 years to life in the Bedford Hills correctional facility.

Westchester County officers escort a handcuffed Jean Harris to court in March 1981 to learn her sentence for the fatal shooting of Dr. Herman Tarnower, creator of the Scarsdale Medical Diet. Despite her protestations that the slaying was accidental, Harris was convicted of second-degree murder and sentenced to 15 years to life.

INFANTICIDE OR WILD DOG SLAUGHTER?

AUSTRALIAN COURTS HAD DIFFICULTIES DETERMINING WHETHER AN INFANT GIRL WAS KILLED BY HER MOTHER OR BY WILD DOGS

The Chamberlain family went on a camping trip to beautiful Ayers Rock in the wild Australian outback. Michael Chamberlain, 36, was a pastor in the Seventh Day Adventist Church in Mount Isa in western Queensland. He was vacationing with his wife, Alice Lynne, 32, their two boys, Aidan, 6, and Reagan, 4, and infant daughter, Azaria, two months old. It was there, on August 17, 1980, that the dingo baby murder happened, if indeed it did happen.

"Lindy," as Alice Lynne Chamberlain became known in the headlines of the Australian newspapers, told the police that tiny Azaria was carried off by a dingo, a wild canine said to be more wolf than dog. The abduction supposedly occurred while Lindy and her husband were preparing the evening meal and the children were asleep in a tent. A search turned up no sign of the missing baby.

A week later, bloodstained and ripped clothing identified as Azaria's was found near a dingo lair three miles from where the Chamberlains had camped. A subsequent inquest produced a coroner's ruling that the infant had been the victim of a marauding dingo.

However, further tests on the clothing and bloodstains by Dr. Kenneth Brown prompted police to call another inquest. This time, Lindy was held over for a trial on the charge of murdering her baby, and Michael was charged with being an accessory after the fact, even though no possible motive could be found.

A jury convicted Lindy of murder and her husband of being an accessory. Judge Muirhead sentenced her to life in prison at hard labor and gave Michael a suspended 18-month sentence. After her fourth child was born, Lindy was released from prison on bail, but an appeals court returned her there in 1983.

Then, in February 1986, a chance discovery in a gully at the foot of Ayers Rock brought a sensational epilogue to the murder case that had shocked the world. While investigating the death of a climber

Lindy Chamberlain leaves court with her husband Michael in February 1982 after learning that she will be charged with murdering her two-month-old daughter and he with being an accessory after the fact.

THEN, IN FEBRUARY 1986, A CHANCE DISCOVERY IN A GULLY AT THE FOOT OF AYERS ROCK BROUGHT A SENSATIONAL EPILOGUE TO THE MURDER CASE THAT HAD SHOCKED THE WORLD.

who fell to his death from Ayers Rock, officers found a baby's knitted matinee jacket, the kind that Lindy had insisted from the start Azaria had been wearing. It would have kept the animal's saliva off the baby's other inner garments, thus, finding the jacket helped Lindy's story. The prosecution had claimed that no such jacket ever existed and that it was part of the mother's made-up story.

The Australian government announced a new inquiry into the case. More importantly, it declared a permanent remission of Lindy's sentence and an order that she never be returned to custody, regardless of the inquiry's outcome. Lindy was free. The latest inquiry found that a dingo could have indeed carried off the baby.

MURDER BECAME THE LOSER'S OBSESSION

In 1975, Mark David Chapman had served as an area coordinator at an Arkansas resettlement camp for Vietnamese refugees. After killing John Lennon, Chapman stood on the sidewalk near his victim's body calmly reading *The Catcher in the Rye* until the police arrived.

JOHN LENNON'S ASSASSIN PRAYED TO SATAN FOR STRENGTH TO CARRY OUT HIS POINTLESS DEED

Mark David Chapman was born in Fort Worth, Texas, in May 1955. Although his family moved around a lot, Mark made friends easily and experienced what seemed to be a normal childhood.

By the time he reached fourth grade, however, Chapman began to change. Other children often picked on him and called him names, and he began to feel inferior, a trait he would carry with him into adulthood. Afraid to fight back, Chapman became withdrawn and created a fantasy world of his own where he ruled "little people" who lived in the walls of his bedroom.

Unable to cope with his inadequacies as he grew into adolescence, Chapman turned to drugs. As a freshman in high school, he began sniffing glue, smoking marijuana, and snorting cocaine. Less frequently he took heroin, LSD, methamphetamines, and barbiturates—basically whatever drugs he could obtain. After he burned himself out, Chapman became a religious fanatic.

By the time he reached adulthood, Chapman was doomed to failure at every turn. He did poorly at junior college and dropped out, had an unstable marriage, and couldn't seem to hold a job. Chapman became physically abusive to those closest to him, and he eventually attempted suicide.

Feeling shut out and betrayed by nearly everyone connected to him, Chapman traveled to New York in December 1980. Although it was a grim motive, he was determined to succeed at something. He finally decided he would kill former Beatle John Lennon, whom he perceived as "phony and insincere," in order to become well known.

On December 8, 1980, Chapman went to the Dakota apartment building at 72nd Street and Central Park West where Lennon and his wife, Yoko Ono, lived. Chapman was packing a Charter Arms .38, which he had bought only two days earlier, concealed in the pocket of his coat.

Pacing beneath the Dakota's archway, Chapman spotted the singer-songwriter leaving the building early in the day and obtained Lennon's autograph. Unable to carry out his plan of murder at that time, Chapman went back to his hotel room and prayed to Satan for the strength that he needed to shoot John Lennon.

Then determined more than ever, Chapman, carrying his highly cherished copy of J. D. Salinger's *The Catcher in the Rye,* returned to the Dakota later that afternoon and began his vigil anew. Appearing to be just another autograph hound, Chapman waited all day for Lennon to return. Finally, at about 10:50 P.M., he saw Lennon and Yoko pull up in front of the apartment building in their limousine.

Yoko climbed out of the car first and was about 40 feet ahead of Lennon when he exited the vehicle. As Lennon approached the Dakota's archway, he looked directly at Chapman. But by then it was too late. Chapman had taken the .38 out of his coat pocket and began firing in rapid succession. When it was over, five shots had been fired.

As John Lennon crumbled to the sidewalk in front of his home and his horrified wife, Chapman's only thoughts were, "The bullets are working." At a tremendous cost to the world, not to mention Lennon's family and friends, Mark David Chapman had finally found success. After pleading guilty to murder, Chapman was sentenced to a life term at the Attica prison in upstate New York.

John Lennon, former Beatle. At their first meeting, Lennon thought Mark David Chapman was a fan and gave him his autograph. Several hours later, when the two met again, Chapman took a Charter Arms .38 out of his coat pocket and opened fire.

. . . AND THEY DIDN'T LIVE HAPPILY EVER AFTER

WHEN SUNNY VON BULOW WAS FOUND UNCONSCIOUS, HER HUSBAND, CLAUS, WAS SUSPECTED OF TRYING TO KILL HER FOR HER MONEY

On the morning of December 21, 1980, Claus von Bulow found his wife, Martha "Sunny," sprawled across the bathroom floor of their Newport, Rhode Island, mansion. Although still breathing, she was icy cold and in a deep coma. Claus von Bulow rushed her to the hospital, where she suffered a cardiac arrest. After being stabilized, Sunny von Bulow was given glucose "pushes"—a treatment to determine if an unconscious patient's illness involves low levels of sugar in the blood. The glucose actually lowered, rather than raised, Sunny's blood sugar level. That was an indication of excess insulin in her blood.

As a result, von Bulow was charged with the attempted murder of Sunny by injecting her with insulin. Many people believed that von Bulow—a charming but penniless Danish aristocrat—had married wealthy heiress Sunny for her money. They reasoned that he attempted to murder his wife for the same reason.

The high level of insulin in Sunny's blood was the heart of the prosecution's case. Two medical experts testified that they felt that the excessive insulin had been injected. Von Bulow's lover also testified that she had given him an ultimatum to leave his wife the same month that Sunny was stricken.

During von Bulow's trial, it was revealed that Sunny had lapsed into a similar coma a year earlier. Sunny had recovered on that occasion, but her children and her maid became suspicious of Claus. The maid testified that he had delayed calling the doctor even though she had begged him to do so. The maid also testified that she saw a little black bag among Claus von Bulow's possessions. The bag contained drugs, hypodermic needles, and on two occasions, a bottle marked "Insulin."

The defense pointed out that three weeks before the last coma, von Bulow had rushed his wife to the hospital after finding her unconscious from an overdose of aspirin. Why would he save her life and

Claus von Bulow in April 1985 as he leaves a gift shop in his Rhode Island hotel to go to court and begin his second trial for the attempted murder of his wife Martha "Sunny."

CLAUS VON BULOW'S LOVER ALSO TESTIFIED THAT SHE HAD GIVEN HIM AN ULTIMATUM TO LEAVE HIS WIFE THE SAME MONTH THAT SUNNY WAS STRICKEN.

then try to murder her three weeks later? Defense witnesses also testified that Sunny often injected herself with drugs. As for the motive of money, von Bulow claimed that he had plenty of money. Sunny had given him a trust fund of two million dollars as an outright gift. In addition, his income was more than $120,000 a year.

On March 16, 1982, Claus von Bulow was found guilty of twice attempting to murder his wife. He was sentenced to 20 years in prison. Von Bulow appealed the guilty verdict; in 1985, he was granted a new trial. During the second trial, a medical expert testified that he thought Sunny's first coma had been caused by a lack of oxygen to her brain when she was unconscious for a long period of time. The medical expert believed that the second coma had been the result of a cardiac arrest induced by drugs and alcohol and complicated by lying on a cold bathroom floor. Claus von Bulow was acquitted in this second trial. Sunny von Bulow still lies in a coma.

THE YORKSHIRE RIPPER

AN INTROVERTED ENGLISHMAN DEVELOPED AN OBSESSION FOR KILLING PROSTITUTES AS A SEXUAL THRILL

Peter Sutcliffe, "the Yorkshire Ripper." Despite an intense manhunt, his reign of terror lasted over five years. Admittedly, the police work was not always the best. However, the larger problem was that Sutcliffe, like so many serial killers in recent times, outwardly gave little hint of his inner torment.

Peter Sutcliffe was born in Yorkshire, England, on June 2, 1946. He was his mother's favorite, the oldest of five children. At age 15, Sutcliffe left school, a lonely, shy boy who drifted from one job to another. At age 21, he started dating a 16-year old Czech girl named Sonia Szurma, but they waited seven years to get married. One night, when the girl was on a date with someone else, the highly jealous Sutcliffe went to a prostitute but he failed to have intercourse. The prostitute took his money without returning his change. When she taunted and humiliated Sutcliffe, the hatred he felt at that moment toward prostitutes remained with him and soon festered into murder.

Sutcliffe first attacked a hooker in 1969, hitting her on the head with a sock filled with gravel. Two years later, on a drive with a friend through the red-light district, he hit another woman in nearly the same way—this time with a brick in a sock. A year after marrying, Sutcliffe began his long, vengeful reign of terror by hitting and slashing two prostitutes. A few months later, he committed his first murder. In the wee hours of October 29, 1975, Sutcliffe struck hooker Wilma McCann on the head with a hammer. When he pulled up her clothes and stabbed her breast and abdomen, he was literally committing rape with a knife; it was an unexpected sexual thrill for him.

In the five years that followed, Sutcliffe earned the title of "the Yorkshire Ripper" by mutilating 14 women, mostly hookers; only three survived. After a narrow escape from being caught, Sutcliffe didn't murder again for a year. A student was his last victim.

On January 2, 1981, while routinely checking license plates, Sergeant Robert Ring and Police Constable Robert Hydes arrested Sutcliffe as he picked up a prostitute. When they suspected his identity after finding a knife that he had hidden, Sutcliffe admitted that he was the Yorkshire Ripper. Found guilty on May 22, Peter Sutcliffe was jailed for life.

ASSASSINATION ATTEMPT ON PRESIDENT REAGAN

AN UNLIKELY ASSASSIN, JOHN W. HINCKLEY, JR., TURNED OUT TO BE MORE DISTURBED THAN PREVIOUSLY THOUGHT

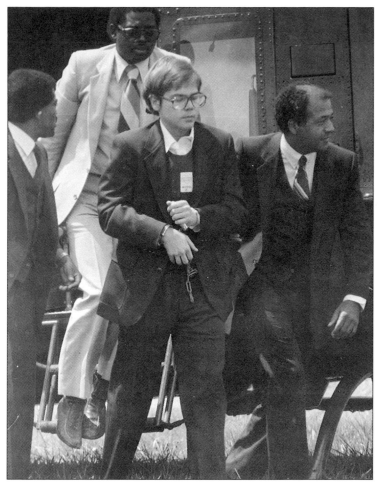

John Hinckley arrives by helicopter at the Quantico Marine Base, Virginia, in August 1981. The label on Hinckley's chest shows that he's wearing a bulletproof vest to prevent him from being fatally shot like Lee Harvey Oswald.

John W. Hinckley, Jr., 25, had seemed to be the ideal American boy. He was quiet, polite, and never went through the drugs-booze-bad-girls stage that so many teenage boys did. The son of an oil executive, Hinckley had a wealthy, loving family. He showed no attributes of a potential presidential assassin.

Yet on March 30, 1981, Hinckley pulled a gun and, in a few seconds, left four men wounded. FBI agent Timothy McCarthy, D.C. po-

President Ronald Reagan a few weeks before John Hinckley tried to kill him. Amazingly, Reagan didn't even know that he had been shot until doctors found a bullet wound under his left armpit. The president survived the assassination attempt without any lasting ill effects.

liceman Thomas Delahanty, Press Secretary James Brady, and President Ronald Reagan were all shot.

Reagan didn't realize he had been hit until doctors found a bullet wound below his left armpit. He thought the pain was from being tackled and slammed to the concrete by a Secret Service agent. The .22 caliber bullet lodged in Reagan's left lung was removed by surgeons. Reagan recovered completely.

McCarthy and Delahanty recovered from their wounds, but the bullet in Brady's brain partially paralyzed him. Brady still suffers from his injury.

Hinckley, captured immediately by the Secret Service, had achieved his goal of international infamy. An investigation showed that Hinckley had attended several colleges for about seven years before dropping out of all of them. The only memorable impression he left were two papers he had written: a review of Adolph Hitler's *Mein Kampf* and a report on the Auschwitz death camp.

On October 9, 1980, Hinckley had been arrested at an airport in Nashville, Tennessee, and charged with the possession of three concealed handguns. Though President Carter was also in Nashville, no connection was ever suspected. Four days later, Hinckley turned up in Dallas where he bought the pistol used in his attempted assassination of Reagan.

Obsessed with actress Jodie Foster, Hinckley somehow developed the idea that Reagan had mistreated Foster. Hinckley had written to Foster, "I will probably die for what I am about to do. It is now 12:30 P.M., an hour before I go to the Hilton Hotel."

Hinckley did not die for his act. His attorneys pleaded insanity, and Hinckley is now confined in a mental institution.

THE MAN WHO LIVED AS HE WROTE

TALENTED INMATE-AUTHOR JACK HENRY ABBOTT COMMITTED COLD-BLOODED MURDER AS HIS BOOK RECEIVED RAVE REVIEWS

In 1979, Jack Henry Abbott, a 35-year-old inmate who had been incarcerated for all but 5½ months since his first jail term in 1956 at age 12, wrote to Norman Mailer, who was then working on *The Executioner's Song,* his book about Gary Gilmore. Mailer saw enough promise in the writing samples that the Irish-Chinese Abbott had sent him to persuade Random House to publish a selection of them. In the early summer of 1981, Abbott's book appeared under the title *In the Belly of the Beast.*

Owing in large part to Mailer's recommendation that he was a "powerful and important American writer," Abbott was paroled in June 1981 to a halfway house on the Lower East Side of Manhattan that overlooked the Bowery.

Hired by Mailer to do research for *Ancient Evenings,* a novel about Egypt, Abbott soon demonstrated that as a consequence of his long incarceration he was unequipped to deal with even the ordinary aspects of life when not at work. He once called his literary agent to say that he had run out of toothpaste and needed help on how to obtain more. At the same time, however, Abbott was quite able to fend for himself on the streets of New York. He had stabbed a man to death in prison and was always careful to arm himself with a paring knife before he left the halfway house.

On the night of July 17–18, 1981, Abbott went out with two women friends to the Great Jones Bar. After several hours of drinking and dancing, the three went to Bini Bon, an all-night diner on Second Avenue. There, Abbott got into a staring contest with a waiter named Richard Adan, a 22-year-old actor-playwright and son-in-law of the Bini Bon's owner. At his trial in January 1982, Abbott testified that he had initially thought Adan's look was one of hostility because Abbott was there with two attractive women. When Adan asked if Abbott wanted to go outside and then stepped behind the counter to get

Jack Henry Abbott testified that the U.S. marshal who arrested him in Louisiana asked him to autograph a copy of *In the Belly of the Beast,* Abbott's book.

something, Abbott assumed that he had been challenged to a fight and that Adan had just armed himself.

Once the two were on the street, Adan pointed to a dumpster in a darkened area around the corner. Thinking that was where the fight was to occur, Abbott headed toward the dumpster and then turned with his knife in his hand when he sensed that Adan was behind him. After stabbing Adan in the heart, Abbott commented to himself on "the precision of the man's movements," as Adan fell to the sidewalk and died. Abbott then fled. Two months later, he was apprehended in Louisiana while working as a casual laborer.

Abbott's claim that the killing was in self-defense was contradicted by Wayne Larsen, the only eyewitness. Larsen gave an articulate account of Abbott stabbing Adan without provocation as Adan tried to return to the Bini Bon. Abbott himself, during his last day on the stand, revealed that he had realized the previous night, while reviewing the trial testimony to that point, that the stabbing was a tragic error on his part. Adan had been staring so intently at him, he finally understood, because his Irish-Chinese facial features reminded Adan of his own wife who was also half Chinese. As for the invitation to come outside, Adan had intuited, when Abbott unflinchingly returned his gaze, that Abbott needed to urinate. Because the Bini Bon had no restroom, men were directed to go behind the dumpster. Adan had not been sneaking up on Abbott; he had been merely following Abbott to make sure that he found the correct spot.

Abbott made a credible, even sympathetic witness. Several jurors were visibly moved during his testimony, particularly when he detailed the tortures that he had endured during his 14 years of solitary confinement in prison. Not even a glowing character reference from Mailer could overcome Larsen's chilling depiction of the Adan's stabbing. Abbott was convicted and sentenced to life imprisonment.

Actor-playwright Richard Adan gave a customer at the diner where he worked as a waiter a look that was interpreted as a challenge to a fight. The customer, Jack Abbott, later realized that Adan's look had meant something quite different and that Adan's slaying had been a tragic mistake.

ABBOTT'S LITERARY TALENT ON DISPLAY

In The Belly of the Beast was a kind of manual on what one critic called "the outlaw mystique." It fluctuated between Marxism and physical violence. In a very frightening sense, the book was both an indictment of incarceration and a plea for it. Ironically, a rave review of *In the Belly of the Beast* appeared on the newsstands in the Sunday Book Review section of the *New York Times* even as Abbott was plunging his knife into Richard Adan's heart.

THE ATLANTA CHILD MURDERS

THE KILLINGS OF AFRICAN-AMERICAN YOUTHS STOPPED AT 28 WHEN THE ATLANTA POLICE ARRESTED A BRILLIANT YOUNG AFRICAN-AMERICAN MAN

A handcuffed Wayne Williams in the back seat of a sheriff's car as he leaves jail to begin the sixth week of his trial.

Wayne Williams was born in 1958 in Atlanta, Georgia, to Herman and Fay Williams, two schoolteachers in their mid-forties. He was a brilliant but spoiled only child who craved instant success. While growing up, this plump African-American youth was featured in magazines and on television for setting up a home-built radio station and selling advertising time. After leaving school at age 18, Williams grew obsessed with police work. He also studied photography and how to use television cameras. At one time, he called himself a talent scout and tried to promote a pop group to sing soul music. One would-be singer, Patrick Rogers, who answered Williams's offer of "free" interviews for singing careers, was murdered.

In July 1979, when the decomposed bodies of two African-American teenagers, Edward Smith and Alfred Evans, were found near a lake in Atlanta, residents were apathetic about the murders. In September, when Milton Harvey, another African-American teenager, disappeared, people still didn't notice. Then Yusef Bell, the

WITNESSES PLACED THE NEWLY FOUND VICTIMS WITH WILLIAMS. DOG HAIRS ON THE VICTIMS' BODIES MATCHED HAIRS IN WILLIAMS'S HOME AND CAR.

gifted son of a civil rights worker, failed to come home. His body and that of Milton Harvey were found about the time that nine-year-old Jeffrey Mathis vanished. Disappearing one after the other were Angel Lanier (the only victim who was raped), Eric Middlebrooks, Christopher Richardson, Aaron Wyche, and LaTonya Wilson.

By then, a year had passed, and African-Americans nationwide believed that the murders were racially motivated. The police disagreed, believing that people would have noticed a white man snatching children in an African-American neighborhood.

On July 30, 1980, Earl Terrell disappeared. A month later, Clifford Jones vanished; his strangled body was found the following day. Twenty policemen were added to the task force. A reward was offered, and a curfew was imposed. Although police believed the killer to be an African-American teenager whom the children trusted, others held to the racial theme because only one child had been sexually assaulted. The disappearances continued: Darron Glass, Charles Stevens, Aaron Jackson, and Lubie Geter. By May 1981, 26 bodies had been discovered and one was missing. The police were discouraged, since they had done all they could to check out all the leads.

Police were close to a Chattahoochee River bridge on May 22 when they heard a splash. They questioned Wayne Williams, 23, who was climbing into a nearby station wagon. After letting him go, they put him under surveillance. On May 24, the bodies of Nathaniel Cater, 27, and later, Jimmy Payne, 21, were found in the river. Witnesses placed the newly found victims with Williams. Dog hairs on the victims' bodies matched hairs in Williams's home and car. Several African-American teens testified that Williams had approached them for sex. Although the evidence was circumstantial, Williams was convicted of killing Payne and Cater. In March 1982, Williams received a life sentence, and the murders ceased.

SPEED, DRUGS, DELOREAN, AND THE FBI

WHEN JOHN DELOREAN'S AUTO COMPANY NEEDED MONEY, DID DELOREAN USE ANY METHOD—LEGAL OR ILLEGAL—TO GET THE CASH?

John Z. DeLorean was the creative genius behind many of the "muscle cars" of the 1960s. Eventually, DeLorean decided to start his own automobile company. With a factory in Northern Ireland, his company made a hot new sports car named after DeLorean himself. When the company ran into serious financial difficulties, DeLorean sought a way to raise money. He allegedly became involved in a drug deal with James Hoffman—a former neighbor and friend of DeLorean. On October 19, 1982, agents from the FBI and the Drug Enforcement Administration (DEA) arrested DeLorean on charges of possession of cocaine and conspiracy to distribute cocaine.

The prosecution's chief evidence consisted of five videotapes and 57 taped telephone conversations in which drug transactions were supposedly discussed. The source of the tapes was Hoffman, who had been wired by the FBI. Hoffman had told DeLorean about a crooked banker (actually an FBI agent) who could help finance the drug deal. Federal agents also posed as drug dealers. DeLorean's defense was that he thought the banker was legitimate. His defense also contended that Hoffman had initiated the drug deal and had threatened the lives of DeLorean's family if DeLorean pulled out of the deal.

The trial revealed that Hoffman was a convicted drug dealer and a professional informant who set up his acquaintances for government sting operations. Hoffman admitted that he had erased part of the audiotapes and that he had asked for some of any proceeds from DeLorean's bust. Hoffman also allegedly told a federal agent, "I'm going to get DeLorean for you guys." The snitch said he was paid over $110,000 in "expenses" for his role. And the agent who posed as the corrupt banker admitted that he had altered his notes.

The federal government admitted that Hoffman was a crook, believing that he would be most effective in helping to nail DeLorean. It didn't work. DeLorean was acquitted of all charges.

John DeLorean speaks to reporters after sitting through the selection of the jury that will try him on cocaine trafficking charges. Seemingly caught red-handed in a government sting operation, the auto company mogul was later acquitted when the jury found the chief prosecution witness too repugnant to be credible.

THE WORST MASS MURDER IN WASHINGTON STATE'S HISTORY

FOURTEEN VICTIMS WERE SHOT A TOTAL OF 29 TIMES AS THEY LAY FACEDOWN ON THE FLOOR

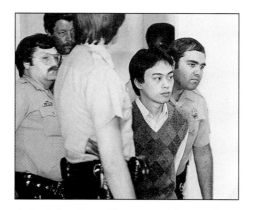

Benjamin Ng, given a life sentence without parole.

Wai-Chiu Ng, received seven consecutive life terms.

It was 12:30 A.M. on February 19, 1983, when Benjamin "Bennie" K. Ng, Kwan Fai "Willie" Mak, and Wai-Chiu "Tony" Ng (the Ngs were not related), walked into the Wah Mee Club in Seattle's Chinatown. Their sole objective was to rob the private gambling club, known for its high stakes, and leave no witnesses.

After binding the hands of the 14 patrons and employees, the three Hong Kong immigrants, all in their twenties, methodically fired bullets into each of their victims' heads at close range. Thinking that everyone was dead, they quickly packed up all the money they could find. The three murderers left with about $10,000, considerably less than the $50,000 to $100,000 that they had believed they would find. Unknown to the killers, one elderly man was still alive.

After the gunmen left, the lone survivor managed to free his hands and crawl out the front door. He was soon found by a passerby who notified the police. When the surviving victim's condition had stabilized and he was able to speak, he positively identified Benjamin Ng and Kwan Mak as two of the gunmen. Wai-Chiu Ng was later identified by other police sources as the third gunman.

During the search of the apartment belonging to Benjamin Ng's girlfriend, detectives discovered a considerable sum of money on her bedroom dresser. Ng told them he had earned it as a dealer at the Hop Sing Club. However, when police found a shoebox containing over $10,000 in cash, Ng had no explanation. Likewise, he could not explain two handguns, ammunition, and a rifle found in the apartment.

The lone survivor of "Seattle's Chinatown Massacre" testified and Benjamin Ng and Kwan Fai Mak were each convicted of 13 counts of murder. Kwan Mak, portrayed as the mastermind, was sentenced to death. Benjamin Ng was sentenced to life imprisonment with no chance of parole. Wai-Chiu Ng was convicted of 13 counts of robbery and sentenced to seven consecutive life terms.

A GREAT GERMAN HOAX

NAZI SYMPATHIZER KONRAD KUJAU ALMOST FOOLED THE PRESS WITH HIS FORGED HITLER DIARIES

Konrad Kujau was a freelance writer and aspiring author. He made his living by day as a military relics dealer in Stuttgart, West Germany. Kujau labored diligently all night long pounding away on his typewriter.

For more than three years, Kujau obsessively spent his nights composing a historic work that was set in the Nazi era. He wrote his docudrama in diary form. The epic was painstakingly researched and accurately detailed. When he was finished, the author rewrote his masterpiece in long hand and bound it in cheap imitation leather. The work filled 60 volumes.

The book was a literary success. *Stern,* West Germany's largest newsmagazine, published excerpts in April 1983. The *Sunday Times* of London and *Paris Match* tried to outbid each other for reprint rights. The book attracted unprecedented international attention. Kujau was paid about one million dollars for his work. His success was short-lived, however, as he tried to pass off his works as Adolph Hitler's previously undiscovered private diaries.

The forgeries had been so well done that he managed to fool Hugh Trevor-Roper, the eminent historian who declared that the documents were authentic. That statement skyrocketed the price of the books. However, when West German government officials tested the diaries' ink, paper, and bindings, they were declared to be "grotesque, superficial forgeries."

Kujau was jailed for fraud after his hoax was exposed. His initial story was that he was merely a middleman who had bought the diaries from some East Germans and then sold them to Gerd Heidemann, a *Stern* reporter. He said the reporter knew the diaries were fakes, a charge the reporter denied.

Kujau was a man who needed to be admired. When Kujau was younger, he told friends that he was an artist and calligrapher when

Konrad Kujau just prior to being convicted of defrauding publishers by passing off his work as Adolph Hitler's previously undiscovered diaries. The court sentenced Kujau to 4½ years in prison. While serving his time, he continued to profit from the hoax by writing about how he pulled it off.

KUJAU SPENT THOUSANDS OF DEUTSCHE MARKS ON CHAMPAGNE AND WOMEN, TELLING TALL TALES ABOUT HIS ACQUAINTANCES IN HITLER'S INNER CIRCLE.

In 1989, Konrad Kujau, holding a forged Dali, opened an art gallery in Stuttgart, Germany, specializing in forged paintings.

he really was a blacksmith, waiter, and window washer. Kujau wore tuxedos to impress his neighbors. He even stretched the truth about his family. The brother he described as a general in the East German Army was actually an assistant policeman at a railway station. Kujau spent thousands of deutsche marks on champagne and women, telling tall tales about his acquaintances in Hitler's inner circle.

Fascinated by anything connected with the Nazi military, Kujau was successful in the 1970s as a dealer in Nazi artifacts. He had a reputation as an eccentric who enjoyed wearing an SS uniform. Kujau owned an extensive collection of uniforms, which he said had been worn by top Nazi officials, including one he swore had been worn by Hitler himself. There is no record, however, that the 45-year-old Kujau had ever served time in Germany's armed forces.

Kujau continued his literary career in his jail cell. He wrote articles for a West German newspaper admitting his guilt and detailing exactly how he did it. This true article earned him $45,000.

DEADLY SEX GAMES

CHRISTOPHER WILDER'S SEXUAL RECREATION BECAME A KILLING GAME WHEN HE COULDN'T TELL THE DIFFERENCE BETWEEN FANTASY AND REALITY

Christopher Wilder was born in 1945 in Australia. His mother was Australian; his father a U.S. Navy man. After World War II ended, the family was stationed in the United States. Intelligent, but dyslexic, he dropped out of school and became a carpenter. Wilder returned to Australia and fell deeply in love. When that relationship ended, he wed on the rebound; the marriage was later annulled.

A good-looking surfer, Wilder found it easy to pick up women. He had long-term relationships with women who resembled his early love. However, Wilder also had a secret sex life that began during his teens—a "game" in which he pretended to be a modeling agent in order to have sex with pretty young women. Once he was arrested for participating in a gang rape. His sentence included electroshock treatments, which he later used on his victims. After returning to the U.S., Wilder continued with his secret games. Tried for rape in 1977, he was acquitted.

By 1984, Wilder was a wealthy 39-year-old playboy contractor with an attractive home in Boynton Beach, Florida. He had a good reputation and many friends. However, his secret sexual obsession had worsened. He fantasized about violence and domination, and he had trouble perceiving where his fantasies ended.

Accused of kidnapping two models, Beth Kenyon and Rosario Gonzales, in March 1984, Wilder began an odyssey of terror that extended from Florida to California and back to New Hampshire. Despite being on the FBI's Most Wanted List and the target of the biggest manhunt since Dillinger, Wilder continued to lure aspiring models until April. He allegedly kidnapped, sexually tortured, and/or killed at least 12 women. Three lived; two were never found.

On April 13, 1984, Wilder had almost reached the Canadian border in New Hampshire when he killed himself while trying to shoot a highway patrolman who was struggling with him.

FBI photo of Christopher Wilder. Wilder's charm was so hypnotic that even though photos of him and stories of his crimes were widely circulated, he continued to find young women who were ready to become victims.

BILLIONAIRE BOYS CLUB

Joe Hunt, charismatic leader of the Billionaire Boys Club, confidently listens to opening statements in his trial for murdering Ron Levin. Hunt's bubble of confidence burst when the jury brought in its verdict. Even though Levin's body was never found, Hunt drew a life sentence for the crime.

WEALTHY YOUNG MEN'S AMBITIONS BECAME DEADLY AS THEIR QUEST FOR SUCCESS GOT OUT OF HAND

They jokingly called themselves the Billionaire Boys Club (BBC). The 30 or so young men in their twenties who joined this investment confederation all came from wealthy families. They had an inherited desire to succeed in a big way and to do it quickly. The cost, however, was high when they committed two cold-blooded murders that smashed their dreams.

Joe Hunt, the leader of the BBC, developed a plan to make them rich with a take-all philosophy of "the end justifies the means." A manifesto presented by Hunt at the organizational meeting in Los Angeles in March 1983 laid out the concept: a network of individuals bound together by "Paradox Philosophy" (getting what you want, whatever the means), and its basic unit was a "cell" (five members). A Billionaire Boys Club business enterprise was called a "shape." The output of a shape was the realization of more money than was put in. BBC leaders were called "shadings," and a shading had to be "the embodiment of Paradox Philosophy." In those elements were incorporated the BBC's format for ruthless murder.

Hunt first brought murder into full focus when he found out that a Los Angeles con man named Ron Levin—for whom Hunt had invested money in commodities that earned $13 million—had bilked him of his promised half of that windfall. Levin stalled, promising eventual payment. On the evening of June 6, 1984, Joe Hunt and another BBC member, Jim Pittman, supposedly went to Levin's apartment and forced the 42-year-old con man to sign a $1.5 million check drawn on a Swiss bank account. Then they took him into a bedroom where they executed him with a silenced .25 caliber pistol as he lay facedown on the bed. The two BBC members hauled the body to a previously dug pit in an isolated canyon. Before burying it, they riddled the corpse with shotgun fire to prevent identification.

In the middle of June, a 23-year-old Iranian man, Reza Eslaminia, was introduced into the BBC. He soon proposed a plan to force his father, Hedayat Eslaminia, a former high-ranking Iranian official, to turn over his assets (estimated in the millions) to Reza, who would split it with the BBC. After careful planning, Hunt, Reza, and three other BBC members allegedly kidnapped the elder Eslaminia on July 30, 1984. They crammed him into a trunk, which they loaded into their car. Then they headed for a Los Angeles hideout where they planned to torture the elder Eslaminia in order to gain control of his money. However, the kidnapping victim suffocated in the trunk en route. The killers dumped the dead man's body into a steep canyon. Later, after Hunt and the others told the BBC membership about the murders, some worried members contacted the police, dispelling earlier conjecture that the elder Eslaminia had fallen victim to Iranian assassins. Police were directed to the dumping spot where Eslaminia's bones were found and identified.

After the arrests of the guilty parties, Joe Hunt was tried and found guilty of first-degree murder in the death of Levin, whose body was never recovered. Hunt received a life sentence in June 1987. In 1988, Reza Eslaminia was sentenced to life, with no possibility of parole, for the murder of Hedayat Eslaminia. Pittman's trial for the Levin slaying was pending as of the last report, as was Hunt's for the Eslaminia murder. One BBC member was given immunity and placed under the witness protection program for testifying against those charged with the murders.

Reza Eslaminia turns around to look at his mother after he was sentenced to life without the possibility of parole for the kidnapping-murder of his father, a former high-ranking Iranian official. The elder Eslaminia suffocated to death before he could be tortured into surrendering control of his fortune to his son.

MURDEROUS RAMPAGE AT McDONALD'S

James Oliver Huberty, the down-on-his-luck family man who staged one of the largest mass shootings by an individual in U.S. history. Like so many individuals who moved to California hoping for a miraculous change in their lives, Huberty found only further frustration and disappointment.

THE RANDOM, SENSELESS KILLING OF 21 INNOCENT PEOPLE AT A McDONALD'S RESTAURANT WILL LONG BE REMEMBERED

James Oliver Huberty was born in the Midwest in 1942. At age 41, he faced a crisis: The plant where he worked in Massillon, Ohio, closed down and he lost his job. Unable to find a suitable position in his hometown, and hearing about the thriving economies of Texas and California, Huberty moved his family to San Ysidro, a suburb of San Diego just north of the Mexican border. When they arrived in December 1983, Huberty was anxious and determined to make a new beginning.

At first, Huberty found work as a security guard in the quiet town, but the job didn't last long. Not knowing where to turn when he was fired, Huberty became extremely frustrated and unhappy. He felt that the move had been his last chance.

On July 18, 1984, an angry-at-the-world Huberty left home carrying a rifle, pistol, shotgun, and a great deal of ammunition. He told his wife that he planned to go "hunting for humans." She had no idea her disturbed husband was dead serious.

Huberty didn't go far for the hunt. The local McDonald's restaurant was close to his home. Huberty began shooting indiscriminately, aiming his fire furiously both inside and outside the crowded restaurant. In no time at all, 21 people died, and 19 were wounded in the attack. Most of the victims were children. It was one of the largest mass shootings by an individual on record. Huberty died when he was struck by a hail of bullets from the hastily summoned SWAT team.

MURDER INFORMATION FOR SALE

LARRY EYLER, A SUSPECTED MULTISTATE MURDERER OF 23 YOUNG MEN, TRIED TO TRADE INFORMATION FOR HIS OWN LIFE

On August 21, 1984, a janitor of an apartment complex in Chicago, Illinois, noticed a muscular man carrying several plastic bags from a neighboring complex to a nearby trash dumpster. The manner in which the man walked to the dumpster indicated that the items in the bags were heavy. After the man walked back to his apartment, a janitor from the man's complex found the bags and decided to examine them. To his horror, he found that the plastic bags contained the dismembered body of a teenage boy.

The man seen carrying the plastic bags was later identified as Larry Eyler, a 31-year-old housepainter. Illinois authorities had previously focused on Eyler as a suspect in a prior murder of a young man and had indicted Eyler in that case. In February 1983, a local judge had reduced Eyler's one-million-dollar bond to $10,000, an amount that Eyler was able to pay in order to gain his freedom.

After the janitor's August 1984 discovery of the dismembered body, Chicago authorities obtained a search warrant for Eyler's apartment. They found human skin in the tub in the laundry room and bloody water in the basement basin. The body in the plastic bags, which had been cut into eight pieces, was identified as that of 15-year-old Daniel Bridges.

Bridges, who had been sexually abused as a young boy, had spent the last four years of his life as a child prostitute. Somehow Bridges had been lured to Eyler's apartment, where he was murdered. An autopsy revealed that Bridges had died from a stab wound to the back, despite multiple stab wounds to the chest. Eyler was tried and found guilty of the murder of the Chicago teenager. He was sentenced to death and for years awaited his fate on death row in the Pontiac Correctional Center in north-central Illinois. Eyler had already been a suspect in 22 other murders of young men and boys in Indiana, Wisconsin, Kentucky, and Illinois.

Larry Eyler after being taken into custody in August 1984 by Chicago police officers. Out on bail at the time for an earlier murder charge, Eyler was seized when a Cook County grand jury ordered him indicted for the murder of Daniel Bridges. Eyler is suspected of committing at least 23 murders.

In October 1990, a Chicago author published the book *Freed to Kill* about Eyler, which lead Indiana authorities to reopen the unsolved homicide of Steve Agan. In December 1990, Eyler began to cooperate with the Indiana authorities about the Agan murder in hopes that he would not be executed in Illinois. Eyler told of his involvement in the 1982 murder of Steve Agan, a 28-year-old car-wash employee in Terre Haute, Indiana, who was found December 28, 1982, in an abandoned building in a remote area near Newport, Indiana. Agan had been bound, gagged, mutilated, and killed.

After he negotiated a plea bargain with Indiana officials, obtaining a 60-year sentence for his role in Agan's death, Eyler gave a detailed confession. Eyler named Robert David Little, a 52-year-old Indiana State University professor, as the man who had been involved in killing Agan. The convicted killer gave a scenario of the homosexual-related murder that he and the university professor had committed. After they promised Agan that he would be paid to engage in sex, they drove the victim to a barn. They then photographed their step-by-step torture of the helpless Agan, taking turns stabbing him until he died.

Eyler had lived with the professor in Terre Haute and later moved to Chicago in 1983. Between 1982 and 1984, Eyler commuted between Terre Haute and Chicago, and he would pick up young men or boys on the highway. He would transport them to any rural location, where they would be bound, tortured, and killed, usually by multiple stab wounds.

On December 13, 1990, Eyler offered Illinois officials his confession to 20 unsolved murders and agreed to implicate Little in five others, in exchange for reducing Eyler's death sentence to life imprisonment. However, Eyler was rejected on January 8, 1991. Eyler remains on death row in the Pontiac Correctional Center in Illinois. Little's trial for his part in Agan's murder begins April 9, 1991.

Daniel Bridges in a photo taken from a television monitor. The 15-year-old male prostitute had been interviewed by a Chicago television station for a special on child pornography. Soon after Bridges appeared on TV, his dismembered body was found wrapped in a trash bin near Larry Eyler's apartment.

THE MAYFLOWER MADAM

ARISTOCRATIC SYDNEY BIDDLE BARROWS RAN A HIGH-CLASS CALL-GIRL OPERATION AND WAS EXPOSED, ALL TO THE DELIGHT OF THE MEDIA

Sydney Biddle Barrows was born on January 14, 1952, in Hopewell, New Jersey, to genteel parents whose ancestors had arrived on the *Mayflower*. When Sydney was four, her father left her mother and money became a problem. Her grandparents helped, and shy and insecure Barrows was reared as a proper young lady. She attended private schools and was presented as a popular, fun-loving, and self-reliant debutante at the annual ball of the Mayflower Society.

Having spent all the money in the college fund that her grandmother had left her, Barrows procured a loan and enrolled at the Fashion Institute of Technology in Manhattan, and graduated highest in her class. She made strides in her fashion career until she was fired when she refused to involve herself in a kickback scam. Unable to find work, Barrows discovered that a friend was making good money answering phones for an escort (actually, call-girl) service. Barrows tried answering the phones as an adventure, and she stayed. However, her boss had poor taste and showed no respect for the clients or the girls. Talking to the other girls, Sydney found that, other than dealing with the boss, they found the work fun.

In 1979, Barrows decided that she could operate a much more refined and businesslike venture, so she started her own business, called Cachet. Barrows taught her carefully selected young women how to dress, how to wear makeup, and how to behave before, during, and after having sex with their clients. Cachet's clients, whose identity and background were checked carefully, were required to behave properly. Barrows was proud that her escorts often attended important functions with rich, powerful, and prominent men.

When Barrows was arrested on October 11, 1984, the media had a field day with her impeccable background. Since her crime had no "victims," she was fined only a nominal amount for a misdemeanor. Later, Barrows earned quite a bit of money when she wrote a popular book about her escort business.

Sidney Biddle Barrows toasts her freedom with a friend, Tom Bird, at a victory party at the Limelight nightclub in New York on July 19, 1985. The Mayflower Madam was celebrating a court agreement in which her felony prostitution charges were reduced to a misdemeanor charge of promoting prostitution.

THE SUBWAY SHOOTOUT

IN A PERSONAL VIGILANTE ACTION, BERNHARD GOETZ SHOT FOUR AFRICAN-AMERICAN MEN WHO HE THOUGHT WERE INTENDING TO MUG HIM

Bernhard Goetz announces that he will bring legal action against Darrell Cabey, one of four African-Americans whom Goetz had shot on a subway train. The move was made to counter Cabey's $50 million civil suit against Goetz, which is still pending. Cabey was paralyzed by one of Goetz's bullets.

On December 22, 1984, Bernhard Goetz, 37 and white, sat in a subway car in New York City. Seconds after the train rattled off, four African-American men—Darrell Cabey, 19; James Ramseur, 18; Troy Canty, 19; and Barry Allen, 18—approached Goetz. Goetz believed that the four young men intended to mug him. In retaliation, Goetz pulled out a pistol and fired at the four. Emergency brakes brought the subway train to a screeching halt, allowing Goetz to exit and disappear. In his wake were the four African-Americans, on the floor and bleeding. Darrell Cabey was paralyzed by one of Goetz's bullets.

Goetz fled to Vermont but returned to New York two days later. As a result of various tips, police had left a note on Goetz's door. The note prompted Goetz to backtrack to Vermont and then to New Hampshire. Finally, on December 31, Goetz turned himself in to the local police in Concord, New Hampshire.

After Goetz's arrest, the media reported the criminal records of the four African-American men, portraying them as muggers on the prowl for "whitey." Goetz was hailed by many as a hero. Some members of the African-American community, however, claimed that the shooting was racially motivated.

Goetz posted bail and was released on January 7, 1985. Eventually, Goetz faced 13 charges, including attempted murder, assault, and criminal weapon possession. The trial commenced on April 27, 1987, and ended June 16. Goetz claimed that he had acted in self-defense. He had previously been robbed and beaten in 1981 in the subway, and he was certain this group had intended to do the same.

Bernhard Goetz was found guilty of third-degree criminal weapon possession. He was sentenced to six months in jail, 4½ years probation, and 280 hours of community service. He also paid a fine of $5,075 and was ordered to receive psychiatric counseling. Goetz still faces Darrell Cabey's $50 million civil suit.

RAPE RECANTED

CATHLEEN CROWELL WEBB RECANTED HER TESTIMONY THAT HAD SENT GARY DOTSON TO JAIL ON A RAPE CHARGE

On July 9, 1977, 16-year-old Cathleen Crowell reported to the police authorities in a suburb of Chicago, Illinois, that she had been sexually assaulted. She gave a detailed account of the kidnapping and rape, as well as a description of the assailant and his vehicle. Later, she identified her attacker—Gary Dotson—in a photo lineup. The teenager identified a second man in a lineup as an accomplice of the rapist. Dotson was arrested and held for trial.

During the trial, the victim testified to the injuries to her breast, stomach, and legs during the alleged attack. She told the court that Dotson had cut words onto her stomach. In Dotson's defense, five witnesses swore that he had been with them on the evening of the rape. Nevertheless, Dotson was convicted of rape and kidnapping, and he was sentenced to 25 to 50 years in prison. Crowell's testimony had been instrumental in achieving a guilty verdict.

In March 1985, six years after the trial, the victim—then in her early twenties, married, the mother of two children, and a born-again Christian—told her minister that she had wrongfully accused a man of rape. Later, Cathleen Webb (nee Crowell) went on national television and confessed that she had lied about the rape. The following month, she appeared in court and told the original trial judge that she had fabricated the rape story.

During her recantation, Webb stated that she had ripped her clothing, placed scratches on her breast with her fingernails, and cut words on her stomach with a broken bottle in order to fake the rape evidence. Webb claimed that she had engaged in sex with her boyfriend around that time and thought she was pregnant. Fearful of the situation, the rape story evolved. Despite Webb's recantation of her earlier testimony, the trial judge did not grant Dotson a new trial.

In May 1985, Illinois Governor James Thompson presided over a clemency hearing for Dotson. Cathleen Webb spent five hours on the

Gary Dotson in April 1985, the day before he and Cathleen Crowell Webb were to appear at a second hearing on evidence that cast doubts on Webb's recantation of rape charges against Dotson. Webb had retracted her sworn testimony of six years earlier that Dotson had raped her on July 9, 1977.

WEBB CLAIMED THAT SHE HAD ENGAGED IN SEX WITH HER BOYFRIEND AROUND THAT TIME AND THOUGHT SHE WAS PREGNANT. FEARFUL OF THE SITUATION, THE RAPE STORY EVOLVED.

Cathleen Crowell Webb listens intently at a May 1985 hearing of the Illinois Prisoner Review Board while her attorney John McLario refills a water glass.

witness stand in Dotson's defense. Details of the self-inflicted letters scratched on her stomach in 1977 became a focal point during the hearing. It was pointed out that if these letters had been self-inflicted, the victim would have had to write them upside down and backward. Another issue was her identification of Dotson's accomplice. The person that Webb had identified as the accomplice was a close friend of Dotson. Investigators also discovered that the television program that Dotson's alibi witnesses claimed to have watched with Dotson did not air until two months after the rape.

The truth concerning what happened that summer night in 1977 may never be known. On May 12, 1985, Governor Thompson stated that Dotson had already served more than the average time for a rape conviction, and so he granted Gary Dotson clemency.

SPYING WAS A FAMILY THING

JOHN A. WALKER, A NAVY OFFICER IN NEED OF MONEY, MASTERMINDED WHAT WAS PERHAPS THE MOST DAMAGING SPY RING IN AMERICAN HISTORY

John A. Walker joined the Navy in 1955. His career was commendable until December 1967. At that time, he was a watch officer in the message room of the operations headquarters for the U.S. Navy's Atlantic Fleet. All U.S. Navy ships operating in the Atlantic Ocean were directed from that two-story building in Norfolk, Virginia. Concerned over marital and financial problems, Walker impulsively stole a secret document. He took the document to the Soviet embassy in Washington, D.C., and announced to a Soviet official, "I want to sell you top secrets—valuable military information."

Thus began Walker's life as a spy. Walker once said that he would have been a criminal no matter what field he worked in. If he had been a banker, he would have stolen money; if he had had access to drugs, he would have been a dope dealer. Although spying was a somewhat unusual crime, the simple truth was that Walker needed the money to maintain his lavish lifestyle and womanizing.

The Soviets accepted Walker's offer. Over the next two decades, Walker stole and delivered highly classified secrets to the Soviets at designated drop sites. He picked up a bundle of cash after each drop; his payoffs ran into the thousands of dollars. Walker also brought others into the operation. He recruited his son Michael and his brother Arthur (Michael's uncle), both of whom served in the Navy. Naval communications specialist Jerry Whitworth also became part of the spy ring.

For nearly 20 years, while in the Navy and after he had left the service, John Walker supplied the Soviet Union with top-secret military information. Through his espionage network, Walker sold data crucial to America's national security. Included among the information sold was a detailed plan on how the Navy would respond if a war started in Central America, as well as schematics of the missile defense system aboard the USS *Nimitz* and its known weaknesses.

John A. Walker returns to the Montgomery County Detention Center in Rockville, Maryland, after attending a pre-trial hearing on his espionage charges. The former U.S. Navy officer sold top-secret documents to the Soviets for nearly 20 years in order to maintain his lavish lifestyle.

Walker also sold the Soviets a study of how America's spy satellites could be sabotaged, and actual authentication codes needed to launch U.S. nuclear missiles. The spies also sold key U.S. cryptographic secrets that Soviet agents used to decode one million coded Navy dispatches. There was also information concerning how the U.S. Navy planned to attack the Soviet Union in the event of war.

By 1985, the marriage of John and Barbara Walker had ended in divorce. Barbara Walker, concerned about the Walker children, contacted the FBI. Barbara's alcoholism was a source of skepticism for the FBI. However, after the FBI contacted daughter Laura Walker, whom her father tried to recruit, federal agents moved into action. Early on the morning of May 20, 1985, John Walker was arrested by the FBI after making a drop at a site near Rockville, Maryland. His arrest was followed by the arrests of Jerry Whitworth, Michael Walker, and Arthur Walker.

John Walker agreed to plead guilty in exchange for a lighter sentence for his son. John Walker received two life terms plus 100 years. All sentences were to be served concurrently, making him eligible for parole in ten years. Michael Walker received two 25-year terms and three 10-year terms, all to be served concurrently; he would be eligible for parole after eight years. Jerry Whitworth was sentenced to 365 years in prison; he would not be eligible for parole until he reached age 107. Arthur Walker was given a sentence of life in prison.

A former high-ranking KGB official who had defected to the U.S. told the FBI that the Walker espionage ring was "the most important operation in the KGB's history."

Jerry Whitworth being escorted from the San Francisco Federal Building following his arraignment on charges of conspiracy to commit espionage. The Naval communications specialist was the only member of the spy ring whom John Walker recruited from outside his own family.

THE WOMAN WHO LOVED GORILLAS

GORILLA EXPERT DIAN FOSSEY TRIED TO PROTECT HER MAGNIFICENT APES, ONLY TO DIE A MYSTERIOUS DEATH IN AFRICA

When she died, Dian Fossey had been the director of the Karisoki Research Center, a station for the study of mountain gorillas in Africa, for 18 years. Under Fossey's direction, the center became internationally known and respected for its scientific findings.

In 1963, Fossey made her first trip to Africa. She felt an immediate kinship with the magnificent apes. She met Louis Leakey, the eminent British anthropologist who had revolutionized the study of human origins. She returned to Africa in 1966 and set up a camp, funded meagerly by Leakey and the National Geographic Society.

Living conditions were primitive, the environment was alien, and the isolation was total. During Fossey's years in Rwanda, Africa, civil war broke out and she was captured and sexually molested.

After several years, the relationship between Fossey and the gorillas reached a stage where they let her sit with them while they ate, played, and made love. Her scientific work was excellent, highly detailed, and accurate. She wrote several articles for *National Geographic* and a very popular book called *Gorillas in the Mist*.

Fossey hated poachers who came into her territory to trap gorillas in order to ship them to foreign countries. Sometimes they only wounded the animals, leaving them to die. Fossey devoted a great deal of energy to destroying traps and snares and to raiding poachers' villages. Her obsession made enemies out of the natives, the poachers, the government, and even those in her own camp.

On December 26, 1985, someone broke into Fossey's cabin and killed her with her own machete. Though there have been many theories about the murder and some people were arrested, no one has ever been convicted. Authorities feel it could have been someone that she had alienated, a hired assassin, or just a thief. Her brutal murder remains one of Africa's great unsolved mysteries.

Dian Fossey fraternizes with mountain gorillas in the Virunga Mountains in Rwanda in 1982. Three years later, she was murdered with her own machete. Many suspects emerged, among them one of Fossey's research assistants. However, at this writing, the crime is still unsolved.

THE PREPPIE MURDER CASE

THE DECADENT LIFESTYLE OF NEW YORK'S PREP SCHOOL STUDENTS LED TO A DEATH IN CENTRAL PARK

Robert Chambers arrives at Manhattan Criminal Court for a pre-trial hearing. Chambers ultimately negotiated a plea bargain. He pleaded guilty to manslaughter and was sentenced to five to 15 years in prison.

Robert Chambers was born in Queens, New York. Chambers's mother, Phyllis, was socially ambitious. She enrolled Robert in the "best" schools, where many prominent families sent their children. Phyllis did charity work and made friends with the "right" people.

Although Phyllis spoiled Robert and excused his faults, she also demanded a great deal of him. At an early age, Chambers began using drugs. He was expelled from one school, and then another. Chambers hung out with young people he had known from his prep school days, many of whom used drugs. They frequented a bar called Dorrian's Red Hand, drinking until late at night. Sleeping around was a common practice. To keep up with the expenses connected with this lifestyle, Chambers stole from the homes of his wealthy companions.

Jennifer Levin was part of this social circle. She fell for the 19-year-old Chambers—a handsome, daring bad boy. The pair dated a few times. Although she was very interested in him, he seemed indifferent. On August 26, 1986, Levin and Chambers left Dorrian's Red Hand together about 4:30 A.M.

Later that morning, Levin's body was found in Central Park with her clothes bunched around her waist. Eighteen hours later, Chambers confessed to killing her; he claimed it was an accident. They had gone to Central Park, where Levin's sexual advances were not welcomed by Chambers. Trying to stop her, Chambers said he flipped her over his head, accidentally killing her.

A combination of poor police investigative work and an experienced defense lawyer undermined the prosecution's case. The jury deliberated for days without reaching a verdict. Finally, a plea bargain was worked out. Chambers pleaded guilty to manslaughter, but he had to admit in court that he had "intended to cause serious physical injury to Jennifer." Chambers was sentenced to five to 15 years in prison; he will be eligible for parole in 1993.

THE TWO-BILLION-DOLLAR S&L FRAUD

CHARLES H. KEATING, JR., WAS CHARGED WITH STEALING BILLIONS IN A NEW, MODERN WAY—ALLEGEDLY WITH THE HELP OF U.S. SENATORS

Federal bank examiners from San Francisco were summoned by Arizona Senator Dennis DeConcini to meet with him and four other U.S. senators. The meeting with the five senators—who would later be dubbed "the Keating Five"—took place April 9, 1987, in DeConcini's office. The discussion centered on the bank examiners' performance in their investigation of the Lincoln Savings and Loan in Irvine, California. Lincoln Savings and Loan was owned by Charles H. Keating, Jr. The lawmakers had directly and indirectly received gifts and contributions from Keating totaling about $1.3 million.

News reports quoted DeConcini saying to the examiners during the meeting, "Actions of yours could injure a constituent." John Glenn—astronaut hero and senator from Ohio—supported DeConcini when he said, "You should charge them or get off their backs." And Michigan Senator Donald Riegle demanded, "Where are the losses?" Senators Alan Cranston of California and John McCain of Arizona also participated in the meeting.

The losses about which Senator Riegle asked soon became apparent. As a result of transactions performed by Keating's Lincoln Savings and Loan, this now-bankrupt institution will have to be bailed out at a cost expected to exceed two billion dollars. Keating's alleged convoluted manipulations purportedly led to this disaster. According to the bank examining agent, "Lincoln was flying blind on all of their different loans and investments," with no underwriting on most. Also, Lincoln's practices "violated the law, regulations, and common sense." The examiners noted that Lincoln's reported $49-million profit in 1986 was simply a matter of bookkeeping trickery.

Charles Keating appearing before the House Banking Committee hearings on his Lincoln Savings and Loan Association in California. The banking magnate invoked his constitutional rights against testifying and further declared that, in the event of an adverse ruling against him, he would fight it until the day he died.

The complex financial maneuvers reportedly masterminded by Keating began in 1976 in Phoenix, Arizona. Keating built a home-construction company into American Continental Corporation, which bought Lincoln Savings and Loan for $51 million in 1984. When the Reagan administration relaxed banking regulations, Keating supposedly used his S&L to invest in junk bonds, raw land, and such superdevelopment projects as the Phoenician Resort, originally a $500-per-night (now less than $200) hotel in Scottsdale, Arizona.

Keating's many deals reportedly caused the greatest loss ever suffered by American investors. American Continental went bankrupt while the Securities and Exchange Commission was looking into the failure of Lincoln. Some 22,000 people held $200 million in bonds outstanding from Lincoln. Many of the bondholders were small investors who had lost their life savings.

The U.S. government seized the Lincoln Savings and Loan on April 14, 1989, and various branches of the U.S. government set in motion assorted suits and actions against Keating. Charles Keating wound up with 42 charges of fraud against him. At age 66, the lean, aggressive Keating—a former Navy fighter pilot and Olympic swimmer—responded with the combative instinct that had brought him success. He stated, "I will fight [any adverse ruling against me] until the day I'm dead."

Unable to post a bond of five million dollars, Keating was incarcerated for a short period. His lawyers convinced a federal court to reduce the bond to $300,000, which freed Keating. Disputing all charges, Keating argued that he'd done nothing wrong. Meanwhile, delays and legal hurdles continue to clog the way to ending this financial fiasco. Some government officials believe that the end to Keating's catastrophic problems might be years away.

Ohio Senator John Glenn, one of "the Keating Five."

THE KEATING FIVE

Perhaps the most disturbing aspect of the failure of Charles Keating's Lincoln Savings and Loan concerns the involvement of five U.S. senators. "The Keating Five"—Arizona Senators Dennis DeConcini and John McCain, Ohio Senator John Glenn, California Senator Alan Cranston, and Michigan Senator Donald Riegle—intervened with bank regulators on behalf of Charles Keating's Lincoln Savings and Loan. Did Keating "buy" the help of these senators with contributions totaling some $1.3 million? Or were the senators merely assisting a constituent in his dealings with the federal government?

The Senate Ethics Committee, chaired by Senator Howell T. Heflin, with Robert S. Bennett serving as the panel's special counsel, must decide if any of the five senators acted improperly when intervening with the regulators. The Ethics Committee—taking testimony from the five senators as well as other witnesses—continues its hearings as the Keating saga unfolds. The committee can recommend various actions for the full U.S. Senate to take, including censure or expulsion of the Keating Five.

THE DEATH OF LITTLE LISA

LAWYER JOEL STEINBERG, HIGH ON DOPE, BATTERED TO DEATH HIS ILLEGALLY ADOPTED DAUGHTER, SIX-YEAR-OLD LISA

On November 2, 1987, six-year-old Lisa Steinberg—a pretty girl with hazel eyes and shoulder-length hair—lay comatose and naked on the bathroom floor of a Greenwich Village apartment. Hedda Nussbaum, the common-law wife of lawyer Joel Steinberg and the "adoptive" mother of Lisa, dialed the 911 emergency phone number and stated that Lisa had stopped breathing.

Officers responding from New York City's Sixth Precinct and paramedics from St. Vincent's Hospital were revolted by the condition of the apartment. The place was filthy, foul-smelling, dark, and cluttered with broken chairs and furniture; it was far below acceptable living conditions. The media later dubbed it "the Cave." Emergency attempts to revive the child failed, and she was rushed to the hospital. The attending physician found severe beating trauma to Lisa's head and body, and immediately suspected brain damage. But despite all attempts, Lisa was dead, a victim of child abuse.

The investigation following Lisa's death revealed Steinberg's shady past. He had somehow bypassed the New York bar examination. His mob connections led to drug abuse that eventually grew to freebasing cocaine nightly. Steinberg violently beat Hedda Nussbaum and virtually controlled her life from the time they met in 1975. Even as Steinberg enrolled her in his lifestyle of drug abuse, the drug addiction took control of both their lives.

Another aspect of Steinberg's devious past concerned his illegal adoption of Lisa. Steinberg took possession of baby Lisa when the biological mother—young and unmarried—released her child to Steinberg after he promised to place the baby with Catholic parents.

Joel Steinberg being escorted from a Manhattan police station after he and his common-law wife Hedda Nussbaum were charged with the attempted murder of their illegally adopted daughter Lisa. The charge was upgraded to murder when the six-year-old child died from her injuries.

When the recipient parents failed to pay his illegal $50,000 fee, Steinberg kept the baby and had thugs beat up the parents. Steinberg gave Lisa his last name but never adopted her.

Hedda Nussbaum, addicted to drugs and trying to care for Lisa, was frequently absent from her job as an editor. Her drug addiction and child-rearing responsibilities also made her unable to perform her job whenever she did go to work. Eventually, Nussbaum was fired. Steinberg's increasing drug abuse led to more frequent and severe beatings of Nussbaum. His physical abuse was accompanied by psychological abuse attacking her self-esteem. Steinberg ruptured Nussbaum's spleen, smashed her nose, gave her a cauliflower ear, knocked out several teeth, fractured nine ribs, and broke her jaw. He also burned her face, leaving her grotesquely scarred. Attempts by Nussbaum's family and friends to help her were thwarted by Steinberg.

Although Nussbaum's appearance told the story of her horrible life with Steinberg, the focus of the investigation centered on Lisa. Steinberg had literally beaten a defenseless child to death. Early reports stated that he had beaten Lisa with an exercise bar, but that was later corrected: He had beaten her "with his bare hands."

Steinberg was arrested on a murder charge. On October 17, 1988, the trial began in a Manhattan courtroom before Judge Harold J. Rothwax. A parade of witnesses, including police, doctors, and neighbors, and the silent testimony of pictures pointed to Steinberg's brutality. The climax of the trial came during Nussbaum's testimony, which detailed Lisa's injuries and her lying unconscious for hours before help was summoned.

Steinberg was found guilty of manslaughter in the first degree. He was sentenced to 8½ to 25 years in the Dannemora State Prison with a recommendation of no parole.

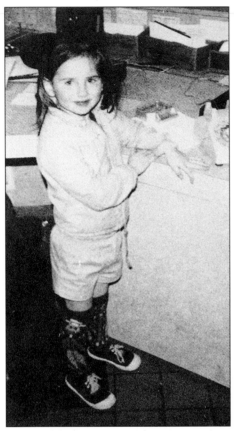

Lisa Steinberg in the state trooper barracks in Orange County, New York. Minutes earlier, police had removed her from a car that Joel Steinberg was driving when a toll-booth collector reported that she appeared to be in distress. Less than two weeks after this photograph was taken, Steinberg beat the child to death.

TERROR IN THE CLASSROOM

MENTALLY DISTURBED LAURIE DANN WENT ON A SHOOTING RAMPAGE, KILLING ONE AND WOUNDING SIX OTHERS BEFORE TAKING HER OWN LIFE

On May 20, 1988, Laurie Wasserman Dann, a 30-year-old divorcée, walked into a second-grade classroom of the Hubbard Woods Elementary School in Winnetka, Illinois, an affluent Chicago suburb. The teacher, Amy Moses, thought Dann was somebody who wanted to observe the class. Dann was given a seat, but she sat for only a few moments. Without a word, Dann rose, left the room, and walked into the boy's lavatory with a gun drawn. When first grader Robert Tross, age six, entered, she shot him in the chest and stomach, leaving him and the weapon—a .357 Magnum—on the floor.

Then Dann returned to the classroom, shut the door, and ordered Moses to put all the children in a corner of the room. When the teacher refused, Dann pulled out a small handgun. Moses and Dann struggled; Dann drew another gun. Moses managed to open the door and call for help, but Dann broke free and fired at the children. Four second-graders were seriously wounded. One student, Nicholas Corwin, was killed instantly when he pushed his best friend out of the line of fire.

Dann fled the school and jumped into her car. She accidentally drove a few blocks down a dead-end street and crashed into a tree. After reloading her guns, she ran into a nearby house.

The quick-thinking Dann told the house's residents that she had been assaulted. She said the police were after her for shooting her assailant. One member of the household, 20-year-old Philip Andrew, sensed that something was wrong. He persuaded Dann to make a phone call; she called her parents. After the call, Andrew tried to take Dann's gun, but she shot him in the chest. In the commotion, the other residents hurried outside. Dann then ran upstairs, put the gun in her mouth, and fired. She died instantly. In her wake, Dann killed one person, besides herself, and wounded six. Later investigations showed that Laurie Dann had a lengthy history of mental illness.

When she walked into an elementary school classroom in Winnetka, Illinois, Laurie Dann was presumed to be somebody who came to observe. Invited to sit down, Dann remained quiet for a time and then went into action. The deeply troubled 30-year-old divorcée left a bloody trail before she killed herself.

THE JUNK BOND KING DETHRONED

Junk bond trader Michael Milken grins widely as he leaves the October 1988 Annual Fixed Income Investors Group luncheon at the Grand Hyatt Hotel in New York. The Drexel Burnham Lambert broker was already facing insider trading charges when he spoke to the small investors who attended the luncheon.

MICHAEL MILKEN CREATED A NEW FINANCIAL MARKET AND MADE MILLIONS, BUT THE FRAUD THAT HELPED HIM TO THE TOP EVENTUALLY BROUGHT HIM DOWN

In 1987, 40-year-old Michael Milken was a fabulously wealthy, highly respected investment broker. Drexel Burnham Lambert Group Incorporated, the securities firm that employed Milken, paid him over $550 million in compensation in 1987. From 1983 to 1987, his earnings surpassed a staggering one billion dollars.

As a child, Milken was a whiz kid in math. He prepared tax returns before he was ten years old. His favorite pastime was reading *The Wall Street Journal.* In 1969, Drexel Burnham Lambert hired Milken while he was working on his MBA at the prestigious Wharton School of the University of Pennsylvania.

Milken's specialty became junk bonds, which are bonds that carry a higher risk and offer a higher return than safer, investment-grade bonds. Milken convinced his employers that junk bonds were less risky than they appeared. By 1978, Drexel had sent Milken to Southern California, giving him carte blanche to manage the firm's junk bond operations. Milken established himself at the center of a complex web of traders, corporate raiders, and financiers. He could conduct half a dozen multimillion-dollar deals simultaneously. Milken had the financial clout to raise up to one billion dollars within a few days. His creation of the junk bond market helped make possible the corporate takeover boom of the 1980s.

Every transaction that the financial wizard made meant fat fees for himself and Drexel. Milken frequently represented both the seller and the buyer of junk bonds in the same deal—a deal Milken himself frequently initiated. The situation was ripe for abuse.

Milken, however, appeared to be an upright American entrepreneur. He married his childhood sweetheart, had three children, and didn't smoke or drink. One associate labeled him a "boring health nut." Milken also gave large sums of money to civic and religious causes.

In May 1986, the empire built on junk bonds began to crumble. The Securities and Exchange Commission (SEC) accused Drexel employee Dennis Levine of insider trading. Levine implicated stock market speculator Ivan Boesky. In turn, Boesky, pressured by the federal government, agreed to secretly gather evidence on other illegal transactions.

By September 1988, the SEC had enough evidence to charge Drexel with securities fraud. The indictment listed counts of insider trading, market manipulation, racketeering, and other criminal activities. Milken became the principal target of the most far-reaching securities fraud investigation in U.S. history.

The SEC and Drexel negotiated a plea bargain in December 1988. Drexel pleaded guilty to six felony charges and promised to pay over $650 million in fines. On March 29, 1989, Milken was indicted. He was named the leader of a conspiracy to defraud Drexel's clients, shareholders, and the investing public. In June 1989, Milken left Drexel and formed his own consulting firm. Drexel filed for Chapter 11 bankruptcy on February 13, 1990.

On April 24, 1990, Milken pleaded guilty to six counts of securities fraud, and he agreed to pay $600 million in penalties. Seven months later, Milken was sentenced to ten years in prison and ordered to perform 1,800 hours of community service. Judge Kimba Wood said that she imposed such a harsh sentence to send a message to the securities market that such criminal activity would not be tolerated.

Ivan Boesky before he was accused of insider trading.

IVAN BOESKY: OUT TO SAVE HIS OWN NECK

Michael Milken wasn't the only person that the federal government nailed through Boesky's cooperation. In fact, Boesky implicated some of the biggest names in the financial markets through secret testimony before federal grand juries. Boesky testified against a stock trader who had once been his best friend and who had let Boesky in on some good deals. Boesky also taped hundreds of conversations that supplied the government with invaluable evidence.

In 1986, Boesky copped a plea in exchange for his information about insider trader schemes. He was well rewarded. Boesky received a relatively "soft" prison term of three years. He also refunded $50 million in illegal profits and paid a fine of $100 million to settle civil charges brought against him by the SEC. However, Boesky was prohibited from ever trading U.S. securities again.

KILLER ON THE RUN

JOHN LIST, A RELIGIOUS ACCOUNTANT, WAS ACTUALLY A MASS MURDERER WHO HAD ELUDED CAPTURE FOR 18 YEARS

Officers escort John List to court in Richmond, Virginia, on June 8, 1989. The persistence of a former acquaintance of his second wife led to his unmasking. After killing all five members of his immediate family in 1971, List changed his name, remarried, and remained a fugitive for 18 years before he was apprehended.

On December 7, 1971, patrolmen were dispatched to the Westfield, New Jersey, home of 46-year-old John Emil List and his family. A neighbor had phoned in a report that List's 19-room mansion had been brightly lit for several weeks. The police found the house cold and devoid of life. To their horror, they found five decomposed bodies belonging to List's wife Helen, 46; his daughter Patricia, 16; his two sons, John, Jr., 15, and Frederick, 13; and his mother Alma, 85. It was later established that they had died on or around November 9. All had been shot to death and neatly arranged in a row.

List had vanished. In 1972, less than one year after the killings, a fire mysteriously destroyed the List mansion.

It seemed that List was $11,000 behind on two mortgages—he was facing bank foreclosure on his house. Moreover, List thought that Helen drank heavily. Worse still, his daughter Patricia was an aspiring actress whom List believed was experimenting with marijuana. The morally rigid List could not tolerate all this. In a letter unearthed later, List confessed to his pastor that "by killing them, they would die Christians." List, a devout Christian, apparently had used his faith to justify murder.

List eluded capture for 18 years. Renaming himself Robert P. Clark, he moved to Denver, Colorado, and married Delores Miller in 1985. Later they moved near Richmond, Virginia, where he worked as an accountant.

In April 1989, the television program *America's Most Wanted* focused on List's deeds. Among the viewers was Wanda Flannery, an acquaintance of Delores Clark from Denver. Wanda recognized List as the man who called himself Bob Clark. She notified the FBI, and Clark was arrested in June 1989. Identified by fingerprints and a scar behind his ear as John List, he was charged with the 1971 murders of his five family members. List is currently awaiting trial.

MURDER BECAME A FAMILY AFFAIR

LYLE AND ERIK MENENDEZ WERE YOUNG, GOOD-LOOKING, AND LIVING THE GOOD LIFE, SO WHY DID THEY ALLEGEDLY SLAUGHTER THEIR WEALTHY PARENTS?

José Enrique Menendez was a Cuban who came to the United States in 1960 when he was 16 years old to avoid Castro's regime. He passed the CPA exam, got married, and had two sons, Lyle and Erik.

Hard work and ingenuity enabled José to rise to the top position of Live Entertainment, a music- and video-software distribution company. Along with his business success came wealth, so José and his wife Mary Louise "Kitty" purchased a five-million-dollar house in Beverly Hills, California.

Lyle, 22, and Erik, 19, were young, handsome, and rich—they didn't have a care in the world. Then, on August 20, 1989, the boys came home from a movie to find that their parents had literally been blown to pieces by over a dozen shotgun blasts.

The boys claimed to have been devastated. The police, however, were suspicious. And with good reason. José Menedez had a $400,000 life insurance policy and his personal assets amounted to $14 million. Curiously, José's last will—which had greatly reduced his sons' share of his estate—had been "accidentally" erased from the family computer. (It later came out that the erasure had been made by Lyle.) This left only José's nine-year-old will, which bequeathed his entire estate to the boys.

On top of all that, the Menendez boys couldn't produce a theater ticket stub removing them from the crime scene. More damning still, a shotgun shell casing was found in one of Lyle's jackets.

Six months later, Lyle and Erik Menendez were arrested, and Ira Reiner, the district attorney, charged them with their parents' murders and asked for the death penalty. Ironically, among Erik's belongings the authorities found a screenplay that he had written entitled *The Perfect Murder.* Not surprisingly, it was about two kids who kill their parents. The fate of the Menedez brothers has yet to be determined.

Lyle, left, and Erik Menendez leave the courtroom after a judge ruled that the taped conversations between the brothers and their psychologist can be used as evidence against them.

A ROADSIDE KILLING

CHARLES STUART'S SUICIDE
MIGHT HAVE BEEN A
CONFESSION OF SORTS TO
THE MURDER OF HIS
PREGNANT WIFE

Charles Stuart and his wife Carol in 1987, two years
before she was slain and he was wounded in their car.
Stuart told his rescuers, who were summoned via a
car phone, that an African-American man had robbed
them. In their zeal to solve the case, the police
enraged Boston's African-American community.

On October 23, 1989, Charles Stuart dialed Boston's 911 emergency number from his car phone. In pain, he said, "my wife's been shot. I've been shot." Stuart, 29, was unable to give his car's location as his wife Carol, 30, lay unconscious from a severe head wound.

The police found the Stuarts and rushed them to a nearby hospital. Charles, who had been shot in the abdomen, survived. Carol, who had been seven months pregnant, did not. Their son Christopher, delivered by cesarean section as Carol lay dying, outlived his mother by only 17 days.

Charles Stuart told police that he and Carol, both white, were returning home from a childbirth class when they were stopped by an African-American man. Stuart said that the man forced them to drive to an isolated area before he shot and robbed them.

Racial tensions flared in Boston as police indiscriminately detained over 200 African-American men who fit the gunman's description. Stuart identified one of those arrested in a lineup, but no formal charges were filed. Eventually, the investigators suspected Stuart himself, who had collected an insurance payment of $82,000 only three days after the shootings.

The investigators' suspicions were confirmed when Stuart's brother Matthew told police that Charles had given him Carol's handbag to throw into the Pines River. The bag was recovered along with a .38 caliber revolver that had been reported missing from a safe in Kakas & Sons furriers, which Charles had managed.

Although it had then become clear to the authorities that Stuart had shot himself and murdered his wife for the money, he was neither charged nor brought to trial. Before the police could arrest him, on January 4, 1990, approximately three months after his wife's death, an apparently guilt-tormented Charles Stuart committed suicide by jumping into the Mystic River.

DOUBLE-DEALING DRUG DEALER

MANUEL NORIEGA, DEPOSED DICTATOR OF PANAMA, DECEIVED THE U.S. THROUGH HIS ALLEGED DRUG DEALING, WHICH LED TO HIS DOWNFALL

Manuel Antonio Noriega began working for U.S. intelligence agencies in the 1950s, passing on information about fellow students while attending a military academy. In 1976, when George Bush was director of the Central Intelligence Agency (CIA), Noriega worked as a CIA agent, and, over the years, he was reportedly paid between $300,000 and several million dollars by the CIA and the U.S. Army.

Panama had the ability to function as a listening post for developments throughout Central America and the Caribbean. In 1983, Noriega's alliance with Cuba's Fidel Castro was strong enough that Vice President George Bush phoned him three hours before the U.S. invaded Grenada. Bush requested that Noriega call Castro and warn him not to interfere. Noriega made the call.

Throughout the 1980s until 1987, the Reagan administration argued that Noriega cooperated fully with U.S. efforts to stem the flow of drugs into the U.S. This "assistance" allowed the U.S. government to look the other way as Noriega amassed more power and became more brutal than ever in Panamanian affairs.

Noriega had strong contacts with the Colombian drug cartel. He allegedly used his power to seize narcotics and to arrest drug smugglers. However, it was reported that only minute amounts of the seized drugs were destroyed or surrendered to the proper authorities. And the drug traffickers Noriega arrested were minor dealers who were rumored to have failed to pay off Noriega.

In May 1989, Noriega declared the Panamanian presidential election void, charging foreign interference. With the help of his "Dignity Battalion" of 8,000 fanatical, brutal soldiers, Noriega made himself dictator of Panama. However, his fellow Panamanians were less than satisfied with his ruthless way of ruling. On October 3, 1989, a group of Panamanian patriots attempted to overthrow the dictator. The coup failed, and Noriega executed its leaders.

Manuel Noriega poses for a U.S. Justice Department mug shot. The ousted Panamanian dictator had dodged his arrest for years on charges of drug trafficking. As a last resort, he took sanctuary in the papal embassy in his homeland for 11 days before finally agreeing to surrender to U.S. forces.

AN AMERICAN NAVY LIEUTENANT WAS PULLED OUT OF A CAR BY PANAMA DEFENSE FORCES WHILE HIS WIFE WAS THREATENED WITH GANG RAPE. THOSE ACTS WERE ALL PRESIDENT BUSH NEEDED.

Those actions forced the U.S. to begin planning a means of removing Noriega from power. While awaiting an excuse to act, the U.S. government secretly plotted an invasion of Panama. Noriega soon gave the U.S. the pretext it needed.

Noriega declared that the economic sanctions that the U.S. had imposed on Panama in April 1988 had created a "state of war" between the two countries. He also charged that the U.S. had instigated the unsuccessful October 1989 coup. Foreigners in Panama were threatened, harassed, and held hostage. One American sailor was killed, and several civilians were wounded by Noriega's men. An American Navy lieutenant was pulled out of a car by Panama Defense Forces (PDF) while his wife was threatened with gang rape. Those acts were all President Bush needed.

On December 20, 1989, some 12,000 U.S. troops were dispatched to supplement the 12,000 American soldiers already stationed bases in Panama. The plan was to have these combined forces launch a massive simultaneous assault on all PDF strongholds.

The Pentagon had hoped the PDF would crumble under the onslaught, but the determined dictator resisted. The battle turned into a nasty street fight in densely populated Panama City. After several days of fighting, the massive attack by the U.S. forces was victorious. However, Noriega—whose capture had been deemed critical by President Bush—eluded the net. Noriega and four aides sought refuge in the papal embassy in Panama on December 24. The fugitives carried an assortment of weapons and suspicious-looking vials of injectable liquids. Under the Vatican tradition of granting sanctuary to anyone fleeing persecution, Monsignor José Sebastian Laboa had no choice but to accept his unwelcome guests. However, Laboa demanded that Noriega and his aides relinquish their weapons, which they reluctantly did—except for a submachine gun found later under Noriega's bed.

For 11 days, Laboa tried to convince Noriega to give himself up. Meanwhile, United States Secretary of State James Baker sent a letter to the Vatican arguing that Noriega was not a political refugee but a common criminal fleeing prosecution. Baker assured Laboa that if Noriega left the papal embassy, he would be arrested—not killed—by U.S. forces. Laboa continued to pressure Noriega, showing him that he could not escape from the surrounded building. Laboa told Noriega that his only choice was to surrender either to the U.S. forces or to the new Panamanian government.

On January 3, 1990, some 15,000 people demonstrated outside the embassy. Laboa told Noriega that the papal embassy staff might move out, leaving Noriega on his own. Noriega gave in. Wearing his full-dress general's uniform, Noriega surrendered. He was taken to a U.S. military base in Panama City, where he was formally arrested. Noriega was then flown to Homestead Air Force Base in Florida.

Back in February 1988, federal grand juries in the U.S. had returned indictments against Noriega and 15 of his confederates. The 15 counts had covered the general's activities from 1981 to 1986. The charges included accepting a $4.6 million bribe from Colombia's drug cartel in return for protecting cocaine shipments and drug runners and for laundering the cartel's money through Panamanian banks. Other charges had stated that Noriega allowed the cartel to shift its narcotics operations to Panama after the Colombian government had ejected the cartel following the 1984 assassination of Colombia's Minister of Justice. Noriega had also been charged with attempting to smuggle 1.4 million pounds of marijuana into the U.S. aboard a jet that had been purchased with illegal drug revenues.

On January 5, 1990, on the grounds that Noriega was a political prisoner, his lawyer refused to enter a plea in federal court in Miami, so a plea of not guilty was entered by the court. Noriega is still awaiting trial, which is scheduled to begin June 24, 1991.

AN UNWELCOME GUEST IS OUTWITTED

Although Monsignor José Sebastian Laboa was forced to accept Manuel Noriega under the Vatican policy of granting asylum to anyone fleeing persecution, he didn't have to like it. For 11 days, Laboa applied psychological pressure and logic in order to convince Noriega to give himself up.

Noriega was given a stark ten-foot-by-six-foot room with no windows, a broken television set, and, with temperatures in the nineties, no air conditioning. Noriega was given only a Bible to read. "Poor Noriega," said a diplomat posted in Rome. "No drugs, no booze, no sex—and eating Vatican food."

Laboa was the clear winner in the battle of wills. He commented modestly, "I'm better at psychology. He's more cunning than intelligent. Without his pistol, he is manageable by anyone."

INDEX

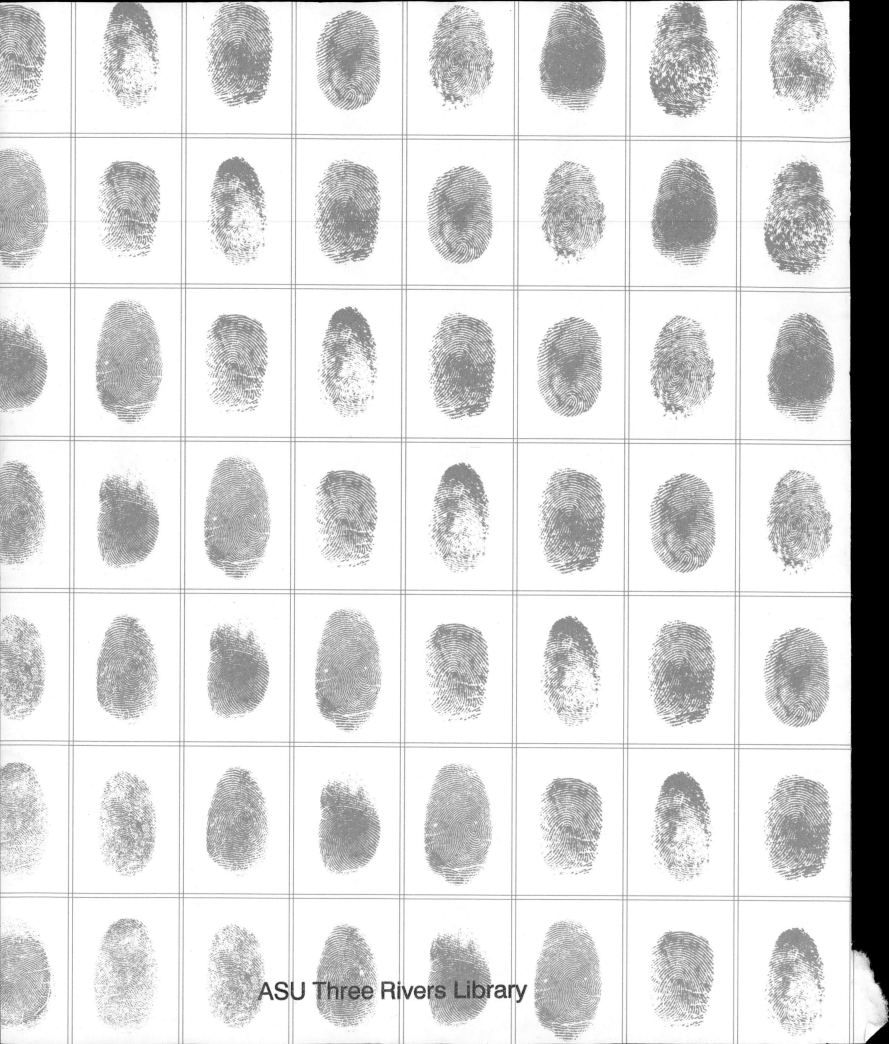